fun with the family
Connecticut

Praise for the *Fun with the Family* series

"Enables parents to turn family travel into an exploration."
—Alexandra Kennedy, Editor, *Family Fun*

"Bound to lead you and your kids to fun-filled days, those times that help compose the memories of childhood."
—Dorothy Jordon, *Family Travel Times*

Help Us Keep This Guide Up to Date

We would love to hear from you concerning your experiences with this guide and how you feel it could be improved and kept up to date. Please send your comments and suggestions to:

editorial@GlobePequot.com

Thanks for your input, and happy travels!

fun with the family

Connecticut

hundreds of ideas for day trips with the kids

Eighth Edition

Doe Boyle

travel

Guilford, Connecticut

All the information in this guidebook is subject to change. We recommend that you call ahead to obtain current information before traveling.

To buy books in quantity for corporate use or incentives, call **(800) 962-0973** or e-mail **premiums@GlobePequot.com**.

Editor: Amy Lyons
Project Editor: Lynn Zelem
Layout: Joanna Beyer
Text Design: Nancy Freeborn and Linda R. Loiewski
Maps: Rusty Nelson © Morris Book Publishing, LLC
Spot photography throughout © Photodisc and © RubberBall Productions

ISSN 1540-2169
ISBN 978-0-7627-6463-1

Printed in the United States of America
10 9 8 7 6 5 4

Contents

Preface viii

Introduction xi

Fairfield County:
Gold Coast and Green Woods 1

Litchfield County:
Artful Pleasures and Historic Treasures 58

Hartford County:
Capital Ideas in the Heart of Connecticut 100

New Haven County:
Urban Culture and Country Adventure 142

Middlesex County:
Riverside Villages and Shoreline Towns 182

Tolland County:
Simple Dreams and Country Comforts 212

Windham County:
River Valleys and Rural Byways 228

New London County:
Coastal Voyages and Country Sojourns 250

Index 293

About the Author

Doe Boyle is a lifelong Connecticut resident and an accomplished writer and editor. She is author of Globe Pequot's *Guide to the Connecticut Shore* as well as a dozen children's books.

Acknowledgments

Many thanks are owed to the scores of people associated with the attractions listed in these pages. Space restraints prevent a listing of their names, but all—from executive director to publicity manager to docent—provided a gracious welcome, much information, and the opportunity to enjoy their facilities as "ordinary" families would.

Thanks are also due the folks at the tourism districts throughout the state, who graciously accept my phone calls and keep me on their mailing lists and web updates. All of them are prompt, encouraging, and professional in providing cheerful and generous assistance.

Special thanks this time around to Anne Lee of the Central Regional Tourism District; the incomparable Janet Serra of the Western Connecticut Convention & Visitors Bureau; and Eliza Cole, Janice Putnam, and Karin Burgess, with particular gratitude to Karin, of the Eastern Regional Tourism District.

Credit must also be given to the dedicated rangers of the Connecticut State Park and Forest System. With each edition of this guide they have renewed my faith in the possibility that we can preserve and protect our land and educate and entertain our citizens at the same time. Each one of these knowledgeable individuals was friendly, enthusiastic, and committed to maintaining the parks for family use.

The folks at Globe Pequot Press are owed thanks as well. The work of its editors and designers is in truth as important as my own. I am grateful for their attention to the bones and spirit of this work. Special gratitude is due Amy Lyons for her generosity and encouragement and to Lynn Zelem for careful and thorough copyediting.

For their great leads, advice, and opinions, I thank the legions of friends and other folks who tell me their adventures, clip articles and reviews, and send me scurrying to see what they have seen. For their unflagging optimism and affection, I thank my husband and my daughters. Their loving support is essential to the happy completion of my work, and, as I have written before, they remain my finest traveling companions.

For Tee, yet again and always.

Preface

In Noah Webster's 1828 *American Dictionary of the English Language,* the word *adventure* is defined, in part, as follows: "an enterprise of hazard; a bold undertaking in which hazards are to be encountered and the issue is staked upon unforeseen events." What better description exists of the social phenomenon known as the family day trip, where two or fewer adults headily depart for an outing with an assemblage of one or more children, a map, a travel guide, maybe a camera, a jugful of lemonade, a six-pack of sandwiches, and an abundance of high expectations for fun?

In most families, a variety of ages, interests, and tastes need to be considered at the outset, or the family day trip will threaten to collapse under the weight of varying expectations even before the family car has left the driveway. On some days, simple variables like weather and traffic conspire against the best-laid plans for an enjoyable day.

Perhaps no certain way exists to predict the hazards that may beset your family adventures, but *Fun with the Family Connecticut* will at least reduce them. Basically, this is a pre-sifted collection of destinations selected by a team of family-fun experts. All the treasures of Connecticut are, in fact, too numerous to be covered in a book this size—even in this thoroughly updated eighth edition. Some categories—annual fairs and festivals, for instance—could fill a book of their own. The selection process, therefore, was both objective and subjective. In some cases, inclusion represents a unique or outstanding attraction, superior facilities, or a broad range of appeal. Exclusion usually represents a decision to limit similar attractions within a certain radius or to reduce what might otherwise result in an overemphasis on one category in the book as a whole. Nearly every town in Connecticut, for example, has a wonderful historical society or historic home. Nearly every county has more than one nature center, bird sanctuary, or wildlife preserve. Christmas tree farms and pick-your-own farms are everywhere, as are toy shops, amusement arcades, and family-friendly eateries. The selection process has resulted in a final list of more than 400 attractions and events, nearly all of which were recently visited by the author and her team of experts. In addition to these are more than 300 suggestions for lodgings and restaurants. Your team of experts should peruse the options and pick those that suit you and your family best.

Even a cursory look through the pages of this book will reveal an obvious emphasis on the state of Connecticut itself and on its varied attractions. Don't be deceived, however. Less obviously, the spirit of the book resides in the heart of its title—it is a celebration of family and a celebration of fun within the context of that unit. How lucky you are that Connecticut is the tool you will use for insight into yourselves as a family. Not only will you learn much about science, nature, and history as you travel the picturesque byways of this pretty New England state, but you will also learn much about each other.

As you read this guide, be assured that I have made every effort to be clear in my descriptions and evaluations of the attractions, restaurants, and accommodations selected for inclusion in these pages. I've made it my business to explore this state thoroughly and thoughtfully with the interests of children in mind. The task of writing this guide has been approached with both enthusiasm and integrity, and I've written the reviews of each entry as positively and fairly as I am able. No matter how appealing or interesting the reviews may seem, you alone as the user of this guide are best equipped to consider the ages, interests, dispositions, and physical and intellectual development of your children. You alone can decide whether a certain attraction may enchant and delight your children or frustrate and disappoint them. *Fun with the Family Connecticut* will, I hope, help you make happy choices, but be sure to trust your own instincts and knowledge of your family.

Scientist and naturalist Rachel Carson wrote, "If a child is to keep alive his inborn sense of wonder, he needs the companionship of at least one adult who can share it, rediscovering with him the joy, the excitement, and the mystery of the world we live in." In that vein, I invite you to use this travel guide to your own advantage. Urge each other toward new experiences. Challenge yourselves to explore what you have not yet discovered. Learn about a topic you have never been taught. Open your eyes to sights you have never before paused to consider. Most important, use this guide to nurture the curiosity, the playfulness, and the imagination of every member of your family. These are the gifts that will sustain you.

Enjoy the journey.

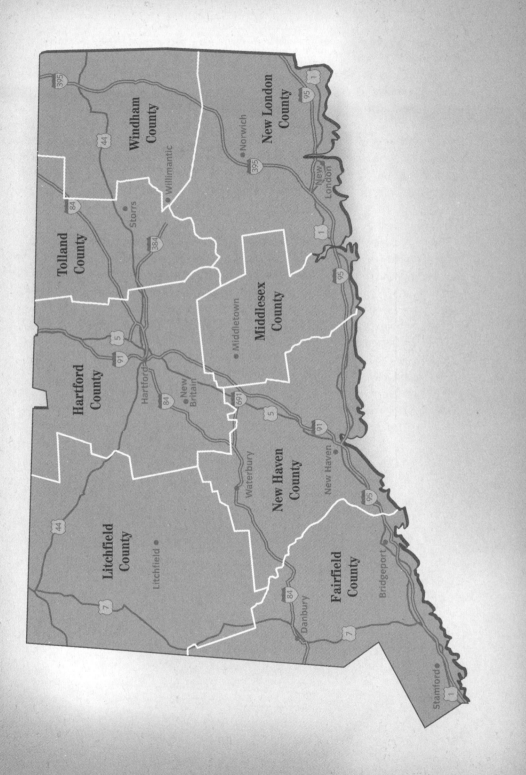

Introduction

Connecticut's Bounty

You're already a step ahead of many travelers if you've chosen to tour Connecticut. The rich history of the region has woven a tapestry of attractions that range from typically Yankee to uniquely sophisticated. Among these are boat, train, and trolley rides; science centers and planetariums; canoe trips and river raft races; amusement parks and carousels; art museums; zoos; beaches; skiing and skating centers; and performing arts.

Many attractions reflect Connecticut's remarkable multicultural populations and their histories. Once home to dinosaurs and mastodons, the prehistoric fertile valleys were later roamed by the nomadic ancestors of the Algonkian people. The Mohegan tribe of the Algonkian nation called the region Quinnehtukqut, meaning "along the long tidal estuary." The area's indigenous population is represented in many exhibits and festivals throughout the state.

The arrival of the Dutch in 1614 and the establishment of the Hartford Colony by Thomas Hooker in 1636 led to the founding of the Connecticut Colony in 1639 and the subsequent decimation of the native population. Despite the shameful nature of that transition, much of value about the European influence can be learned today. Wave after wave of immigrants enriched the development of the state. Scholars, inventors, artists, industrialists, scientists, farmers, and others whose deeds made American history have left their mark. So, along with miniature golf courses and water slides, museums, historic sites, and farms appear with regularity on the list of attractions families will enjoy. In fact, you may have trouble deciding where to visit first.

Using This Book

Arranged by county in a roughly west-to-east progression and then by geographic proximity of towns within each of the eight county chapters, each entry includes basic information such as addresses, telephone numbers, websites, hours, and admission rates. Then there is a brief but detailed review of what families can expect to see (or learn or explore). Bear in mind that the age recommendations are somewhat subjective based on the author's experience or suggested guidelines.

The maps at the beginning of each chapter are a quick reference to the towns covered in each county. Not intended to replace a good highway map or to provide routes for driving tours, the maps should help you gain a general sense of the area.

At the end of each chapter are listings of additional sources of information.

Connecticut's State Parks
and Historic Sites

The rangers at Connecticut's state parks and historic sites are some of the most dedicated professionals employed by the State of Connecticut, committed to preserving safe public access to 200,000 acres of state-owned lands. Stewards of 2,000 miles of rivers and streams, 800 miles of hiking trails, 1,300 campsites, and 100 public boat launches, they are dedicated to implementing Governor M. Jodi Rell's 2006 initiative called No Child Left Inside (check the website www.ct.gov/dep/NoChildLeftInside). Designed to encourage families to enjoy the recreational resources of Connecticut's state parks, the initiative offers a Great Park Pursuit game (see the website for all current Pursuit locations and dates) that encourages outdoor exploration at designated parks for a period of seven weeks each summer. Before you set out on a trip to any of Connecticut's state parks or historic sites, be sure to check the Connecticut State Parks website (http://dep.state.ct.us/stateparks) for current information on park hours and services, including any closings or delayed openings. Always carry a heavy-duty plastic bag to pack out trash; bring along drinking water and toilet tissue. Do not allow children to swim when no lifeguards are present. Obey signs that indicate closed trails and restrooms.

Rates

Throughout this book dollar signs provide a sense of the price range at various establishments. For meals, prices are per individual dinner entrees. Keep in mind that meal prices generally do not change seasonally but that lunch may be less expensive than dinner. For lodging, rates are for a double room, European Plan (no meals), unless otherwise noted. In addition, guests are charged state sales tax, not included in the room rate. Lodging rates usually are seasonal, with higher rates prevailing during the warm months, at holiday and school vacation times, or in winter near ski centers. Be sure to inquire about special rates. Camping rates are listed under individual attractions and reflect nightly campsite fees. Rates for attractions represent the range per person for both adults and children. Free admission for younger children, if offered, is noted separately. If a facility hopes for a donation, that too is noted. Keep in mind that many "free" facilities do indeed welcome the public at no charge but also depend on visitors' generous donations.

Remember also that rates change frequently, and the range reflects the prices charged in fall 2010.

If you are planning to stay at an inn or a bed-and-breakfast, call before your visit, and be honest about the number and ages of the children in your family. In hotel rooms with two double beds and perhaps a couch and plenty of floor space, families may be able to sleep three or four small children, for whom there may be no extra charge. In the smaller hostelries, however, space in guest rooms is often more modest; many rooms contain only one double or queen-size bed. Cribs and rollaway cots are available at (nearly) all of the listings in this book, and a charge of $10 to $20 is usually added for each.

Please note that all restaurants in Connecticut are smoke-free.

Rates for Accommodations

$ Less than $75
$$ $75 to $100
$$$ $100 to $125
$$$$ More than $125

Rates for Attractions

$ Less than $5
$$ $5 to $10
$$$ $10 to $20
$$$$ More than $20

Rates for Restaurants

$ Most entrees less than $10
$$ $10 to $15
$$$ $15 to $20
$$$$ More than $20

Season Pass **for State Parks**

Frequent visitors to Connecticut's state parks may want to purchase a season pass that can be used in every state park for the entire Memorial Day through Labor Day season. The pass (currently $67 per Connecticut vehicle/$112 per out-of-state vehicle for one-year admission to all parks) exempts users from any additional parking fees for individual parks. Unlimited visits to the parks are allowed, and no parks are excluded, except that in Gillette Castle State Park, Fort Trumbull State Park, and Dinosaur State Park, the pass covers only the entrance fee to the outdoor areas. Tours of the castle itself or to the Exhibit Dome of Dinosaur Park or the Exhibit Center at Fort Trumbull incur an additional fee. Caregivers and grandparents who are 65 and older can get free Charter Oak passes, which allow unlimited access to all state parks and forests. For information on obtaining passes, contact the State Parks Division at (860) 424-3200 or check the website at www.ct.gov/dep.

Museum **Pass Program**

Before you head out with a pocketful of cash, stop at a local or nearby library. Most libraries in the Connecticut Library Consortium participate in the Museum Pass Program, stocking up on passes to the state's best, most popular, and even obscure attractions and offering them to residents (and sometimes even nonresidents) who can check them out with their library card. Most passes offer free or reduced-cost admission for adults and children. Policies vary from library to library: some allow passes to be reserved 24 hours in advance; most require that passes be returned to the library that lent them, typically the same day or the day after they are borrowed. Call or check the websites of your local or nearby library to view their policies and peruse their list of passes.

Special Needs and Equipment

If your family has special needs, call before you depart. Families with infants and toddlers may also benefit from an inquiry about the use of strollers, knapsacks, child carriers, and so on. Inquiries about the use of cameras and audio and video equipment may also spare you any disappointment.

A Word to the Wise

Although the hours and prices listed in this guidebook were confirmed at press time, we strongly recommend that you call ahead to obtain current information before traveling. Exhibits and facilities change—even locations shift and, unfortunately, some places close down altogether. Restaurants and lodgings are especially changeable, and websites sometimes include outdated information. Don't hesitate to let us know if you discover changes you'd like to pass along for future editions.

Attractions Key

The following is a key to the icons found throughout the text.

SWIMMING		**FOOD**	
BOATING/BOAT TOUR		**LODGING**	
HISTORIC SITE		**CAMPING**	
HIKING/WALKING		**MUSEUM**	
FISHING		**PERFORMING ARTS**	
BIKING		**SPORTS/ATHLETICS**	
AMUSEMENT PARK		**PICNICKING**	
HORSEBACK RIDING		**PLAYGROUND**	
SKIING/WINTER SPORTS		**SHOPPING**	
PARK		**PLANTS/GARDENS/NATURE TRAILS**	
ANIMAL VIEWING		**FARM**	

Fairfield County

Gold Coast and Green Woods

Widely known as Connecticut's wealthiest, busiest, and most densely populated area, Fairfield County offers a distinctive mix of attractions that belies the stereotyped reputation that gave parts of it the nickname the Gold Coast. True, vast estates fight for space alongside sleek corporate headquarters and manicured suburban enclaves, but much more is also here along this coastal plain, the gateway to New England.

Out-of-state visitors looking for a taste of New England within 60 miles of Manhattan can stop here to sample the Yankee charms of industry, prosperity, and abundance so evident in Fairfield County. This part of the state has long been popular as a playground

TopPicks for fun in Fairfield County

1. **Stepping Stones Museum for Children**
2. **Audubon Center of Greenwich**
3. **Stamford Museum and Nature Center**
4. **Schooner** *Soundwaters*
5. **The Maritime Aquarium at Norwalk**
6. **Sheffield Island Cruise and Lighthouse**
7. **Westport Country Playhouse Family Festivities**
8. **The Beardsley Zoological Gardens and Carousel**
9. **Levitt Pavilion for the Performing Arts**
10. **Squantz Pond State Park**

FAIRFIELD COUNTY

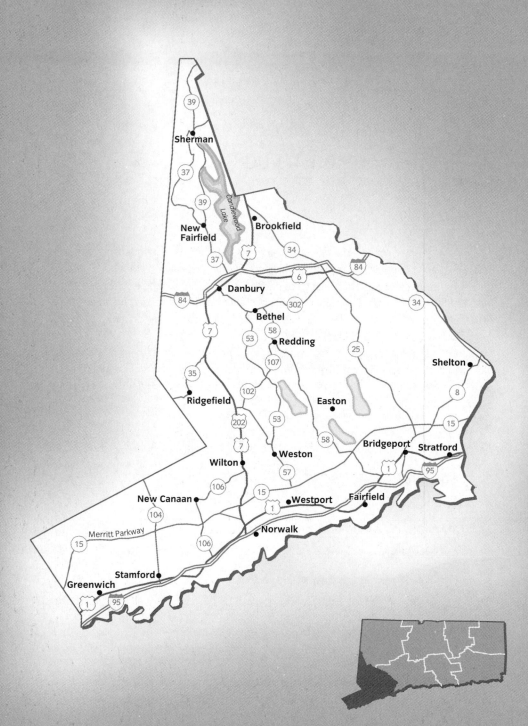

for those seeking the forest, fields, and flowers in spring; the sea and sun in summer; the glorious foliage and bounties of the harvest in autumn; and the snowy serenity of the lanes and pastures in winter. Throughout the seasons, the famed Gold Coast offers a multifaceted gestalt of glitz and glade to suit all tastes and ages.

Some families may wish to search for fun in the county's metropolitan areas. The urban movers and shakers of Stamford, Norwalk, and Bridgeport woo travelers wary of the city by providing state-of-the-art museums, aquariums, playgrounds, and performing-arts stages equal to those in Boston and New York. Families adventuring among the city-based destinations will find well-marked streets, good lighting, safe parking, and top-notch facilities to ensure worry-free enjoyment of the city.

Families on the lookout for activities centered on the aquatic and nautical delights of Long Island Sound will find myriad opportunities for fun on and in the waters off the Gold Coast. First-time visitors may want to get their feet wet, so to speak, aboard tour boats that range from an ecological research vessel to a steam-powered cross-Sound ferry or a replica three-masted schooner. Families with their own boats can enter the Sound at a score of docks, marinas, and public launching sites. Fishing charters, daylong and overnight cruises, and sailboat and kayak rentals can be arranged through many operators. Families content with simpler pleasures can take beach gear to any of several public areas for castle-building and beachcombing in the sand.

When the charms of life on the water no longer float your boat, trade your sea legs for a landlubberly stroll through attractions wholly or partly dedicated to the marine and tidal ecosystem. You'll gain Sound-related education at Greenwich's Bruce Museum and at Norwalk's Maritime Aquarium and the Stepping Stones Museum.

Care to leave behind the bustle of both city and seaside? Fairfield County has hidden pleasures north of the I-95 and Route 1 highways. Nature centers, wildlife refuges, and bird sanctuaries also provide shelter for world-worn seekers of solitude.

If you can't go far, at least take the slow lane to the back roads of Greenwich, New Canaan, Stamford, Westport, and Fairfield. If you can, go farther—to Easton, Redding, Ridgefield, Bethel, Brookfield, and the roads that lace around Candlewood Lake in New Fairfield. A yearlong tribute to Mother Nature lies around each bend of these pretty-as-a-picture roadways. Perfect for hiking, bicycling, and cross-country skiing, these trails, paths, and byways meander through maple and conifer forests, farmlands, and orchards, and alongside rivers, streams, and waterfalls. Far from the clamor to the south, families who take these roads less traveled can savor the joys of outdoor recreation in the Eastern Woodlands.

A Heart-to-Heart Chat about Arteries

Lower Fairfield County has some interesting road signage on its main arteries, signage that may prove confusing to newcomers. The three main routes that run the length of the county from its New York border on the west throughout the remainder of the county as it extends east are I-95 (also called the New England Thruway and the Connecticut Turnpike), the Merritt Parkway (SR 15), and Route 1 (also known as the Boston Post Road, the Post Road, King's Highway, East or West Main Street or Avenue, or some other name altogether). All these roads run east–west, but they have signs that say they go north–south. This smacks of some twisted Yankee humor along the lines of "You can't get there from here," but it's not. The roads are labeled that way because in general they lead north from New York and south from Boston. To confuse matters further, in Fairfield County the entrance signs to both the Merritt Parkway and I-95 usually read "North—New Haven" and "South—New York." Pull out a map and look at the names of the towns and cities along both routes. Be sure that you know whether you intend to travel east or west to or through these towns. Then, when you hop up on the highway or parkway, go north if you mean to go east and go south if you wish to go west. It's a perverse little system, ain't it?

A Word to the Driver

The main arteries for visitors traveling through Fairfield County are also the main arteries for commuters traveling from their jobs in New York and New Haven to their bedrooms in suburbia. Traffic, especially northbound, on I-95 and the Merritt Parkway (Route 15) is nearly always heavy from 4 to 7 p.m. on weekdays year-round. Heavy-but-steady becomes stop-and-go or even bumper-to-bumper even earlier on Friday and before holidays from Memorial Day through Columbus Day as city dwellers hit the road in search of sun and fun in New England.

Whenever possible, avoid I-95 and the Merritt during these hours. Instead, stay busy in one place—dinnertime is a convenient excuse for staying put—or take Route 1 if you must head out at this time.

Should you become enmeshed in wall-to-wall machinery at some point, it is often best to stay on the road you have chosen—just rock steady with good tunes to pass the time. The other road is likely to be as crammed as the one you wish to exit, although switching can be effective if an accident has caused the delay. Tune the radio to a station with a traffic report and get the scoop. If you are near Stamford, Route 137 (Washington Boulevard to High Ridge Road) will take you between I-95 and the Merritt. In Norwalk, Route 7 or Route 53 will get you on a true north–south track between the two highways. In Fairfield, Route 58 (Black Rock Turnpike) connects the two roads, and in Bridgeport the Route 25 Connector at exit 27A is the route to take.

Greenwich

Visitors approaching Fairfield County from the New York border won't have far to drive for a full day of family-perfect activities. Home to corporate executives, artists, writers, athletes, and actors, the prestigious town of Greenwich is enriched by the varied interests and talents of its wealthy inhabitants. Adding to Greenwich's riches are its most beautiful assets: rolling hills, verdant woodlands, and 32 miles of shoreline along Long Island Sound and its estuaries. Although here, as elsewhere, much of the coast and woods is privately owned, there is plenty that visitors can share in this top-drawer community.

Bruce Museum of Arts and Science (ages 5 to 12)

1 Museum Dr.; take I-95 exit 3 or Merritt exit 31; (203) 869-0376; www.brucemuseum.org. Open year-round, Tues to Sat 10 a.m. to 5 p.m. and Sun 1 to 5 p.m. Last admission at 4:30 p.m. Closed Mon and major holidays. $$; children under 5 free. Free to all on Tues.

One of the most sophisticated museums in the region, the Bruce houses approximately 15,000 objects in three categories: fine and decorative arts, cultural history, and environmental sciences. Pre-Columbian and Native American artifacts, American paintings, including Cos Cob Impressionist works, prints, and sculpture, French and American costumes, pottery, Tiffany glass, and more are in the art galleries. Changing exhibitions feature such diverse collections as textiles, dollhouses, photography, and mechanical banks.

In the permanent galleries, which focus on natural history and science from ancient to modern times, you'll learn about the past 500 years of local history and ecology. The minerals gallery preserves a collection of ores, crystals, precious stones, and fluorescent minerals. An archaeological dig tucked into the coastal exhibit depicts the discovery of the Manakaway site on Greenwich Point and includes artifacts unearthed during the excavation. Interactive exhibits allow visitors to experience the evolution and ecology of Long Island Sound. These galleries also include a simulated wigwam of the Eastern Woodland Indians, a cross-section of a tidal marsh ecosystem, a marine touch tank, a diorama that takes audiences from dawn to dusk in a coastal woodland ecosystem, and an ecological awareness gallery focusing on tree and water communities.

The Bruce offers a museum store and a continuous schedule of festivals, workshops, concerts, and children's programs. The museum also runs a small nature center at the beach at Greenwich Point. Perfect for families with young children, the **Seaside Center** offers free educational activities about the environment for visitors of all ages. A touch tank is maintained at the site along with other modest displays on marine life, but the best parts of a visit here are the guided beach and marsh walks, sensory hikes, nature crafts, beach-seining activities, and environmental games. The Seaside Center is open from early July through late Aug on Wed through Sun from 10 a.m. to 4 p.m. For information on its schedule of programs, check the website or call the museum. Nonresidents must pay the Greenwich Point Park day-use fees ($$$).

The Bruce Memorial Park and Playground (all ages)

Immediately adjacent to the Bruce is a great place to rest, run, or picnic. Views of a tidal marsh and Long Island Sound provide the backdrop. Leave your car at the museum or park on the street. Free.

The Beaches **of Greenwich**

Responsible use and limited parking space have proven the best tools for protecting Greenwich's beautiful coastal parks. Residents are required to purchase seasonal passes ($–$$$$); nonresidents willing to pay the day-use fees ($ admission per person, plus $$$ vehicle parking fee), charged only from May 1 through Oct 31, can enter the town beaches on any given day as long as parking spaces are available. Per-person park passes and daily vehicle parking passes must be purchased (by cash or check only) at the town hall or the Eastern Greenwich Civic Center; they are not available at the beaches or at the ferry dock. Daily per-person park passes are not required before 7 a.m. or after 5 p.m., even in the summer season, but you will still need to have a prepurchased vehicle parking pass to visit in the evening. The 147-acre park at **Greenwich Point** is a good bet for families. Excellent for fishing and bird watching, it also features a large swimming beach with concessions, restrooms, and play areas; the **Seaside Center** (see Bruce Museum entry); ponds; a seaside garden; an arboretum; and biking paths. Open from 6 a.m. to sunset, the park is connected to the mainland by a strip of land known as Tod's Driftway. Take Sound Beach Avenue south 1.8 miles from Route 1 to a right turn on Shore Road, then onward to the park entrance. You can also go to Byram Park (Byram Shore Road) for the same fees. In addition to its beach, it has a freshwater pool and tennis courts. It opens at 9 a.m.

Audubon Center of Greenwich (all ages)

613 Riversville Rd. at John Street, Merritt exit 28; (203) 869-5272; http://greenwich.audubon .org. Open year-round Mon through Sat, 9 a.m. to 5 p.m.; Sun, noon to 5 p.m. Kimberlin Nature Education Center closed Easter, Thanksgiving, Christmas, and January 1. $, free to National Audubon Society members.

In Greenwich's northern reaches, 15 miles of trails lead through 686 acres of woodlands, meadows, ponds, and streams, and 7 miles of trails are located on the 285 acres of the main sanctuary area on Riversville Road. Here too, the Kimberlin Nature Education Center houses an exhibit gallery, a demonstration beehive, a bird observation window, a model backyard wildlife habitat, and the excellent Nature Store.

Several loop trails provide options for varying schedules and hiking abilities. None of the trails are strenuous, but some are moderately difficult. The Discovery Trail leads past a pond replete in summer with bullfrogs, duckweed, and dragonflies. Stay on the trail long enough and you'll walk right across the top of a pretty waterfall at the edge of Mead Lake. The landscape here is extraordinarily pretty and restful, and the trees are

Great fun, too, are the beaches at **Great Captain's Island** and **Little Captain's Island.** The ferry service (mid-June to Sept; $) at the **Arch Street Dock** takes visitors to **Island Beach** on the 3-acre island or to the more primitive 17-acre island, where families may enjoy swimming, picnicking, and walking the trail to the 19th-century lighthouse. To park at the ferry lots, board the ferry, and debark at the island beaches, you each must have a prepurchased daily park pass ($$), you each must pay the per-person ferry fare ($), and you must pay a vehicle parking fee ($$$) at the ferry lots. A family of two adults (16-64) and two children (5-15) will thus pay $50 for this opportunity. A concession operates on Little Captain's Island, but pack a picnic and beverages for a day on Great Captain's Island. If you would like to cruise the harbor and islands, you can take the ferry service's two-hour **Cruise to Nowhere,** offered from early June through early Sept; all passengers pay one low fee ($$); children under 5 are free. Tickets are available at the Arch Street Dock from 10 a.m. on the day of the cruise; be sure to come for tickets early in the day. For more cruise and ferry service information, call (203) 661-5957, or to see the schedule go to www.greenwichct.org and click through the links to the Ferry Service pages. For information on daily park passes and vehicle parking passes, call the Park Pass Office at (203) 622-7817. To sort through all the details at your leisure, check www.greenwichct.org and click through the links to the Parks and Recreation pages.

among the most awesome specimens in Connecticut. Return in autumn for the spectacular foliage and for the annual hawk migration that can be observed from the Quaker Ridge Hawk Watch Site.

Audubon Center offers hikes, bird-watching activities, butterfly programs, aquatic studies, day camps, and workshops for children and adults. Call or check the website for a calendar of these events.

Fairchild Connecticut Wildflower Garden (all ages)

North Porchuck Road. Open daily, dawn to dusk. Free. Audubon Center visitors are welcome to walk the trails of a second parcel just a mile away on North Porchuck Road.

This 135-acre tract offers 8 miles of trails through native flowering plants and ferns. Established by Benjamin Fairchild in the early 1900s as an example of naturalistic landscaping, Fairchild Garden is especially lovely in the spring. On the two properties, more than 900 species of plants, 35 species of mammals, and 160 species of birds have been recorded.

Connecticut **Art Trail**

A nationally recognized art trail links 15 Connecticut museums. Five sites are in Fairfield County, where some say the American Impressionism movement was born. Fourteen of the sites are covered in this book: the Bruce Museum (Greenwich), Bush-Holley House Museum (Greenwich), Aldrich Contemporary Art Museum (Ridgefield), Weir Farm National Historic Site (Wilton), Yale Center for British Art and Yale University Art Gallery (New Haven), Florence Griswold Museum (Old Lyme), Lyman Allyn Art Museum (New London), Wadsworth Atheneum (Hartford), Hill-Stead Museum (Farmington), William Benton Museum of Art (University of Connecticut/Storrs), Slater Memorial Museum (Norwich), Mattatuck Museum Arts and History Center (Waterbury), and the New Britain Museum of American Art (New Britain). For more information on the trail and special events, itineraries, and packages offered in association with each museum, check the website www.arttrail.org.

Greenwich Historical Society and Bush-Holley House Museum (ages 7 to 12)

39 Strickland Rd. in Cos Cob; (203) 869-6899 (visitor center, ext.18); www.greenwichhistory .org. Gallery, visitor center, and house museum open year-round Wed through Sun, noon to 4 p.m. Bush-Holley House tours at, 1, 2, and 3 p.m. Wed through Sun from Mar through Dec and Fri through Sun only in Jan and Feb. Closed Easter, July 4, Thanksgiving, Christmas, and January 1. $$; children 6 and under free.

If the visual arts or pre-Revolutionary history and colonial lifestyles interest you, visit this National Historic Landmark. Owned and operated by the Greenwich Historical Society, whose mission is to interpret the house and its uses through the past three centuries, the 1732 structure is a classic central-chimney saltbox. Once home to farmer and mill owner David Bush and later a boardinghouse operated by the Holley family, the house is also the site of one of the first American Impressionist art colonies. Childe Hassam and J. Alden Weir, among others, painted here from 1890 to 1925. Examples of their works are displayed, along with an authentic re-creation of Elmer MacRae's studio and a fine collection of household implements, tools, furniture, and textiles. A charming visitor center orients families to the house as well as to the art colony and local history, and tour guides fashion the tours to families whenever children are present. Be sure to ask for the scavenger hunt game that enlivens the visit for youngsters. Changing exhibitions are launched annually; check the website to see if the current exhibit seems well suited to your family's interests. Check there too for the calendar of family and school-vacation programs, which may include craft workshops, storytelling, and puppet shows, among other activities.

Children may also attend the two-week Summer History and Art Camp ($$$$) to learn about 18th-century colonial life, history, and art. Designed for kids in grades two through seven each session is divided into a Colonial and Early American Week and an Art Colony

Week. Hearth cooking, painting, drawing, printing, fishing, ice cream–making, and other art may be among the activities. Your family may also enjoy the summer farmers' markets held here twice weekly and the **free** Candlelight Open House in mid-December, which offers costumed guides, refreshments, and entertainment from 4 to 7 p.m.; check the website for the dates.

Putnam Cottage (ages 7 to 12)

243 East Putnam Ave. (Route 1); (203) 869-9697; www.putnamcottage.org. Tours from May through Nov on Sun from 1 to 4 p.m., or by appointment anytime. $, children under 12 free.

Built circa 1692, Putnam Cottage was used during the Revolution as a meeting place of military leaders, including former resident Major General Israel Putnam, who was second in command to George Washington when, shortly after the Battle of Lexington, he led the Connecticut militia to Boston in 1776 and took on the British at the Battle of Bunker Hill. Once a colorful figure in Connecticut legend as well as a valiant military leader, Putnam also wintered with Revolutionary forces near Bethel (see entry on Putnam Memorial State Park), and he apparently slew Connecticut's last wolf (see sidebar in Pomfret section of Windham County chapter). Children may enjoy visiting the house on the last Sunday in February for the reenactment of Putnam's famous ride down the steep stone cliff east of the cottage; they will be delighted to see redcoats and rebels—in full regalia—skirmish on the grounds.

On more ordinary Sundays, you can see Putnam's desk, Bible, glasses, the mirror through which he supposedly saw the British coming, and his military uniform. The cottage, restored to appear as it might have looked in 1700, has unusual fish-scale shingles, fieldstone fireplaces, and an 18th-century herb garden on its pretty property.

Where to Eat

Meli-Melo. 362 Greenwich Ave.; (203) 629-6153. This very French, very friendly creperie is great fun for kids and the food is incredibly delicious. Try the ham and Swiss cheese crepe or the fabulous banana and Nutella wheat crepe. Magnifique. Fresh-made soups,

Garden Education

If you and your children are among the many families enjoying the revival of home gardening, you may enjoy a visit to the **Garden Education Center of Greenwich** (130 Bible St. in Cos Cob; 203-869-9242; www.gecgreenwich.org). Incorporated into the 200-acre Montgomery Pinetum, which offers lovely walking trails, it is dedicated to promoting horticulture, conservation, and the arts through varied educational programs and special events. An art gallery, a gift shop (open weekdays, 9:30 a.m. to 3:30 p.m.), and a greenhouse (open Mon, Wed, Thurs, and Fri from 10 a.m. to 2 p.m.) are on the grounds.

salads, sorbets. Very festive juice bar. Open daily from 10 a.m. to 10 p.m. $

Pasta Vera. 48 Greenwich Ave.; (203) 661-9705. Open daily for lunch (except on Sun) and dinner, this is the best place for pasta and pizza. Adults will enjoy favorites with excellent sauces. Paninis, salads, soups, tons of takeout. $–$$

Penang Grill. 55 Lewis St.; (203) 861-1988. This popular and inexpensive Malaysian restaurant will suit any food explorers with a taste for spicy Thai/Indonesian/Chinese favorites. Lunch and dinner daily. $–$$

Pizza Factory. 380 Greenwich Ave.; (203) 661-5188; www.pizzafactorygreenwich.com. This cheerful, casual place with red-checked tablecloths and deep-dish and thin-crust pies also offers salads, pastas, paninis, and calzones; perfect for families. Lunch and dinner daily. $–$$$

Where to Stay

Delamar Greenwich. 500 Steamboat Rd.; (203) 661-9800; www.thedelamar.com. This luxury hotel on Greenwich Harbor offers 82 deluxe rooms and suites among other top-quality services and amenities, plus, from June through Oct, complimentary harbor cruises on a vintage yacht. $$$$

Harbor House Inn. 165 Shore Rd., Old Greenwich; (203) 637-0145; www.hhinn .com. 23 rooms including 3 suites (one roomy enough for families of five) in Victorian mansion near sandy beach. Private baths, some with whirlpool, complimentary breakfast. Bicycles available. Open year-round and very welcoming to children. $$$$

Hyatt Regency Greenwich. 1800 East Putnam Ave., Old Greenwich; (203) 637-1234 or (800) 233-1234. Luxurious, tasteful, convenient to everything. 373 rooms (13 suites), restaurants, fitness room, indoor pool, day spa. Complimentary continental breakfast. $$$$

Stanton House Inn. 76 Maple Ave.; (203) 869-2110. 22 rooms, plus 2 suites, in vintage mansion close to town. Breakfast included. Private baths, outdoor pool, beach passes. $$$$

Stamford

The glitziest city in Fairfield County and the second largest in the state, Stamford offers excellent opportunities for family fun in both its southern and northern extremes, along with a handful of lesser-known choices in between. In the city's center, just 5 miles east of Greenwich, museums, galleries, performing arts centers, shops, and restaurants sprinkled among the downtown corporate office towers sparkle with a sophisticated vitality. Down by the shoreline, brightly polished since some coastal blight was cleared away 20 years ago, visitors play at glittering marinas, on sun-washed beaches, and on the waves of the Sound. In the coming decade, a huge waterfront redevelopment, on a 90-acre site called Harbor Point, promises to draw even more attention toward the shore, as office buildings, hotels, and residential and retail spaces rise near the water, along with new marinas and parks. And if none of that thrills you, the city's northern hills hold the hidden pleasures of Stamford's surprising woodlands. In every season, there's a reason to visit Stamford.

Stamford Center for the Arts (all ages)

The Rich Forum, 307 Atlantic St.; The Palace Theatre, 61 Atlantic St.; box office (203) 325-4466 or offices (203) 358-2305; www.scalive.org. $$$–$$$$.

The Rich Forum and the Palace Theatre add a dash of panache to Stamford's cultural attractions. Opened in 1992, the Rich Forum is a performing arts and communications complex that includes the 757-seat Truglia Theatre and the intimate Leonhardt Studio. Its elegant Rossi Salon offers a panoramic view of downtown, and its Rosenthal Gallery overlooks the lush Mercede Promenade, its main lobby that also serves as a performance space. From September through June, the Rich Forum hosts highly acclaimed theater productions featuring top performers from around the world. Many of these full-stage performances from Broadway and London are suitable for the whole family.

   The Palace Theatre is a fully restored architectural masterpiece with incredible acoustics. Permanent home to the Stamford Symphony Orchestra, the Connecticut Grand Opera, the New England Lyric Operetta Company, the Stamford City Ballet, and the Connecticut Ballet, the Palace offers single-night or short-run performances of music, dance, drama, and other family entertainment such as circuses, magic shows, and musical comedies. The Palace also offers a variety of arts infusion programs, classes, and workshops in the summer for children ages 4 through 20 with interests in the dramatic arts. Check the Education page of the website for a list of the current programs.

Curtain Call Theater at the Sterling Farms
Theatre Complex (ages 8 to 12)

1349 Newfield Ave.; (203) 329-8207; www.curtaincallinc.com. Open year-round. $$$–$$$$.

Specializing in theater for the lighthearted, Curtain Call does four main-stage productions each year, along with musicals and interactive murder mysteries. Ticket prices may be the best theater bargain in the state; subscriptions are even better deals; students pay half the adult price—so just $14 per show. Both stages have comfortable seating and recently improved sight lines. The cabaret-style Dressing Room Theatre stages several classics each season, for audiences who bring their own dinner, snacks, and beverages to the show. In the Kweskin Theatre, full-scale musical productions such as *1776, Annie, Noises Off,* and *A Chorus Line* entertained audiences of all ages in the 2010–2011 season. Ask about the appropriateness of individual shows if you'd like to take young children.

Schooner *SoundWaters* and
SoundWaters Coastal Education Center (all ages)

For schedules and information on both schooner and education center, see www.sound waters.org. Schooner: Dock S1, Brewer Yacht Haven Marina, on Batemen Way at the foot of Washington Boulevard. All cruises $$$$ per person. (Note: No children under the age of 5 are allowed aboard the *SoundWaters;* sunset cruises are intended for adults, and alcohol may be brought aboard.) Reservations and advance payment are required; call (203) 406-3335. For weather and sail updates, call the Schooner hotline at (203) 406-3333. Education Center: 1281 Cove Rd. in Cove Island Park; (203) 323-1978; open Tues through Sat, 10 a.m. to 5 p.m. From Labor Day to Memorial Day, parking at Cove Island is free both to Stamford

residents and nonresidents. In season, day visitors must pay a parking fee to enter Cove Island; registrants for camps and multisession programs receive parking passes.

If the smell of the salt breeze draws you toward the water, try to catch a ride on the 80-foot *SoundWaters,* a replica of a three-masted sharpie schooner that offers two-and-a-half-hour public cruises from early June to mid-Oct. Led by trained naturalists, the afternoon cruises focus on the ecology, history, culture, and future of Long Island Sound. You can help raise the sails, haul in the trawl net, and examine the catch in four stations that focus on various aspects of marine life and ecology.

The **SoundWaters Coastal Education Center** is located at Cove Island Park (see Cove Island Park sidebar). History, natural science, and marine and maritime exhibits are among the displays here. Aquarium tanks showcase freshwater and saltwater creatures; come to see the fish get fed every Saturday at 1 p.m. Check the website for the calendar of family arts and ecology programs, concerts, special events, guided canoe trips, and summer day and overnight camps.

Stamford Museum and Nature Center (all ages)

39 Scofieldtown Rd.; (203) 322-1646; www.stamfordmuseum.org. Open year-round. Museum and galleries: Mon through Sat and holidays, 9 a.m. to 5 p.m.; Sun 11 a.m. to 5 p.m. Heckscher Farm and Nature's Playground: daily 9 a.m. to 5 p.m. Closed Thanksgiving, Christmas, and New Year's Day. Planetarium shows on the second Sun of each month year-round at 3 p.m.; $, plus museum entrance fee. Observatory hours, weather permitting, are 8 to 10:30 p.m. from May 1 to Labor Day; $ with no entrance fee. Museum and Nature Center, $$; children 4 to 17, $; children 3 and under free.

This 118-acre property has features like no other Connecticut park. Heckscher Farm, for instance, is a working 19th-century farm re-creation that includes a 1750 barn on

Cove Island Park

A single paper bill with an image of Andrew Jackson on it will buy your family a whole day's access to **Cove Island Park,** one of the state's best beach bargains. Along with two sandy beaches and wide lawns for kite-flying, outdoor games, and general lolling about, you'll also find shaded picnic areas, a mile-long loop trail for walking and running, a rollerblading/bicycling path, a playground, fishing and bird-watching areas, a Long Island Sound interpretive trail with marker exhibits, and even a tram that takes you to these places and spaces. The SoundWaters Coastal Education Center is also here (see separate entry), providing exhibits on the salt marsh, intertidal mudflats, and estuarine embayments of the Sound, Holly Pond, and the Cove River. From Memorial Day weekend until Labor Day, nonresident daily passes to the park can be purchased at the park gate from 9 a.m. to 7 p.m. There's no charge after Labor Day.

hillside pastureland, a working organic garden, and 50 animals, including cows, horses, pigs, goats, chickens, geese, and sheep. In its midst is a country store and a tiny gem of an exhibit dedicated to 18th- and 19th-century farm life and tools. The Overbrook Nature Center is an information hub with exhibits that orient visitors to the site and serves as a starting point for the center's full calendar of programs, guided walks, and self-guided hikes. Its award-winning Nature's Playground is a wooded 1-acre children's play area with elaborate—and completely fun—nature-based exploration areas. Dig in a sandpit for fossil and dinosaur bone replicas; discover insect galleries and honey-combs; climb into a hawk's nest; rest in a chipmunk burrow; slide down an otters' slide; make a dam; race a boat; explore a tree house, a beaver lodge replica, and a rope spi-der's web. The Animal Embassy is an environmental education center with live exotic animals; demonstrations are commonplace when the exhibit is open Tues through Sun from 10 a.m. to 2 p.m. In addition to those outdoor areas are 3 miles of woodland trails that include a pond habitat with a picnic area, a streamside boardwalk with benches, handrails, braille signs, sensory stations, and the quarter-mile universally accessible Wheels in the Woods trail. The center's trails also connect to those of the adjacent Bartlett Arboretum.

Inside the Bendel Mansion is the Stamford Museum, with fine art exhibitions, Ameri-cana, and nature exhibits. Several dioramas are the highlight of its Native American gallery, which includes artifacts from four major North American Indian groups. All exhibi-tions include a children's corner that makes each topic understandable to youngsters. The museum is also home to a planetarium and an observatory with the largest telescope east of the Mississippi.

Held among all these areas are many annual events and regularly occurring weekly programs. Sunday Explorers, from 11 a.m. to 3 p.m., is a drop-in program offering staff-led and self-guided activities on a different topic each week. Astronomy Nights at the Observatory on selected Fri evenings offer exploration of the night sky, planets, and stars. Come back throughout the year for such events as Spring on the Farm Day, a Harvest Fes-tival, Maple Sugar Sunday, and Dolls, Toys, and Teddy Bears, a holiday event. Along with monthly Outdoor Adventures programs and summer camps, these events are all listed on the website calendar.

Bartlett Arboretum and Gardens (all ages)

151 Brookdale Rd.; (203) 322-6971; www.bartlettarboretum.org. Open year-round, daily, 9 a.m. to sunset. Visitor center open 9 a.m. to 4:30 p.m. Mon through Fri, except on holidays. Greenhouse open weekdays only from 9:30 to 11 a.m. Adults, $$; free to children under 12. Leashed pets are welcome. Access for people with mobility impairments is limited; call ahead to arrange accommodation to any special needs.

Just down the road from the Stamford Nature Center is this gorgeous state-owned arbo-retum, recently improved in beautiful and inventive ways. Within the sanctuary of natural-growth oak, maple, beech, and hickory woodlands and wetlands are a conifer garden, a native wildflower garden, and a nut tree collection. Five miles of trails help families to explore. A shallow reflecting pond at the end of the Woodland Trail is a perfect destination for young children, as is the boardwalk that leads through the red maple Swamp Trail. The self-guided Ecology Trail combines portions of each of these trails. Pick up a guidebook at the visitor center so you can enjoy the descriptions of 27 stations along the trail. ("Bee" sure to check out the arboretum's honeybee hives in the wildflower meadow.)

If your group includes children under 12, borrow a nature activity backpack from the visitor center before you set out on a walk. Crayons, scratch pads, a magnifying glass, and a wonderful set of cards with games and activity suggestions enhance the experience for the whole family.

Take a stroll through the greenhouse to see its incredible cacti and succulents, and stop at the visitor center to see its rotating art exhibitions.

By summer 2011 the arboretum's Silver Education Center should be up and running. Among its excellent camps, after-school, and drop-in programs ($$$$) for children ages 5 to 10 are Summer Fridays (9 a.m. to noon), when children are engaged in such themed experiences as vegetable gardening, pond ecology, birding, and composting. The arboretum also offers one-hour guided walks suitable for the whole family throughout the year, typically on Sun at 11:15 a.m. and sometimes at twilight on Thurs. A donation is suggested. Check the website for a schedule of these walks. An annual Garden Fair is offered in early May, and two concert series ($) suitable for the whole family are held every Sun in July and Aug. Pack a picnic and come for Morning Music from 10 to 11 or Evening Music from 5 to 7. Check the website for concert dates and event details.

Where to Eat

Brasitas. 954 East Main St.; (203) 323-3176. This friendly, welcoming establishment is casual enough for families and delicious enough for anyone. The Caribbean/Latin American fare includes child-friendly quesadillas, empanaditas, wraps, corn cakes, tacos, soups, and salads. Fresh, wholesome, and delightful at lunch and dinner daily, inside the cozy dining room or outside in warm weather. $$–$$$

City Limits Diner. 135 Harvard Ave.; (203) 348-7000. Delightfully retro and refreshingly contemporary choices are on the huge menu at this absolutely sparkling 1950s-style establishment attached to the La Quinta Inn. Perfect for families, it seats 220 for casual snacks, breakfasts, lunches, and dinners at typically modest diner prices. Open 7 a.m. to 11 p.m. Sun through Thurs and until midnight on weekends. $–$$$

Tat's on Summer. 184 Summer St.; (203) 325-2222. This busy, cheerful all-you-can-eat Chinese buffet right downtown provides lunch daily from 11:30 a.m. to 4:30 p.m. and dinner daily from 4:30 p.m. Children's meals are discounted 25 percent to 50 percent, depending on their age. $

Where to Stay

Courtyard by Marriott Stamford Downtown. 275 Summer St.; (203) 358-8822. 115 rooms, including suites with whirlpool baths or terrace balconies, in the heart of downtown. $$$$

Holiday Inn Stamford Downtown. 700 East Main St.; (203) 358-8400. 372 newly renovated rooms, 3 suites, restaurant, fitness room, indoor pool. $$$$

La Quinta Inn & Suites. 135 Harvard Ave.; (203) 357-7100. 158 rooms; 30 suites.

Restaurant, fitness room, indoor pool. Continental breakfast. $$$$

Stamford Marriott Hotel & Spa. 243 Tresser Blvd.; (203) 357-9555. 508 units,

including 6 suites, fitness room, sauna, indoor and outdoor pools. Lower weekend rates. $$$$

New Canaan

Exquisite in nearly every way is the gracious and affluent suburb of New Canaan, just 8 miles northeast of downtown Stamford via Route 137 or 106. Its busy village center is chock-full of boutiques, restaurants, bakeries, and bookstores, many of which are specially designed to fulfill the whims of children. If you hate malls but love to shop, spend a day in New Canaan. Two of the best downtown places are luckily paired: Be sure to browse at **Elm Street Books** (35 Elm St.; 203-966-4545) and take whatever you buy to **Rosie** (27 Elm St.; 203-966-8998), just next door. Pull up a few chairs to the window-seat banquettes to read while you eat. When you are rested and refreshed, stash your books in a backpack and explore two of Fairfield County's treasures.

New Canaan Nature Center (all ages)
144 Oenoke Ridge; (203) 966-9577; www.newcanaannature.org. Discovery Center and gift shop open year-round, Mon through Sat from 9 a.m. to 4 p.m. Closed on major holidays. Trails and grounds open daily, dawn to dusk. Free.

A respite from the thrust and parry of lower Fairfield County's version of civilization, the Nature Center's 40 acres of diverse habitats include 2 miles of trails and boardwalk through meadow, woods, and marsh. Its compact size makes the center accessible to small children while remaining of interest to older visitors.

Outside are a Birds of Prey exhibit and an Animal Care Building for the rehabilitation of injured creatures, as well as a solar greenhouse, a bird-watching platform, two ponds, a wildflower garden, a butterfly field, a maple syrup shed, an orchard, a cider house, and an herb garden. Inside the visitor center, the excellent Discovery Room offers exhibits and activities in the natural sciences. See a living bee colony, crawl through a "burrow," make leaf rubbings, handle animal homes and hides, or make animal tracks with rubber stamps and ink. Learn about soil, seeds, minerals, geology, migration, and animal defense mechanisms; check out snakes, newts, turtles, and fish in several habitat tanks.

The Education Building and Annex are used for the center's nature nursery-school program for children ages 3 to 5 and for natural-science birthday parties, after-school activity programs, and parent-child programs. Check the website for details of these, plus the full slate of walks, day camps, live animal demonstrations, and occasional hiking trips.

Check also for the dates of such annual events as the marvelous Fall Fair (mid-October), Winter Wonderland (mid-December), and Syrup Saturday (early February).

New Canaan Historical Society (ages 7 to 12)

13 Oenoke Ridge; (203) 966-1776; www.nchistory.org. The Town House is open to the public year-round, Tues through Sat from 9:30 a.m. to 4:30 p.m. On Sat only, the building closes from 12:30 to 2 p.m. The other buildings are open for docent-led tours by appointment. Donation.

This complex includes five buildings housing seven museums and a library. The Town House includes a library and exhibition room; a Costume Museum that spans 200 years of American life; and the Cody Drug Store, which contains fixtures, salves, ointments, scrip books, patent medicines, and even the ice cream parlor from the original 1845 store, once on New Canaan's Main Street. The 1764 Hanford-Silliman House, furnished in the style of its 18th- and 19th-century inhabitants, includes a beautiful collection of dolls, toys, and quilts. The Tool Museum houses the tools of the housewright, cabinetmaker, wheelwright, wainwright, tanner, farmer, cooper, farrier, and shoemaker. The fully operational New Canaan Hand Press is a re-creation of a 19th-century printing office; the 1878 John Rogers Studio and Museum, dedicated to the famed "people's sculptor" of the same name, houses a fine collection of Rogers's work actually sculpted in the studio. The 1799 Rock School is an original, fully furnished New Canaan one-room schoolhouse. On the town's Irwin Park property is Gores Pavilion, a mid-century-modern structure that serves as a museum of modern architecture with a focus on New Canaan's notable architectural legacy of Modernist homes.

The society offers living-history reenactments and encampments, after-school workshops, and special event days (such as an annual ice cream social) when all buildings are open to the public. Call ahead to arrange a family tour of all the buildings.

Where to Eat

Garelick and Herbs. 97 Main St.; (203) 972-8200. Great eat-here or take-out sandwiches, soups, baked goods, salads. Open Mon through Sat, 8 a.m. to 7 p.m.; 9 a.m. to 5 p.m. on Sun. $

Gates. 10 Forest St.; (203) 966-8666. Just outside the village, this place is colorful and noisy, the food is excellent and original, and a children's menu keeps youngsters happy. Lunch Mon through Sat; dinner daily; Sun brunch. $–$$$

Reid's Country Kitchen. 17 Elm St.; (203) 966-6163. A charming blast from the past, this old-fashioned malt shop/cafe has been serving American comfort food for more than 50 years. Open daily from 7 a.m., serving everything families like best, three meals a day. $

Rosie. 27 Elm St.; (203) 966-8998. Stop at this merry place for breakfast, lunch, or carrot cake, which certainly counts as a nutritious meal all by itself. A classic American children's menu includes scrumptious house-made mac and cheese; lunches include fresh soups, great paninis, and wonderful and whimsical cupcakes. Don't miss it—and buy a book next door on your way out or in. Open Tues through Sun. $–$$

Taste of Asia. 73 Elm St.; (203) 966-8830. This spotless eatery offers Szechuan-style cuisine, a handmade-noodle bar, and usually on weekends only, Shang-hai dim sum. Open daily for lunch and dinner. $–$$. If it's SRO here, try Plum Tree (70 Main St.) or Ching's Table (64 Main St.).

Where to Stay

The Roger Sherman Inn. 195 Oenoke Ridge; (203) 966-4541. This classic country inn offers deluxe accommodations in luxury rooms and suites welcoming to families; rollaway beds and cribs are available. Complimentary continental breakfast as well as fine dining ($$$$) daily in an award-winning restaurant. $$$$

Norwalk

Even were the city not chock-full of terrific attractions, Norwalk's interesting history and charming coastline would make it a perfect family destination. As it is jam-packed with all these qualities, however, there is no doubt that Norwalk is one of Connecticut's most popular cities with tourists. This guide includes only the top attractions and events in town. The city's center is 7 miles east of downtown Stamford and 5 miles south of the center of New Canaan.

The Maritime Aquarium at Norwalk (all ages)

10 North Water St.; (203) 852-0700; www.maritimeaquarium.org. Open daily except Thanksgiving and Christmas Day. Regular hours are 10 a.m. to 5 p.m.; from July 1 to Labor Day open until 6 p.m. Environmental Education Center; cafeteria; museum store. Seal feedings: 11:45 a.m. and 1:45 and 3:45 p.m. daily; shark feedings: 12:40 p.m. on Sun. IMAX films: see website for shows and schedule. Admission charged to the aquarium alone, to the IMAX alone, or to both together. $$–$$$, children under 2 are free.

The flagship of the artsy SoNo neighborhood, this aquarium/theater/maritime museum is a celebration of the fragile ecosystems of Long Island Sound and its estuaries. Overlooking Norwalk Harbor, this attraction includes 22 aquariums with more than 125 species of marine life.

Stroll from one habitat re-creation to another, beginning at the salt marsh and culminating at a 110,000-gallon tank with sharks, stingrays, and other creatures of the open ocean. Watch harbor seals swim in a pool and river otters tumble and slide in a simulated woodland and shoreline habitat. View the underwater ballet of loggerhead sea turtles, and handle sea stars, horseshoe crabs, and other tidal pool inhabitants in a touch tank.

In the maritime museum area, watch crafters build wooden boats in the centuries-old tradition of New England boatbuilders. Discover the names and uses of boats such as the dory, sandbagger, and sharpie as you learn about marine navigation and Norwalk's oyster industry.

Changing exhibitions and related programs are frequent and wonderful. Birthday parties and overnight visits can also be arranged. Special events, lectures, camps, and workshops are commonplace here, and many are tailored to children of specific or all ages.

Before you go home, watch both classic and current IMAX films, well known for their dramatic you-are-there effects.

All Aboard the *Oceanic*

The Maritime Aquarium offers two-and-a-half-hour public marine-life study cruises on its research vessel, the 40-foot trawler *Oceanic.* On winter weekends from December through March, see the seals that inhabit the Sound during the coldest months. In summer, learn about the ecology of the Sound as you collect water samples, haul a trawl net, and examine the catch in the shipboard touch tank. Summer cruises leave daily at 1 p.m. from July 1 through Labor Day and on Sat only in May, June, Sept, and Oct. Board the *Oceanic* at the aquarium's dock on the Norwalk River near the IMAX theater entrance. Make reservations online at www.maritimeaquarium.org or call (203) 852-0700, extension 2206. $$$$.

Sheffield Island Cruise and Lighthouse Tour (all ages)

Seaport Dock, just south of the Maritime Aquarium at the corner of Washington and Water Streets; call the Norwalk Seaport Association (203-838-9444) for schedule, information, and reservations, which are highly recommended, or check www.seaport.org. On weekends and holidays, from early May through mid-September, cruises depart at 11 a.m., 2 p.m., and 3:30 p.m.; on weekdays from mid-June through Labor Day, cruises depart at 11 a.m. and 3 p.m. Seating is first come, first served. Arrive a half-hour early to allow time for parking in the nearby Maritime lot. Adults, $$$$; children 4 to 12, $$$; children under 4, $.

Join up to 49 passengers on a single-deck covered catamaran for a 45-minute narrated cruise to the outermost of the Norwalk Islands, where one can disembark for beachcombing, bird watching, picnicking, or touring the 1868 stone lighthouse.

On the outbound trip, the knowledgeable crew and captain offer lively stories about the wildlife areas of Norwalk Harbor, the historical details on landmark structures, and the legends of the islands.

Once on dry land at Sheffield Island, passengers can spend time as they choose. Most folks take the tour of the lighthouse. Several of its 10 rooms are open to the public, and four flights of stairs lead to the lovely black-capped light tower. Decommissioned in 1902, when a new light was built a quarter-mile inshore, the original light is no longer in the tower. If you prefer to relax in the tranquility of an island idyll, bring along a picnic and spread a blanket in the 3-acre picnic grove for a leisurely lunch or brunch. Limited refreshments (water, chips, and such) are sold on the island, so you may want to bring snacks. You can also swim (at your own risk—no lifeguards are here) or comb the beach. An environmentally friendly restroom is on the island.

The 60-acre island also includes the **Stewart B. McKinney National Wildlife Refuge.** Within its boundaries is a 2,000-foot nature trail with an observation deck, or you can encircle the refuge by walking the perimeter of the island. Don't forget to note the time your cruise will depart if you set out on such an excursion: The last cruise departs the island at 5:15 p.m. on weekdays and 5:45 p.m. on weekends and holidays. The seating area on the catamaran is covered to protect you from sun, wind, or inclement weather. A bathroom and a snack-and-drinks bar add to your comfort. Check the website for the schedule of sunset cruises and such special family events as Christmas in July and a haunted lighthouse cruise.

Lockwood-Mathews Mansion Museum (ages 6 and up)

295 West Ave., in Mathews Park, near the junction of I-95 (exit 14 North or exit 15 South) and Route 7; (203) 838-9799; www.lockwoodmathewsmansion.com. Open Apr 1 through Dec 31, Wed through Sun from noon to 4 p.m., with tours at noon, 1, 2, and 3 p.m. Closed on major holidays. Gift shop. $$, children 8 and under free.

If any child in your family would like to see a castle, come here. A National Historic Landmark, this remarkable four-story stone chateau redefines splendor and elegance. Originally built in 1864 for Legrand Lockwood, Wall Street investment banker and railroad

SoNo Historic District and
SoNo Arts Celebration

Like the Sheffield Island lighthouse, this waterfront area is listed on the National Register of Historic Places, and its comeback from decay is a tribute to the city of Norwalk. Centered on Washington, Water, and South Main Streets, SoNo is a picturesque neighborhood of boutiques, restaurants, galleries, and interesting attractions. The **SoNo Switch Tower Museum,** at 77 Washington St., tucked high above the roadway at the railroad overpass, is an interesting slice of history. At this circa 1896 switch tower for the New Haven Railroad, learn how these towers switched trains from one track to another and see the only Armstrong switch lever machine in the state. For more information on this historic structure, call its visitor center at (203) 246-6958 or check www.westctnrhs.org/tower.htm. It is open weekends from noon to 5 p.m., May through Oct. Free.

If you like the arts, come to SoNo during August for the free three-day **SoNo Arts Celebration**. Hundreds of juried fine artists exhibit their work in a sidewalk show spanning several blocks. Live-music performances, an antique auto parade, storytelling, dance exhibitions, a film fest, and a giant puppet parade are all part of the festivities. The children's area has hands-on projects designed for young artists. Similar events and festivities occur at the **Splash! Festival** held annually in June for free; a real treat among the many harbor-front activities is the Hong Kong–style dragon boat race. For information on the neighborhood and its events, call (203) 866-7916 or visit www.southnorwalk.com.

magnate, the lavish Victorian mansion features the craftsmanship of the finest American and European artisans of the time. Incredibly fine inlaid woodwork, marble floors, frescoed walls, gold-leaf ceilings, crystal chandeliers, and fine decorative arts (such as charming music boxes the tour guides will play for you) are found throughout the 62 rooms that surround the mansion's magnificent skylit octagonal rotunda. You can even come for a special Underbelly Tour of the astonishing basement, with its brick ovens, wine cellar, vault, and bowling alley.

Hour-long guided tours of the most impressive of the mansion's rooms are preceded by a short film describing the house's ongoing restoration. Annual events include a wonderful flea market (free admission) on the fourth Sunday in August. Other exhibitions, festivals, lectures, and special tours are held each year; check the website for current information.

Stepping Stones Museum for Children (ages 1 to 10)

303 West Ave., in Mathews Park; (203) 899-0606; www.steppingstonesmuseum.org. Open 10 a.m. to 5 p.m. daily from late June through Labor Day; from the day after Labor Day through late June, open Tues from 1 to 5 p.m. and Wed through Sun from 10 a.m. to 5 p.m. Also open on most Monday holidays. Closed on January 1, Easter, Thanksgiving, and Christmas. $$, children under age 1 are free.

One of the most popular attractions in the state for families with young children is this marvelous interactive learning center. Designed to meet the intellectual, physical, and emotional needs of young children and based on the idea that children learn best through hands-on investigation and discovery, this museum is a "please touch" fantasyland. Firmly rooted in down-to-earth philosophies regarding a child's sense of wonder and curiosity, Stepping Stones branches upward and outward from the point of view that kids love to and need to use all their senses as they learn.

In diverse exhibits that explore the arts, science and technology, and culture and heritage, children can immerse themselves in sensory-rich environments guaranteed to educate as well as entertain. The museum's only permanent exhibit is its entrancing Color Coaster, a 27-foot-tall kinetic sculpture in constant motion near the entrance to this wonderland, which underwent a renovation and expansive addition in 2010. Beyond the coaster are an engaging and exciting variety of new and favorite learning labs, galleries, theaters, and outdoor play, discovery, and learning areas.

Indoor and outdoor activities, theater performances, concerts, workshops, and a parent-teacher resource center are among the unique aspects of this museum. The Age of Reason museum store is beyond excellent, and the Stepping Stones Cafe provides inexpensive snacks and light meals. Stepping Stones is a sure bet for families.

The Norwalk Museum (ages 8 and up)

41 North Main St. at Marshall; (203) 866-0202; www.norwalkct.org/norwalkmuseum. Open year-round Wed through Sun from 1 to 5 p.m. Reference library. Free.

The small but innovative Norwalk Museum seeks to educate and entertain visitors by presenting the past hundred or so years of Norwalk history from a commercial and artistic

Aw, Shucks! **Oysters!**

Another of Norwalk's famed festivals is the **Norwalk Oyster Festival,** held annually the weekend after Labor Day. Celebrating Long Island Sound and its seafaring past, the waterfront events include an arts and crafts show, tall ship tours, an oyster shucking contest, and the typical foods and hoopla of summer festivals. Call (203) 838-9444. $–$$, children under 5 are free.

point of view. Located in a historic building a block from the Maritime Aquarium, the museum's Merchants' Court gallery celebrates goods invented or manufactured in Norwalk. From hats to scales to high-powered binoculars to light fixtures, each display brings to mind the glory days of local artisans and industries that added to the city's economy. The Dunne's Hardware exhibit re-creates the authentic interior of a store that existed in the city from 1912 to 2003. The Lockwood Gallery of changing exhibitions has more of an artistic focus, typically with Norwalk or Connecticut themes.

Where to Eat

Chocopologie. 12 South Main St.; (203) 838-3131. This lively cafe proves that chocolate is a food group. It serves breakfast (all day), lunch, and dinner (soups, sandwiches, salads, quiche), but best of all are the handmade chocolates. Yum. Come watch the process that takes place in the chocolate workshop. $–$$

Fat Cat Pie Co. 9 Wall St.; (203) 523-0389. At lunch and dinner, thin-crust pizza artfully designed to your specs with seasonal, often-organic, and locally made "toppers." Great soups and organic salads, and, steps away at Fat Cat Joe, coffees of all sorts, plus breakfast pies and great breads. $

Lime. 168 Main Ave.; (203) 846-9240. Come here for delicious natural foods and vegetarian specials from the simple to the gourmet. Soups, salads, excellent breads, and Middle Eastern and Mediterranean specialties, plus seafood, steak, chicken, and grilled cheese and nachos. Lunch and dinner Mon through Sat; dinner only on Sunday. $–$$$

Lushe's SoNo Diner. 70 North Main St.; (203) 354-9474. Seemingly open 'round the clock and perfect for breakfast, lunch, and dinner for families, this retro-styled space offers extensive children's entrée choices, plus classic dessert faves like banana splits, rice pudding, and real ice cream sodas. $–$$

Strada 18. 122 Washington St.; (203) 853-4546. For pizza and calzones that are a little more gourmet in a setting that is a little more adult, come here for thin crusts and inventive toppings, good salad combos, great gelato, house-made sorbets, and biscotti. Lunch and dinner daily, noon to 9:30 p.m. (later on weekends). $–$$$

Where to Stay

Courtyard by Marriott-Norwalk. 474 Main Ave.; (203) 849-9111 or (800) 647-7578. 145 units, restaurant, fitness room, indoor pool. $$$$

Hilton Garden Inn Norwalk. 560 Main Ave.; (203) 523-4000. This award-winning hotel offers 170 luxurious rooms with fridge, microwave, and coffeemaker. $$$$

Norwalk Inn & Conference Center. 99 East Ave.; (203) 838-5531 or (800) 303-0808. 69 units, restaurant, fitness room, coffee shop, outdoor pool. Complimentary full breakfast on weekdays. $$$$

Wilton

First settled by Europeans in 1651 and later established as a parish of Norwalk in 1726 by a group of 40 families, Wilton remains, in the 21st century, a small town of 27 square miles in the Norwalk River Valley. Mostly residential, it is a generally quiet place with some quint-essentially New England features that visiting families may enjoy. Two such attractions are described in some detail in the following paragraphs, but for those who may spend a weekend or more in this vicinity, mention is due of the **Wilton Historical Society's Heritage Museum** (224 Danbury Rd.; 203-762-7257). At this site are two historic homes that showcase an extensive collection of decorative arts and domestic implements from 1740 through 1900. Between them, the 1757 Raymond-Fitch House and the 1735 Betts-Sturges-Blackmar House contain 12 period rooms furnished to show the passage of time through Wilton's early history. Locally made stoneware and redware plus an extensive collection of costumes, textiles, dolls, toys, and dollhouses are also displayed. Both homes host special events and exhibitions throughout the year.

Weir Farm National Historic Site (ages 5 and older)

735 Nod Hill Rd.; (203) 834-1896; www.nps.gov/wefa. Except for Thanksgiving, Christmas, and New Year's Day, the grounds are open daily year-round dawn to dusk. Visitor center open Wed through Sun from 9 a.m. to 5 p.m. from May through Oct, and Thurs through Sun from 10 a.m. to 4 p.m. from Nov through Apr. Walking tours May through Oct, Wed through Sun at 11 a.m. and 3 p.m. and on Wed, Fri, and Sun at 1 p.m. Check the website for the walking-tour schedule in colder months. On Thurs and Sat at 1 p.m., year-round, the guided Stone Walls Walking Tour is offered. Every Sun from 1 to 4 p.m., take part in art activities and instruction. Free.

The first and only national park in Connecticut and the only one in the country dedicated to a painter, Weir Farm is the former home of noted American Impressionist J. Alden Weir (1852–1919). One of the foremost painters of his time, Weir acquired the farm in 1882 in the area known as Branchville between Wilton and Ridgefield. His summer retreat from New York City, Weir Farm is the subject of many of his paintings.

On 60 acres straddling the Wilton/Ridgefield border, the secluded site includes Weir's farmhouses, studios, and barns, all among the rocky meadows and rolling woodlands of the lower Danbury Hills. If you need a place to restore the soul, come here to stroll, bird watch, and visit the place where Weir also raised his three little girls.

A video introduction to Weir Farm's history and importance is offered at the Burlingham House visitor center, which also includes historic photographs of the farm and changing exhibitions of the work of visiting artists. Be sure to pick up a copy of *Passport to Weir Farm*, a kids' activity booklet designed especially for visitors ages 8 to 12, or ask for a Junior Ranger booklet that helps youngsters earn a National Park Service badge during a two-hour visit here.

Professional and amateur artists are welcome to bring easels and paints. The Weir Farm Historic Painting Sites Trail features 12 sites identified as the original inspiration for works of art done at the farm. The self-guided trail is easy walking through woods, fields, and wetlands, past gardens and historic structures, and along old stonewalls and fences. A trail guide with color reproductions of the paintings is available at the visitor center ($).

The **free** walking tours and stonewall tours are lively and informative. On the latter, while exploring the farm's landscape, you also learn about the various kinds of walls laid here between 1775 and the 1930s.

Bring a picnic if you want to spend the day. Wear socks and walking shoes, and bring insect repellent. The socks may be a must for some of you—we encountered poison ivy in many places. If you arrive without art supplies and your children are inspired to draw, ask at the visitor center for the loan of a sketch pad and crayons. You might also ask about art classes offered for children and adults periodically throughout the year.

Woodcock Nature Center (all ages)
56 Deer Run Rd., Wilton; (203) 762-7280; www.woodcocknaturecenter.org. Trails open dawn to dusk daily. Visitor center open year-round Mon through Fri and, in the cooler months, on most Sundays, from 9:30 a.m. to 4:30 p.m. Donation requested.

Located in both Ridgefield and Wilton, this small preserve is great for young children. It has 2 miles of trail and swamp boardwalk, a pond, an interpretive center with exhibit areas, and a store with nature-related books, gifts, and supplies. Botany walks, bird watching, geology and wildlife talks, and similar programs are among the usual activities. A junior naturalist program and summer day camp are offered for children.

Where to Eat

Bon Appetit Café. 5 River Rd.; (203) 563-9002. Why fly the whole family to Paris? Just come here for a taste of France, tucked next to Stop & Shop. Sit on stools at the counter or at one of its petite tables. It's tiny but magnifique. $$–$$$

The Schoolhouse at Cannondale. 34 Cannon Rd. at Cannondale Village; (203) 834-9816. Once a one-room schoolhouse built in 1871, this unique place on the Norwalk River has gussied itself up for an adult clientele, especially at dinnertime, but Sunday brunch and an outdoor patio at waterside make it an elegant place for families to dine on special afternoons. Lunch on Fri and Sat; Sun brunch, 10 a.m. to 3 p.m. $$$–$$$$

Soup Alley. 239 Danbury Rd.; (203) 761-9885. Soup is the word here, Mon through Fri, 10:30 a.m. to 6 p.m., and Sat until 4 p.m. Along with nearly a dozen soups daily, you can buy salads, an entree or two, a sandwich or two, beverages, and desserts to take out or to eat in. $

Where to Stay

Four Points Hotel by Sheraton. 426 Main Ave., which is Route 7, in Norwalk; (203) 849-9828 or (800) 325-3535. Located near exit 40 of the Merritt Parkway, this hotel has 127 units, including 5 suites. Restaurant, exercise room. $$$$

Westport

Bordering Norwalk on the west and Fairfield on the east, shore-hugging Westport usually needs no introduction. Long famous as a haven for writers, actors, artists, and other glitterati, it is well known as the suburb of suburbs with a dash of panache rivaled only by its imitators. Year-round and seasonal activities ensure that there's always fun for the family here. In keeping with the town's arts heritage, the **Westport Arts Center** (51 Riverside Avenue; 203-222-7070; www.westportartscenter.org; open daily) offers year-round arts opportunities for children, so be sure to check their calendar for Kinder-create and Super Saturday workshops, gallery talks, and concerts. Check the website of the **Westport Historical Society** (www.westporthistory.org) for family events and info about its museum (FYI: It has a working antique train model that is super-neat). In and out of doors, families will find plenty to enjoy in Westport, especially in these top spots for day-trippers.

Earthplace: The Nature Discovery Center (all ages)

10 Woodside Lane; (203) 227-7253; www.earthplace.org. Open year-round. Grounds, 7 a.m. to dusk daily. Building, Mon through Sat from 9 a.m. to 5 p.m. and Sun from 1 to 4 p.m. Closed on major holidays. Building admission, $$; children 1 to 12, $; admission to grounds is free for all.

The 62-acre wildlife sanctuary at this facility includes 2 miles of trails for all ages. A Swamp Loop Trail, an open field habitat, and a universal-access trail called Wheels in the Woods are among six easy hiking options. A wildflower courtyard and a bird and butterfly garden showcase native and introduced plants, and a Birds of Prey area features bald eagles, owls, hawks, and vultures.

Inside Earthplace's 20,000-square-foot museum is an exhibit hall with such interactive areas as the Tiny Treehouse and the Explorer's Clubhouse. A live-animal hall with many species of indigenous creatures offers frequent special demonstrations. Changing displays focus on ecology and animal biology. A working water-quality lab, a wildlife rehab center, and a gift shop are also here.

Best of all, though, are the workshops, guided walks, outdoor classes, and summer camp programs. Beach walks, family campfires, maple-sugaring, bird banding, a holiday fair, and more are open to all visitors. If none of those options appeal, still come to this little slice of wilderness—wild turkeys, pheasants, red foxes, deer, hawks, songbirds, and more await you.

Sherwood Island State Park (all ages)

Off I-95 exit 18. Turn south at the end of the ramp to enter the park; (203) 226-6983. Open daily year-round, 8 a.m. to sunset. Day-use fees, $$–$$$ per vehicle. Off-season parking is free, except on weekends in May and Sept. Public restrooms, changing rooms, outdoor showers, first-aid station, lifeguards, and concession stand from Memorial Day through Labor Day; only restrooms available in winter.

This 234-acre park's 1½-mile beach is preceded by two picnic groves, a softball field, bocce and horseshoe courts, and plenty of open space for kite flying, volleyball, badminton, and bicycling. In the Sound, you can swim, fish, snorkel, and scuba dive (but scuba divers must register with the rangers).

The park's appeal to families is enhanced by a ½-mile interpretive nature trail that points out flora, fauna, and special areas of importance to Long Island Sound and its estuaries. In the park's east pavilion, a nature center, linked to the trail, celebrates the marine environment. Among the indoor displays are a marine aquarium, marsh tank, and touch tank with local marine species. Outdoors, a bird observation deck provides an overview of the shore habitat. Tree and bird guides and maps are available to help you identify what you see. Naturalist-guided walks and talks are scheduled each season.

Westport Country Playhouse (ages 4 and up)

25 Powers Court, off Route 1; box office: (203) 227-4177 or (888) 927-7529; www.westport playhouse.org. Family Flex Passes are $260 each. Groups of 10 or more save up to 30 percent off the regular ticket price. For group sales information, call (203) 227-5137, extension 120. For Family Festivities productions, check the website. $$$.

For more than 75 years, this wonderful, old-time summer-stock playhouse has offered professional productions starring such legends as Henry Fonda, Helen Hayes, Jessica Tandy, Gene Kelly, Liza Minnelli, and Cicely Tyson, among many others. First located in a cow barn–turned–tanning factory and then a rustic theater with post-and-beam construction and bench-style seating, the playhouse was completely renovated and expanded in 2005 and is now on the Connecticut State Register of Historic Places.

Actress Joanne Woodward and other theater supporters have worked tirelessly to bring the theater to new heights. Now the playhouse is a year-round venue with state-of-the-art technology paired with its traditional country-roots charm. Theater lovers can

CT Coastal Access Guide

For a convenient guide to all of Connecticut's coastal access points, be sure to look up www.lisrc.uconn.edu/coastalaccess/index.asp. Organized by town and by category, the lists help you find all the places where the public may safely and legally gain access to coastal sites for boating, fishing, swimming, hiking, and beachcombing. The list includes access points on the lower Housatonic, Connecticut, and Thames Rivers as well as to Long Island Sound.

enjoy the usual bill of fare: musicals, comedies, and dramas, and a slate of Family Festivities with a special focus on theater-goers in grades 1 through 7. Among the Family Festivities of the 2010 season were *Charlotte's Web*, based on E. B. White's classic novel; *A Diary of Anne Frank*, based on the famed account of a Holocaust experience; and *The Lion, The Witch, and A Wardrobe*, based on the C. S. Lewis novel. The 2010 Family Festivities ticket prices were $10 for special "Together at the Table" performances (which include a communal buffet dinner before the performance) and $16 for other family productions. Matinee tickets for other main-stage shows, such as 2011's production of Shakespeare's *Twelfth Night* are also $16 for students.

Levitt Pavilion for the Performing Arts (all ages)

Jesup Road, behind the Westport Public Library; (203) 226-7600; (203) 221-4422 for concert hotline; www.levittpavilion.com. Free.

If theater ticket prices are too high for your budget (and even if they're not), don't miss the festival atmosphere at the Levitt. One of the most ambitious summer entertainment venues of its kind, it is planning an even bigger and better transformation in 2012, with the opening of a brand-new performance stage, entrance pavilion, landscaped riverwalks, and such long-awaited amenities as indoor restrooms. On the banks of the Saugatuck River, this open-air series offers more than 50 evenings of entertainment from late June through late Aug. Bring a blanket, chairs, and a picnic to the lawn in front of the band shell and enjoy performances suitable for the whole family. Tuesday is Potpourri Night—maybe swing, maybe the community band, maybe stories for children; Wednesday is Family Night (mime, puppetry, magic, storytelling); Thursday is classical/cabaret/theater; Friday is Party Time (folk, reggae, bluegrass, or rock 'n' roll); Saturday is pop/rock/blues; and Sunday is big band/blues/jazz. On Monday there is no show. Occasional special events— one or two—do charge admission. Wednesday and Sunday performances are usually at 7 p.m., and most others are at 8 p.m. Friday and Saturday are designated as alcohol-free evenings.

Where to Eat

DeRosa's. 577 Riverside Ave.; (203) 227-7596. Great pastas, superb pizza, great folks here, doing everything right for more than 20 years. Open daily from 11 a.m. for lunch and dinner. $$

Oscar's Delicatessen. 159 Main St.; (203) 227-3705. If you love classic kosher delis with excellent sandwiches and great matzo-ball and chicken soups, come straight to busy, crowded, here-forever Oscar's, right downtown. Open daily 6:30 a.m. to 5:30 p.m. (5 p.m. on Sun). $

Tutti's Ristorante. 599 Riverside Ave.; (203) 221-0262. Hungry kids will be happy kids in this family-style, family-friendly, family-owned trattoria, offering unfussy but excellent Italian classics for lunch or dinner Mon through Sat. $$

Where to Stay

The Inn at Longshore. 260 Compo Rd. South; (203) 226-3316. Twelve rooms (3 suites) in this lovely country inn overlooking the Sound. Playground, pool, tennis, golf, boating, beach swimming. Complimentary breakfast buffet. $$$$

The Westport Inn. 1595 Post Rd. East; (203) 259-5236 or (800) 446-8997; www

.westportinn.com. Full-service hotel with 115 units, indoor pool, sauna, fitness room, Bistro restaurant. Complimentary deluxe continental breakfast. Weekend packages; **free** bicycle rentals. $$$–$$$$

Fairfield

Settled in 1639, Fairfield is one of Connecticut's oldest towns, so it's not surprising to find beautiful historic homes and still-quaint village centers within its boundaries. Populated mostly by farmers, tradespeople, sailors, and shipbuilders through much of the 18th century, the town was burned by the British in 1779. Rebuilding was slow but determined, and soon the community had rallied as Southport and Black Rock Harbors helped to reestablish Fairfield's place as an important port of entry. Two centuries later, Fairfield's shoreline location still influences life in this thriving, comfortable community.

Ogden House and Gardens (ages 6 and older)

1520 Bronson Rd.; (203) 259-1598; www.fairfieldhs.org. Public tours from June through Sept on Sun from 1 to 4 p.m. Check website for exceptions. $.

A meticulously restored historic site for those interested in pre-Revolution life, Ogden House, owned and operated by the Fairfield Museum and History Center, is a 1750 saltbox farmhouse furnished to portray the lives of its first inhabitants, Jane and David Ogden. An 18th-century kitchen garden and a native wildflower garden are also on the picturesque property overlooking Brown's Brook near Mill River.

Beachin' It

Long attractive for its 8 miles of shoreline, Fairfield has five public beaches that allow residents and visitors to enjoy the Sound. Call the Fairfield Parks and Recreation department at (203) 256-3144 for current parking policies and prices. $$$–$$$$.

Penfield Beach (Fairfield Beach Road) and **Jennings Beach** (South Benson Road) offer pavilions, concessions, restrooms and showers, playgrounds, and convenient parking. **Southport Beach** (Pequot Avenue) is quieter, less crowded, and has great sandbars for young children, plus restrooms and a concession. It's also just past the historic village center of Southport—a pleasant place to stroll and pick up some picnic goodies at the **Spic and Span Market** (203-259-1688; open Mon through Sat), also on Pequot Avenue.

In addition to annual events celebrating the gardens and the seasons, Ogden House offers an annual Colonial Life Camp during the summer. Designed to take children back to the time of Jane Ogden, the program offers cooking, tin lantern piercing, taffy pulling, and 18th-century games. An ongoing schedule of hands-on workshops for children has included teddy bear repair, gravestone study, and principles of archaeology.

Fairfield Museum and History Center (ages 6 and older)

370 Beach Rd.; (203) 259-1598; www.fairfieldhs.org. Open Mon through Fri from 10 a.m. to 4 p.m., and Sat and Sun from noon to 4 p.m. Closed on major holidays, except Labor Day. $; children under 5 are free. Three annual community events, free to all. Separate fees for some programs and workshops.

In its 13,000-square-foot home behind the Fairfield Town Hall, this museum has spacious exhibition galleries, a classroom for education programs, an extensive library and

Take to **the Sea**

For great lessons on physical, spiritual, and environmental fitness, get the family out on Connecticut's waterways in a traditional, fossil-fuel-free vessel of one sort or another. Kayaks, canoes, rowboats, sailboards, and small sailboats are offered as rentals throughout the state. Some of the best outfitters in Fairfield County also offer lessons, camp programs, and guided tours. A few offer winter as well as warm-weather opportunities. All are well worth the fees and reservations that may be required.

Below Deck. 157 Rowayton Ave., Rowayton; (203) 852-0011; home of Downunder Kayaking, for rentals, lessons, guided tours.

Darien Windsurfing. Nearwater Lane, Weed Beach, Darien; (203) 655-6757; junior sailing and windsurfing lessons.

Kayak Adventure, LLC. 24 Poplar St., Norwalk; (203) 852-7294; lessons and tours for teens with their parents.

Longshore Sailing School. 260 Compo Rd. South, Longshore Club Park, Westport; (203) 226-4646; lessons and guided tours.

Norwalk Sailing School. Calf Pasture Beach Road, Norwalk; (203) 852-1857.

Outdoor Sports Center. 80 Danbury Rd., Wilton; (203) 762-8797; rentals only.

Small Boat Shop. 144 Water St., Norwalk; (203) 854-5223; parent/child kayaking tours; lessons; rentals.

Sound Sailing Center. 54A Calf Pasture Beach Rd., Norwalk; (203) 838-1110.

genealogy research center, and a lovely gift shop, all within a striking post-and-beam building incorporated into a cultural and historical campus that includes the Sun Tavern, Burr Mansion, and town hall, among other important Fairfield landmarks. The museum holds a permanent collection of 15,000 objects from pre-Revolutionary days to the present, including costumes, furnishings, and decorative arts.

Researchers interested in Connecticut history and genealogy will love its library, but families will most appreciate its main exhibit, *Landscape of Change,* and its workshops, education programs, musical entertainments, story hours, encampments, and reenactments. Check the website for the current calendar of events.

Birdcraft Museum and Sanctuary (all ages)

314 Unquowa Rd.; (203) 259-0416; www.ctaudubon.org/visit/birdcraft.htm. **Open year-round Tues to Fri from 9 a.m. to 1 p.m. $.**

Just south of I-95, this 6-acre enclave was founded in 1914 as the first songbird sanctuary in the United States. More than 120 species of birds have been documented on this tiny property, and you'll be sure to see at least some of those if you visit here. Limited hours mean families with school-aged kids can only come during summer and school vacations, but you'll be glad you came if you can find a little slice of a weekday morning. Along the trail through the woodlands, see huge maples, century-old rhododendrons, sassafras, and highbush cranberry. Linger a while on the wooden boardwalk above a shallow pond, or sit at the gazebo and listen to the birds and frogs.

Inside the turn-of-the-20th-century museum, designated a National Historic Landmark, are four galleries that feature the birds and mammals of New England, grouped in diorama displays by habitat and seasons. The murals here are exceptional, as is the gallery of African animals. These exhibits fulfill the dream of Mabel Osgood Wright, founder of the Connecticut Audubon Society and founding member of the American Conservation Movement. It is in the property's vintage cottage, reincarnated as a visitor center, that guests are introduced to Ms. Wright's important contributions to conservation and are oriented to the varied attractions. The cottage's Nature Observatory space includes a hands-on classroom for natural history and crafts workshops, a library, an observation deck, and a nature gift shop and bookstore.

Hands-on children's programs, story hours, and summer camps fill the needs of young naturalists, and one-hour guided tours can be arranged by appointment. Come the second Sat of May for International Migrating Bird Day, a festival of bird watching, crafts, a book sale, and lessons on how to attract birds to your own yard.

Connecticut Audubon Center at Fairfield and
Roy and Margot Larsen Wildlife Sanctuary (all ages)

2325 Burr St.; (203) 259-6305. **The nature center is open year-round, at no charge, Tues through Sat, from 10 a.m. to 3 p.m. The sanctuary is open daily, year-round, from dawn to dusk; suggested donation, $.**

Located in the Greenfield Hill neighborhood in the north end of town, this beautiful 160-acre tract of New England woodland was created on reclaimed farm property. Juxtaposing habitats and trails to allow people maximum opportunity to experience the diversity without disturbing the refuge, this wildlife sanctuary features 6 miles of trails (plus a 1-mile universal access loop trail) that lead visitors to marshes, ponds, streams, vernal pools, meadows, and coniferous and hardwood forests.

At the Connecticut Audubon Center, you can see natural science exhibits, live animal displays, and a nature book and gift shop. A Discovery Room with hands-on activities is under development as well. Outside are a greenhouse (with seasonally rotated themed plantings), demonstration bird-and-butterfly-friendly gardens, and a non-releasable birds of prey compound with such species as falcons, owls, and hawks.

Summer camps, workshops, naturalist-guided walks, junior naturalist programs, and field trips are frequent, as are birthday parties, which can be arranged from September through June only. Check the website calendar for the current schedule of events.

Where to Eat

Centro Ristorante. 1435 Post Rd.; (203) 255-1210. Located downtown (near Sherman Green), this casual but elegant Italian restaurant offers homemade pastas, good salads and seafood, pizzas, burgers, and a children's menu. Patio in warm weather. Open Mon through Sat for lunch and daily for dinner. $$–$$$

Colony Grill. 1520 Post Rd.; (203) 259-1989. Owned by four lifelong friends who played

The Dogwood **Festival**

Graced by vintage homes as well as modern mansions, the winding roads of northern Fairfield take you through lightly populated residential enclaves and into a perfect antique village center punctuated by one of the nation's most stately and classic Congregational churches. Known as Greenfield Hill, the area is heavily planted with dogwoods and is famed for its annual **Dogwood Festival** in mid-May. A great outing for Mother's Day or any other reason, it provides opportunities to enjoy the beauty of springtime in Connecticut.

To celebrate the gorgeous pink-and-white blossoms of more than 30,000 dogwoods, the Greenfield Hill Congregational Church (1045 Old Academy Rd.; www.greenfieldhillchurch.com) plans a four-day schedule of festivities that includes an arts-and-crafts show, a plant sale, walking tours and luncheons, musical programs, children's games, and a white elephant sale. Buy food here or bring a picnic. Bring along a camera to capture the day forever. For information, call the church (203-259-5596) and ask for the Festival Committee telephone number. Admission and parking are free.

on the Trumbull, CT, Little League team that won the World Series championship in 1989, this place delivers thin-crust pizzas right to your table, with your selection of 12 classic toppings. Open daily from 11:30 a.m. through midnight. $$

Firehouse Deli. 22 Reef Rd.; (203) 255-5527. Open daily, Mon through Sat 7 a.m. to 5 p.m. and Sun 8 a.m. to 4 p.m. Sandwiches, tacos, salads. Takeout or sit-down self-service. Outside seating in warm weather. $

Frank Pepe Pizzeria Napoletana. 238 Commerce Dr.; (203) 333-7373. Finally, another chance of getting a flavorful slice or two of famed Frank Pepe's crisp New Haven pizza. Way beyond good, this is pizza at its finest. Lunch and dinner daily. $–$$

Isabelle et Vincent. 1903 Post Rd.; (203) 292-8022. Just go—trust me. *Authentique patisserie—superbe!* Tues through Sat, 6 a.m. to 7 p.m.; Sun until 5 p.m. $

Where to Stay

Best Western Black Rock Inn. 100 King's Highway Cut-Off; (203) 659-2200. Built in 2005, this 100-percent nonsmoking motel is convenient to all Fairfield and Bridgeport attractions, beaches, transportation. 60 rooms; complimentary continental breakfast; fitness room. In-room fridges. $$$$

Fairfield Inn. 417 Post Rd.; (203) 255-0491 or (800) 347-0414. Clean, independently owned motor inn. 80 units, outdoor pool. Complimentary continental breakfast. Circle Diner on the premises. $$–$$$$

The Inn at Fairfield Beach. 1160 Reef Rd.; (203) 255-6808. 14 suites with fully appointed kitchenettes in immaculately renovated Fairfield landmark near Penfield Point. Daily, weekly, and monthly rates. Open year-round. $$$$

Merritt Parkway Motor Inn. 4180 Black Rock Turnpike; (203) 259-5264 or (888) 242-4742. Perched atop a hill at the north end of town. 40 units, restaurant. Complimentary continental breakfast. $$$

Bridgeport

The wealth of activities offered to tourists in Bridgeport is suited to no one better than children. In recent years each of the best attractions has expanded or improved in some way, and the blue street signs help usher visitors to the good, clean fun that can still be found here despite the political scandal that has tarnished this shoreline city.

Unknown to most folks who skirt the city on I-95 and the Merritt Parkway are the facts that Bridgeport has the longest public waterfront in the state, more protected historic districts than any other Connecticut municipality, and two expansive parks designed by famed landscape artist Frederick Law Olmsted. It's not too early to celebrate Bridgeport's gradual and ongoing recovery from blighted pockmark to merry dimple in the cheek of the Sound, as its devoted entrepreneurs and investors and its diverse ethnic communities infuse the city's culture with energy and vitality. The center of the city is a mere 4 miles from downtown Fairfield.

Discovery Museum and Planetarium (all ages)

4450 Park Ave., exit 47, Merritt Parkway; (203) 372-3521; www.discoverymuseum.org. Open year-round Tues to Sat 10 a.m. to 5 p.m. and Sun noon to 5 p.m.; also Mon 10 a.m. to 5 p.m. in July and Aug. Closed on major holidays. $$; children under 5 free.

Hands-on in nearly every way, this museum contains interactive exhibits in the areas of science and art, all designed with a special focus on visitors ages 4 to 12. Children and other visitors of all ages can make discoveries about space science, physical sciences, electronics, electricity, magnetism, and light, for instance, through the museum's frequently changing exhibitions. From ancient dinosaurs to space-age travel, you are sure to find simplified hands-on science for the youngest visitors along with engaging and intriguing displays for older learners.

At the **Henry B. DuPont III Planetarium,** daily shows offer a dramatic look at the heavens; programs change throughout the year. Cinemuse high-definition movies play frequently in a small auditorium; these films are often matched in theme to current exhibitions, as are the fine arts exhibits hung in the Balcony Gallery. The museum is also the site of a **Challenger Learning Center,** a computer-simulated mission control and space station where participants perform experiments and collect data as astronauts would. You can arrange a mini-mission for a group or birthday party, or arrange a Wonder Science Party on one of several themes.

Inside the museum are a small gift shop and a cafeteria space where you may bring in your own picnic lunch or snacks; vending machines in this area offer limited snacks and beverages of minimal nutritional benefit. Outside are some easy and short nature trails that may help you burn off some empty calories; plans are afoot in this area for a solar-system planetary trail, which may be in place by the time you visit. Check the museum website for current events, movies, and exhibitions.

Harbor Yard **Ballpark and Arena**

Near the city's revitalized waterfront, the 5,300-seat **Harbor Yard stadium** is the home of the **Bluefish** Atlantic League team. It features box seats, club seats, skyboxes, a supervised play area, a barbecue picnic area, food concessions, restrooms, and on-site parking. Check its website (www .bridgeportbluefish.com) for tickets and a game schedule or call the Bluefish ticket office at (203) 345-4800. Also in this sports complex is the **Arena at Harbor Yard,** where the **Bridgeport Sound Tigers** of the American Hockey League take to the ice as the premier affiliate of the New York Islanders. Their 40-game season runs from October through April. For hockey tickets, check www.soundtigers.com or call the Sound Tigers box office at (203) 334-GOAL. The sports complex is located at 500 Main St., off exit 27 on I-95. $$–$$$$.

Captain's Cove Seaport (all ages)

1 Bostwick Ave.; (203) 335-1433; www.captainscoveseaport.com. Seaport shops and restaurant open roughly May 1 to September 30 from 11 a.m. Closing time varies with the
weather. Free admission and parking. Boat rides and charters, $–$$.

Busiest in summer, this unusual attraction at the edge of historic Black Rock Harbor is
part marina, part shopping arcade, part seafood restaurant, and, in small part, a museum
of sorts. Captain's Cove is the baby of Kaye Williams, an imaginative Black Rock native
and lobsterman who began the cleanup of this derelict area in the 1980s. Along with the
marina and a boat repair shop are a 500-seat seasonal restaurant, harbor cruises, and a
lively boardwalk filled with 20 tiny boutiques, including a candy store, an ice cream shop,
and all sorts of purveyors of nautical gear, toys, clothing, crafts, and other classic summer-
at-the-shore gifts.

If you'd like to get out on the water, you can take a harbor tour on *Chief,* a 35-passenger
vessel that offers 45-minute cruises ($–$$) on the weekends for folks 6 years of age and
older. You'll learn harbor lore while exploring the waters of historic Burr Creek. Or, your
family may prefer a fishing trip ($$$$) on the *Middlebank II* (www.middlebank.com). The
sunset trip, from 4:30 to 8:30 p.m. on weekends only from Memorial Day through Columbus Day, is most popular with families; for that and the seven-hour daily trips, children
under 12 ($$$$) are welcome; children under 6 are free. Whenever you come, have a
quick look upstairs at the restaurant's 40-foot model of the *Titanic,* then enjoy your fish-
and-chips and such outside on the deck or on the restaurant's lower family level. The
boardwalk offers live entertainment every Sunday afternoon, 3 to 7 p.m., and the shops
are generally open whenever the restaurant is open.

Notable among the many vessels in the marina is the **STV *Unicorn,*** a double-masted
gaff-rigged schooner built in 1947 with metal salvaged from captured German U-boats
after World War II. It's not always in port because it is a sail training vessel—and the only
tall ship in the world with an all-female, all college-educated professional crew. Deck tours
are rare, but the friendly crew will be happy to answer questions, and, of course, you can
admire the ship from dockside. If you have preteen or teenage daughters, you may want
to learn about the weeklong Sisters Under Sail leadership expeditions, which are quite
remarkable (check www.tallshipunicorn.com for details). The laudable mission of the *Unicorn* and its owners, Dawn and Jay Santamaria, is to develop young women's confidence
and decision-making skills; that they choose to do so often on the gentle waters of Long
Island Sound is Connecticut's good fortune. The ship is also available for private day-sail
charters and overnight cruises.

Open only for guided tours ($) by appointment, the Seaport's restored Victorian **Dun-
don House** is a small maritime museum that contains exhibits on the maritime history of
Black Rock Harbor as well as Long Island Sound's environment, economy, fisheries, and
oyster beds. Photographs depict the history of three local lighthouses that guided sailors
and fisherfolk, and a collection of interesting items salvaged from nearby waters provides
an eye-opening look at nautical litter. Also here are the Sailaway sailing school (see www
.teamsailaway.com or call 203-209-3407); the city's Aquaculture high school for regional
youth wanting to learn marine skills and sciences; and the **Gustave Whitehead hangar.**

The last typically (but not in 2010) houses a replica of the glider built and flown by Bridge-port native and aviation pioneer Whitehead, supposedly before the Wright brothers took their famed flight at Kitty Hawk, North Carolina.

The Beardsley Zoological Gardens (all ages)

1875 Noble Ave.; (203) 394-6565; www.beardsleyzoo.org. Open from 9 a.m. to 4 p.m. daily, except for Thanksgiving, Christmas, and New Year's Day. New World Tropics building open 10:30 a.m. to 3:30 p.m. Adults, $$; children, $$; children under 3 free. Zoo-only visitors do not have to pay the parking fee ($ for Connecticut vehicles, $$ for out-of-state vehicles) charged to users of Beardsley Park.

Continually improving, this facility has marvelous exhibits throughout its 52-acre site inside Beardsley Park. Dedicated to wildlife research, conservation, and education, Connecticut's only zoo participates in an international program called the Species Survival Plan. Rare or endangered species such as Amur tigers from Russia's Far East, along with North American red wolves, scarlet ibises, and sandhill cranes, live here with 120 other species. Inside the New World Tropics building, for instance, is an outstanding open-aviary South American re-creation, where toucans, monkeys, tortoises, ocelots, golden lion tamarins, and marmosets live with tropical birds. In the Wolf Observation Learning Facility, floor-to-ceiling windows in the Wolf Cabin provide close-up views of red wolves and timber wolves.

You can also explore the Alligator Alley wetlands trail to see river otters, alligators, and another free-flight aviary. Hike the Predator Walk, which features hunter species, and the Hoofstock Trail, which borders the habitat of llamas, bison, deer, and antelope. The New England Farmyard enclosure is a petting zoo that features bunnies, goats, geese, and sheep. In the warm months, the delightful Bug House features native insects. Plans are also under way for a new Asian plateau exhibit and an Arctic tundra exhibit.

Pony rides, an outdoor classroom, a gift shop, the Peacock Cafe, and a universal-access picnic grove are also on the grounds, as is the Hanson Exploration Station, used for the zoo's special programs. Check the web calendar for lectures, demonstrations, drop-in programs, and such fee-based programs as Zoo Tots and Zoo Crew, and sign up for e-mail delivery of *CTZooTimes,* a monthly newsletter.

Not to be missed here is the pavilion that houses exhibits from the antique **Pleasure Beach carousel** as well as its operating modern replica. Admire magnificently restored animals from the original ride, then hop onto the reproduction for a wonderful whirl ($). It is open seasonally from 10:30 a.m. to 4 p.m.

Barnum Museum (all ages)

820 Main St.; (203) 331-1104; www.barnum-museum.org. (Note: The Barnum Museum is currently closed temporarily and all of its educational programs are suspended in order to preserve the collection and repair the building following a 2010 tornado that caused damage. A grand reopening is expected in mid- to late 2011. Before planning a visit, please call ahead or check the website to learn about P.T. Barnum's extraordinary life and accomplishments.) Open year-round 10 a.m. to 4:30 p.m. Tues through Sat and noon to 4:30 p.m. on Sun. Also open on many Monday holidays. $, children under 3 free.

Prepare to enter the "Greatest Show on Earth" and one of New England's best themed museums. If you have only one day to spend in Bridgeport, make sure you make this museum one of your stops. Designed to immerse the visitor in the experience of its exhibits, the Barnum creates the effect of a journey back in time.

Dedicated to the life and times of P. T. (Phineas Taylor) Barnum, the museum also celebrates the remarkable industrial heritage of Bridgeport and the culture of the circus in general. The first floor concentrates on Barnum the showman, entrepreneur, politician, and journalist. The successful juggler of half a dozen careers during his 81 years, Barnum started the circus when he was 60! According to Barnum, his circus was "the most expensive and marvellous combination of the world's wonders ever brought together." You'll be easily drawn in to his magic from the minute you step inside the museum.

A real elephant right in the lobby and a display of Barnum's famed Feejee Mermaid set the tone, and it only gets better from there. Make sure the kids watch the excellent short clip from the A&E biography of Barnum so they get a fix on who P. T. really was. On the second floor you'll get a sense of the once-great city of Bridgeport in its heyday. A fabulous exhibit of all the products invented here will surprise visitors of all ages. On the third floor, enter the circus. See a real Egyptian mummy, Tom Thumb and Lavinia Warren's clothing and furniture, memorabilia of Jenny Lind, and the incredible 1,000-square-foot Brinley's circus, a hand-carved five-ring extravaganza, done completely to scale and massive even in miniature.

Better than ever, especially since its restoration in 2010-11, the Barnum Museum continues to delight and challenge the imagination. Be sure to step right up and see its interactive exhibits and intriguing changing exhibitions, usually in keeping with Barnum's fascination with popular culture. Check the website for events designed especially for children, and be sure to join its Kids Club, which, for a single annual payment of $15 (plus one adult admission at the time of your visit) offers **free** admission to the museum and to all programming throughout the year for children in grades K-5.

The Barnum Festival

If you are charmed by Barnum's hoopla, return to the city for its annual **Barnum Festival,** a multifaceted celebration that includes the Great Street Parade on or near each Fourth of July. Among parades held across the nation, this event has historically been second in size only to Macy's Thanksgiving Day extravaganza. Road races, a fabulous marching band competition called Champions on Parade, a Jenny Lind voice competition, a children's Wing-Ding parade and carnival at the Beardsley Zoo, and fireworks are on the calendar of events. Check www.barnumfestival.com for the complete list of events and details on obtaining tickets for events that require them. For other information, call the Barnum Festival Society at (203) 367-8495.

Lights Up **at the Klein**

Bridgeport's beautifully restored Art Deco–style **Klein Memorial Auditorium** (910 Fairfield Ave.; 203-366-4647; www.theklein.org; $$–$$$$), long the home of the Bridgeport Symphony Orchestra and operated now by the Fairfield County Theater Company, is enjoying a jubilant renaissance. Single-night or short-run productions here include musical, theatrical, and dance performances. At least one winter holiday spectacular or concert is offered each season, and a production especially for children typically is staged by a well-known traveling company. Check the website for details of the current season; tickets can be purchased through the box office or in some cases online. Unless they are sold out, tickets for all shows can also be purchased at the door 90 minutes before show times. Free parking is available.

Downtown Cabaret Theater (all ages)
263 Golden Hill St.; (203) 576-1636; www.dtcab.com. Open year-round, Fri through Sun; children's series Oct to May. Performances Sat and Sun at noon and 2:30 p.m. $$$, subscriptions also available. Call the box office from Tues through Sun, 10 a.m. to 4 p.m., or buy tickets online. Secure parking ($) is located in the City Hall lot across the street.

This theater produces shows, from Broadway hits to musical revues, nearly every weekend of the year. Matinee and evening performances are given cabaret-style; patrons sit at tables and bring their own picnics and refreshments. Many performances are suitable for children older than 8, and a special 5:30 p.m. performance is staged for families. You can bring your dinner here, enjoy the show, and still have everyone at home and in pajamas at a reasonable bedtime.

The most popular pull for families, though, is the award-winning Cabaret Children's Company. For more than a quarter century, this troupe of adult actors has offered an enormously successful slate of musical matinees for children ages 4 to 12. Nearly every weekend from mid-October through mid-May, you can enjoy exceptional original and classic productions. Bring lunch, snacks, beverages—or birthday cake—and enjoy the merriment.

Playhouse on the Green (all ages)
177 State St.; (203) 333-3666; tickets: (866) 811-4111; www.playhouseonthegreen.org. $$$–$$$$, subscriptions also available.

Located in an amazingly revitalized historic district in the heart of downtown, the Playhouse on the Green is a 225-seat theater created inside a 1911 bank building across from the beautiful McLevy Green. The playhouse is a year-round venue, offering affordably priced dramas and comedies suitable for adults and teens. In addition, performances specifically aimed at families with young children are offered occasionally during the year.

Throughout the year, weeklong arts education programs are offered to students in grades K-8. Check the website for Playhouse Greenhouse and Project Broadway.

The Bridgeport to Port Jefferson Steamboat Company (all ages) ⚠

Water Street Dock; (203) 335-2040; or 102 West Broadway, Port Jefferson; (631) 473-0286; www.bpjferry.com. Operates daily year-round. Call for reservations, rates, and schedules. $–$$$$.

The huge white boats at the pier just a block from the downtown transportation terminal offer ferry service across Long Island Sound. Used for both excursions and commuter transportation, the ferry functions as both pleasure cruiser and as a means of getting by car to the prettier parts of Long Island more quickly than you'd go via New York City or the Throgs Neck Bridge. Three ferries run 32 round trips between Bridgeport and Port Jefferson each day. From Bridgeport, the boats usually depart every hour on the half-hour between 6:30 a.m. and 9:30 p.m. Each ferry has enclosed passenger decks, topside sun decks, restrooms, and food service in onboard restaurants and bars.

Travel on foot, with bicycles, or with your car to Port Jefferson, a small village of shops and restaurants that caters to day-tripping crowds. Call the numbers above to obtain a brochure describing the Port Jeff attractions. **Theatre Three** (516-928-9100) presents reasonably priced ($$$–$$$$) well-known hits suitable for almost the whole family (children under age 6 are not permitted at Main Stage productions). Children's matinee productions ($$) are offered in July and August for the entire family. Go to shop and stroll, have some dinner, see a show, and sail home by starlight. It makes a sensational day trip.

The sailing time on the ferry is about an hour and 15 minutes each way. Charters, moonlight cruises, and dance cruises are available.

Seaside Park

At Bridgeport's southernmost tip lies **Seaside Park,** a 325-acre expanse designed by Frederick Law Olmsted and Calvert Vaux and donated to the city by P. T. Barnum. The park is reached through the magnificent Perry Memorial Arch over Park Avenue. Designed by Henry Bacon in 1916, the same year he designed the Lincoln Memorial in Washington, the arch is the gateway to the 2.5-mile peninsula that features a shoreline drive, a wide, white-sand beach, playing fields, concessions, and walking paths. Nonresidents wishing to drive through or spend a day at the park must stop at a checkpoint to purchase a day-use pass ($$ for CT vehicles, $$$ for out-of-state vehicles from Memorial Day weekend through Labor Day weekend). Be sure to find the bronze P. T. Barnum statue along the shoreline drive. Swimming is occasionally prohibited, but the park is widely used year-round, from dawn to sunset. Call the Bridgeport Parks Department (203-576-7233) for more information.

Where to Eat

Bloodroot. 85 Ferris St.; (203) 576-9168. Come to this hidden wonder, tucked near the sea, for delicious vegetarian fare for lunch, dinner, and Sunday brunch, with locally grown, lovingly sourced everything. Closed Mon; no lunch on Wed; only brunch on Sun. $$

Joseph's Steakhouse. 360 Fairfield Ave.; (203) 337-9944. This old-fashioned steak-house gets rave reviews from all directions. Friendly father-of-five owner encourages sharing between parents and kids; famed home fries and crisp salads can complete a meal that makes the whole clan happy. Lunch on weekdays; dinner daily. $$$–$$$$

Taco Loco. 3170 Fairfield Ave.; (203) 335-8228. In the historic Black Rock neighbor-hood, come to this casual, colorful place for authentic Mexican classics: tacos, enchi-ladas, fajitas, tortilla soup, and excellent paella. Outdoor terrace. Lunch and dinner daily. $–$$

Take Time Cafe. 211 State St.; (203) 335-7255. Open from 6:30 a.m. to 4:30 p.m. on weekdays, this downtown coffeehouse/bakery has outstanding bagels, sandwiches, muffins, and other kid-friendly fare, perfect for breakfast, lunch, and picnics. $

Vazzy's. 513 Broadbridge Rd.; (203) 371-8046. This family-owned Bridgeport fixture has the city's best pasta and hands-down best pizza. Lunch and dinner daily. $$

Where to Stay

Bridgeport Holiday Inn. 1070 Main St.; (203) 334-1234 or (800) HOLIDAY. Convenient downtown location. 256 rooms, fitness room, indoor pool, restaurant. Kids **free**; week-end packages with tickets to attractions. $$$

Trumbull Marriott. 180 Hawley Lane, Trum-bull; (203) 378-1400. Convenient to parkway, Route 8, and Bridgeport attractions. 311 rooms, 6 suites; fitness room; indoor and out-door pools. Kids **free**; weekend packages. $$$–$$$$

Stratford

This small municipality on the easternmost border of Fairfield County often gets lost in the shuffle as travelers rush past it on I-95 in an effort to beat the traffic in or out of New Haven and Bridgeport. Despite its long history as one of Connecticut's oldest shoreline communities, Stratford keeps a modest profile in the tourism sector. That situation could change if two special projects develop. First is the long-awaited reopening of the Ameri-can Stratford Festival Theater, a re-creation of the Bard's famed Globe Theatre in London. The Town of Stratford continues to maintain the property surrounding the theater, which sits on a bluff above the lower Housatonic River. Look for news on the websites www .stratfordfestival.com or www.townofstratford.com. The second project is in keeping with Stratford's long association with the aviation industry. The Connecticut Air and Space Cen-ter is under organization at the former site of the Vought-Sikorsky plant, where Connecti-cut's official state aircraft—the World War II fighter plane, the F4U Corsair—was made from 1939 to 1948. Check the website www.ctairandspace.org for the latest information

Stratford's **Best-Kept Secrets**

The sand spit at **Long Beach** offers one of Fairfield County's best beach-combing opportunities. Park at the base of Washington Parkway among the restaurants near Marnick's Rodeway Inn and walk from Point No Point, at the eastern end of the seawall, toward the west, where Stratford's Long Beach stretches toward Bridgeport's Pleasure Beach. Except for the occasional interruption of an airplane returning to or leaving the nearby airport, you'll be alone with the wind, surf, and wildlife in this secluded spot.

As you return from a weekend beach walk, the music from **Long Beach Skateland** (55 Washington Parkway; 203-378-9033; $$) may tempt visitors both young and old to add wheels to their feet and take a few turns around this old-fashioned roller-skating rink. To protect their specially coated wooden floor, the owners allow only traditional quad skates, which are available for you to borrow at no extra charge. Most skate sessions feature contemporary Top Forty hits; Sunday evenings offer the charming lilts of organ music. Year-round, sessions are Fri 7 to 9:30 p.m., Sat 2 to 4 p.m. and 7:30 to 10 p.m., and Sun 2 to 4 p.m. and 7 to 9 p.m.

On the east-facing cove that cups the mouth of the Housatonic River, Stratford's **Short Beach Park** (Park and Recreation Department: 203-385-4052) offers families the best day-tripping bargain of all the public beaches along the Connecticut shore. Nonresidents pay a modest day fee per vehicle ($) to use the beach and the park's ball fields, tennis courts, basketball courts, and playground. Picnic tables and grills are also available, and a concession operates in the summer months. For an extra charge, visitors can use the park's nine-hole golf course or its miniature golf course. The park is open year-round, dawn to dusk. Lifeguards are on duty mid-June through Labor Day; during this time the restrooms and outdoor showers are also operational.

A quirkier place to consider for history and transportation buffs is Stratford's **Merritt Parkway Museum,** operated by the Merritt Parkway Conservancy. This "lobby museum" is located in the Ryder's Landing shopping area at 6850 Main St. A 10-foot guide to the parkway is mounted on the wall there, and a 30-minute video tells the story of the parkway's construction, its engineering challenges, its famed bridges, and its preservation. For more information, call (203) 661-3255 or check www.merrittparkway.org. The museum, by the way, is just a short walk from the **bike and pedestrian path** that leads from Ryder's Lane across the **Sikorsky Bridge,** which spans the Housatonic River between Stratford and Milford.

on this museum, which promises to feature Connecticut's contributions to the science of aviation. Until the completion of those endeavors, families can still enjoy other interesting destinations in this pleasant town.

Children's Garbage Museum (ages 5 to 12)

1410 Honeyspot Rd. Extension, I-95 exit 30; (203) 381-9571 or (800) 455-9571; www.crra.org/ education. Open to school groups daily in the academic year; open to families from noon to 4 p.m. Wed through Fri (Sept through June) and 10 a.m. to 4 p.m. Tues through Fri (July and Aug), plus Family Fun Days on selected Saturdays and December holiday openings. $; 3 years and under, free.

This museum features 22 interactive exhibits that teach children about the importance of recycling and the responsible treatment of garbage. One of the exhibits is a soft-sculpture compost pile in which children can crawl into a simulated worm tunnel to see how organic matter decomposes into soil. The museum's mascot is Trash-o-saurus, a 24-foot-long dinosaur constructed from trash.

Visitors generally spend about an hour at the hands-on exhibit area, then take a tour of the next-door Southwest Connecticut Regional Recycling Plant, where recyclables are sorted and prepared for sale to remanufacturers. Most visitors then return to the museum to create a craft or buy a gift made from recycled or reusable material.

Boothe Memorial Park and Museum (all ages)

5774 Main St., Putney, a northern section of town; (203) 381-2046 for tours and museum information, or (203) 381-2068 for Stratford parks department; www.townofstratford .com or http://boothememorialpark.org/index.html. Park grounds open year-round daily from approximately 8 a.m. to dusk. Buildings open for guided or self-guided tours June 1 through October 1; Tues and Fri 11 a.m. to 1 p.m. and Sun1 to 4 p.m. Free.

This 32-acre park overlooking the Housatonic River was once the site of an estate owned by two wealthy, and apparently eccentric, brothers whose family had successfully farmed the site for more than 300 years. Today this National Historic Landmark includes two of the original Boothe homesteads, plus a trolley station, a tollbooth plaza, a model lighthouse, a miniature windmill, an icehouse, an outdoor basilica with an organ house, an 1844 chapel, a barn with a weaving loom and other objects related to 19th-century farm life, a working blacksmith shop, a clock tower museum, and an amazing redwood monument called the Technocratic Cathedral! An observatory hosts the Boothe Memorial Astronomical Society's meetings and public open houses. Check the society's calendar for free open-house nights, when young and beginner astronomers are invited to observe stars and comets or whatever else the night skies reveal. Check www.bmas.org for more information.

Surrounding this intriguing conglomeration are acres of parkland offering gardens; walking paths; picnic groves with tables, barbecue grills, and shelters; a playground; ball-playing areas; and restrooms. The buildings and restrooms close in November, but ice-skating and sledding are allowed in the winter, weather permitting.

National Helicopter Museum (all ages)
2840 Main St., at the eastbound side of the tracks at the old Stratford Railroad Depot; (203) 375-5766 or (203) 767-1123; www.nationalhelicoptermuseum.org. Open Memorial Day through October 15, Wed through Sun, 1 to 4 p.m. Donation requested.

If you have aircraft buffs in your clan, an hour at this small museum, located in the old red Stratford Railroad Depot, will be enjoyable if you can't make it up to the New England Air Museum in Windsor Locks. Exhibits trace the development of the helicopter and the life of aviation pioneer Igor Sikorsky, founder of Stratford's famed Sikorsky Aircraft industries. Museum displays include the cockpit of the V-22 Osprey (an airplane that hovers like a helicopter), several helicopter engines, and miniature models of Sikorsky's helicopters. Also on display are drawings of early helicopter prototypes (such as da Vinci's Helix) and photographs of helicopters used in various military operations.

Where to Eat

Knapp's Landing. 520 Sniffens Lane; (203) 378-5999. At the mouth of the Housatonic River at Sniffens Point, this establishment offers seafood, pasta, chicken, steaks, soups, sandwiches, and salads. Open-air deck in warm weather. Lunch and dinner daily. $$

Marnick's Restaurant. 10 Washington Parkway; (203) 377-6288. Owned by the same family for more than 50 years, this right-on-the-water favorite serves reasonably priced steaks, seafood, sandwiches, salads, and burgers. Waterfront patio in warm weather. Open daily. $–$$

The Peppermill Steak and Fish House. 225 Longshore Blvd.; (203) 870-8445. A Westport fixture for 40 years, this steak and seafood house has relocated to the Stratford Ramada Inn. Familiar American fare, children's entrees; lunch on weekdays ($–$$) from 11 a.m. to 3 p.m.; dinner daily ($$$–$$$$) from 5 to 10 p.m.

Where to Stay

Rodeway Inn. 10 Washington Parkway; (203) 377-6288. In the interest of travelers shopping by brand-name recognition, Marnick's family-owned motel on the Sound has changed its name, but it's still the same old-fashioned (but fully renovated) waterfront hostelry, as it has been for half a century. 29 rooms, restaurant. Waterfront rooms have balconies, microwaves, and refrigerators. Private beach for swimming and shore fishing. $$

Stratford Ramada. 225 Lordship Blvd.; (203) 375-8866 or (800) 2RAMADA. 145 rooms, restaurant, indoor pool. Continental breakfast. $$–$$$

Shelton

In another of Fairfield County's bucolic corners lies the growing town—a small city, really—of Shelton, easily accessible from the Merritt Parkway and Routes 8 and 110. North of Stratford and east of Trumbull and Monroe, the city is also bounded by the Housatonic River, which is among its greatest natural resources. Suburban developments and

Freshly **Pressed**

Any cider you drink in Shelton may have come from **Beardsley's Cider Mill and Orchard** at 278 Leavenworth Rd. (Route 110). The Beardsley clan has run this operation since 1849, so they have had plenty of practice pressing cider at their mill, as well as baking delicious pies. You can pick (weekends only) more than 30 different varieties of heirloom and other apples in the orchards here—or just buy a bagful in the shop. While you munch a crisp apple or try your free sample of unpasteurized cider, you can watch the pressing operation in the mill. Learn about the method they employ to protect you from bacteria (it's all in the lighting system, you might say). You'll be hard-pressed to leave without stocking up on locally made honey, maple syrup, jams, jellies, and applesauce. Excellent cookies, pies, cheesecake, and cider doughnuts are good accompaniments to your jugful of cider, too. Open from Sept through Dec, Mon through Fri noon to 6 p.m. and weekends from 10 a.m. to 6 p.m. For more information, call (203) 926-1098 or check the website, www.beardsleyscidermill.com.

shopping areas encroach on land that was once—not too long ago—woodland and farmland, but efforts like those of the Shelton Land Trust (www.sheltonlandtrust.org) and the City of Shelton Open Space Plan do protect some of the earlier ambience of its hilly countryside. Check the land trust website for additional ideas for fun with the family on Shelton's remaining farms and trails. For a sense of the town's early history and culture, you might also visit the **Shelton History Center** (70 Ripton Rd.; 203-925-1803), a lovely 1-acre enclave with five collected historic structures, including the 1872 Trap Falls Schoolhouse, the 1822 Marks-Brownson House, and the circa 1860 Wilson Barn, with a permanent exhibit called *Three Centuries of Shelton, From Farming to Industry and Beyond,* which traces town history from early European settlement through the 20th century. Excellent educational programs and summer camps are offered for families and children.

Jones Family Farms

Main farm: 606 Walnut Tree Hill Rd.; Pumpkinseed Hill farm: 130 Beardsley Rd.; (203) 929-8425; www.jonesfamilyfarms.com. Free admission; pay per pound for the produce you buy; all cut-your-own trees, $60 in 2010. Strawberries, early June through mid-July; blueberries, mid-July to late August; call for picking hours and conditions; pumpkins, late September through Halloween; Christmas trees, mid-November through December 24. Please leave pets at home during pumpkin season; leashed pets are allowed on the tree farm but not in the historic barnyard, winery, or gift shop. Farmers' market in summer.

During the growing season, this family-fun place is one of the most popular outdoor attractions in the state. From June through December, come here to enjoy the great outdoors and connect with the farmers who work so hard to bring food to our tables. You can help them out by picking your own strawberries and blueberries on the main farm in the summer season, and then come to Pumpkinseed Hill to pick pumpkins in the fall. During the winter holidays, return for one of the state's largest selections of perfect Christmas trees. The Jones family has been farming these parcels since the mid-1800s, when Welsh-Irish immigrant Philip Jones staked a claim here. Now his great-great-grandson Terry and Terry's son, Jamie, have taken on the stewardship of this 400-acre Century farm.

You may learn something valuable about sustainable agriculture while you're here having fun. "Be good to the land, and the land will be good to you" is the farm motto, and it shows in the family's approach to pest management, crop rotation, and preservation of soil structure. You may check out the fine soil of Shelton's White Hills on a ramble through 200 acres of Christmas trees, 15 each of berries, or the 25 acres of pumpkin patches, or you might prefer to take a hayride ($) or walk the corn maze ($) in the autumn. A UNICEF Children's Festival the last weekend in October offers fun activities such as gourd tosses, pumpkin decorating, sing-alongs, and **free** wagon rides; in winter, stop at the old dairy barn to browse in the Holiday Gatherings gift shop and have a cup of hot mulled cider at the Christmas canteen.

Indian Well State Park

Howe Avenue (Route 110); (203) 735-4311; www.ct.gov/dep; open daily year-round from 8 a.m. to sunset. Weekend and weekday per-vehicle parking fees ($$) from Memorial Day through Labor Day.

This state park with 153 acres along the Housatonic River gets its name from the waterfall and splash pool at its base. According to legend, an ill-fated romance between two young Native Americans met its end at this site, but local native inhabitants never actually used this water place as a well. Likely they enjoyed the same activities you might enjoy here today: picnicking near the cascades; boating, fishing, and swimming in the river; and hiking on the Paugussett Trail through the woodlands. (A 2.5-mile section of the 8-mile trail, which ends in the town of Monroe, is accessible near the entrance to the park; no fee is charged for access to the trail, a portion of which crosses the Stevenson Dam.) A volleyball court and a picnic shelter with grills and tables are also here, along with restrooms. The swimming area has lifeguards and a concession in the summer months. No camping is allowed.

SportsCenter of Connecticut

784 River Rd. (Route 110); (203) 929-6500; www.sportscenterct.com. Open 365 days a year; hours vary for each sport and activity; call or check the website. Each individual activity fee is generally $–$$$.

If your own backyard is letting you down and the woods and ponds of Shelton don't beckon, come here, where everything is go-go-go! In a bright-lights, big-city style, this enormous recreation complex offers glitzy pay-as-you-play opportunities year-round, sunup to sundown, for active families with a yen for physical challenges. The world's only double-decker ice rink is here, and it's a doozy. Both indoor rinks, stacked one over the other, are NHL-sized and offer public skating hours six days a week, year-round, plus pickup hockey games several times each month. Eighteen holes of miniature golf are available day and night year-round, weather permitting; the outdoor course features a waterway and falls and lots of pretty landscaping. If it rains on your game, you can ask for a poncho or a **free** game token. If you prefer real golf, hit a bucket of balls at the driving range or take lessons at the Junior Golf Academy. At Fun Bowl, in the Golf Center, even small children feel successful when they roll three-pound balls down the lane: Automated bumpers block the gutters for beginners, and automated scoring makes it easy to keep track of all the fun the kids are having. Eight outdoor batting cages can pitch you balls at your choice of 28 to 91 miles per hour; you rent the opportunity to swing at these for a half-hour or an hour at a time. If you prefer jungle games, head to the Rinks building for Lazer Tag. The 5,000-square-foot indoor forest here provides plenty of room to act out the dramas you invent as you navigate the tree-lined, rock-walled pathways to base camp. If your team has extra energy, SportsCenter also rents two full-size basketball courts, and they melt the ice on one of the rinks in the springtime for in-line hockey leagues.

You can have birthday parties here as well, and meals of the fast-food sort are available at the Rinks Food Court. What, no pool, rock-climbing wall, or go-karts? Those are the only fun missing here!

Where to Eat

Sassafras Restaurant & Ice Cream Parlor. 13 Huntington Plaza; (203) 929-3249. For three meals plus J. J. Lawson's gourmet ice cream, there's no better place for families than this independently owned eatery serving casual American fare. Breakfast and lunch, daily from 7 a.m.; dinner, Mon through Sat. $–$$

Trattoria Roma. 232 Leavenworth Rd.; (203) 929-5177. In the White Hills Shopping Center, this family-owned trattoria offers pizza as well as authentic family-style Italian cuisine in a casual setting. Lunch, Tues through Fri; dinner from 4 p.m. Tues through Sun. $$

Where to Stay

Courtyard by Marriott. 780 Bridgeport Ave.; (203) 929-1500. 161 units (12 suites), restaurant, lounge, fitness room, indoor pool. $$$–$$$$

Hilton Garden Inn Shelton. 25 Old Stratford Rd.; (203) 447-1000. 142 units (3 suites), refrigerator, microwave; restaurant, fitness room, hot tub, indoor pool. $$$$

Holiday Inn Express. 695 Bridgeport Ave.; (203) 925-5900. 128 suites with refrigerator, microwave; indoor pool, fitness room. $$$–$$$$

Easton/Redding/Weston/Bethel

The area between Fairfield in the south and Danbury in the north is sliced vertically in two by Route 58, a great road through lovely countryside. Routes 53 and 57 north from Westport also lead you toward the quiet pleasures of life north of the rat race. If you have spent a few days in the cities on the Sound, give yourselves a break and head for the farthest reaches of the county. Meander awhile—along green-canopied lanes in summer, beside snow-capped fences and stone walls in winter. The following itinerary will take you to some of the county's most interesting and engaging sites, and descriptions of those places follow. If you begin your day traveling north from Fairfield on Route 58, you'll pass through Easton's stately conifer forests surrounding the Hemlock and Aspetuck reservoirs. If you've started out early, stop in Easton at the Olde Bluebird Inn Restaurant (363 Black Rock Turnpike; 203-452-0697) at the junction of Route 58 and Route 136 for some home-cooked breakfast vittles. Once you're back in the car, pause again just a quarter-mile or so up the road at the aeration fountain spouting high into the air at the edge of the Hemlock reservoir. Let its music soothe your soul, then return to the car and stop just a mile or so northward at the Aspetuck Valley Apple Barn (see Pick-Your-Own Pleasures sidebar) to pick up some picnic gruel and hiking fuel.

Continue northwest on Route 58 about 7 miles until you reach Putnam Memorial State Park, near the Redding and Bethel town lines. Known as Connecticut's Valley Forge, it's

Mark Twain Library

Redding's town library differs from other Connecticut libraries because famed Redding resident Samuel Clemens funded it. Formed as a private association library funded by "friends," the original library building built in 1911 still exists within the now-expanded library. Called the Mark Twain Room, that portion of the library houses many titles about Twain and by him, as well as 200 volumes from his personal collection of favorites. You may ask for a free guided tour of this area when you come, and, if you come in May/June or November/December, you may see one of the two annual themed exhibits about some aspect of Twain's life or his work. Outside the library is a popular site for photographers: a sculpted bronze bench that incorporates figures of Twain, Tom Sawyer, and Becky Thatcher. The library sits quite prettily on the banks of the Saugatuck River, so you may also want to wander here or picnic here; benches are provided at riverside. If you're intrigued, you'll find the library at 439 Redding Rd. (Route 53); (203) 938-2545; www.marktwainlibrary.org. It's open year-round Mon through Wed and Fri and Sat, 10 a.m. to 5 p.m., and until 8 p.m. on Thurs, and on Sun (except in the summer) from noon to 5 p.m.

well worth a stop, even if it's a brief one at the museum and visitor center. From the park, take a left from Route 58 onto Route 107 (also called Putnam Park Road). If you are a member or are arriving for one of its two annual public festivals, you could go from here to New Pond Farm, a private outdoor environmental education center in West Redding. (You'd take a right onto Lonetown Road and drive .2-mile to a left onto Limekiln Road, then travel just under 2 miles to Route 53 [Redding Road] and take a left onto Route 53 South. Drive .8 mile and take a right on Umpawaug Road, then another right onto Marchant Road.) Otherwise, take Route 107 West to Route 53 South and travel south for about 5 miles. Along this stretch of road, you'll pass the Mark Twain Library (see sidebar) and then the Redding Roadhouse (a good place for lunch now or dinner later). Continue to a right turn onto Godfrey Road and then another right on Pent Road; there, take a walk through Connecticut's largest contiguous nature preserve, owned by the Nature Conservancy.

Putnam Memorial State Park (ages 7 to 12)

492 Black Rock Turnpike (Route 58 between West Redding and Bethel near Route 107 junction); (203) 938-2285, or (866) 287-2757 for the State Parks Division; http://putnampark.org. Park open daily 8 a.m. to dusk; museum open from Memorial Day to Columbus Day from 11 a.m. to 5 p.m. on weekends only. Pit toilets; picnic tables. Free.

Families who love studies and stories of the American Revolution will love a visit here, especially if you have read Christopher Collier's award-winning middle-grade novel, *My Brother Sam is Dead,* set around these parts. Site of the 1778–79 winter encampment of General Israel Putnam's Northern Brigades of the Continental Army, the park includes a nearly new visitor center and a small museum built on the original picket post from which the sentries guarded the barracks and magazine. In the museum you'll see exhibits related to the Revolutionary War and the encampment. On weekends in July and August from 10 a.m. to 3 p.m., colonial craftspersons demonstrate varied skills (blacksmithing, weaving, cord-winding, pottery) and portrayals of Revolutionary-era soldiering. Reenactments of the Revolutionary War encampment, with artillery demonstrations and cavalry and infantry camp life activities, are presented during the annual Patriots' Weekend, usually in July or later in the fall. On a self-guided tour of the area, you can also see the remains of the gunpowder magazine, a reconstruction of the officers' barracks, a guardhouse reproduction, and the remains of the soldiers' huts. Even without a passion for history, you may enjoy the park's 183 acres; come in summer for fishing, hiking, and picnicking or in winter for cross-country skiing.

Israel Putnam Statue

A magnificent bronze statue of "Old Put" shaking his fist at the British while atop his trusty steed stands at the entrance to Putnam Memorial State Park. Not surprisingly, the sculptor is notable herself. Anna Hyatt Huntington created the statue at the age of 94.

New Pond Farm (all ages)

101 Marchant Rd., West Redding; (203) 938-2117; www.newpond.org.

In West Redding, this 102-acre private nonprofit property is a members-mostly environ-mental education center and outdoor classroom open to local and nearby members and, twice yearly, to the visiting public. A designated Connecticut Dairy Farm of Distinction, its peaceful habitats include pasturelands, woodlands, and wetlands, as well as perennial gardens, a bog garden with carnivorous plants, a large vegetable and fruit plot, a colonial herb garden, and a Shakespeare garden. Members can come here for farm programs in its historic barns, which house sheep, chickens, roosters, and dairy cows; buy freshly pasteurized milk and yogurt in the Dairy Annex; or sign up for veg-etable and herb programs in the Shared Harvest Program. Native American programs for members also take place here, often in the farm's re-created Eastern Woodlands encampment, complete with native-style dwelling places. Also open to members only are classes, programs, and family-friendly activities like barn dances, art shows, and monthly astronomy programs. In the summer, children ages 8 to 12 can attend a residential camp; three 10-day sessions are offered ($$$$); older children, in grades 7, 8, and 9 can come for a Summer Shakespeare camp ($$$$). Members ($60 annual fee per family) are welcome to hike the farm's 2.5 miles of trails and can arrange themed birthday parties here on a variety of topics; members also enjoy discounts on programs. Each year, the farm offers just two special events open to the public: a Harvest Festival in mid-October and the Founder's May Fair in mid-May. Both festivals ($ per person over age 3, or $$$$ per family) include hands-on activities, demonstrations of traditional farm chores, skills, and crafts, and food and music options suitable for the whole family.

The Nature Conservancy's Devil's Den Nature Preserve (all ages)

33 Pent Rd., Weston; (203) 226-4991; www.nature.org/wherewework/northamerica/states/ connecticut/preserves. Trails open dawn to dusk daily; preserve office open 9 a.m. to 5 p.m. Mon to Fri. Free.

This beautiful refuge includes 1,756 acres of woodlands, wetlands, and rock ledges sepa-rated by valleys with swamps and streams that sustain nearly 200 species of birds and mammals and nearly 500 species of trees and wildflowers. The site of prehistoric native encampments and a 17th-century colonial settlement, the preserve has a mill pond, a lovely ravine with a tumbling cascade, and 21 miles of trails, including loop routes for every age, fitness level, and time schedule. Occasional guided walks are offered (check the website), but most folks take to the trails on their own; just pick up a trail map in the park-ing lot at the map shelter. The staff asks that you register before entering the trails. No pets, bicycles, or mechanized vehicles are permitted here. There are no restrooms, and no camping is allowed.

Pick-Your-Own Pleasures

Some of Fairfield County's farms offer great opportunities for parents to introduce children to local agriculture and the special satisfactions of the recently revived farm-to-table movement. The recipes you can pick up down on the farm may be beneficial to your family's sense of well-being—and you're sure to have a good time learning where your food comes from and how it's grown. Choose from farms that offer pick-your-own crops or ones that at least offer right-from-the-farmer market stands.

Free Connecticut Farm Maps offer current lists of berry, vegetable, and tree farms, plus orchards and sugarhouses. Call (860) 713-2503 to request a map from the Connecticut Department of Agriculture.

- **Blue Jay Orchards.** 125 Plumtrees Rd., Bethel; pick-your-own information: (203) 748-0119; www.bluejayorchardsct.com. Open daily from Aug through late Dec from 9:30 a.m. to 5:30 p.m. This conventional-methods farm grows apples, pears, and pumpkins; its roadside market offers pies, jams, syrup, honey, sweet cider, and cider doughnuts. Come for an Apple Festival in late September, hayrides to the pumpkins in October, and a Christmas tree sale in December. Sometimes the joint is jumping—hayrides, painted pumpkins, red-cheeked kids having a ball. Sometimes it's sleepy as a dog in August, and the only thing moving is the dust on the road. Either way, the apples are crisp and the pies are delicious.

- **Warrup's Farm.** 51 John Read Rd., West Redding; (203) 938-9403; www .warrupsfarm.com. Open Tues through Sun, July through Oct, this certified organic farm offers vegetables, flowers, pumpkins, free-range poultry, and maple syrup (demonstrations 10 a.m. to 5 p.m. the first three weekends in March). To reach it travel down a beautiful country lane; see barnyard animals; take a hayride in pumpkin season.

Where to Eat

Dr. Mike's Ice Cream. 158 Greenwood Ave., Bethel; (203) 792-4388. Stop here for what the doctor recommends—Dr. Mike, that is. If you love rich coat-your-throat ice cream, you're going to love Dr. Mike's prescription. Noon to 10 p.m. daily in summer; shorter winter hours. $

Georgetown Saloon. 8 Main St., Redding, at the junction of Routes 57 and 107 in village of Georgetown; (203) 544-8003. Kids will like the Western-themed decor, the huge menu of American favorites, and the kids' karaoke, if you're here on the right day. Lunch and dinner daily; weekend brunch. $–$$

- **Holbrook Farm.** 45 Turkey Plain Rd. (Route 53), Bethel; (203) 792-0561; www.holbrookfarm.net. Open Mar through Nov, Mon through Sat 10 a.m. to 6 p.m. Bakery and farm market with local honey, meats, cheeses, flowers, jams, soaps, and produce fresh from their fields.

- **Maple Row Tree Farm.** 538 North Park Ave., Easton; (203) 261-9577; www .mrfarm.com. Christmas trees, wreaths, garlands, oxen- or tractor-drawn wagon rides, hot cider. Open daily from the day after Thanksgiving to Christmas Eve, this 200-acre farm is the perfect setting for finding the perfect tree.

- **Silverman's Farm.** 451 Sport Hill Rd. (Route 59), Easton; (203-261-3306); www.silvermansfarm.com. Young children especially enjoy this popular site, with an animal farm, a seasonal cider mill, and 60 acres of pick-your-own peaches, plums, nectarines, sunflowers, apples, pumpkins, gourds, and Christmas trees. Open daily year-round, except Thanksgiving, Christmas, and New Year's Day. In the fall, watch the cider pressing process and take a tractor-drawn wagon ride through the fields and orchards. At the animal farm ($), see a small menagerie of domestic and exotic creatures. Picnic tables, washing stations, and restrooms are available. At the farm market, buy produce, house-made pies, jams, salsas, honey, and syrup—and mums, wreaths, and poinsettias in season. Call ahead for the pick-your-own schedule or to arrange a birthday party here.

- **Aspetuck Valley Apple Barn.** 714 Black Rock Turnpike (Route 58), Easton; (203) 268-9033. This produce store is open Apr through Dec, daily from 9:30 a.m. to 5:30 p.m. In all three seasons, it's stocked with fresh fruits and veggies, local honey, maple sugar candies, and other great trail food.

Olde Bluebird Inn Restaurant. 363 Black Rock Turnpike, Easton; (203) 452-0697. A classic roadside favorite since 1919, this place serves up awesome breakfasts and filling lunches. Gotta try the fruit-packed pancakes. Open daily from 7 a.m. to 2 p.m., except Sun 8 a.m. to 1 p.m. $–$$

Plain Jane's. 208 Greenwood Ave., Bethel; (203) 797-1515. Owned for 30-plus years by two sisters who know how to cook for families, this restaurant is a standout for homemade, healthy American cuisine. Lunch and dinner, Mon through Sat, 11 a.m. to 9 p.m. Early-bird specials 4 to 6 p.m. $$

Redding Roadhouse. 406 Redding Rd. at the junction of Routes 53 and 107; (203) 938-3388. Traditional New England fare in a place where Mark Twain himself is reported to have tarried. Lunch and dinner daily; Sunday brunch, 11 a.m. to 2 p.m. $$$–$$$$

Where to Stay

Best Western Stony Hill Inn. 46 Stony Hill Rd., Bethel; (203) 743-5533 or (800) 528-1234. 36 units. Restaurant, outdoor pool, continental breakfast; 40 acres with pond. $$$

Microtel Inn & Suites. 80 Benedict Rd.; (203) 748-8318; www.microtelinn.com. 78 newly renovated rooms; deluxe continental breakfast, special packages. $–$$

Ridgefield

While the northern sections of Fairfield County's coastal cities and towns become more rural as you leave the Route 1/I-95 corridor, it's not until you're inland 10 miles or so that you notice Fairfield County's split personality. From points north, Fairfield County is downright bucolic except for the city of Danbury. Small towns with pretty greens and white clapboard churches dot the countryside. The pace slows. The air is clean. You might even forget you are in the most densely populated county of the state. If you've been in the truly small and quiet interior towns of the county, meander along Routes 107 and 102 to reach one of the state's nicest medium-sized suburbs—the affluent, sophisticated, and yet friendly Ridgefield.

Visitors with children will enjoy the pedestrian-friendly nature of Ridgefield's pretty town center, where most of its attractions, shops, and restaurants are clustered. Its Aldrich Museum enjoys national renown for its art as well as for its exceptional family education programs; its historic Keeler Tavern Museum is especially welcoming and accessible to children; and its many boutiques and restaurants, both sophisticated and simple, have friendly proprietors who clearly cater to a family-oriented clientele. Spend the day just strolling here on the lovely town green or in pretty **Ballard Park,** right in the center of the village. Have lunch, check out the shops, and be sure to leave time for both museums. If you live nearby, be sure to check out the incredible lineup of performers and productions at the **Ridgefield Playhouse** (203-438-5795; 80 East Ridge; www.ridgefield playhouse.org). Baby boomers will especially enjoy some of the musical headliners, but families will also find much to enjoy.

The Aldrich Contemporary Art Museum (ages 6 to 12)

258 Main St. (Route 35); (203) 438-4519; www.aldrichart.org. Open year-round, Tues through Sun, from noon to 5 p.m. $–$$, children under 18 free. Free to all on Tues. Ask Me Gallery tours, Tues and Sun 2 to 4 p.m.

Surprising to find in the center of a residential suburb like Ridgefield is this sophisticated museum founded in 1964 by Larry Aldrich, an innovative connoisseur of fine art. The internationally renowned Aldrich focuses its attention on new talents and currents in art and culture. In 2004 the Aldrich moved its exhibitions into a magnificent addition linked to a renovated historic structure. Twelve galleries, a hundred-seat performance space, an education center, a screening room, a 22-foot-high project space, and an outdoor sculpture garden are among its features.

In addition to exhibitions of the work of emerging and mid-career artists, the Aldrich is dedicated to contemporary video artists and performing artists. World-class concerts, performances, readings, and films are offered on a regular schedule. Children's art days, studio visits, and interactive family tours add to the museum's appeal to visitors of all ages.

Keeler Tavern Museum (ages 5 to 12)

132 Main St; (203) 438-5485; www.keelertavernmuseum.org. Tours by costumed guides from Feb 1 through Dec, on Wed, Sat, and Sun from 1 to 4 p.m. (last tour at 3:30 p.m.). Lantern-light tours in early Nov. Closed Easter Sunday, July 4, Thanksgiving, Christmas, and in Jan. $.

Reputed as the most hospitable stop on the coach route between New York and Boston, Ridgefield's historic tavern was built about 1713 and operated as one of the most important inns in Connecticut for 130 years. A hub of community life in Ridgefield and a meeting place for patriots in Revolutionary War days, the tavern was fired on by British troops during the Battle of Ridgefield. A small cannonball remains imbedded in a corner post of the house. The tavern's taproom is a cheerful reminder of the comforts the inn offered to weary 18th-century travelers. Although the tavern was modified several times in its history (once by famed architect and former owner Cass Gilbert), its main rooms are furnished according to the period closest to its early days. Visitors can also see the ladies' parlor, the dining room, the bedchambers, and the kitchen. Woodenware, cooking implements, and other domestic utensils illustrate the colonial lifestyle. Be sure to stroll through the lovely walled garden Gilbert designed for his wife.

Where to Eat

Deborah Ann's. 181 Main St.; (203) 438-0065. For the sweetest treats ever, go straight to this cheerful shop. Every kind of deliciousness is here, from bonbons, truffles, and turtles to gummies, jellies, and all flavors of beans. All of that plus locally famed and absolutely epicurean Mr. Shane's Homemade Ice Cream. Open daily, year-round. $

Early Bird Cafe. 88 Danbury Rd.; (203) 438-1395. It's a little more out of the way of the main village, but it's just off Route 35, and some folks drive miles for the delicious French toast and omelets. Open Tues through Fri from 6 a.m. to 9 p.m.; Sat from 6 a.m. to 3 p.m.; and Sun from 7 a.m. to 2 p.m. $

Southwest Cafe. 109 Danbury Rd.; (203) 431-3398. For family dinners, this is the best bet in town. Kids under 12 have their own menu of southwestern and Tex-Mex favorites like flautas, fajitas, tacos, and such. Great salads, wraps, soups, and much more. Lunch and dinner daily; live music on Thurs and Sat evening. $$–$$$

Where to Stay

Days Inn. 296 Ethan Allen Highway; (203) 438-3781. Convenient to I-84, 36 units with fridges and such, complimentary continental breakfast, restaurant. $$

West Lane Inn. 22 West Lane, Route 35; (203) 438-7323. Elegant four-diamond inn, 16 rooms (3 efficiencies) with private baths, continental breakfast. $$$$

Danbury

From the Ridgefield area, take Route 35 north to Route 7 north, or if you're coming north from Bethel, take Route 53 north about 3 miles to Danbury, a small city famous for its nearly 200-year history of hat manufacturing. Now better recognized for the corporate headquarters that were drawn here by low real estate prices and a convenient location on I-84, Danbury has some family destinations that reflect its interesting past.

Danbury Museum and
Historical Society Authority (ages 7 to 12)

43 Main St.; (203) 743-5200; www.danburyhistorical.org. Open in the summer for tours Tues through Sat, 10 a.m. to 4 p.m. and at other times of the year by appointment for tours on Tues, Wed, and Thurs. Donation.

This interesting collection of buildings, massively restored, includes the 1785 John and Mary Rider House with 17th- and 18th-century furnishings and costumes. The John Dodd Hat Shop has terrific exhibits explaining Danbury's world-famous hat-making industry, the impact hat-making had on the growth of related industries, and the history of hats from a fashion point of view. A Revolutionary War exhibit includes facts you never knew about the Daughters of the American Revolution, and a fascinating woodworking exhibit of carpentry and joinery tools offers lessons about time-honored handcrafts.

Among the most important buildings here is the restored Marian Anderson Studio, where the famed opera singer rehearsed for the 50 years in which she made Danbury her home. Exhibits in the studio tell about her magnificent contralto voice, her career, and her struggles and triumphs in her journey toward racial equality. If you want your children to learn more about her, read Russell Freedman's outstanding biography for young readers, *The Voice That Challenged a Nation: Marian Anderson and the Struggle for Equal Rights* (Clarion, 2004), or *When Marian Sang: The True Recital of Marian Anderson*, a picture book by Pam Nunoz Ryan (Scholastic, 2002).

Danbury Railway Museum (all ages)

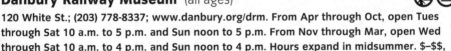

120 White St.; (203) 778-8337; www.danbury.org/drm. From Apr through Oct, open Tues through Sat 10 a.m. to 5 p.m. and Sun noon to 5 p.m. From Nov through Mar, open Wed through Sat 10 a.m. to 4 p.m. and Sun noon to 4 p.m. Hours expand in midsummer. $–$$, children 2 and under free. Special holiday excursions may be higher.

Who doesn't love trains? Whatever magic they have, it is something very attractive to most children and quite a few mature adults. Here in Danbury you can explore the restored Union Station, restored to just about what it looked like when it was built in 1903 for the New York, New Haven & Hartford Railroad. Alfred Hitchcock's thriller *Strangers On a Train* was filmed in and near this station in 1950, when the station was still an important stop for the New Haven Railroad. By the 1980s, though, the city and its rail service were in decline, and the engine house and freight house here had been torn down. Listed on the

National Register of Historic Places since 1995, when interest in its history was revived, the station is in business again.

Check out the nifty memorabilia in the station, and operate three model railroad layouts. Then, tour the 6-acre railroad yard filled with 70 vintage railcars, boxcars, a locomotive, and other artifacts. A sleeping car and an observation car from the 20th Century Limited that ran between New York and Chicago are part of the collection. Train rides range from short rides in the yard, hour-long excursions out of the yard, and daylong trips that head for the Hudson River Valley. Thomas the Tank Engine rides, Easter Bunny rides, Halloween Pumpkin Patch train rides, and Santa trains decorated in the rail yard are part of the family fun here. Check the website for the current schedule.

Ives Concert Park (all ages)

Mill Plain Road, Westside Campus, Route 6; (203) 837-9226; www.ivesconcertpark.com. $$$$, children 3 to 12 $$–$$$, children 2 and under free.

On the campus of Western Connecticut State University, the center offers top-drawer entertainment in an open-air, gazebo-covered stage throughout the summer months. In the colder months, other concerts, plays, and other musical productions take place at Western's Berkshire Theatre or at the Ives Concert Hall on the midtown campus. Named in honor of Pulitzer Prize–winning composer Charles Ives, considered the father of American music, the Ives center hosts symphonies, jazz, folk, blues, theater, dance, and popular artists on its summer stage. Ticket prices and performers vary, but you can always count on exceptional quality and value. A free Family Fair in September features community artists and musical performers as well as the Ives Festival Orchestra. You can bring lawn chairs and picnics to any concert, but no pets, grills, alcoholic beverages, or glass containers.

Where to Eat

Bangkok. 72 Newtown Rd.; (203) 791-0640. This colorful and cozy restaurant has served authentic Thai favorites for 20 years. The staff dresses in traditional costumes, and the atmosphere is warmly convivial. Lunch, Tues through Fri; dinner Tues through Sun. $$

Chuck's Steak House. 20 Segar St.; (203) 792-5555. Excellent steaks, chicken, grilled seafood, and famous salad bar. Open daily for dinner from 4:30 p.m. $$$–$$$$

Stanziato's Wood-Fired Pizza. 35 Lake Ave. Extension; (203) 885-1057. One of the best pizzerias in the state—no worries—plus house-made salads, soups, and sauce, all locally sourced or wonderfully imported.

Open Mon through Fri from noon and Sat from 4 p.m. $

Where to Stay

Ethan Allen Hotel. 21 Lake Ave. Extension; (800) 742-1776. 193 rooms and suites, restaurant, fitness room, outdoor pool. $$$$

Holiday Inn. 80 Newtown Rd.; (203) 792-4000. 114 units, including 11 executive rooms with king-size beds and sofas; outdoor pool. Kids stay free. Complimentary continental breakfast with omelet station. $$$$

Quality Inn and Suites. 78 Federal Rd.; (203) 743-6701 or (800) 4-CHOICE. 72 units, indoor pool, fitness room, continental breakfast. $$$–$$$$

Brookfield/New Fairfield/Sherman

Six miles north of Danbury (taking Route 7 north), Brookfield town center has developed rapidly in the past 10 years, especially along the Route 7 corridor. However, the Brookfield countryside remains rural, or at least suburban, in character, and the beauty of Candlewood Lake and Lake Lillinonah adds to the town's charm. Farther to the west and north are the two small towns of New Fairfield and Sherman. Although their centers, linked by Routes 37 and 39, have charms of their own, there is no doubt that their greatest attractions are Candlewood Lake and Squantz Pond State Park.

Mother Earth Gallery and Mining Company (ages 6 to 12)
806 Federal Rd., Route 7; (203) 775-6272; www.motherearthcrystals.com. Open Mon and Wed through Sat from 10 a.m. to 6 p.m. and Sun noon to 5 p.m. Closed Tues. The mine closes at 4:30 p.m. on Sun and at 5:30 p.m. on the other days. $$$ (prospecting), $$$$ (birthday parties).

This looks like an ordinary storefront with an inventory of pretty neat stuff—crystals, minerals, shells, candles, wind chimes, nature-related toys, and environmentally friendly merchandise with a New Age touch. It's also something more.

It has a mine in it, full of crystals and minerals and semiprecious stones. And you can go prospecting with a bucket and a miner's hard hat complete with headlamp. A birthday celebration in the Miner's Shack party room buys you a Planet Earth cake and juice, a game of Rocko, a video trip around the world to learn about real mines and gem production, and a chance to go prospecting for amethysts, obsidian, calcites, fossil shark teeth,

Candlewood's **Story**

Nearly 1,400 men created the lake in the woodlands and farmlands nestled between the rolling hills of Brookfield and New Fairfield. Five hundred lumberjacks hand-felled 4,500 acres of trees, burning the lumber in massive bonfires. Dams were constructed, and in 1928 the first pumping operation began bringing water from the Housatonic River. Soon the Connecticut Light and Power Company was able to generate electricity by letting the water pour down an enormous pipe called a penstock and into an immense turbine.

Almost immediately the incredible beauty of the newly formed lake lapping the wooded shoreline caused land prices to skyrocket. Development escalated rapidly as the area began drawing homeowners as well as vacationers to the pretty coves of the 60-plus miles of shoreline along the 11-mile-long lake. This valuable new landmark was christened **Candlewood** after the native candlewood trees whose sapling branches had sometimes been used as candles by early settlers.

Fishing at Squantz Pond
and Candlewood Lake

Some fishers say you can't have a bad day fishing in the lakes in this neck of the woods. It's not unusual to land a 10-pound trout, so anglers young and old come to try their luck for one of these trophy fish. Bass also love these waters, and bass tournaments are common summer events as hundreds of boats crowd this vast waterway for both the sport and the great dinners that result from fishing in it. Pickerel, carp, catfish, bluegills, and white and yellow perch proliferate as well. Fish from your boat, the shoreline, or public piers and docks. Remember that Squantz Pond has a special pier for handicapped anglers.

Call the **Candlewood Lake Authority** (860-354-6928) for more information on either lake. The state Department of Environmental Protection website (www.ct.gov/dep) will steer you to both the *CT Boater's Guide* and *CT Angler's Guide,* which provide details for both bodies of water. On the DEP site you can also find state boat-launch sites and info on the marinas that provide fuel, boating goods, boat rentals, and boat services. The DEP online store also offers for sale its *Fisheries Guide to the Lakes and Ponds of Connecticut.* It's a great buy especially for anglers with plans to travel from place to place throughout the state.

or other treasures. Not your birthday? Go prospecting anyway. Serious collectors and beginners alike will love the exceptional minerals and gemstones sold here, and, if you are tempted to really go prospecting in the Connecticut hills, Mother Earth also sells the materials you'd need to find or polish your own gems.

Candlewood Lake (all ages)

Built in 1926 to provide hydroelectric power to the region, Candlewood is the largest artificial lake in Connecticut. Now bordered by private residences, it's pretty as a picture in every season and popular with vacationers and day-trippers even in the quiet of winter. Use Route 39 to travel the length of the western side of the lake; smaller side roads branch off Route 7/202 on the eastern side.

Much of the lakefront is held in private hands, although house, cottage, and cabin rentals are common. Families interested in renting by the week or month can check local newspaper listings or contact area real estate agencies. You can also check out www.candlewoodlake.org.

The five towns (Brookfield, New Fairfield, Sherman, Danbury, and New Milford bordering the lake also have beaches. Some of these are opened to out-of-town visitors at a daily rate. Public boat launches are also available at some of the town beaches on the perimeter, and docks are on the east shore at Down the Hatch Restaurant and near the Candlewood Inn caterers.

Squantz Pond State Park (all ages)

Route 39; (203) 797-4165; www.ct.gov/dep. From Memorial Day weekend through Labor Day, day-use parking fee from 8 a.m. to 6:30 p.m., $$–$$$ (higher fees on weekends).

This pretty area of low hills and woodlands surrounds Squantz Pond, a 5-mile arm of Candlewood Lake. The park offers a public boat launch from which boaters can gain access to Candlewood by passing under the Route 39 causeway that crosses the narrowest connection of the two bodies of water. Other wonderful summer fun here includes riding Jet Skis, waterskiing, fishing, swimming, scuba diving, hiking, and picnicking. In winter the park is perfect for ice-skating, ice fishing, and cross-country skiing. The main entrance to the park is off Route 39 in the town of New Fairfield. From the southern junction of Routes 37 and 39, take 39 north about 4 miles to the entrance. If you're at the north end of the loop, in Sherman, take 39 south about 6 miles.

Along the shore are picnic groves, barbecue areas, a guarded swimming area, and a bathhouse with changing rooms and restrooms (but no showers). There is a wheelchair-accessible pier for fishing. Easy to moderate hiking trails along the lakefront and into the beautiful Pootatuck Forest start at the north end of the picnic area on the pond's western shore.

A food concession provides typical fare such as burgers, dogs, and fries in the summer. It often stocks necessities like foil and charcoal for those who want to barbecue.

Pedal boats and canoes rent for $10 an hour; canoes can also be rented for the day for $30. Squantz Pond is actually better for canoeists than is Candlewood. The high-speed powerboats on the larger lake create so much wake that canoeists have a safer, saner day with the smaller numbers of boats that remain on Squantz.

Sherman Historical Society and
The Old Store Museum (ages 6 and up)

10 Route 37; 860-354-3083; www.shermanhistoricalsociety.org. Open on the second weekend of each month from May through Dec. Store (Route 37; 860-350-3475) open Apr through Dec, Thurs through Sat, noon to 4 p.m.

A local history museum with seasonal exhibits, living history programs, and summer camps can be found at the 1829 David Northrop House, and across the road is the circa 1810 Old Store Museum and Giftshop, a truly charming mercantile store with a second-floor gallery of rotating exhibits and artworks. Programs at the historical society take kids back to colonial days, as they learn what life might have been like in Sherman two centuries ago. Woodworking, outdoor cooking, ecology studies, native plant collection, puppet making, and old-fashioned games and foodways are among the pleasures and pastimes learned here.

Sherman Playhouse (age 8 and up)
5 Route 39 North, near Route 37; (860) 354-3622; www.shermanplayers.org. $$$ (less for students).

From April through December this community theater presents new and classic plays and musicals. Curtain time is 8 p.m. on Friday and Saturday. Sunday matinees are at 3 p.m.

Where to Eat

The American Pie Company. Junction of Routes 37 and 39 in Sherman; (860) 350-0662. In the same building as the post office, this eatery has everything kids love at breakfast, lunch, and dinner. Chicken pot pie, shepherd's pie, homemade soups, salads, sandwiches, great desserts. Open daily from 7 a.m. to 9 p.m.; no dinner on Mon. $–$$

Down the Hatch. 292 Candlewood Lake Rd.; (203) 775-6635. Great lake views and great food in northern Brookfield. Fresh fish, big burgers, and perfectly grilled chicken. Outside deck. Open daily for lunch and dinner in season. Closed Mon and Tues in early fall. Closed entirely Nov through Mar. $–$$

189 Sports Cafe. 189 Federal Rd., Brookfield; (203) 775-7072. For folks who'd prefer a slightly less casual ambience, this reincarnated favorite features a great chef and hearty American fare. Excellent seafood, pastas, chicken, and steak, plus a children's menu and kid-friendly appetizers. Lunch and dinner daily. $$–$$$

Rickyl's Brookfield Luncheonette. 800 Federal Rd.; (203) 775-6042. American cuisine, including omelets, fresh-fruit pancakes, homemade soups, creative sandwiches, and salads. Open Tues through Fri for breakfast and lunch. Breakfast only on Sat and Sun. $

Where to Stay

Newbury Inn. 1030 Federal Rd., at Routes 7 and 202 in Brookfield; (203) 775-0220; www.newburyinn.com. Renovated in 2007, this hotel offers 46 units, including 6 suites/efficiencies and some rooms with whirlpool spas or private patios; complimentary deluxe continental breakfast served in breakfast lounge with fireplace. On 5-acre grounds, a mile from Candlewood Lake. $$$–$$$$

General Information

Western Connecticut Convention and Visitors Bureau. P.O. Box 968, Litchfield, CT 06759; (860) 567-4506; www.visitwesternct.com; www.litchfieldhills.com; www.visitfairfieldcountyct.com; www.facebook.com/LitchfieldHills.FairfieldCounty.

Connecticut Welcome Centers in Fairfield County are located at I-84 Danbury (eastbound), I-95 Darien (northbound), Merritt Parkway Greenwich (northbound).

Litchfield County

Artful Pleasures and Historic Treasures

From its northwest corner where it meets the Berkshire Mountains of Massachusetts to the fertile valleys formed by the Housatonic and Farmington Rivers as they dissect the foothills, Litchfield County is famed for its beauty, history, and tranquility. Punctuated by charming colonial towns, picturesque lakes, and thousands upon thousands of acres of farms, forests, and parks, it is an intriguing mix of rural and affluent culture. Resorts, restaurants, antiques shops, and country inns draw visitors from all over to share in the wealth, while farm markets, country fairs, and nature preserves draw visitors eager to taste the salt of the earth.

TopPicks for fun in Litchfield County

1. **Appalachian Trail**

2. **Kent Falls State Park**

3. **Mohawk Mountain Ski Area**

4. **Mount Tom State Park**

5. **Quiet Sports in the Housatonic Valley—Breadloaf Mountain Lodge**

6. **Fishing at Twin Lakes—O'Hara's Landing**

7. **Local Farm Old-Style Life Skills Workshops**

8. **Lee's Riding Stable**

9. **Tubing the Farmington River—Satan's Kingdom Recreation Area**

10. **Institute for American Indian Studies**

LITCHFIELD COUNTY

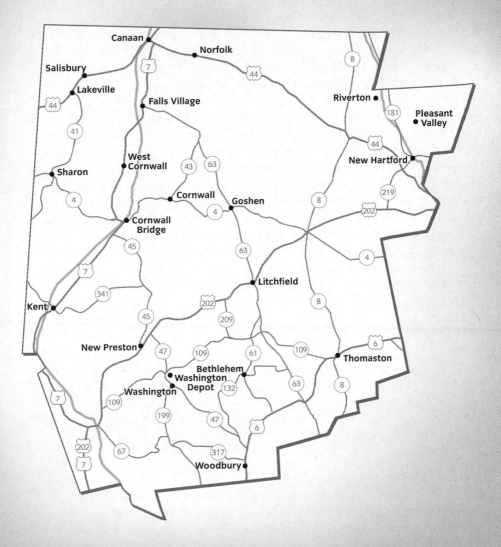

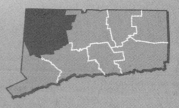

Families have much to gain by exploring the Litchfield Hills. Leave behind your health clubs and home-based gymnasium equipment, and come here instead to keep fit and trim in the fresh air. Outdoor recreation opportunities abound in every pristine corner of the county. Hiking, bicycling, canoeing, fishing, kayaking, whitewater rafting, tubing, downhill and cross-country skiing, horseback riding, swimming, and camping entice health-minded families to the Litchfield Hills.

Other families may be drawn to the spark of creative and spiritual energy that seems to reside in the nooks and crannies of the county. Fine artists, country crafters, writers, musicians, actors, and other folks driven by the Spirit and the Muses—even gardeners, vintners, chefs, and Benedictine sisters—have made their homes in these woodlands and have set up shop so that visitors might have the pleasure of enjoying their artistry. Potteries, stained-glass studios, woodcarving shops, glassworks, and galleries and boutiques showcasing all of their creations proliferate side by side with playhouses, concert halls, cooking schools, wineries, arboretums, and ornamental gardens. If your aim is to inspire the budding talents within your family, you will find no lack of opportunity to encourage one another to believe in the importance of creative careers and vocations. If you have no ulterior motive except to enjoy the displays and performances, a grand tour of the county's theaters, ateliers, and galleries will leave you awestruck.

Those of you excited by history, especially Native American lifeways, colonial settlement, and the American Revolution, will love Litchfield County. Historic homes, ruins and archaeological sites, excellent museums, and festivals celebrating the past are ubiquitous here. This book will cover only a select number of these sites and events. This volume's selection is intended to be what the author considers the best sites for families.

Lastly, Litchfield is the perfect place for wanderers. Dress in the casual garb of the vagabond and meander down the scenic highways and waterways that lead to places only more lovely at each bend in the road or river. The Western CT Convention & Visitors Bureau has created a booklet of tours suitable for car, foot, boat, and bike. Each of these adventures renews both body and soul. Do yourselves a favor and journey here.

Woodbury

Using Routes 25, 34, or 8 to get to I-84, you might make Woodbury your first stop in Litchfield County. Larger and more populated than many Litchfield County towns, Woodbury was settled in 1673 and was once known for its agriculture and its production of cutlery and cloth. Day-tripping families will discover that the town is now famed as the place to go for antiques.

Woodbury's Famous Antiques and Flea Market (all ages)
Held at the junction of Routes 6 and 64; (203) 263-2841; www.woodburyfleamarket.com. Open every Sat mid-Mar through mid-Dec, weather permitting (most vendors come from Apr through mid-Dec), from 7 a.m. to 3 p.m. Free admission and parking.

Families wary of entering crowded shops full of expensive goods may enjoy a trip to this child-friendly outdoor market of up to 150 vendors. Go early for the best selection or late for the best bargains. Antiques are well mixed with junk; new stuff is well mixed with authentic collectibles. Two food stands make it easy for you to come for breakfast or stay for lunch.

The Glebe House Museum and Gertrude Jekyll Garden (ages 6 and up)

Hollow Road off Route 6; (203) 263-2855; www.theglebehouse.org. Open from 1 to 4 p.m. Wed through Sun from May through Oct. Open weekends only in Nov from 1 to 4 p.m. Open by appointment Dec through Apr. $.

This 1745 minister's farmhouse, or glebe, is an exceptional example of 18th-century architecture and is especially welcoming to children. The mood inside the house is warm and inviting. Artifacts are laid out in positions of use, and children are enthusiastically addressed on tours tailored to the interests and schedules of visitors. Historically important as the site of the first election of an American bishop of the Episcopal Church in 1783, the house has many fine (and simple) furnishings and a charming gift shop/bookstore. Its beautiful perennial garden is the only one in the United States designed by renowned English landscape designer Gertrude Jekyll.

Most important for interested families is a summer History Camp for children ages 6 to 14. Two weeklong sessions of colonial activities offer an eye-opening experience of 18th-century daily life. (You can also come for Art in the Garden Camp.) Return in late October for "All Hollow's Eve," a one-night extravaganza that includes refreshments, storytelling, and candlelight tours of the museum, other nearby sites, and the Old Burying Ground. This is a spooky but delightful experience, suitable for younger children as well as older—but parents should be the judge of individual children's capacities for scary stories and ghostly happenings.

Woodbury Ski and Racquet Area (ages 3 and up)

785 Washington Rd., Route 47; (203) 263-2203; www.woodburyskiarea.com. Open weekdays from 10:30 a.m. to 10 p.m., Sat from 9 a.m. to 10 p.m., and Sun from 9 a.m. to 4:30 p.m. $$$–$$$$.

This year-round recreational facility attracts thousands of outdoor sports enthusiasts each year. In winter its 14 alpine downhill trails are especially popular with children and with beginner and intermediate skiers. Lessons, rentals, and night skiing specials are offered, and a double chairlift, two rope tows, a handle tow, and snowmaking equipment keep the pace active all season long. Two major half-pipes and a quarter-pipe provide excitement for snowboarders. A base lodge and ski shop flesh out the amenities that keep Woodbury on a par with other Connecticut ski areas. Ask about the Winter Carnival in January—a weeklong extreme extravaganza.

Three tubing and sledding courses with a dedicated lift are also available, from a gentle glide for beginners to a two-lane, bobsled-like run for thrill-seekers. Seven kilometers of groomed cross-country trails are also on the property; these improved trails are lighted and have snowmaking, tracking, and tilling.

A year-round skateboarding park and an in-line skate course are also here. In the warm seasons, you can also camp, swim, picnic, and play tennis and paddle tennis. Concerts, from rock to reggae, are also offered from time to time in the summer. Check the website to see what's on the calendar.

Flanders Nature Center (all ages)

Church Hill and Flanders Road, off Route 6; (203) 263-3711; www.flandersnaturecenter.org. Trails open daily year-round, dawn to dusk. Free.

Nature lovers will enjoy this center's two sanctuaries at Van Vleck Farm and Whittemore, where trails lead through 1,000 acres of woodland, bog, a nut tree arboretum, and more. Bird and wildflower walks, a fall festival, and a variety of programs such as maple-sugaring in March are among the opportunities for discovery. The Trail House offers a nature shop and some small exhibits; it's open Sat from 9 a.m. to 5 p.m.

Where to Eat

Carmen Anthony Fishhouse. 757 Main St. South; (203) 266-0011. As perfect for families as for discerning adult diners, this casually elegant establishment is open for lunch and dinner daily year-round. Fresh fish, soups, salads, pastas, and a special selection of kids' favorites. $$–$$$

Dottie's Diner. 740 Main St. South; (203) 263-2515. Of course. Best doughnuts ever, anywhere. Everybody knows it. Those, plus two versions of chicken pot pie, almost as good as homemade, and great mac and cheese, in the old Philips place. Breakfast and lunch daily and dinner, Tues through Fri. $

New Morning. 738 Main St. South; (203) 263-0673. Check the Provender fresh-food counter for soups, scones, salads, sandwiches, wraps, and much more, all natural and organic and mostly locally sourced. Eat breakfast, lunch, and early dinner at tables inside or out. Open daily from 8 a.m. (10 on Sun). $–$$

Ovens of Woodbury. 660 Main St. South; (203) 263-2540. Open daily from 6 a.m. Here you can decide if this baker makes the best baguettes in the state; many buyers say it's so. Coffee, tea, croissants, cakes, cheese, and pastries and breads of every description. $

Where to Stay

Curtis House. 506 Main St.; (203) 263-2101. One of Connecticut's oldest hostelries, this rambling 1754 colonial inn and carriage house in the heart of Woodbury offers guest rooms that range from small with shared bath to huge or linked with private bath. Restaurant. $$–$$$$

Longwood Country Inn. 1204 Main St. South; (203) 266-0800; www.longwood countryinn.com. Small families with children over age 10 looking for accommodations in a refined setting might ask for guest room numbers 3, 5, and 6 in this restored 1789 colonial. Full country breakfasts are included in the room rate. $$$$

Kent

I don't believe there's a family alive who won't find something to please every member in the beautiful town of Kent. About 12 miles north of New Milford on Route 7, the village center was once little more than a bump in the road. But it hums now with the activities generated by the shops, galleries, restaurants, bakeries, and natural and historical attractions that line Route 7 as it passes through one of northwest Connecticut's most interesting villages. Beautiful in all seasons, it was once called the number one fall-foliage town by *Yankee Magazine.* Come and see; you may agree.

Bull's Bridge (all ages)

Officially in Gaylordsville, 3.8 miles south of Kent's center; just off Route 7 on Bull's Bridge Road. Free.

Originally built in 1760 by Isaac and Jacob Bull to carry iron ore and charcoal over the Housatonic, the current bridge, believed to date from 1842, is one of two remaining covered bridges open to traffic in Connecticut. The view of the river and its powerful whitewater cascades and ravines is perfect from the bridge. A small scenic loop trail leads to other views of the woodlands, rapids, still water, and wildlife in the area. A parking area on the western side of the bridge allows you to stop here safely and walk to several clearly marked sites and trails. A second hiker parking area is located a bit farther along Bull's Bridge Road at the entrance to the Appalachian Trail section (see sidebar), marked with white blazes. Use extreme caution at the river edge; stay on the marked trails and *do not ever* step into the rapids or onto river rocks.

Kent Village Center

On Route 7, also called Main Street, mostly north of the Route 341 intersection.

In the center of Kent, stroll through the shops and galleries. All lovely, some are especially suited to families. **Toys Galore and More** (860-927-4091) is self-explanatory. Sometimes they put bubble solution and giant bubble wands outside in the brick plaza—so fine for fun. Other favorites are **Foreign Cargo** (860-927-3900), which has great funky and exotic import clothing, unusual jewelry, and an upstairs gallery of American antiques and Asian, African, and Pacific Island art. If the kids enjoy them or can allow you to enjoy them, at least peek into the art galleries. Our favorite is the **Heron American Craft Gallery** (860-927-4804), which offers top-quality handcrafts in all price ranges. When the gallery gazing and boutique hopping leave you weary, head for the restaurants.

Sloane-Stanley Museum (ages 5 and up)

Route 7, north of Kent center; (860) 927-3849. The museum itself is open Fri through Sun from 10 a.m. to 4 p.m. mid-May to Oct 31. The grounds remain open until 4:30 p.m. during that time. $.

Just north of the village on the left side of the road where the railroad tracks border Route 7, stop for a look at one of the most surprisingly moving exhibits in the state. Gathered

It's **Revolutionary**

Historically important because of the integral role it played in the Revolutionary War, Kent supplied the Continental Army with iron ore, goods, and soldiers. It also offered a strategic location on a main waterway to Long Island Sound and on the marching road between Lebanon, the army's supply depot, and Washington's headquarters in New York. Now, nearby and along this same route, lies a sizable stretch of the **Appalachian Trail,** including the longest river walk on the whole 2,144-mile hiking path. You can enter this easy-to-moderate 7.8-mile portion of the trail near Bull's Bridge. You'll find the trailhead off of Route 341 west. Go to Skiff Mountain Road, and bear right at the fork to the Appalachian National Scenic Trail. The trail is marked with white blazes, and the area closes at sunset.

through the efforts of the late author/artist Eric Sloane, the collection includes tools made by colonial Americans as early as the 17th century.

Revealing much about the early settlers' experiences and their adaptation to their new home, the tools are fascinating in their diversity, their ingenuity, and in their beauty. Each object has been finely crafted, mostly by hand, primarily from the hardwoods of the Eastern Woodlands. The presence of each cabinetmaker, each farmer, each cook seems to fill the post-and-beam barn in which the collection is housed. A videotape featuring Sloane himself explains the philosophies behind the artist, his work, and the museum collection.

The museum also includes a complete re-creation of Eric Sloane's art studio along with some of his original works. Outside the museum is a small cabin Sloane built in 1974 with the use of notations found in a young boy's 1805 diary. The simple realities of frontier life are made obvious throughout the austere interior of this display.

A visit to the ruins of the **Kent Iron Furnace** (also on the property) may have some interest (see why in the next sidebar). Long important as a producer of pig iron, the blast furnace is partially restored. A diorama inside the museum explains the process of smelting pig iron and shows how the blast furnace would have worked.

Connecticut Antique Machinery Association
Museum (ages 5 and up)

Route 7, north of Kent center; enter property at Sloane-Stanley Museum; take driveway to right; (860) 927-0050; www.ctamachinery.com. Museum and grounds are open mid-May through October 31, Wed through Sun 10 a.m. to 4 p.m. A donation ($) is gratefully accepted.

One of Connecticut's newest museums is a tiny village of eight new or restored buildings constructed on 8 acres of wooded property adjacent to the Sloane-Stanley Museum. The complex houses the state's largest display of steam and gas engines and tractors, as well as other antique agricultural and industrial machinery and mining equipment. Arranged on the site are such buildings as the Agricultural Hall (a tractor barn housing 50 tractors from the late 1800s to the 1950s), the Cream Hill Agricultural School (the state's first such school, moved here from Cornwall with its original desks, kitchen implements, library, and natural science and curiosities collection), and the Connecticut Museum of Mining and Mineral Science (the largest permanent display in the state of native minerals and rocks, historical bricks, and mining equipment). The last-mentioned includes amazing small dioramas depicting gold mining, brick making, and iron smelting, complete with miniature figures and signage that tells the story of the nation's mining heritage and industry. Among the other buildings are a blacksmith shop, engine halls, an engine house

Hitting the **Iron Heritage Trail**

I assure you that none of my children would have said, "Hey, Mom, let's go check out Connecticut's Iron Heritage Trail! It sounds awesome!" But if you are of the No Child Left Inside philosophy, as I am, and you are yearning for an outdoor romp with a nifty educational/environmental element, then you might consider contacting Ronald D. Jones (860-435-9183), chairman of the **Upper Housatonic Valley National Heritage Area** (P.O. Box 1942, Lakeville, CT 06039; www.upperhousatonicheritage.org). Ask him to send you a trail guide to the Iron Heritage Trail through the Tri-State Salisbury Iron District, in which you and the kids can explore the remains and restorations of the 40-plus blast furnaces, lime kilns, forges, and iron mining and mill sites in northwestern Connecticut, southwestern Massachusetts, and eastern New York. These sites, all within the watershed of the Upper Housatonic River, were in operation from 1735 to 1923. In addition to the furnace in Kent at the Sloane-Stanley site, you can visit the 40-foot-high **Beckley Iron Furnace** on Lower Road in East Canaan, beautifully situated along the pretty Blackberry River. It used to produce 11 tons of pig iron each day and has a terrific "sala-mander" you'll want to learn about. Bring a picnic to this pretty spot, and be sure to choose a bit of iron slag from the pile to take back to school for show-and-tell. You can also hike to the **Mount Riga Furnace** and the **Lime Rock tower,** both in Salisbury. Mount Riga features spectacular views from Bald Peak; Lime Rock once produced thousands of railroad car wheels. The trail guide has a map and clear descriptions of the best sites. Whether you drive the suggested routes from place to place or just hike to specific points, it takes you through some mighty pretty country, not to mention to another era in Connecticut's history. All of the easy to moderate hikes are suitable for young family members. Guided walks are offered from time to time; check the website for information.

for the museum's operating narrow-gauge railway, and an oil pumping station from Pennsylvania.

Most displays are labeled, and educational signage is in place in some areas, but be sure to take the guided tours offered here. They generally last an hour, but volunteers will take into account the ages of your party and your areas of interest. Despite its apparent potential for lots of bells and whistles, this tends to be a quiet place. Demonstrations are given only at special events, such as the three-day Fall Festival (see sidebar).

Kent Falls State Park (all ages)

Route 7 about 5 miles north of Kent's center; (860) 927-3238. Open year-round. A parking fee ($; $$ for out-of-state vehicles) is charged on weekends and holidays only from Memorial Day weekend through Labor Day weekend.

Wander northward from the Sloane-Stanley Museum until you reach this park on the right side of the road. Leave your car at the parking lot right off Route 7 at the base of the wide meadow that slopes down from the hills above. Beyond the meadow are the beautiful cascading waterfalls known as Kent Falls. Beginning in the town of Warren, the mountain stream known as Falls Brook reaches Kent through a series of drops, about 200 feet in total. Each drop is as pretty as the last as the falls descend through a dense forest of hemlocks, creating pools and potholes that openly invite visitors to dip a toe or two or even more into the cold, clear (but not potable) water.

Two trails to take you to the top of the falls are cut through the forest on either side of the stream. We suggest you climb up the .25-mile south trail directly to the right of the falls as you face them from the meadow and descend on the north trail, which you reach by crossing the bridge at the top of the south trail. The trails are fairly steep at points, but not strenuous. Small children will manage well if they rest from time to time. Stairs and railings on the south trail will help those who haven't had a workout in a while. The slightly longer north trail angles off into the woods a bit away from the falls. You'll miss a pretty walk through the New England woodlands if you don't come down this way.

"Swimming" in the strictest sense is prohibited here, but wading (in bathing suits, please) in designated areas is absolutely allowed. Where else can you cavort directly under a waterfall? The deepest pool, depending on the water level in a particular year, can be waist- or even chest-high for adults, so don't take your eyes off small children.

After you cool off, try some fishing in the stream as it nears the meadow. The stream is stocked with trout, and no license is necessary for children under 16. Picnic tables and grills are scattered throughout the meadow and under the trees near the parking lot. Toilets are also available. You have to pack out your own trash, so be prepared. The falls tend to be most dramatic in the spring, by the way, when melting winter snow raises the water level; the forest, however, is most dramatic in fall. In winters when the water freezes, the falls form giant icicles. Maybe you'll just have to return in every season.

Macedonia State Park (all ages)

Four miles northwest of the village off Route 341; park office: (860) 927-3238; campground office: (860) 927-4100. Open year-round; seasonal camping (no pets or alcohol). Free **day-use; camping, $.**

With 2,300 acres, this park has excellent trails offering spectacular views of the Catskill and Taconic Mountains. Camping (80 sites, mid-April to September 30), hiking, stream fishing, picnicking, and cross-country skiing are all available here. Take the loop trail to Cobble Mountain (1,380 feet at the summit) for a view you won't forget. It's just a half-mile to the top, then a mile down on another trail, or you can retrace the way you came. Ask a ranger for a map.

Where to Eat

Belgique Patisserie. 1 Bridge St. at the junction of Routes 7 and 341; (860) 927-3681. The best place for tarts, Belgian pralines, chocolates, ice cream, hot chocolate, and coffees. Open year-round, Thurs to Sun, except for brief closings in Sept and Jan. For treats and eats on other days, try the Millstone Café at 14 Main St. and its adjacent bakery (860-592-0500); they're yummy, too. $

Doc's Trattoria. 9 Maple St.; (860) 927-3810; www.docstrattoria.com. Doc's offers the best pizza in Litchfield County, plus other delicious Italian favorites in a casually sophisticated setting in the center of town. Open daily from noon (1 p.m. on Sun) to 3 p.m. for lunch; dinner, daily from 5 p.m. Innovative salads, pastas, chicken, and seafood keep the place popular with parents; kids love the imaginative pizzas and half-orders that help them leave room for dessert. Reservations are a good idea. $$–$$$

Fife 'n Drum Restaurant and Inn. Route 7; (860) 927-3509. Three-star restaurant in the style of an elegant but homey tavern, wonderful New England classic cuisine at lunch (11:30 a.m. to 3 p.m.), dinner (from 5:30 p.m.), and Sunday brunch. Piano music in the evening, played by the well-known owner/host. Adjacent inn offers lodging, and a lovely shop offers tempting gifts. Closed Tues. $$–$$$

Where to Stay

Cooper Creek Bed and Breakfast. 230 Kent Cornwall Rd.; (860) 927-4334. Open

Which Way Did He Go, **George?**

Local lore documents that George Washington may have nearly lost a trusty steed as he crossed Bull's Bridge one day in March 1781. It's uncertain how the accident happened or whether the horse was Washington's own mount, but it is clear that one of his horses fell into the roiling waters under the bridge as his company made the passage on the way to meet with the French to make plans for naval support against the British. Washington's diary for the day records that the cost of retrieving the horse from Bull's Bridge Falls was $215. The time spent on this rescue and the cost incurred led some historians to guess that the animal may not have been just any ordinary horse.

Fall **Festival**

If you're in Kent the last Friday, Saturday, and Sunday in September, stay for the **Connecticut Antique Machinery Association's Fall Festival.** Sounds awful, right? It's not—at this three-day machinery extravaganza, you may see cider making, threshing, wood splitting, blacksmithing, broom making, or shingle making. Check out the draft animals, antique cars and trucks, homestead displays, and working exhibits of steam and gas engines, farm equipment, steam launches, and motor canoes. Enjoy a cup of the CAMA's famed Engineer's Vegetable Beef Soup or cruise the other food vendors from 10 a.m. to 4 p.m. Call (860) 927-0050. $; children 5 and under are free.

from April through November, this 1820 Greek Revival B&B offers a charming 2-room suite with private bath as well as 3 to 5 guest rooms that have private or shared baths, all within the main house. Families with infants up to 1 year old are welcome to stay Sun through Thurs; families with children ages 6 or older are welcome at any time. The entire house can also be rented to family groups with kids of any age for reunions and weddings and such. Full breakfast. Nonsmoking. 2½-acre property to play in. $$$–$$$$

Fife 'n Drum Inn. 59 North Main St. in the center of the village; (860) 927-3509. 8 large rooms with private baths, restaurant (see above). $$$

Sharon

If your last stop in Kent was Macedonia State Park, you might consider continuing north along Route 341 into New York State, then eastward again on Route 41 back to Connecticut and the town of Sharon. (As the crow flies, Sharon is about 10 miles north of Kent; the surface route is about 15 miles.) Charming and barely there, Sharon existed in the 18th century and has not developed much since. That's a tribute, not a criticism. The beauty of the place and the careful stewardship of the community are apparent in its lovely town green and the historic homes and farms that surround it. Truly, the vistas around these parts are as pretty and bucolic as any in the state, and you might want to come to see them while they are still here. You might enjoy a visit to **Ellsworth Hill Orchard and Berry Farm** (461 Cornwall Bridge Road; 860-364-0025), where you can pick apples, take a wagon ride, and explore the corn maze in autumn or pick berries, plums, peaches, pears, and cherries at varied times throughout the summer; if time is short, just stop at **Paley's Farm Market** (230 Amenia Rd.; 860-364-0674) for some of Connecticut's finest locally grown produce. If your kids are old enough, the show is appropriate, and if the time of your visit is summer-stock time, you might also enjoy a performance at the

TriArts Sharon Playhouse on Route 343 (49 Amenia Rd.; 860-364-7469; www.triarts .net). More than a few steps above the average community-theater offerings, these professional-quality productions are almost always family-friendly fare, including famed Broadway favorites, and the tickets are very affordable. Look here too for a small slate of winter productions and staged readings in the theater's Bok Gallery, and if you live nearby, check out the many children's theater workshops for your young thespians.

Sharon Audubon Center (all ages)

Route 4; (860) 364-0520; www.audubon.org/local/sanctuary/sharon. Trails open dawn to dusk daily year-round; building open year-round, Tues through Sat 9 a.m. to 5 p.m. and Sun 1 to 5 p.m. Closed major holidays. Access to the trails, $. No charge for center's main building.

Like all Connecticut Audubon facilities, the 684-acre Sharon Audubon Center is exceptionally well done, with 11 miles of carefully tended trails and boardwalks. Pond, swamp, marsh, and woodland habitats have clearly marked, self-guided interpretive nature walks. Naturalist-guided tours highlighting such topics as birds, trees, or mammals are also offered.

The center's main building includes a noncirculating library and an excellent gift and book shop. Its Adventure Center features a crawl-through simulated beaver's den, a live honeybee hive, a coral reef aquarium, and other hands-on natural science exhibits.

Outdoors, you can see non-releasable birds in the aviaries. If you come in spring or summer near evening or early morning, you may see beavers at Ford or Bog Meadow Ponds. Warblers tend to stop here on their annual fall and spring migrations, so bird watchers (and listeners) might enjoy a visit at those times. The center also maintains an herb garden, a wildflower garden, and a butterfly and hummingbird garden.

Check the website for such special annual events ($–$$) as the Maple Fest in mid-March (sugaring process, legends, tastings); the Sharon Audubon Festival in mid-August (hands-on crafts, demonstrations, workshops, music, pony rides, food); the Enchanted Forest in mid-October (campfire, hot chocolate, costumed animal characters telling their stories along the trails); and Audubon Kids Day in late October (costume parade, hayrides, hay-bale maze, nature activities).

Where to Eat

Sharon Farm Market. 10 Gay St.; (860) 397-5161. This independent grocery store offers everything you might need for a picnic, plus other freshly prepared meats, meals, sandwiches, cheeses, and salads to take out of their excellent Jam Bakery and Jam Food Shop. Open year-round, 8 a.m. to 9 p.m. Mon through Sat and until 7 p.m. on Sun. $–$$

Twin Oaks Café. 20 Gay St.; try (860) 364-7002. Affordable and tasty meals daily, but don't expect them to pick up the phone. $

When Pigs Fly. 29 West Main St.; (860) 492-0000; www.hudsonvalleybbq.com. Quality Southern-style barbecued meats and *all* the locally sourced fixin's are the real deal here—chef-owned and chef-made. Try the terrific shoepeg corn pudding, skillet cornbread, and the mac and cheese, for sure. Lunch and dinner, 11 a.m. to 7 p.m. (8 p.m. on weekends) Wed through Sun. $–$$

Cornwall Bridge

In a roughly elliptical shape drawn by Routes 7, 128S, and 4, you'll find the separate villages of Cornwall Bridge, Cornwall, and West Cornwall, with one of the three nearby state parks or forests shouldering each of them. Together this trio composes the town of Cornwall. Traveling north from Kent on Route 7, Cornwall Bridge is the first of the three. One of those villages you can easily pass through before you know you have reached it, Cornwall Bridge is a beautiful area with a couple of sites of interest to families.

Cornwall Bridge Pottery (ages 5 and up)

69 Kent Rd. (Route 7); (860) 672-6545 or (800) 501-6545; www.cbpots.com. Generally open daily from 9 a.m. to 5 p.m. year-round, but be sure to call ahead to see what might be going on at a particular time. Your best chance to see Todd at work is Monday through Friday, but the production cycle includes loading and unloading the kiln, moving wood, and other chores. A call ensures that you'll know what you might see on a visit. Free.

On the east side of Route 7 a mile north of the Route 45 junction and a mile south of the junction with Route 4, visit the pottery workshop and see the potters and the 35-foot-long wood-fired kiln at work. I suspect your family will love to see this process.

Todd Piker is owner, potter, philosopher, and excellent businessman. His pots (and plates, bowls . . .) are exceptionally beautiful and eminently useful, and he makes an expanding line for such well-known clients as Dean & Deluca. Browse here or at the pottery's store (see the West Cornwall section) for the pots you might find most usable for the needs of your family. Still-beautiful and useful seconds are available here; perfect pots are at the store.

Housatonic River Outfitters Inc.

24 Kent Rd. at the junction of Routes 4 and 7; (860) 672-1010; www.dryflies.com. Open Mon through Sat from 9 a.m. to 5 p.m., Sun from 9 a.m. to 4 p.m. Longer hours from May through fall.

Come here for top-quality fishing equipment, fly-tying materials, outerwear, fishing vests and other outdoor clothing, maps and books, camping equipment, and luggage. An amazing inventory of anglers' flies includes more than 50,000 in all. They will provide guide services for spin- or fly-fishing the river. All-day guided float trips in comfortable inflatable rafts can be arranged, complete with customized lunches. Licenses are available here. The staff can also arrange lodging and dinner reservations or point you toward activities in the Litchfield Hills.

Housatonic Meadows State Park (all ages)

One mile north of Cornwall Bridge on Route 7; park office: (860) 927-3238; camp office: (860) 672-6772. Open year-round; seasonal camping. Day use 8 a.m. to sunset. Alcohol prohibited. Free day use; camping $.

One of the state's best and most scenic campgrounds is right on the river and offers plenty of opportunities for hiking, fishing, and canoeing. Along one 2-mile stretch only fly fishers are allowed. You can watch them or be one of them (the latter only with a license). Cross-country skiing is popular here in winter. In warmer weather, 95 campsites are available from mid-Apr through Dec. Hikers may like knowing that the park's Pine Knob Loop Trail connects to the Appalachian Trail and passes lovely cascading waterfalls.

Housatonic Meadows Fly Shop and Tightline Adventures Guide Service (ages 8 and up)

Breadloaf Mountain Lodge and Cottages (all ages) ⊕ ⊕

13 Route 7; (860) 672-6064; www.flyfishct.com. Shop open from 8 a.m. Mon through Thurs and from 7 a.m. Fri and weekends. Closings vary with the day and season. Breadloaf Mountain Lodge open year-round.

The folks who run the fly shop here say, "There's no tonic like the Housatonic," a phrase apparently borrowed from Oliver Wendell Holmes, who may indeed have been the first to say it. Happier than ever to help you find out how to enjoy yourselves on the river, these guys will set you up for full- or half-day float trips ($$$$) in drift rafts; come for instruction or hire a guide, or just arrange equipment rentals or purchase a license here. Call well in advance for rentals or float-trip arrangements; you can't just show up at the door. Located right across from the state park entrance and picnic area, the fly shop, by the way, carries a bazillion flies and everything else you'd need for a lifetime of fishing.

These fellows have also invented a very clever and pleasant way to get families and others to stay happy longer: Their beautiful Breadloaf Mountain Lodge and Cottages are hugely popular. A historic lodge and five adjacent cottages are about as charming and as practically appointed as can be. These too come at somewhat of a dear price, but they are totally terrific if you can spare the change, and, so far, not one of the happy families who stayed here has balked at the tariff. Each of the cottages has a fully equipped kitchenette, gas fireplace, and queen-size bed or twin beds, or some combo thereof. All can also accommodate rollaway cots and such for families. Screened porches with built-in daybeds allow for more enjoyment of the setting, well within earshot of the river and wildlife. Personal barbecue grills at each cottage make meal prep fun and easy; coffee and homemade muffins are delivered fresh to your door each morning. Pair this lodging arrangement with a long weekend or even a week or more of quiet-sport fun in this pretty valley, and you're all set for happiness. As mentioned, the folks at the fly shop are pleased to set you up with all kinds of guided or self-guided outdoor recreation, from bird watching and fishing to canoeing, kayaking, cycling, hiking, skiing, and more. The splurge may be well worth it. This place gets my vote for the best outdoor recreation destination in the Litchfield Hills.

Where to Eat

Baird's General Store. 25 Kent Rd.; (860) 672-6578). Open for breakfast, lunch, and early dinner, for takeout, picnic fixings, or to eat here on a front-porch picnic table or at tables at the back of the store. Soups, sandwiches, eggs, steak, and more. Open daily from 6 a.m. to at least 6 p.m. $

Cornwall Inn Restaurant & Tavern. 270 Kent Rd.; (860) 672-6884. Innovative, seasonal New American cuisine from 5 p.m. Thurs through Sun. Sunday brunch is a great deal. Children's menu. $$$

Where to Stay

Cornwall Inn. 270 Kent Rd. (Route 7); (860) 672-6884 or (800) 786-6884; www.cornwall inn.com. The main building of this refurbished 18th-century inn has two options for families, including adjoining rooms connected by a private bath. 3 rooms with 2 double beds in each are in the adjacent motel-style lodge. Outdoor pool and hot tub. Continental breakfast included. Restaurant/tavern (see above). $$$$

Cornwall

In the area closest to the village center called Cornwall is one of Connecticut's best sites for family fun in winter as well as in warmer weather.

Mohawk Mountain State Forest and
Mohawk Mountain Ski Area (all ages)

Ski Area: 48 Great Hollow Rd.; (860) 672-6100 or (800) 895-5222; www.mohawkmtn.com. Open from Thanksgiving Day to early April. Forest: Route 4 at Toomey Road; (860) 424-3200 or (860) 491-3630; www.ct.gov/DEP Open daily, Apr through Nov, depending on snow and mud, 8 a.m. to sunset. No day-use parking fee.

Connecticut's largest and oldest ski area, Mohawk has 23 trails and slopes, five lifts, and snowmaking equipment for 98 percent of the slopes. Families can enjoy day and night skiing, snowboarding, and 5 miles of cross-country ski trails in the Mohawk State Forest. Snowmobiling is allowed in designated areas of the park. Rental ski equipment is available, as are services like waxing and repairs. The PSIA Mohawk Learning Center provides lessons for all ages and skill levels; young children can participate in the SKIwee program.

The historic, renovated Pine Lodge offers skiers a place to rest and get warm; it has a ski-to restaurant and a sundeck. The base lodge has a retail ski shop and headquarters for rentals, lessons, and food services.

From late spring through mid-fall, hiking, mountain biking, fishing, letterboxing, and picnicking draw thousands of visitors to the forest. Famous for its rare and fragile black spruce bog, the forest is laced with trails, including a portion of the Mattatuck Trail and original segments of the Appalachian Trail. A climb to the wooden observation tower at Mohawk Mountain's 1,683-foot summit will leave you speechless, not from the exercise but from the view. Forest rangers will give you a map and directions to the trailhead and to a nature trail. The overlook at the top is also accessible to vehicles via Toomey Road. Picnic tables and toilets are available; and a private food vendor may be here as well in summertime.

Local Farm Old-Style Life Skills Workshops (ages 5 and up)

(860) 672-0229; www.motherhouse.com. See the calendar on the website for workshop dates, times, and locations. $35 per person; $50 for a family of four, with potluck lunch provided by the teacher and participants.

Priceless. Just perfectly priceless. This little corner of the world is a better place, that's for sure, because of the energy, effort, and mission of the remarkable Debra Tyler, who raises and milks Jersey cows, among her many other passions. Debra also offers a series of special classes in satisfying and simple lifeways that some of us might consider old-fashioned (but wish we knew how to do). Throughout the year, Debra and her like-minded colleagues offer workshops in bread-making, bee-keeping, goat-raising, wool-gathering, herbal crafts, and much more. Family Cow workshops, among her most popular offerings, teach the benefits and practicalities of cow ownership. All the workshops are open to families with kids of all ages, and all are hands-on and interactive in nearly every way. You'll breathe easier here in the company of the capable people who will coax you back in time in a real-world, real-simple way. Preregistration is required, and the workshop locations can vary. Debra has a lease arrangement on one of the prettiest farms in Cornwall, but not all workshops take place on this property.

West Cornwall

You have to visit West Cornwall if only to see Connecticut's finest and largest covered bridge. Built by Ithiel Town in 1837 of native oak, the **West Cornwall Bridge** is a beauty beyond a shadow of a doubt, and I don't think anyone is too jaded to feel its magic as it leads you across the river and back in time. I wish I could have heard the clip-clop of horses' hooves instead of the rumble of my car wheels as we made our crossings.

The village at West Cornwall is picturesque and very tiny, and for many travelers the bridge is in fact the main attraction. Traveling families may want to explore the bridge on foot, and you might also enjoy the small park and footpath along the waterway. Extended hikes on the Appalachian Trail are nearby. If you'd like to linger awhile in the village, there's one casual restaurant (see below); Barbara Farnsworth's used- and rare-book store (407 Sharon Goshen Turnpike; 860-672-6571); a post office for you to drop a pretty picture postcard in the mail; the workshop of famed Shaker furniture maker Ian Ingersoll; and a couple of gift and craft shops, including the **Cornwall Bridge Pottery Store** (415 Sharon Goshen Turnpike; 860-672-6545; www.cbpots.com), which offers Todd Piker's lead-free stoneware, plus glassware, woodenware, leather goods, jewelry, furniture, clothing, and other quality crafts.

Clarke **Outdoors**

The beautiful river that flows through the countryside and the Housatonic State Forest may appeal to your sense of adventure. If so, from mid-March through early December, **Clarke Outdoors** can help you enjoy a 10-mile stretch through quiet water and easy whitewater that is perfect for both experienced and novice paddlers. Offering one of the largest selections of canoe and kayak equipment in the Northeast, Clarke's store (860-672-6365; www .clarkeoutdoors.com) just south of West Cornwall on Route 7 is also the registration point where you begin your journey.

You can choose to canoe, kayak, or raft. No more than three people are allowed in each canoe (minimum age allowed is 7). Single-paddler kayaks, sit-yaks, and inflated rafts (minimum age, 3) that can hold four, six, or eight paddlers and passengers are also available. All rates ($$$–$$$$) include life vests and shuttle service that takes you to the put-in in Falls Village and picks you up at the takeout at Housatonic Meadows State Park. (The halfway point is at West Cornwall Bridge, where you can take out for a picnic on the banks.) Hot showers are available back at the Clarke shop.

Reservations are a must on weekends and many weekdays. Call at least a week in advance. American Canoe Association–certified instructors, including former national canoe champion Mark Clarke, provide lessons and guided trips. A kayaking school offers weekend lessons for adults and special groups for children 10 to 17.

Where to Eat

The Wandering Moose Cafe. 421 Sharon Goshen Turnpike (Route 128, or Main Street); (860) 672-0178. Casual, diner-style cuisine perfect for families. Breakfast and lunch, Tues through Fri from 7 a.m. and weekends from 8 a.m. Dinner Wed through Sun from 5:30 p.m. $–$$

Salisbury/Lakeville

If you can, continue north on Route 7, swing left when you reach Route 112, following the signs for Salisbury and Lakeville. Route 112 leads to Route 44, where you'll take a right. Connecticut doesn't have a prettier town than Salisbury. They should place signs at the edge of the town that say "Please do not disturb." A quiet corner of pure sanity, Salisbury is home to beautiful Lake Wononscopomuc, on which is the Town Grove, an incomparable summer recreation spot. Here too is Mount Riga State Park and one of the state's most-hiked trails to Bear Mountain. Charming inns and lovely shops are in both village centers and tucked on their quiet country roads. The Appalachian Trail passes through town, as do several other trails. Call the Salisbury Town Hall for information on these trails and the Heritage Walks that are offered from time to time.

Mount Riga State Park (ages 8 and up)

From the intersection of Route 44 and Route 41 in the center of Salisbury, go north on Route 41 3.2 miles to the Undermountain Trail parking area on the left. No fees; no services. Open year-round dawn to dusk. Be sure to hike with a trail map or other written directions and safe footgear.

If you love the outdoors, you're in the right spot here. Basically this park exists pretty much entirely to provide access to the state's highest summits and most spectacular views. The iron industry had a real hold on this part of Connecticut a century ago, and you can still see the remains of the old charcoal roads, charcoal pits, and ore pits, some of which are now small ponds. This park is very well used by hikers, and trails are well marked, but no other amenities or services are here. Pack in everything you might need for your day. All the hiking here is moderately to truly strenuous, and there is no truly easy route to the summit. See the sidebar for one possible option for hardy hikers.

O'Hara's Landing at Twin Lakes (all ages)

254 Twin Lakes Rd.; (860) 824-7583; www.oharaslanding.com. Open daily in season.

If you can't resist the idea of a day fishing lazily on a pretty-as-a-picture lake high in the hills, come to O'Hara's Marina on picturesque Twin Lakes. Launch your own boat or rent a canoe, a rowboat, or a small powerboat. Pontoon boats that hold eight to ten passengers are also available. You can fish, water-ski, or water-tube, but you need to bring your own equipment or purchase it here. Twin Lakes has some of the best fishing in the state, so a day on the water is bound to be exciting for young anglers. Bring your own gear or purchase bait and tackle at the shop here. If the trophy trout elude you or the sun gets to you, return to shore and have a bite to eat in the snack bar or cafe-style restaurant. The

Connecticut's **Agricultural Fairs**

Each year more than 50 agricultural fairs are held in Connecticut to celebrate the successful labor of the state's growers and their families. Nearly a score of these are classified as major fairs, and the towns of the Litchfield Hills host some of the state's largest and oldest fairs. Bethlehem, Bridgewater, Harwinton, Riverton, and Terryville are among these. Our family favorite is the Goshen Fair, which is always on Labor Day weekend. For more information and a complete guide to Connecticut's fairs, visit the Association of Connecticut Fairs website at www.ctfairs.org.

Bear Mountain and the **Appalachian Trail**

Parts of Salisbury are traveled exclusively on foot by hikers walking Connecticut's 52 miles of the Appalachian Trail. Near the northernmost piece of the trail as it emerges from Massachusetts lies the peak of Bear Mountain, the highest full peak in the state at 2,316 feet. From its topmost point, you can see lots of Connecticut plus New York State and Massachusetts.

Pack a lunch and some water and, from the junction of Route 44 with Washnee Street near the Salisbury Town Hall, take Washnee Street west and drive .6 mile to Mount Riga Road. Follow Mount Riga Road 2.6 miles to Mount Washington Road, take a sharp right to the north and continue 2.8 miles to an old woods road on the right. Park carefully on the side of the road and walk onto the woods road, continuing for 1 mile until you reach the white-blazed Appalachian Trail. The ascent from here to the top of Bear Mountain is the easiest of all the challenging approaches to the summit, but young children may still need to take it slow over the rough trail. It can be tricky following wet weather. Proceed to the top of the mountain, where a stone monument rests, and share a lunch while you enjoy the vistas. Watch children carefully, since some overlooks skirt the mountain's sheer face. Some hikers may actually ascend by the toeholds in that vertical trail. Don't let your children attempt to descend that route. Retrace your path to the woods road and your parked car.

You can also access the peak from the longer Undermountain Trail off Route 41, 3 miles north of Salisbury center, with a parking area on the left. You'll hike about 2 miles, pretty much straight up, then take a right when you see the marker for the Appalachian Trail. From that point, it's about a mile to the Bear Mountain summit.

restaurant (open on weekends from April 15 to October 10 and daily in the three summer months) serves breakfast and lunch only, but you may not want to leave this pretty place until after sunset.

Town Grove (all ages)

Ethan Allen Street, in Lakeville, on Lake Wononscopomuc. Town Grove Manager available at the boathouse to the left of the park entrance. Purchase a season pass ($50 for residents; $300 for nonresidents) or a day pass ($$ per person) at the boathouse. Call the town offices (860-435-5170) for more information. Open from 7 a.m. to 8 p.m. daily in the summer season. Access to the park is limited in the winter season. No dogs allowed.

The Town of Salisbury welcomes nonresidents as well as residents to its lakefront park. You'll find a playground and a picnic area with barbecue grills; a small store offers ice cream and sundries. Boating and fishing are the most common activities here, of course; canoes and kayaks can be rented by the hour, half day, or full day.

Separate swimming areas with lifeguards are available for small children and for older swimmers who might want to venture to the rafts in deeper water. Dressing rooms and restrooms are open in season.

Where to Eat

The Boathouse at Lakeville. 394 Main St. (Route 44), Lakeville; (860) 435-2111. This Adirondack-style restaurant is cheerful and welcoming to families. Great vegetarian dishes, plenty of seafood; soups and sandwiches at lunch. Open daily for lunch noon to 3 p.m.; dinner from 5 p.m. $$–$$$

The Woodland. Route 41, Lakeville; (860) 435-0578. Hearty American cuisine in a casual, country setting for lunch (noon to 2:30 p.m.) and dinner (from 5:30 p.m.), Tues through Sat; Sun, dinner only, from 4 p.m. $$–$$$

Where to Stay

Inn at Iron Masters. 229 Main St. (Route 44), Lakeville; (860) 435-9844; www.innatiron masters.com. 28 spacious rooms with sitting areas, private baths. Outdoor pool, continental breakfast, Hearth Room with fireplace. $$$$

Interlaken Inn, Resort, and Conference Center. 74 Interlaken Rd. (Route 112), off Route 7, in Lakeville; (860) 435-9878 or (800) 222-2909; www.interlakeninn. On 30 acres with two lakes, this resort offers an 82-unit contemporary building, a century-old B&B, and duplexes with fireplaces and kitchens. Restaurant, outdoor pool, sauna, tennis, golf, boating, lake swimming, fitness room. Great weekend packages, especially for families— you can even bring the dog! $$$–$$$$

The White Hart Inn. On the village green in Salisbury, Routes 41 and 44; (860) 435-0030 or (800) 832-0041; www.whitehartinn.com. Elegant country inn in restored vintage building spiffed up from cellar to chimney. Canopy beds, veranda overlooking village. 26 charming rooms with private baths. The restaurant not only serves exquisite meals, three times daily to guests as well as to the public, but much of its seasonal food is locally sourced, in part from the inn's very own farm. $$$$

Canaan/Falls Village

For those who live near the crowded New York–to-Boston corridor of I-95, visiting Canaan is like visiting another country—a very rural, quiet country. Somehow Canaan and the villages (Falls Village, South Canaan, East Canaan) surrounding it soothe the soul, restoring harmony to crowded lives. Fall foliage attracts tourists in droves, but it's pretty here in summer, too. If you live downstate or in the city, you're going to think these pristine hills and woodlands are out of this world. You can smell the green. Drop your plans for anything that smacks of rushing about in the fast lane. You won't find much here in the way of "attractions" really: It's not so much a place to come as it is a place to be. Reserve a campsite or a bed with a hearty breakfast and stay awhile. Hike the trails, take a bike ride, fish for trout, and make your way to the places where the hills come alive with the sound of music—and water.

Falls Village Station Nature Trail, Great Falls of the Housatonic, and Dean Ravine Falls (all ages)

An easy loop for young hikers is the Falls River Station Nature Trail, which can be reached from a parking area on Water Street, off Route 126. Linked to the Appalachian Trail, it's about three-quarters of a mile through fields and forest, with markers and a trail guide that explain the changing landscape from the days of the iron industry to the present reforestation. To see the Great Falls of the Housatonic, which is the state's second-largest river, take Route 126 North a third of a mile or so from its junction with Route 7, then bear left on Main Street; follow the road to Falls Village center, where you'll bear right and go down the hill. At the traffic island, turn left and go under the railroad bridge, pass the hydropower station, and cross the river. Turn right on Falls Mountain Road, and right on Housatonic River Road; park at the scenic overlook. This cascade is especially dramatic in the spring, when the dam above the falls has planned water releases. The water flows over a 60-foot ledge, and short hiking paths take you to an upper viewpoint and a lower observation point. In early springtime, this is nothing short of astonishing: Who would have thought Connecticut's wee mountains and quiet-water rivers could produce such a sound? To get to Dean Ravine Falls, head to Music Mountain (see below), off Route 7, near the intersection of Music Mountain Road and Cream Hill Road. The trail begins to the left of the parking area near the music hall. Follow its blue blazes downhill; it's an easy 10-minute walk to the cascades, which also tumble down a 50-foot drop. There is a picnic area at Dean Ravine.

Music Mountain (ages 8 and up)

Gordon Hall, off Route 7 or 63; (860) 824-7126 on weekdays 9 a.m. to 5 p.m. or (860) 364-2084; www.musicmountain.org. Tickets may be purchased by mail in advance, by telephone for credit-card payments, or picked up at the box office on concert days. $$–$$$.

This legendary and especially soothing compound in Falls Village is not a place exactly, but a festival. The nation's oldest continuous chamber music festival, it also features jazz, blues, baroque, and folk music on its picturesque grounds just off Route 7 near the Housatonic Valley Regional High School. You can also enter from Route 63 near the junction of Route 126.

Founded in 1930 as the permanent home of the Gordon String Quartet, Music Mountain's intimate and acoustically perfect wooden concert hall seats 335 on its softly cushioned pews; its 132 acres of lawn and grove are idyllic. The site is listed on the National Register of Historic Places. Picnic tables are provided for those who'd like to pack a boxed lunch or dinner to enjoy before the performances.

Offered from early June to mid-September, most of the chamber concerts are on Sunday at 3 p.m. Saturday performances are usually at 8 p.m., but some may begin a half hour earlier or later.

Where to Eat

Freund's Farm Market. 324 Norfolk Rd. (Route 44), East Canaan; (860) 824-0650; www.freundsfarmmarket.com. Delicious, especially if you think pie makes a good breakfast and breads and cheese make a great lunch, along with muffins, brownies, fresh local produce, plus pick-your-own raspberries. If the weather is right, you might even take home one of their awesome popcorn cobs. Open Mar through Dec. $

Toymaker's Cafe. 85 Main St., Falls Village; (860) 824-8168. The perfect casual establishment for snacks, soups, sandwiches, muffins, and more, all served up by good people. Open Thurs through Sun for breakfast and lunch from 7 a.m. $

Where to Stay

Inn at White Hollow Farm. 558 Lime Rock Rd., Route 112, Lime Rock; (860) 435-8185. 4 charming rooms, each with private bath, on the upper floor of a lovely white farmhouse. Fully equipped kitchen, dining area, and wrap-around porch on the lower floor. Coffee and baked goods each morning. On-site hiking and fly-fishing. Corn maze nearby. Smoke-free. $$$$

Locust Tree B&B. 131 East Canaan Rd. (Route 44), Canaan; (860) 824-7163; www.locust-tree-bed-and-breakfast.com. 7 rooms with private and shared baths in a gorgeous expanded 1700s farmhouse with double-story wraparound porches. Full country breakfast. Open year-round. $$$–$$$$

Lone Oak Campsites. Route 44, East Canaan; (860) 824-7051; www.loneoakcampsites.com. Open April 15 to October 15, this large family campground has tent and RV sites, plus 40-foot trailers with kitchen, bath, and bedroom, and a cabin with 2 rooms and a fridge. $

Norfolk

Norfolk is inarguably beautiful, nestled in the rolling shoulders and knolls of the Berkshire foothills, looking much the same as it might have a hundred years ago. There's not a lot of action here, but a full day or even a weekend, if you plan ahead, can be enjoyed in this sylvan village 7 miles east of Canaan. If you can, bring bicycles.

If ever a New England village could be fairly described as quaint, it is Norfolk. Beyond the few "attractions" described below, there is a most exquisite public library well worth a peek inside, the quintessential tall-spired, white Congregational church flanked by a lovely fieldstone chapel with Tiffany windows, and yet another state park, Haystack Mountain, just a mile or so up the road.

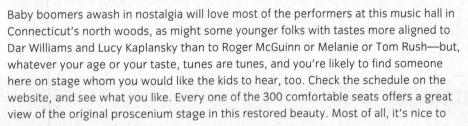

Infinity Music Hall (ages 8 and up)
20 Greenwoods Rd. (Route 44); (860) 542-5531; box office: (866) 666-6306. $$$.

Baby boomers awash in nostalgia will love most of the performers at this music hall in Connecticut's north woods, as might some younger folks with tastes more aligned to Dar Williams and Lucy Kaplansky than to Roger McGuinn or Melanie or Tom Rush—but, whatever your age or your taste, tunes are tunes, and you're likely to find someone here on stage whom you would like the kids to hear, too. Check the schedule on the website, and see what you like. Every one of the 300 comfortable seats offers a great view of the original proscenium stage in this restored beauty. Most of all, it's nice to see the lights on at a venerable old place like this, so the hills stay alive with the sound of music.

The Norfolk Chamber Music Festival (ages 6 and up)

Off the town green at the junction of Routes 44 and 272 on the Ellen Battell Stoeckel Estate; (860) 542-3000; music.yale.edu/norfolk. Concerts Tues and Thurs through Sat in June, July, and Aug. Prices vary; some are free to all ages; all are free to children under 18.

Summer home of the Yale Music School, this magical enclave is the perfectly serene setting for a chamber music festival that invites nationally and internationally famed quartets and quintets of piano, woodwinds, and strings for Friday and Saturday evening concerts throughout July and August. Held rain or shine in the historic redwood and cedar Music Shed, these 8 p.m. concerts are affordable for adults, discounted for young adults, and, amazingly, completely free to children, all summer long, every concert. In addition, on Tuesday and Thursday nights at 7:30 and Saturday mornings at 10:30, Young Artists Recitals feature the Fellows of the Norfolk Summer School playing recognizable favorite standards and an eclectic mix of new and old pieces. Perfect for families, these free concerts require no tickets. Check the website for a schedule.

Almost every summer a free family day includes events especially for children ages 6 to 12. Come for an ice cream social and children's games and activities, plus two performances (one at 2 p.m. and another at 4 p.m.), the first of which is an hour-long preconcert show that previews the featured music and draws children into the theme. No matter which concert you attend, bring along a picnic to enjoy before or after the program.

Dennis Hill State Park (all ages)

2.5 miles south on Route 272 from center of village. Open year-round. Free.

Families will enjoy an easy loop-trail hike of 2 miles along an old lumber road through the woodlands to a fieldstone gazebo that provides a place to picnic and look out over the

Loon Meadow Farm Hayrides and Carriage Rides

What could provide more old-fashioned good fun than a private hayride, carriage ride, or winter sleigh ride, complete with hot cider and antique lap robes? **Loon Meadow** arranges such outings (by reservation only) on Norfolk's village lanes and woodland trails. Four-person carriages, wagonettes, hay wagons, and sleighs are among the vehicles. Call the farm at (860) 542-6085 for the full scoop or check the website at www.loonmeadowfarm .com. $$$$.

views of the hills. Along the way you'll pass through stands of oaks, maples, hemlocks, and mountain laurels and see the remains of a colonial hearth and chimney. When you have nearly returned to the point from which you started, you can walk or drive the paved path to the 1,627-foot summit of Dennis Hill, where, on clear days, an octagonal bungalow with a rooftop observation platform allows you to see three states, views of several towns and villages, and the surrounding mountains—Bear Mountain to the west and Haystack just north of Norfolk, Mount Everett and Mount Greylock in Massachusetts, and the Green Mountains of Vermont.

Both trails are easy to find without maps. The first trail is yellow blazed and begins just beyond a wooden gate; the second is paved, popular, and clearly marked.

Where to Eat

Infinity Bistro. 20 Greenwoods Rd.; (860) 542-5531. Polished wood floors and snazzy, upbeat decor in the Victorian music hall building that's been revived as a Norfolk centerpiece. For inventive American fare at lunch, dinner, and Sunday brunch from Wed through Sun, Sept through May, and extra nights and longer hours in summer. Children's menu. Outdoor seating in warm weather. $$–$$$$.

MizzaPizza. 32 Greenwoods Rd.; (860) 542-6848. Perfect for families. Sandwiches, salads, soups, pizzas, chili; take-out dinners available for alfresco dining before the concerts. Lunch and dinner Tues through Sun from 11:30 a.m. $$–$$$

Where to Stay

Blackberry River Inn. (860) 542-5100 or (800) 414-3636. For two-and-a-half centuries, this colonial inn has welcomed guests to its 27 acres with apple orchard, hiking trails into the hills, trout fishing in its brook, tennis, and outdoor pool. 20 rooms, including pairs of rooms linked by a private bath, are perfect for families with children. Full country breakfast. $$$$

Goshen

Traveling south from Norfolk on Route 272 toward Torrington will take you through a slice of Goshen, which is a slice of heaven. You can follow 272 south to Route 4, which you'll then take west to the center of Goshen at its junction with Route 63. At this point, the scenery and the clean air may lead you to believe you're at the top of the world. A visit to Goshen's most well-known family attraction may convince you that you've actually stumbled upon Eden. It's a mind-boggling place, that's for sure. Some folks prefer Goshen's famed agricultural fair (www.goshenfair.org), on the first weekend in September, but you may enjoy both.

Action Wildlife Foundation (all ages)

337 Torrington Rd., which is Route 4; (860) 482-4465; www.actionwildlife.org. From early June to Labor Day, open daily 10 a.m. to 5 p.m. In Apr, May, Sept, and Oct, open weekdays, 10 a.m. to 2 p.m. and on weekends until 5 p.m. Weekend hayrides ($), weather permitting, in late Sept through Oct. Closed on stormy days. $$.

Located on a 116-acre former dairy farm on Route 4, just west of the Torrington border, this nonprofit game park is home to more than 200 exotic animals that roam relatively freely over about 90 acres currently open to the public. On the 40 acres closest to the park entrance, several fenced or walled compounds provide enclosures for 32 species of such creatures as the scimitar oryx, red stags, Scottish Highlander cattle, fainting goats, zebras, fallow deer, aoudads, ostriches, bison, yaks, elks, reindeer, and Russian boar. Crisscrossed by stone walls, the park has a petting and feeding barn, a picnic area, and several ponds. A drive-through parcel of 50 additional acres features pygmy donkeys and miniature horses. Visitors can walk on pathways throughout the complex; on weekends, tractor-drawn wagon rides are offered.

A building called the Museum and Exploration Center is paired with the foundation's gift shop and snack shop. Displayed here, along with a live reptile exhibit and an iguana habitat, are 50 mounted animal specimens in somewhat limited diorama-style natural settings.

Where to Stay

Mary Stuart House B&B. Route 4, Goshen; (860) 491-2260; www.marystuarthouse.com. This 1798 country home offers 4 bedrooms, 2 private sitting rooms, and a 2-bedroom cottage with kitchen, living room, private bath. Generous country-style continental breakfast. Volleyball and badminton in season. Hot tub. Screened porch. $$–$$$$

Riverton/Pleasant Valley

The Riverton area (east of Route 8 and about 8 miles north of Winsted) is just a plain old nice place to be. Generally described for this book's purposes, the Riverton environs are the roughly rectangular area created by the roads linking Riverton, Pleasant Valley, Barkhamsted, and West Hartland—the perfect spot for a world-weary family to restore some equilibrium.

The village proper of Riverton is a picturesque hamlet centered on Route 20 and West River Road. A couple of restaurants and a general store that sells fishing licenses, firewood, and camping supplies, along with great all-American lunch fare and breakfasts, are all within a spit of this corner. Nearby are a venerable old inn and Peter Greenwood's wonderful glassblowing studio in the historic former Union Episcopal Church. It's all worth a slow stroll.

Something **Fishy**

For 50 years, the village of Riverton has hosted the annual **Riverton Fishing Derby,** held traditionally on opening day of fishing in Connecticut (the third Saturday in April). The West Branch of the Farmington River is stocked with rainbow, brown, and brook trout, and each year 500 or more anglers try to catch the biggest of them all.

Free to all participants and spectators as well, the derby starts with a Fisherman's Breakfast at the Riverton Firehouse at 6 a.m. and ends at 10 a.m. regardless of the weather. No registration or fee is required, but anyone over the age of 16 must have a Connecticut fishing license. If you arrive without a license, you can buy one ($$$$) at the Riverton General Store.

Children under the age of 12 have their own area slightly upriver from the rest of the crowd. Anyone old enough to handle a pole can join the Kid Derby and share in the wholesome fun. Prizes are awarded in adult and youth divisions of this classic event. For information, call (860) 379-4826.

People's State Forest and Stone Museum (all ages)

One mile north of Pleasant Valley on East River Road to the forest's public entrance and the Stone Museum. Park office: (860) 379-2469; park open year-round 8 a.m. to dusk; day-use fee on weekends and holidays, $$. Stone Museum: (860) 379-6118; www.stonemuseum .org; seasonal hours; **free,** donations accepted.

Nearly filling the aforementioned rectangle made loosely by Routes 318, 181, and 20 and cut further by the East and West River Roads that flank the sides of the Farmington River's West Branch, this beautiful park provides access to and views of the 14-mile section of the river that the National Park Service has designated an American Wild and Scenic River. The gorgeous Matthies grove overlooks the rushing water as it twists through the 200-year-old pines—be sure to have lunch here if you've packed a picnic. Anglers hip deep in the water during trout season are a pleasant addition to the majestic view.

Open every Sunday from Memorial Day to Columbus Day and every Saturday and Sunday in July and August, the park's Stone Museum has exhibits on native flora and fauna, natural history, and Native American and colonial history and industry. A seasonal series of slide programs is presented here on Saturday evenings at 8 in July and August, and hikes are led on varied Saturday mornings throughout the summer and early fall.

A blue-and-yellow-blazed trail called the Beaver Swamp Loop follows an old wagon path through the forest, across a bridged brook, and up to a kame terrace that was the site of native encampments from 2,000 BC to AD 600. Remnants of 18 ancient Indian village sites have put this terrace on the National Register of Historic Places. As you descend the trail, still following the blazes, you can see a colonial house foundation and a meat-smoking chamber as well as other natural sites. The Beaver Swamp Trail is easy

Christmas in Riverton

This village-wide festival is quintessential New England for both Christian revelers and anyone, I suppose, who might like to share in the merriment during the winter holiday season. Everything is decorated and candlelit, and you can take a horse-drawn wagon ride, make a craft at the firehouse, blow your own ornament at Peter Greenwood's amazing glassblowing studio, see a puppet show or a performance of Dickens's *A Christmas Carol* by the Riverton Theater at the Congregational Church, or have a bowl of chili at the Chili Fest. You name it—it's Currier & Ives–style fun, typically on the first weekend in December, unless that overlaps with the last weekend in November. Some of the activities listed here have a fee, but much of the fun is **free.** See the Riverton website (www.rivertonct.com) so you can plan ahead.

to moderate, takes about two and a half hours to hike, and is 3.5 miles long. Ask for a detailed description and map at the park office. Descriptions of other trails leaving from the museum area are available on the website.

Cross-country skiing is allowed here in winter.

American Legion State Forest (all ages)
West River Road, Pleasant Valley; (860) 379-0922. No day-use charge; campsites, $.

On the western bank opposite People's State Forest, this quiet camping area has 30 wooded sites along the West Branch of the Farmington River. Clean pine woods, great shower facilities, flat tent sites, and good fishing spots make this a nice family campground. If no ranger is at the park office when you arrive, you just leave your registration in the box with your nightly fee. Open mid-April through December 1, the area has trails to beautiful sights along the river (watch the steep hillsides as you go along some of the paths).

Where to Eat

The Catnip Mouse Tearoom. Route 20; (860) 379-3745. Over-stuffed sandwiches on homemade bread, soups, ice cream, tea. Yum. Tues through Sat, 11 a.m. to 2 p.m. $

Old Riverton Inn. See below. Breakfast for guests only. Lunch and dinner Wed through Sun open to the public; reservations highly recommended. $$

Riverton General Store. Route 20; (860) 379-0811. Open Mon through Fri, 6 a.m. to 6 p.m., Sat until 5 p.m., and Sun from 6:30 a.m. to 3 p.m., for great sit-down breakfast and lunch, and perfect take-out picnic fare. Deli sandwiches, salads, pickles, ice cream, homemade soups, chili, coffee bar, and more in a charming setting with intriguing artifacts from its 120-year history. $

Sweet Pea's. 6 Riverton Rd.; (860) 379-7020. Old-fashioned charm spills from every pore of this 1880 house, and the food is even more delightful than the ambience. Children are warmly welcomed—in fact, they have their own menu. Lunch and dinner, Tues through Sun; brunch on Sun. $$–$$$

Where to Stay

Old Riverton Inn. Route 20; (860) 379-8678 or (800) EST-1796. Doing business for 200 years, this inn, listed on the National Register, has 12 rooms with private baths; some rooms have canopy beds and fireplaces. Open year-round, it enjoys a front-row seat on the rushing river and has an award-winning dining room. Full breakfast. $$$

On the River B&B. 420 West River Rd.; (860) 738-9660. 1 spacious room in 1920s house with views of the river, gardens, and hills, at the confluence of the Farmington and Still Rivers. King-size bed; rollaway cots for the kids. Fireplace; air-conditioning; private bath, porch, and entrance. Country breakfast. Lovely innkeeper. Bring a canoe, fishing poles; relax, have fun. $$$$

New Hartford

This tiny community has put itself on the map as one of the state's most popular sports and recreation destinations. From tubing in summer to skiing in winter, it's a town few families miss in a search for fun in the great outdoors.

Farmington River Tubing—
Satan's Kingdom State Recreation Area (ages 10 and up)
92 Main St. (Route 44); (860) 693-6465; www.farmingtonrivertubing.com. Open every day in July and Aug and on weekends and weekday afternoons only from Memorial Day through June from 10 a.m. to approximately 6 p.m. Call for hours on Labor Day weekend, for limited hours through mid-September, and to check on river conditions. $$$–$$$$.

This adventure is certainly on our top-ten list of best family summer activities in Connecticut—that is, if you're 10 years or older, 4 feet tall, and can swim alone without a doubt no matter your age. On some days, the river is chock-full of other tubing enthusiasts; on others you may be alone except for the dragonflies.

When you arrive at Satan's Kingdom, park in the lot next to the river and the **North American Canoe Tours Inc.** outpost. Wear cutoffs and a T-shirt or change into your swimsuit in one of the changing huts provided at the lot. Put on sunscreen and old sneakers, preferably your own. If you arrive barefoot, NACT makes you put on one of the spare pairs of soggy previously owned sneaks. Put on a life vest (mandatory equipment for everyone), pay your money, then walk down to the river with your tube and put your warm body into the cold water, bottom first, as you sit down in the hole of your tube with your feet up over the side. Sound like fun yet? It is, really—I promise. Now all you have to do is float and soak up the Vitamin D for 2.5 miles in about as many hours. The segment lies within the nationally designated Wild and Scenic River portion of the Farmington River.

The best parts for some are the mild rapids—three sets, with NACT lifeguards on duty in kayaks at the largest set only; others like the placid stretches where mergansers nest and the living is easy. This outfitter won't allow you to bring food on the river, so don't arrive hungry. When your ride is over (at a clearly marked take-out point), haul out with your tube. A shuttle bus takes you back to the starting point.

Ski Sundown (ages 3 and up)

126 Ratlum Rd., 2 miles northeast of New Hartford on Route 219 off Route 44; (860) 379-9851; www.skisundown.com. Open from 9 a.m. to 10 p.m. Sun through Thurs and until 11 p.m. on Fri and Sat, usually from early Dec to late March. For lift rates and special packages, check the website.

For winter fun, Ski Sundown is a convenient alternative to out-of-state skiing. Special trails, FlexTix, and a First-Time package for novice and beginner skiers and snowboarders make Sundown perfect for families new to the sport. Other programs are geared to children of moderate and advanced skills. Even accomplished skiers can enjoy the challenges of the three most difficult trails out of the total 15. Four chairlifts keep lines moving efficiently to the top of the 65-acre property.

Proud of their well-groomed runs and friendly professional staff, the operators also like to crow about their rental shop, which provides skis, boots, bindings, and snowboards, and Ski Shop, which offers similar goods and clothing for sale. A cafeteria helps hungry skiers renew their energy, and a lodge and lounge provide a place to relax with fellow skiers.

All-day, after-school, twilight, and evening sessions include reasonable rates for adults, juniors, preschoolers, and seniors. Bring Grandpa and the baby, too, and enjoy the winter in the Berkshire foothills.

Gently Down the **Mainstream**

For guided canoe, kayak, and bicycle trips in the rolling beauty of northwestern Connecticut, call **Main Stream Canoes & Kayaks** (170 Main St., which is Route 44; 860-693-6791; www.mainstreamcanoe.com) in New Hartford. These folks will set you up for full-day or half-day guided river trips on the wild and scenic Farmington River. Flat-water, quick-water, and rapids tours ($$$$) on upper and lower river segments for canoes and kayaks. Moonlight trips are among the most entrancing options (ask about age limitations). They also rent bicycles for half and full days.

Where to Eat

Chatterly's. Two Bridge St.; (860) 379-2428. This landmark eatery in the old New Hartford Hotel in the center of the village offers great fare for kids—soup, salads, sandwiches, burgers—or full dinners for adults—steaks, roast pork, seafood. Lunch and dinner daily. $–$$

Passiflora Tea Room. 526 Main St.; (860) 379-8327. Local and organic as much as possible and made from scratch every day, the breakfasts and lunches served daily here are the best you can get in town. Sandwiches, soups, salads—and tea. $

Portobello's Ristorante and Pizzeria. 107 Main St.; (860) 693-2598. Great Italian fare of traditional sorts, plus pizza and seafood. Open daily from 11 a.m. to 10 p.m. $$–$$$

Where to Stay

Alcove Motel. 87 Main St., which is Route 44; (860) 693-8577. 15 basic, affordable, clean rooms. Nightly rentals; no long-term residents. $

Chapin Park Bed & Breakfast. 45 Church St.; (860) 379-1075; www.chapinparkbandb .com. In the Pine Meadow historic district of New Hartford, right on its green, is a beautiful blue Victorian B&B awaiting children of all ages. Lovely innkeeper, happy to meet your needs and direct you to attractions and entertainments. Country breakfast; cheerfully quilted beds in spacious guest rooms, each with private bath. $$$–$$$$

Litchfield

From the Pleasant Valley and New Hartford areas, families may want to head south on Route 8 through Winsted and Torrington and then take Route 118 west about 5 miles to Litchfield. Settled in 1719, Litchfield remains one of the prettiest towns in the state, attracting visitors in droves to its meticulously preserved colonial architecture, its boutiques, and its restaurants. Antiques shops, elegant inns, and vineyards lure travelers looking for pastoral pleasures of a sophisticated nature. Judging these elements alone, it may seem an area more suited to adults than to families, but we discovered places everyone should visit. The website www.litchfieldct.com. will lead you to other town information.

White Memorial Foundation
and Conservation Center Museum (all ages)

80 Whitehall Rd., 2 miles west of Litchfield Center off Route 202; (860) 567-0857; www .whitememorialcc.org. Grounds open daily, year-round, from dawn to dusk. Free admission. Museum open daily 9 a.m. to 5 p.m. Mon through Sat and Sun noon to 5 p.m. Winter hours slightly reduced. Museum admission, $.

The state's largest nature preserve, with 4,000 acres, 35 miles of trails, and a public boat launch that provides access to Bantam Lake, White Memorial is a wonderful place to hike, ride horses, cross-country ski, fish, and picnic. Vacationing families may want to camp at its two understated campgrounds that offer lakeside or woodland sites with drinking water, pit toilets, and a camp store. Day-tripping families will enjoy all of the outdoor trails, including the quarter-mile Trail of the Senses, which invites youngsters to touch, smell, and listen at different spots along the pathway. Bird-lovers and photographers will also appreciate a specially landscaped bird observatory area that includes 30 viewing stations.

Inside, families will find plenty to do at the excellent hands-on Conservation Center Museum, housed in the former Whitehall mansion. Dioramas and interactive exhibits on such topics as birds, bees, soil, seeds, and woodland animals can be explored in a bright, open atmosphere. An outstanding natural science library with a special children's section is also here, and guided walks and special programs are frequent. In late September, be sure to come for the annual Family Nature Day ($; **free** to children under 12), which features old-time outdoor games, nature crafts, wagon rides, and much more, from 11 a.m. to 5 p.m.

Bantam Lake and Sandy Beach (all ages)

East Shore Road, Morris; (860) 567-5871; www.bantamlake.com or www.sandybeachatbantam lake.info. Open to the public on weekends only from Memorial Day through the end of June, daily from late June through Labor Day from 9 a.m. to 7 p.m. Daily fee, $ per car or boat; nonresident season passes ($$$$) are also available and can be purchased at the beach or at the Litchfield or Morris Town Halls.

If you want to take a dip or launch a boat in pretty Bantam Lake, leave Litchfield center on Route 202 West, take a left on Alain White Road, and another right on East Shore Road. Just before the bend in the road, you'll find the entrance to Sandy Beach. Actually in the town of Morris, the secluded beach provides 800 feet of clean sand on the shore of Connecticut's largest natural lake.

Lifeguards, bathrooms and bathhouses, and a snack bar are among the amenities. A canoe launch, a volleyball "court," and a picnic area with tables and fire pits make this a great place to spend the day. Return in winter to see the ice boaters clip across the frozen lake or to try your luck at ice fishing.

Lee's Riding Stable (ages 4 and up)

57 East Litchfield Rd. (Route 118); (860) 567-0785; www.windfieldmorganfarm.com. One-hour guided trail rides, $$$$ (7 years and older only); pony rides (7 and younger, mostly), $$ for twice around and $$$$ for a half hour or an hour. Open 365 days per year 9 a.m. to 5 p.m. but reservations for trail rides and appointments for pony rides are preferred.

If you love horses, horseback riding, and truly decent people, go directly to Lee's. Only positive experiences unfold for kids at this peaceful horse farm. The registered Morgan horses are gorgeous, and Lee Lyons, the special angel who runs the whole show, has a down-to-earth approach that makes everyone feel comfortable and want to come back. Trail ride groups are normally limited to six to eight riders, so you don't get that mule-train feeling, and the attitude of the staff is friendly and enthusiastic. No one has a hint of reluctance to take you over the same trails they've seen time and time again—a pleasant change from the bored demeanor of staff at other stables. The trails take you through 5 miles of exceptionally pretty country in and adjacent to Topsmead State Forest.

If the staff is not too busy, they may give you a tour of the stables. English and Western riding lessons are also offered, and the Litchfield Little Britches program offers therapeutic riding for children aged 4 through 18 with special needs (call for information).

Mount Tom State Park (all ages)

Route 202, southwest of Litchfield Center, in Bantam; (860) 868-2592. Open daily April 1 to October 15, dawn to dusk. Parking fee on in-season weekends, $$.

A small lake offers fishing, swimming, scuba diving, and non-motor boating in summer; ice fishing and ice-skating are possible in winter. A beach and picnic area with a snack bar concession, lifeguard, picnic tables, grills, restrooms, and changing houses (but no showers) make this a good family-fun destination.

Those who want more vigorous recreation can take the short hike to the top of the 1,325-foot mountain. The yellow-blazed trail is little more than a mile, but it's a pretty steady climb; older kids may do it in 15 to 20 minutes, younger ones may need a half hour. The extra 30-foot climb up the wooden interior staircase of the black granite tower at the top is well worth it. The view over the treetops is spectacular—you'll be glad you did it.

Litchfield History Museum and Tapping Reeve House and Law School (ages 8 and up)

7 South St. and 82 South St.; (860) 567-4501; www.litchfieldhistoricalsociety.org. Open mid-April through Nov, Tues through Sat 11 a.m. to 5 p.m. and Sun from 1 to 5 p.m. Adults $ for both museums; children under 14 free.

If history lessons intrigue your children, have a brief look at the collections in the seven galleries of the historical museum for insight into the town's culture and community. Afterward, stop at the Tapping Reeve House and Law School if you want to inspire future attorneys to emulate the 130 members of Congress who graduated from this first law school in the nation, open to the public as a historical exhibit. Hands-on activities, role-playing areas, and an introductory short film help make this site engaging for younger visitors. In mid-September, come for a walking tour of Litchfield Center or come for Borough Days, an annual celebration of old-time skills, crafts, games, and music, with reenactors, artisans—even stagecoach tours!

Where to Eat

Aspen Garden. 51 West St. ; (860) 567-9477. Omelets, salads, pizzas, Greek specialties, pasta, seafood. Terrace dining in nice weather. Lunch and dinner daily. $$–$$$

Bantam Bread Company. 853 Bantam Rd.; (860) 567-2737. If you think you can make a meal from delightful French cheeses and the world's tastiest organic breads, tarts, pies, and quiches, bring a picnic basket to this

bakery and prepare for ecstasy. Strawberry rhubarb pie counts as a fruit in my book, and pumpkin custard is a vegetable. Open 8:30 a.m. to 5:30 p.m. Tues through Sat and until 5 p.m. on Sun. $

Saltwater Grille. Route 202; (860) 567-4900. On Litchfield Commons, this family-friendly fish house offers lunch and dinner from noon every day (except no lunch on

Mon). Steaks, flatfish and shellfish of all sorts, salads, sandwiches, chowder, children's menu. Patio in warm weather; paper and crayons on the tables inside. $$–$$$

Where to Stay

The Litchfield Inn. Route 202; (860) 567-4503. Set back from the road, this inn offers 30 rooms with private baths, continental break-fast, and lovely common areas. Inn Between Tavern restaurant (860-567-9040) offers lunch on weekends and dinner daily. $$$$

Washington/Washington Depot/ New Preston/Bridgewater/ New Milford

Often called unspoiled and compared to the alpine lake regions of Austria and Switzer-land, the town of Washington and its village of New Preston, with its most famous attrac-tion, Lake Waramaug, are among Connecticut's most popular day-tripping destinations. If you can't get to Europe to check out whether the comparison works, take my word for it and come here to enjoy the four-season beauty of this delightful area just about 10 miles southwest of Litchfield. If you're exploring awhile in this region, you'll more than likely come upon such towns and hamlets as Warren, Washington Depot, Roxbury, New Milford, and Bridgewater, as well as northern sections of Brookfield, which is officially in Fairfield County, and Southbury, which officially lies in New Haven County. For the purposes of day trips, these towns are closely linked, but be sure you have a good map on the car seat when you head out.

By the way, even though GPS gizmos have taken all the fun and mystery away from our wanderings, you may be hard-pressed to find the below-mentioned CT Route 458 around Lake Waramaug, which is sliced roughly in half by the boundary between the town of Warren and the town of Washington. Route 458 is one of the state's "secret" routes, often unmarked with a numbered sign but no less real. A designated CT Scenic Roadway, it curls all around the 680-acre lake, which is Connecticut's second-largest natural inland body of water. From Route 7 if you are traveling from parts north or south, or Route 202 if you're coming southwestward from Litchfield, find Route 45, which is also called Cornwall Road or, when it reaches the lake area, is called both Lake Road and East Shore Road. Follow Route 45 to North Shore Road, which loops around the lake to Lake Waramaug

Road (past the state park, which actually lies in the town of Kent), which then links to West Shore Road to take you back to Route 45. The drive is about 8 miles.

When Lake Waramaug loosens its grip on your soul, take Route 45 south of the lake to Route 202 and the junction where you'll find New Preston's village center, which is chockablock with antiques shops. The kids will probably want to move right along to other attractions, so head northeast for a bit on 202, then take Route 47 south from Route 202 to Washington and Washington Depot. Don't blink or you'll miss the towns hidden in the twists and turns of these lovely hills. The fourth town in the colonies to be named for George, the pretty little village of Washington is a true New England gem, and the Depot, another hub of regional community life, is in its own way equally charming. (If you have time to linger in the latter, stop at the **Hickory Stick Bookshop** and the **Washington Art Association**.) Artful in many ways, all of these small towns and villages have lovely architecture, pretty shops, and lively cultural calendars. But for families especially, the special treasure here lies in the natural environment.

Lake Waramaug State Park (all ages)

Lake Waramaug Road (Route 478), in Kent, 5 miles north of New Preston center; park maintenance office: (860) 868-2592; campground office: (860) 868-0220. Open year-round from 8 a.m. to dusk; camping from May 15 to September 30. Camping fee, $; day-use fee, $$ on weekends and holidays only from Memorial Day through Labor Day.

Although this state park lies officially in the town of Kent, few travelers would arrive here by way of Kent's village center. The lake itself is bordered on the west by Kent, on the north by Warren, and on the south and east by Washington, which includes New Preston,

Luxury in the **Litchfield Hills**

If you have enormous bundles of cash to burn, you may want to stay at the most expensive—and perhaps the most creative—hostelry in all of Connecticut. At **Winvian** (155 Alain White Rd. in Morris; 860-567-9600; www.winvian .com; $$$$+), you can sleep in a beaver lodge, a cave, a tree house, or one of 15 other themed "cottages" scattered over a 113-acre woodland estate that is beyond the beyond for luxe lodging and dining. Offering blocks of "family-friendly" nights throughout the year, this property has a spa, an award-winning restaurant, and services fit for royalty—if you can spare a month's salary for a night or a week here. If you prefer purely patrician comforts to inventive ones, the **Mayflower Inn & Spa** in Washington (118 Woodbury Rd.; 860-868-9466; www.mayflowerinn.com) will be happy to pamper you as well, for slightly fewer pretty pennies. Loveliness abounds here, if luxury is what you are looking for, and the Shakespeare garden is a delight. Both places have earned Relais & Chateaux designations that ensure you won't have many complaints, if you don't mind the credit card bill.

Family Fun in **New Milford**

This town may be among the best examples of a smallish, family-friendly Connecticut community that is still lovely to visit, even as parts of it teeter toward the edge of overdevelopment. In the early 1990s, when the first edition of this guide was published, our family cruised the state's hill and valley roads looking for the idiosyncratic places nestled in Connecticut's famed nooks and crannies. In those days, we found plenty—and one of those was New Milford's Village Green, where we greatly enjoyed one of its annual Village Fair festival days. But since then, many of the state's narrow, windy roadways have been straightened and widened, and chunks of prime farm and forestland have been plowed down, paved under, and plastered with big-box and name-brand retailers and restaurants. (Connecticut may actually have the highest rate of decrease in farmland in the nation—up to 7,000 acres per year, lost to development.) Sigh. To us, the cultural loss is incalculable, and we cringe more than a little when we return to favorite places that have been steamrolled and face-lifted. In New Milford, the Route 7 corridor is getting way too wide and homogenized for our taste, but, luckily, when you cross that bridge and reach the town center, a lively sense of place and history is preserved in its pretty green, its narrow streets, and its independently owned emporiums. And out in the quieter, greener patches of this roomy town, which has a Farmland Preservation committee (phew!), the pastures still unroll their golden-green colors and fields fill with lovingly grown nutrition for you and me. Here are a few ideas for a weekend in these parts, where a life-affirming whiff of a "typical" Connecticut sense of community can still be savored—at least for now.

In summer or autumn, book a room for the weekend at the Heritage Inn and arrive on a Friday evening. Have a Southwestern-inspired dinner at **Salsa** (54 Railroad Ave.; 860-350-0701), then, if the show seems appropriate for your

the village most closely associated with the lake. It is from New Preston's roadways that most folks find their way to this beautiful spot. To start with the basics, Waramaug, also the name of a chief of the Wyantenock tribe, means "good fishing place." If you're so inclined, this sounds like the plainest fishing tip I've ever heard. In addition to this most popular sport, the park offers opportunities for picnicking, swimming, scuba diving, and sailing (you bring your own gear), and it provides paddleboats (which you rent). Trails for hiking and 77 very nice sites for camping are also available. Nightly camper nature programs are scheduled in summer, and ice-skating, cross-country skiing, and ice fishing are possible in winter.

family, see a play at **TheaterWorks New Milford** (5 Brookside Ave.; 860-350-6863; theaterworks.us) or see what movies are playing at **Bank Street Theater** (46 Bank St.; 860-354-2122;www.bankstreettheater.com). On Saturday morning, get thee to the green and stroll the **Plow to Plate Farmers Market** (9 a.m. to noon June through Oct), which includes free musical entertainment and activities for the kids; buy a book or two at independent bookseller **Bank Street Book Nook** (50 Bank St.; 860-354-3865) and browse the well-stocked shelves at **Play,** a toy shop at 49 Bank St. (860-355-2134). Have a cupcake fix at **Sugar Hoot Bake Shop** (57 Bank St.; 860-355-3000) or a cone or a float at **The Sweet Spot** (60 Railroad St.; 860-799-7170), then head out to the **Pratt Nature Center** (160 Papermill Rd.; 860-355-3137), a wildlife preserve and environmental education area on the East Aspetuck River, where you can hike, picnic, visit with farm animals, and watch wildlife. Or see what is happening at **Hunt Hill Farm Land Trust and Silo Cooking School,** which offers Silo Kids programs. When you come back to town, you'll be hungry enough for **All Aboard Pizzeria** (14 Railroad St.; 860-354-9552), a perfect dinner spot for most families. If you're here in summer, take a blanket to one of the free family concerts on the green on Saturday at 7:30 p.m.; you'll find the lineup on www.newmilford.org. On Sunday morning, head a bit down Route 7 (Danbury Road) to the **Elephant's Trunk Flea Market** (www.etflea.com) to search for treasure at one of the state's oldest and largest outdoor markets. Hold hands here—it's incomparable fun, but it's big and busy. If you're not yet exhausted and your drive home is not too long, head back out to the countryside: make your last stop at **Harris Hill Farm** (116 Ridge Rd.; 860-354-3791), where, if you've chosen to come in October (weekends only), you can navigate their corn maze, take a hayride, and pick a pumpkin. And that's just a taste of New Milford for you. Let's hope it stays this way.

Gunn Historical Museum and Library (ages 6 and up)

5 Wykeham Rd.; (860) 868-7756; www.gunnlibrary.org. Museum open Thurs through Sat 10 a.m. to 4 p.m. and Sun noon to 4 p.m. Closed major holidays. Free.

If you fall in love with the village, a visit to the museum adjacent to the lovely 1908 fieldstone Gunn Memorial Library on the town green will flesh out the area's history and lifeways. Within the also-historical museum building, you will find frequently rotating and exceptionally inventive exhibitions on the people, places, and events of this ancient and beautiful region. Assisted by area artists who embellish each exhibition, the curator here plumbs the extensive collection of decorative arts, household furnishings, utilitarian

O Little Town of **Bethlehem**

About 6 miles east of Washington as the crow flies (14 miles by Route 109 east to Route 61 south), Bethlehem is Litchfield County at its best—gorgeous hills, pretty village, quiet byways of unsurpassed serenity. Its evocative name conjures images of peace and sentiment that its residents play upon in a few special ways. In the months before Christmas, folks deluge the Bethlehem post office with holiday cards they would like to bear the Bethlehem postmark. A Christmas festival in early December celebrates the spirit of the season, and an annual country fair in late summer celebrates the bounty of Bethlehem's fields and orchards. The village is so tiny that you can easily find the shops, the post office, the fairs, and the historic homes. The information below will help you begin to plan a visit, but be sure to check the websites for further facts about each attraction's offerings and activities.

- **Bethlehem Post Office.** 34 East St.; (203) 266-7910.

- **Bethlehem Fair.** Bethlehem Fairgrounds, Route 61; (203) 266-5350; www .bethlehemfair.com. Often the second full weekend in September. $$, accompanied children are free.

- **March Farm.** 160 Munger Lane; (203) 266-7721; www.marchfarms.com. Open May through Dec, 10 a.m. to 5 p.m. for pick-your-own fruit, sunflower maze, corn maze, hayloft playscape, hayrides, animals, and more.

- **Old Bethlehem Historical Society Museum.** Corner of Routes 132 and 61; (203) 266-5188. Open Sun 1 to 4 p.m. from June through Aug. $.

- **Bellamy-Ferriday House and Garden.** 9 Main St. North (Route 61); (203) 266-7596; www.ctlandmarks.org. Open May through mid-October; in May through Aug, on Wed, Fri, and weekends from 11 a.m. to 4 p.m. and in Sept and Oct on the weekends only; also open on Memorial Day, Labor Day, and Columbus Day. One of the 12 notable properties linked as a network called Connecticut Landmarks, this exquisite homestead, its art, and its glorious gardens are on property linked to the nature trails of a nearby land trust; $. Art & Nature Kids Camp in July ($$$$).

- **The Abbey of Regina Laudis and the Monastic Art Shop.** 273 Flanders Rd.; (203) 266-7727; www.abbeyofreginalaudis.com. The Abbey Church of Jesu Fili Mariae on Robert Leather Road is open year-round for daily mass (8 a.m.) and vespers (5 p.m., except Sun 4:30 p.m.). In August its Performing Arts Center offers an annual musical theater production suitable for the whole family. Its Monastic Art Shop and Gallery (203-266-7637), featuring the handcrafts of the Benedictine nuns, is open every day except Wed from 10 a.m. to noon and 1:30 to 4 p.m. The best family attraction here, open to the public at no charge, is the abbey's magnificently restored Neapolitan crèche, which illustrates the Nativity in a dramatic fiber-optically starlit scene of nearly 90 human and animal 18th-century figures beautifully dressed in silks and brocades and placed against the 16-foot backdrop of an Italian hillside. Children of all ages, plus parents and grandparents, will love to search for both reverent and comical characters, all painstakingly reborn at the hand of conservators at New York's Metropolitan Museum of Art, where a similar (but less extensive) collection resides. Displayed in a climate-controlled enclosure inside a restored historic barn, this is a fascinating work of art that families of every faith can appreciate. Open daily 10 a.m. to 4 p.m. from Easter Sunday through January 6, but call ahead to confirm these hours, especially in inclement weather.

If you have built up an appetite exploring this pretty place, try these three establishments, which all offer a warm welcome to families. Most casual is **Theo's Pizza** (15 Main St.; 203-266-5558; open daily 10 a.m. to 10 p.m.; $) for pizza, salads, and Greek and Italian specialties. Theo says, "If you want it, we're going to try to make it!" If you want something a bit more polished, try the **Painted Pony** (74 Main St. South; 203-266-5771; www.paintedponyrestaurant.com; open daily from 11 a.m. to at least 10 p.m.; $$), best known for prime rib, pastas, chicken, seafood, and its special children's menu. And if you would like gourmet delights in an elegant setting refined enough for special occasions but not so stuffy that the owners won't beam at your well-behaved children, try the dinners and wonderful holiday brunches at the **Woodward House Inn** (4 The Green; 203-266-6902; www.thewoodwardhouseinn .com; dinners Wed through Sun; brunches on the major holidays; $$$–$$$$).

artifacts, images, and stories to reveal themes of interest to both adults and children. At the very least, you are sure to see a new and wonderful multimedia display every summer and at holiday time between Thanksgiving and January. Check the website for news of family programs and such annual events as an October cemetery tour, suitable for all ages. Be sure to visit the library, too. Family programs are open to the public throughout the year in the Junior Library (860-868-2310). When you go, visit the Stairwell Gallery, which features the work of notable regional artists—and don't miss the magnificent multi-panel ceiling mural on the third level; restored in 1995, this work by Henry Siddons Mowbray portrays the Greek myth of underworld god Pluto, Ceres, and her daughter Proserpine. Check the website for library hours.

Institute for American Indian Studies (ages 4 and up)

38 Curtis Rd. off Route 199; (860) 868-0518; www.birdstone.org. Open Mon through Sat from 10 a.m. to 5 p.m. and Sun from noon to 5 p.m.; closed on Mon and Tues from Jan through Mar. $.

Magnificently displayed smack dab in the woodlands near Steep Rock Nature Preserve, the permanent and changing exhibitions at this museum are interpretations of the institute's research on the history and culture of Indian America, whose civilization preceded that of the colonists by several thousand years. Exhibits on archaeology and the Algonkian people of Quinnetukut include stories of survival, spirituality, and ingenuity as well as Native American tools, baskets, implements, and art. Inside the museum are a re-creation of a pre-European-contact Algonkian longhouse and a simulation of a northeastern reservation house from the early 1900s, both filled with artifacts used in everyday life. A Children's Discovery Room features interactive exhibits about woodland creatures and plants and the ways that Algonkian peoples used these gifts.

Outside, an authentically constructed 17th-century settlement with three wigwams, a longhouse, a rock shelter, native-plant trails, and a garden provides further exploration of the proud 10,000-year history of these people. Craft workshops, dances, films, storytelling, and summer camps are also on the schedule.

Steep Rock Reservation (all ages)

(860) 868-9131; www.steeprockassoc.org. Open dawn to dusk year-round. Small parking area off River Road. No facilities. Free.

After a morning at the Indian studies institute, you might want to stay in the great outdoors to reflect on all you've learned about the fragile, life-sustaining ecology of the Eastern Woodlands. Linked to the institute property by a common border, this 700-acre natural preserve is one section of a two-parcel land trust owned and maintained by the Steep Rock Association. Dedicated to preserving and protecting, for the good of future generations, the beauty and integrity of this important ecosystem and all of its flora and fauna, the association has opened its trails to hikers. With pathways that hug the Shepaug River and climb to Steep Rock, the sanctuary offers incredible vistas that should keep families mindful of their integral role in conservation of our remaining wild places. Come here to the cool woods to hear the whispering wind in summer, enjoy the glorious blaze of the foliage in autumn, linger as the snows fall silently in winter, and walk softly beside the wildflowers as the new leaves open in the springtime. The association fears that overuse of these lovely footpaths may force them to close to the public, so please remember to walk respectfully only on cleared trails, pack out every scrap of what you carry in, and take nothing but memories with you as you leave.

Shepaug Bald Eagle Observation Area (all ages)

Off I-84 exit 13 or 14; River Road, Southbury, in the Shepaug Recreation Area. Observation area open from 9 a.m. to 1 p.m. on Wed, Sat, and Sun (except New Year's Day) from the last week in Dec through mid-Mar. Free, but reservations required. For reservations, which can be made from early Dec, call (800) 368-8954, Tues through Fri, from 9 a.m. to 3 p.m.

During the coldest months, nature lovers should bundle up well and go see the annual reunion of bald eagles that gather near the Shepaug Dam, especially from January through mid-March. Through a program managed by Northeast Utilities, guided by the Connecticut Department of Environmental Protection, and staffed by volunteers from the Connecticut Audubon Society, visitors can come to the NU Shepaug Bald Eagle Observation Area near the Shepaug hydroelectric station on the Housatonic River in Southbury. The dam area is attractive to wintering birds because the station's operation prevents the water from freezing, making fishing below the dam easy for the birds. One of the largest concentrations of wintering eagles in Connecticut may be seen at this site.

A blind equipped with spotting scopes is set up to provide excellent viewpoints, and exhibit panels on the eagles' habits and conservation issues help to educate visitors. NU staff and CAS volunteers are on hand to assist visitors, and they are always happy to answer questions. You might also want to bring binoculars and a camera (and mittens!). In addition to the eagles, you may see red-tailed and sharp-shinned hawks, goshawks, great blue herons, and a great variety of waterfowl.

Where to Eat

Bridgewater Village Store. 27 Main St. South (Route 133), Bridgewater; (860) 354-2863. Right on the green of the last dry town in the state, this charming store is the place to come for down-home breakfasts, gourmet deli sandwiches, salads, homemade baked goods, ice cream, coffee, teas, a local newspaper, and much more in a vintage store that has preserved all the right old-fashioned touches even as it has updated with modern conveniences and comforts. Built in 1899, it has worn wood floors, tin ceilings, and a delectably tempting candy counter where you can buy locally made Bridgewater Chocolates. Eat inside or out or spread your blanket on the green. Open Mon through Fri 6 a.m. to 6 p.m.; Sat 7 a.m. to 5 p.m.; Sun 7 a.m. to 4 p.m. $

G.W. Tavern. 20 Bee Brook Rd. (Route 47), Washington Depot; (860) 868-6633. Traditional favorites like chicken pot pie, steaks, pastas, soups, salads, and a cheerful staff that welcomes children. Children's menu and lots of side dishes make choosing easy. Lunch and dinner daily; brunch Sat and Sun. $–$$

The Pantry. 5 Titus Rd., Washington Depot; (860) 868-0258. Gourmet fare in a simple setting often used by adults with fancy tastes and deep pockets. Good for families needing picnic fare. Delicious bakery treats, salads, and sandwiches. Open 10 a.m. to 6 p.m. Tues through Sat. Table service from 11 a.m. to 5 p.m. $

Where to Stay

The Heritage Inn. 34 Bridge St., New Milford; (860) 350-3097; www.theheritage innct.com. Perfect for visitors to Lake Candlewood, Squantz Pond, and the "greater" Washington area, this lovely small inn in the heart of New Milford is owned by the folks who own the Newbury Inn near Lake Candlewood. 20 guest rooms and 8 deluxe suites, all with private baths, in historic building, where young children are warmly welcomed. (No cribs are available.) Kids under 16 stay free. A deluxe hot continental breakfast is complimentary. $$$–$$$$

Thomaston

East of Bethlehem (take Route 61 south, then Route 6 east through Watertown and onward to Route 8) is the town of Thomaston, named for clockmaker Seth Thomas. Thomas's clocks were made right in Thomaston with brass gears manufactured in the mills of Waterbury. Today those two communities are linked in other ways. One of these links is a railway: the original Naugatuck Railroad that opened in 1849 to connect Bridgeport with all the towns north to Winsted. Located in the beautiful and still rugged Naugatuck Valley, Thomaston welcomes families to its historic downtown (where one can see the famed Seth Thomas clock tower and its magnificently restored opera house), its Victorian railroad station, and the vintage train that offers travelers splendid views of the scenic Naugatuck River, its wildlife, and the communities along its banks.

Railroad Museum of New England/
Naugatuck Railroad Scenic Excursion (all ages)

242 East Main St.; (860) 283-7245; www.rmne.org. Operates May through Oct, most Saturdays and/or Sundays at noon and 2 p.m.; Tues, 10 a.m. Foliage, Pumpkin, and Halloween excursions in Oct; Northern Lights and Santa Express excursions in Dec. $$–$$$$; children 2 and under, free.

This moving museum is a scenic 20-mile round-trip railroad excursion that resulted from the signing of a 30-year lease that gives the Naugatuck Railroad Company operating rights over a 150-year-old track that departs from the 1881 Thomaston Passenger Station in downtown Thomaston.

Grab the kids and jump aboard for the great sights and sounds of this grandly exciting one-hour-and-fifteen-minute adventure. What is it about train rides that is so appealing? Maybe it's the bells and whistles or the clackety-clack, maybe the huge sighs and shudders of the enormous locomotives, maybe just the heart-tingling joy of heading off to new horizons on a beast so mighty it can scale mountains. Ride this baby with your eyes and ears wide open to all the fabulous wonders around you—from inside one of the factory complexes near the historic brass mills of Waterbury to the Mattatuck State Forest's cool green canopy in summer or blazing patchwork of scarlet and bronze in autumn. Travel past small towns with charming old houses and tiny depots, and onward across—yes, right across the face of—the spectacular Thomaston Dam.

The train consists of restored historic New England passenger and freight cars pulled by historic New Haven and Maine Central locomotives. Onboard, on the regular rides, you'll hear a few stories about the importance of this line in the golden days of industry in the Naugatuck Valley; on special excursion days, the narration and the music varies (and the fares are a bit higher). Reservations are not required, but you can buy tickets in advance online or by phone; for the themed excursions, reservations are recommended.

Thomaston Opera House (ages 4 and up)

158 Main St.; (860) 283-6250; www.thomastonoperahouse.org. Open year-round. Season tickets for varied series, plus individual tickets ($–$$$) for all productions. Box Office, Mon through Sat 1 to 6 p.m.; or buy tickets online.

Built in 1884, the beautifully restored Thomaston Opera House is a perfect venue for families. Shows are affordable, especially compared to Broadway and even Bushnell prices, and more family-friendly shows are staged here than in any other theater in the state. The opera house is gorgeous, with frescoed ceilings, an incredible pipe organ (ask about the organ concerts), and amazing acoustics. If it was good enough for Enrico Caruso and Marian Anderson, it's good enough for Connecticut families.

General Information

Western CT Convention & Visitors Bureau. P.O. Box 968, U.S. 202, Litchfield, CT 06759; (860) 567-4506; www.litchfieldhills .com. Call or write for the tours booklet, which provides itineraries for walking, hiking, driving, and boating tours of the area. Also ask for a **free** getaway planner called *Unwind*.

Connecticut Angler's Guide. Published by the State Department of Environmental Protection Bureau of Natural Resources Fisheries Division, this booklet describes everything you'd need to know about fishing in the state of Connecticut. Call (860) 424-FISH to request a copy.

Hartford County

Capital Ideas in the Heart of Connecticut

S liced into unequal parts by the Connecticut River, the north-central region of Connecticut is a region of diversity including farming communities, towns with a long history of industry, and a city of pre-Revolutionary importance as a seat of government. This diversity makes for perfect touring conditions, as it offers something for all tastes, interests, and ages.

Hartford itself offers a full slate of attractions typical of an urban cultural center. The arts, sciences, history, and industries of the city, its suburbs, and the nation are well represented on its long list of museums and exhibits. Traveling families should try to plan at least a day in the state's capital city, keeping in mind that even if you were

TopPicks for fun in Hartford County

1. **Lake Compounce Theme Park and Entertainment Complex**
2. **Huck Finn Adventures**
3. **Imagine Nation Museum**
4. **Talcott Mountain State Park and Heublein Tower**
5. **New England Air Museum**
6. **Old State House**
7. **Mark Twain House**
8. **Connecticut Science Center**
9. **New Britain Museum of American Art**
10. **Dinosaur State Park**

HARTFORD COUNTY

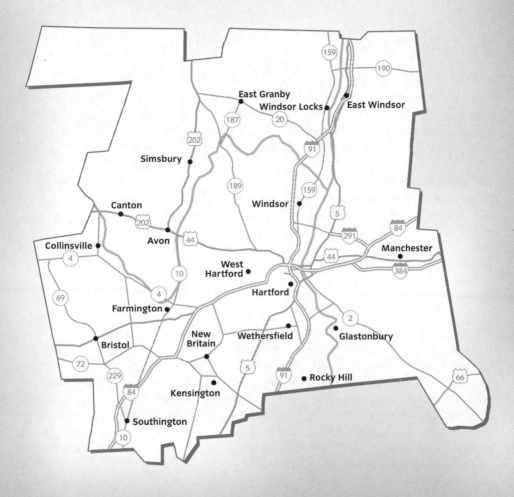

East Granby
Windsor Locks
East Windsor
159
190
187
20
202
Simsbury
91
189
159
Windsor
5
Canton
202
84
291
Avon
44
Collinsville
44
Manchester
4
10
West
Hartford
384
4
Hartford
69
2
Farmington
New
Britain
Wethersfield
Glastonbury
Bristol
5
72
91
Rocky Hill
229
Kensington
66
84
10
Southington

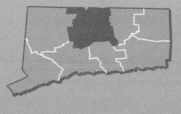

to visit only the most important museums and family-fun sites, you could easily spend three days here.

In the towns surrounding Hartford, you will find attractions that reflect each community's unique history and importance. Defined by such tourist district names as Tobacco Valley or Olde Towne, every area of this county provides opportunities for family fun.

Southington

The town of Southington lies halfway between New York and Boston just east of I-84, a location that even in pre-highway days helped it become an important industrial community, producing cement, tinware, and carriage hardware in the 19th century and aircraft parts, electronic equipment, and medical instruments in the 20th. With all the work they do, folks in these parts need a time and place for play. Southington offers both.

Ski Mount Southington (ages 4 and up)

Off I-84 exit 30; follow signs to 396 Mount Vernon Rd.; business office: (860) 628-0954 or (800) 982-6828; snow phone: (860) 628-SNOW; www.mountsouthington.com. Open from early Dec through Apr for skiing.

If hiking in summer or skiing in winter appeals to your family, Mount Southington is a good place to start. Fourteen downhill trails with five surface lifts and two chairlifts provide a convenient and state-of-the-art alternative to out-of-state facilities for young families who don't want to travel too far to ski.

Night skiing, snowboarding, and ski parties are all part of the business here. Be sure to check the website for the great variety of specials, passes, flex tickets, and other chances to make skiing and boarding affordable. More than 100 professional instructors give group and private lessons, for 3- to 12-year-olds in the kid-centric Glacier Learning Area and learn-to-race programs on four electronically timed courses for ages 8 to adult. Snowmaking machines keep the slopes active from early December through much of early spring. A Terrain Park with tabletops, spines, and rails has made this an especially popular site for boarders. A snack bar/cafeteria and the Mountain Room restaurant give you a chance to refuel, and a ski shop and rental shop help you get the equipment you need. Come to the annual Ski Swap in late October for great deals on equipment.

Where to Eat

Anthony Jack's Wood-Fired Grill. 30 Center St.; (860) 426-1487. Family-owned and family-friendly American-cuisine restaurant right downtown. Booths and brick walls, Angus steaks and fresh seafood cooked over oak and apple fires. Children's menu ($); daily specials; dinner, Wed through Mon; lunch, Wed through Sat. $$–$$$

Bonterra. 98 Main St.; (860) 426-2620. This Italian bistro is also family-owned, family-friendly, and right downtown in the clock tower building on the town green. Traditional favorites with house-made pasta and sauces; children's menu; crayons. Lunch, Tues through Sat; dinner, Tues through Sun. $$–$$$

Nuts about **Apples**

Every October, Southington's population swells by many thousands as the annual **Apple Harvest Festival** attracts an estimated 100,000 revelers. Since 1968, this six-day street festival has celebrated the Southington apple crop in every way possible—a parade (on the first weekend), arts and crafts (on the second weekend), a carnival, a road race, a variety talent show, fireworks, apple foods and ethnic foods, music, and dancing. Admission is free. Follow the crowds to the town green on Route 10. Depending on the way the weekends fall on the calendar, the festival is usually held the last weekend of September and the first weekend in October, including the Fridays. For this year's schedule and information, check the official website: www.apple harvestfestival.com.

The festivities extend to the orchards themselves. In late summer and fall, two in Southington have apples to pick or buy, plus cider, candies, other produce, and gifts. **Roger's Orchards** is at 336 Long Bottom Rd. (860-229-4240; www.rogersorchards.com); **Karabin Farms** is at 894 Andrews St. (860-621-6363; www.karabinfarms.com), and there you can take wagon rides to their pick-your-own apples, peaches, and pumpkins, beginning Labor Day weekend.

Where to Stay

Holiday Inn Express. 120 Laning St.; (860) 276-0736 or (800) 221-2222. 122 units, outdoor pool, continental breakfast. $$$

Residence Inn by Marriott. 778 West St.; (860) 621-4440. 94 suites with full kitchens. Pets welcome. Exercise room, indoor pool. Buffet breakfast. $$$–$$$$

Bristol

Though firmly in Hartford County, the small industrial city of Bristol is classified by the State Tourism Commission as part of Connecticut's Northwest. The city's history as a center of venerable Yankee industries, however, gives it a distinctive character much more in line with Hartford than with rural Litchfield. To arrive here from Southington, take Route 10 north to Route 229, and you'll reach Bristol about 8 miles from that junction.

American Clock & Watch Museum (ages 4 and up)

100 Maple St.; (860) 583-6070; www.clockandwatchmuseum.org. Open daily from about Apr 1 through Nov 30 from 10 a.m. to 5 p.m. except Easter and Thanksgiving Day. $, children under 8 free.

In honor of those industrious craftsmen, you might start a day in Bristol here. More than 1,400 clocks and watches are beautifully displayed in a 19th-century colonial home with two modern wings filled with the largest of the ticking, striking, and chiming clocks.

A forest of grandfather clocks shares one wing with a marvelous representation of an 18th-century wooden-works clock workshop that displays ledger books, manuals, and clocks in various stages of finishing. Back in the main house, a charming clock shop is re-created with hundreds of clocks that would have been sold in the 1890s, including the original fixtures from an actual 1890s shop in Plymouth, Connecticut.

The collection is magnificent and very appealing to children. A guided or cell-phone tour takes about one hour. We found clocks shaped like Old King Cole, a bumblebee, a frying pan, a pumpkin, a violin, a town crier . . . the list could go on and on. The museum also contains the largest collection of Hickory Dickory Dock clocks held anywhere. Children may enjoy finding familiar figures such as Mickey Mouse, Bugs Bunny, Barbie, and other licensed characters among the antique cabinet clocks, pocket watches, and wristwatches.

The New England Carousel Museum (ages 4 and up)

95 Riverside Ave. (Route 72); (860) 585-5411; www.thecarouselmuseum.org. Open Mar through Dec, Mon through Sat 10 a.m. to 5 p.m. and Sun, noon to 5 p.m. Closed major holidays. $; children under 4 are free. This admission fee covers entrance to all the entities in this complex.

One of the nation's largest displays of antique carousel pieces has its home in the **Bristol Center for Arts and Culture.** The golden age of the carousel, from 1880 through the 1930s, is portrayed in the restored hosiery mill—the "Stockingnet Factory"—that houses both this museum and the restoration workshop of carousel expert Bill Finkenstein, as well as two other small museums and fine arts galleries. The main hall of the Carousel Museum contains a changing parade of Coney Island, Philadelphia, and Country Fair–style figures so colorful and stately that one cannot help but be drawn into their magic. Many horses have been rescued and restored here, or kept on long-term loan from private collectors, a situation that constantly infuses the museum with new life. The simplicity of the hall underscores the grandeur of the horses, chariots, band organs, and rounding boards. You can't help but smile and you might even feel like dancing when you hear the beautiful band organ music that fills the hall. Guides tailor tours to the age and interests of the visitors. Children are invited to feel a horsehair tail and to guess at details of carousel construction. A re-creation of a carver's workshop reveals the secrets of the craft; the particular details of master carvers such as Illions, Stein and Goldstein, Denzel, and Looff are pointed out.

Call for information on the museum's birthday parties, which include crafts, games, and tours. On an upper floor of the building, be sure to explore the **Museum of Greek Culture** and the **Museum of Fire History,** which includes a collection of firefighting

Connecticut Carousels

The carousel museum may make you ache for a ride, but you can't do it there. Luckily, you're in a great state for carousels. Although by the end of the 19th century more than 3,000 carousels operated in the United States, fewer than 100 still exist. Connecticut is home to three antiques, plus a few more recent and brand-new ones, such as the one in the Danbury Fair Mall, the one at Lake Compounce (see description later in this section), and the one at Lake Quassapaug (see Middlebury section of New Haven County chapter). Of the three antique carousels, two are currently operating at Lighthouse Point Park in New Haven and at Bushnell Park in Hartford. The third, the restored Pleasure Beach carousel, is partly displayed in Bridgeport's Beardsley Zoological Gardens, next to the operating reproduction that twirls in the Carousel House. At Sound View Beach in Old Lyme is a 1925 kiddie-sized carousel that is pure summertime fun for the wee ones.

equipment and memorabilia dating from the 1800s to the present. Downstairs are two fine art galleries, including the work of local artist Glo Sessions and others. All of these are open at the same hours as the Carousel Museum.

Imagine Nation Museum (ages 1 to 10)
1 Pleasant St.; (860) 314-1400; www.imaginenation.org. Open Wed to Fri 9:30 a.m. to 5 p.m.; Sat 11 a.m. to 5 p.m.; Sun noon to 5 p.m. $, infants under 1 free. Admission may be higher during special events.

Operated by the Family Center of Bristol and affiliated with the Boys & Girls Club of Bristol, the Imagine Nation Museum is a nonprofit hands-on learning facility targeted to the youngest of visitors. Its focus is on interactive exhibits that encourage exploration and experimentation in the sciences of sound, air, and motion.

The Sandsational Pendulum allows children to experiment with pendulum motion and art, and at the Gravity Well, they'll discover the principles of gravity and inertia. At the Tuning Fork Table, visitors experiment with sound vibration, learning the principles of frequency and resonance, and at an oversize glockenspiel, they can explore musical notation. The Stretch-It Pegboard employs rubber bands to form original shapes and patterns; Whisper Dishes invite visitors to learn how to channel sound waves; and Air Time uses table tennis balls, blowers, and launch tubes to show how directed air produces power. One of the museum's most popular exhibits is Play Your Way, which allows kids to role-play as their favorite athletes along with a digital-image backdrop. In the Kids Zone, children can don construction hats, safety goggles, and work aprons and build structures from plumbing pipes, plastic and wood blocks, Erector sets, and gears. And the creative arts center provides recyclable materials for self-directed activities as well as some

conducted by museum staff. Candle- and jewelry-making, bookmaking, weaving, rug hook-
ing, and basketry classes are offered in this area.

As if that weren't enough, the museum also has a collection of international dolls; a
cyber-lab of PC workstations; a greenhouse where visitors learn about ecology, botany,
and conservation; a water-play area with bubble wands and giant bubble machines; a
jungle-theme playscape with tunnels, a slide, and climbing wall sections; a birthday party
room; and a dark room with black lights and glow-in-the-dark toys where visitors can
explore luminescence and phosphorescence. There's even a real 1940s soda fountain that
serves up kids' lunches and ice cream treats. You have to come play here—it's great!

Lake Compounce Theme Park and Entertainment Complex (all ages)

**822 Lake Ave. (Route 229 North), 2 miles from I-84 exit 31; (860) 583-3300; www.lake
compounce.com. Open most days from Memorial Day to late Aug, then weekends and holidays only until late Sept. Call for specific hours and days of operation. Ride-all-day rates:
$$$$; children 3 and under free. Season passes good for unlimited visits, $$$$. Evening
rates and group rates also. Parking, $.**

Lake Compounce upholds its record as the oldest continually operating amusement park
in the United States. Besides the old-fashioned fun in the sun encouraged by its 28-acre
lake and its sandy beach, the park operates more than 30 new and newly restored rides,
including its 1911 carousel with Wurlitzer organ, a 1927 white wooden Wildcat roller
coaster, and its century-old open-air sky trolley. Along with those are new and nearly-new
temptations for thrill-seekers: Boulder Dash (the East Coast's longest and fastest wooden
coaster); Zoomerang coaster with corkscrew turns; Splash Harbor wave pool and Tunnel
Twister water slides; Thunder Rapids raft ride; Mammoth Falls flume ride; Rainbow Riders
balloon ride; and the Zoomers Gas 'n' Go mini-Corvette ride. The Vacation Village Lakeside
Theatre features changing acts from circuses to magic shows; a 100-foot Ferris wheel
competes with the 750-foot ascent of the Southington Mountain Sky Ride; the Shoreline
Trolley car shuttles passengers to a 2,400-seat picnic pavilion. Young visitors will enjoy the
Kiddieland Circus World, with rides for children under 48 inches. A miniature golf course
and paddleboats (both an extra charge) add to the entertainments.

Bring along a bathing suit or a change of clothes and a towel so you can enjoy a ride
on the water slide or a dip in the lake. Lockers and changing rooms are provided. Several
food concessions and a large full-service restaurant provide lots of choices for snacks,
meals, and beverages. Groups of 25 or more can request special rates, so visitors might
consider the reduced price a good excuse for a neighborhood outing, a family reunion, or
a birthday bash.

Where to Eat

Carmine's Italian Grill. 650 Farmington
Ave.; (860) 314-1501. Traditional Italian specialties, offered in wonderful family-sized
portions, along with salads and fresh bread,
plentiful for sharing with the whole table. Children's menu. Open daily for lunch and dinner.
$$–$$$

Super Natural Market and Deli. 430 North Main St. in Northside Square; (860) 582-1663. Excellent hot and cold buffet and deli with small eating area; perfect for takeout or picnics, or pull up a stool and eat here. Terrific soups. Open Mon through Fri 8 a.m. to 6 p.m. and Sat 9 a.m. to 5 p.m. $

Where to Stay

Clarion Hotel. 42 Century Dr.; (860) 589-7766. 120 units, including 2 suites. Fitness room, sauna, indoor pool. Full breakfast available ($) at Jillian's Restaurant on premises. $$–$$$

Canton/Collinsville

Fishing and antiquing are probably the most popular tourist activities in the Canton/Collinsville area near Route 179 north of Burlington and west of Avon, but they are not likely to sustain the long-term attention of everyone in the family. Luckily, some other options make the area a crowd-pleaser anyway.

Huck Finn Adventures (all ages)

(860) 693-0385; www.huckfinnadventures.com. Open in spring, summer, and fall. Call for reservations and directions. Mini solo kayaks, catamaran canoes, a wooden raft, and an inflatable raft are also available. $$$$

First of all, this operation is run by an easygoing fellow with a great appreciation for the beauty and adventure to be enjoyed in the outdoors. An all-around nice guy, John Kulick offers leisurely trips specially designed for families with young children or beginner canoeists. You choose from 3-, 5-, or 9-mile trips in waist-high flat water along a quiet section of the sandy-bottomed Farmington River between Avon and Simsbury.

Everything you need for the self-guided outing is provided, except the picnic or snacks you bring along. The outfitter sets you up with stable 17-foot canoes, paddles, and life vests. The canoes have seats in the middle for the kids, so two adults and two young children are usually comfortable in one canoe. Instruction on paddling, put-in, and take-out is offered at the outset for novices, but this is gentle enough for little risk to true beginners.

You'll paddle past King Philip's Cave high up on the Talcott Mountain Ridge. On the ride back to your put-in spot, the driver of your shuttle van will tell you the story of Metacomet, also known as King Philip. A bloody three-year war began near this spot in 1675, when Metacomet came into violent contact with the English settlers. When Simsbury, among other towns, was set afire in 1676, Metacomet supposedly watched from a cave atop what is now called Metacomet Ridge. You might want to stop in the small park near the old iron bridge along the way for a picnic at the Pinchot Sycamore, the largest tree in Connecticut. Actually located in Simsbury in the Weatogue section on Route 185, the tree's circumference is 25 feet, 8 inches. It is 93 feet tall and its branches spread 138 feet. A picnic area with tables is there for your use.

Two adults paddling at a leisurely pace can do these trips in two to three hours (paddling time), but you're welcome to spend the day picnicking and exploring, or drifting like Huckleberry himself. Twilight, firefly, and moonlight trips can also be arranged. Whitewater instruction usually takes place in May and June as water conditions allow.

Collinsville Canoe and Kayak (all ages with some limits)

41 Bridge St. (Route 179); (860) 693-6977; www.cckstore.com. Seasonal hours, depending on weather and water conditions; call to inquire. $$$–$$$$.

This outfitter offers guided and self-guided canoe and kayak trips on flat water, whitewater, and the Sound. Self-guided trips on flat water are commonly taken from the put-in points near the Collinsville Canoe store on Route 179. Guided tours are offered on the Farmington, Mystic, Bantam, and Four-Mile Rivers as well as Selden Neck, Great Island, and other areas. Reservations are necessary for all guided tours and are highly recommended, especially for weekends, even for the self-guided Farmington River flat-water trips.

The age minimum for kayaks and canoes is up to parental discretion, but the child must be able to fit snugly into a life vest. They also offer instruction for children ages 5 and older in beginning canoeing and kayaking for whitewater, flat water, and the sea.

Canton Historical Museum (ages 6 and up)

11 Front St.; (860) 693-2793; www.cantonmuseum.org. Open Apr through Nov, Wed through Sun from 1 to 4 p.m.; open until 8 p.m. Thurs. Dec through Mar, Sat and Sun from 1 to 4 p.m. $, children under 6 free.

If you're intrigued by the history of the area after a day on the river, visit this marvelous museum. A complete, original post office, a general-store re-creation, a blacksmith area, a barbershop area, a Victorian bride's parlor with wedding dresses, a late-19th-century kitchen setting, and tons of farming equipment, medical equipment, household implements like looms and spinning wheels, and much more await your perusal on the one-hour guided tour. A special children's area includes dolls, toys, and other items of interest, and a true highlight is an operational model train diorama of the whole Collinsville village and countryside as it appeared about 1900.

Roaring Brook Nature Center (all ages)

70 Gracey Rd.; (860) 693-0263; www.roaringbrook.org. Open year-round Tues through Sat 10 a.m. to 5 p.m. (also Mon from July through Aug) and Sun 1 to 5 p.m. Hiking trails open daily, dawn to dusk. $.

Canton's sanctuary is perfect for families. An excellent longhouse typical of the Eastern native people is among the Changing Land and Wildlife indoor exhibits, which reveal how the past 500 years of land use have affected the flora and fauna of southern New England's woods. Another exhibit explores the natural and cultural history of the Farmington River. Among the interactive areas are fascinating walk-in dioramas, including a beaver wetland re-creation and an ancient forest and Native American area. Here too are a wild animal attraction area, a live-animal area with native creatures, and a small gift shop. Out in the exceptionally pretty sanctuary are five miles of trails, including a wildflower trail and a native-plant butterfly trail, especially lovely in spring and summer. Ask for wildlife and flora guides and checklists before you head out to the beautiful Werner's Woods property. Indoor programs and guided walks are offered throughout the year. A full slate of concerts ($–$$$), some especially designed for young children, is one of the most unique features of this nature center. See the website for its schedule and such other annual events as the Hobgoblin Fair in October.

Where to Eat

The Bagel Deli. 220 Albany Turnpike (Route 44), Canton; (860) 693-8905. In the Canton Village Shopping Center, this bagel shop/cafe offers breakfast and lunch options every day and can help you pack a pretty good picnic. Bagels and bagel sandwiches of every description; great deli sandwiches and soups. Eat here at a few tables, or pack it out. Open from 6 a.m. to 2 p.m. on weekdays; 6 a.m. to 2 p.m. on Sat, and 7 a.m. to noon on Sun. $

Crown & Hammer Restaurant and Pub. 3 Depot St.; (860) 693-9199. In the former freight station, this busy local favorite is open Wed through Sun for lunch and dinner. Great setting; great burgers, wraps, crab cakes, and fried green tomatoes, of course. $$–$$$

Feng. 110 Albany Turnpike, Canton; (860) 693-3364. Open from 11:30 a.m. daily for lunch and dinner. Asian at its best. $–$$

La Salle Market and Deli. 104 Main St., Collinsville; (860) 693-8010. Open daily year-round; from 6:30 a.m. Mon through Fri, and from 7 a.m. on weekends, this friendly throwback to the good old days has five eat-in tables or take-out service if you need picnic food. Bagels, muffins, breakfast and deli sandwiches, salads, dogs, burgers, and more (like pizza in the evenings only). Open-mike entertainment on Friday until 10 p.m. $

Where to Stay

Hillside Motel. 671 Albany Turnpike (Route 44); (860) 693-4951. 11 units in this neat, clean, owner-occupied motel. No-frills basic place to rest your head comfortably and safely. Complimentary coffee in the morning. $

Avon

Named for the river in Stratford, England, Avon originated in 1645 as a section of Farmington. First known as Nod, for North District, it grew substantially in the following century when the new stagecoach route from Boston to Albany came through town. Along with the Albany Turnpike came prosperity for the farmers and traders of the region, who capitalized on the needs of the travelers passing through town. Inn and tavern keepers, blacksmiths and harness makers, merchants, and even bandits all benefited from the construction of the road we now call Route 44.

Avon has retained all signs of the affluence it achieved in its past. Now a bedroom community populated largely by commuting professionals, it is plump with restaurants and shops catering to a comfortable clientele. For tourists, this means wonderful food and great shopping, plus a few places the kids might really enjoy. One caveat: It's best to be here in summer or fall.

Avon Cider Mill (all ages)

57 Waterville Rd. (Route 10); (860) 677-0343. The mill's market is open daily, mid-September to October 31 from 9 a.m. to 6 p.m.; November 1 to December 25, they close at 5 p.m.

When the trees show signs of turning, come here. From apples trucked in from upstate New York, the Lattizori brothers make 35,000 to 40,000 gallons of cider every year, starting in mid-September. You can actually watch them make the cider in the press their grandfather bought in 1919, but you'd have to get up pretty early in the morning. Cider-making begins at 2 a.m. and is usually done by 7 a.m. Set the alarm if you want to see the press in action. If you like to sleep a little longer, just plan on tasting the wonderfully sweet cider—the ultimate chaser for the melt-in-your-mouth cider doughnuts sold here as well.

The market also offers local produce and crafts, pumpkins, and fall accoutrements like Indian corn, gourds, mums, and more. Later in the season, they truck in the Christmas trees. After Christmas, the Lattizoris rest a bit; they close shop until spring, when they bring out plants for your gardens. In midsummer, local produce, such as sweet corn, tempts the tourists right off the road.

Pickin' Patch (all ages)

276 Nod Rd., off Route 44; (860) 677-9552. Pick-your-own fields and farm store open daily in season from 9 a.m. to 6 p.m. Open 9 a.m. to 5 p.m. in Nov and Dec.

In the same vein, only more so, you might like to stop by the Pickin' Patch, just a mile and a half up Nod Road, which begins at the Avon Old Farms Inn at the corner of Routes 10 and 44. Owned by Janet and Don Carville, the farm has been in the Carville family since 1666 when their ancestors came from Hartford after accompanying Thomas Hooker to Connecticut.

This farm—and its busy store—is a fountain of riches, namely nearly everything growing under the sun from asparagus to zucchini. Come here to pick yourself or choose from the store, from mid-April to December 24. The 10th-oldest family farm in Connecticut, the farm grows the largest variety of berries, vegetables, and flowers in the state. Strawberries, blackberries, blueberries, squash, spinach, collards, peas, cucumbers, tomatoes, peppers, and much more are sold at half the cost of retail if you pick them yourself.

The joint really starts hopping when pumpkin season begins. On weekends in October from 10 a.m. to 5 p.m., take a **free** ride on a tractor-driven hay wagon out to the fields to pick your own pumpkin.

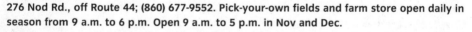

Farmington Valley Arts Center (ages 6 and up)

25 Arts Center Lane, in Avon Park North office/industrial complex. Buildings #25 and #27 are the Arts Center; (860) 678-1867; www.fvac.net. Studios open year-round by chance or by appointment; store open year-round Wed through Sat, 11 a.m. to 5 p.m. and Sun noon to 4 p.m. In Nov and Dec, open Mon through Sat 10 a.m. to 5 p.m., Thurs until 8 p.m., and Sun noon to 5 p.m.

Historically important as former factory buildings, these century-old brownstone structures now house the studios of about 25 resident professional artists. Painting, ceramics, weaving, and sculpture are just a few of the media explored here. Classes are offered for children and adults at every level—beginners as well as advanced. Artists work on individual schedules, but someone is almost always here to watch. You are welcome to stroll from studio to studio throughout the year, especially on weekends from February through October or as many as seven days a week in November and December. Open Arts Day in early June is a festival event with demonstrations, classes, musicians, dancers, a theater performance, and other arts experiences. Check the website calendar for **free** (or very affordable) Art Nights, at which adults and children ages 6 to 17 are welcome. From the first Saturday in November until Christmas Eve, a holiday exhibit called the Art of Giving/The Giving of Art features musicians, luminaria, and festivities on opening night, plus sales of contemporary American crafts thereafter in the Fisher Gallery and in the FVAC store. The pottery, jewelry, toys, prints, clothing, and other work here are made by U.S. crafters only. Ask for a course catalog in the FVAC office or check the website. The teen and children's summer classes at the Learning Center Annex are wonderful.

First Company Governor's Horse Guards (all ages)

Military Reservation, 232 West Avon Rd. (Route 167 between Routes 4 and 44); (860) 673-3525; www.govhorseguards.org. Public viewing of drills on horseback every Thursday evening, usually shortly after 7:30 throughout the year. Open horse show in June. Call for schedule or check the website. Visitors welcome at other times daily to view horses. The driveway to the compound is at 280 Arch Rd.

If you are in Avon at a time that coordinates with the activities of the Governor's Horse Guards, stop for a look. The nation's first cavalry unit organized in 1658 as the mounted guards of Connecticut Colony, the original 30 or so riders and horses served both as ceremonial escorts and in active duty in the War of 1812, World War I, and World War II. The company's current responsibilities are mostly decorative. Their choreographed maneuvers are amazingly intricate "dances" performed at such events as presidential and gubernatorial inaugurations. You are welcome to watch them practice their astounding routines at the compound. Each Thursday evening, the caretaker and the mounted troopers go through the drills, both inside the barn and outside. You can also ask for a tour of the compound on other days if you are visiting nearby; an advance call is a good idea.

Where to Eat

Avon Old Farms Inn. 1 Nod Rd., at the junction of Routes 44 and 10; (860) 677-2818; www.avonoldfarmsinn.com. This classic is one of the 10 oldest restaurants in the country, offering New American cuisine in a beautiful setting. Lunch and dinner, daily, from Labor Day through June only; Sunday brunch year-round. $$$$

Bakers Dozen Bagel Company. 315 West Main St.; (860) 676-2245. This spic-and-span family-owned bakery has made 35 varieties of bagels on-site for the past 25 years. Bagel sandwiches, stuffed bagel pockets, soups in winter, and more. Eat in or out for breakfast, lunch, and beyond. Open daily from 6:30 a.m.; closings vary (earliest is 2 p.m. on Sun). $

Max a Mia Ristorante and Cantinetta. 70 East Main St. (Route 44); (860) 677-MAXX. Northern Italian contemporary cuisine is what they call it; we call it delicious. Fresh focaccia,

excellent salads and pastas galore, thin-crust pizza made in wood-fired oven. Open for lunch, dinner, and Sunday brunch. $$–$$$

Where to Stay

Avon Old Farms Hotel. 279 Avon Mountain Rd., at the junction of Routes 44 and 10; (860) 677-1651; www.avonoldfarms hotel.com. Across the street from the Avon Old Farms Inn, which is a restaurant, is this cream-of-the-crop, 160-unit luxury hotel very welcoming to families. Continental breakfast in atrium lobby. Outdoor pool, sauna, fitness room. FERME Farm-to-Table Restaurant and pub, with half-size portions and children's menu (open to public year-round, three meals daily). $$$$

Simsbury

Six miles north of Avon, Simsbury is an appealing suburb of 22,000 people, many of whom work in Hartford, just 20 minutes south. Established in 1670 by English colonists, Simsbury was built on land long populated by native peoples, who had no understanding of the English concept of land claims when they began to share local tribal lands with the new-comers. Their misapprehension of the situation led to turbulence that culminated in their burning of Simsbury on March 26, 1676. Sad to say, the native people underestimated the tenacity of the settlers and were nearly eradicated in the bloody King Philip's war that ensued. Reconstruction of colonial Simsbury commenced in 1677 when it was clear that no further resistance was possible. The settlers of Simsbury soon had a community that flourished, as did industries of copper mining, smelting, steel production, copper coinage, silver plating, and safety fuse manufacturing. Now largely residential, Simsbury offers to the public one of the best historical settlements in the state.

The Phelps Tavern Museum (ages 6 and up)

800 Hopmeadow St. (Route 10); (860) 658-2500; www.simsburyhistory.org. Open year-round, Tues through Sat from noon to 4 p.m. Last full tour at 3:15 p.m. Closed holidays. $–$$.

Once called Massacoh Plantation, this property has eight structures—some reproduction, some original, and some transported here for the purpose of creating a museum. A tour of the property usually begins at the replica 1683 meetinghouse wherein the Simsbury founding fathers decided matters of church and state and from which supposed witch Goody Griffin is said to have departed by flying through its keyhole.

The 1771 Elisha Phelps House, occupied by the Phelps family for nearly 200 years, is restored to the period of 1830–40 when it served as a hotel/tavern for travelers on the New Haven–Northampton Canal. The site also includes a Victorian carriage house with an authentic tin peddler's cart, a 1740 one-room schoolhouse, a barn, an icehouse, a 1795 cottage also owned by the Phelps family, and a re-creation of the safety fuse manufactory with fixtures, records, and furnishings of the original factory.

Tours by (sometimes) costumed guides of the Simsbury Historical Society are excellent, though a full tour for children under 8 may be longer than they can bear. Feel free to ask for a short version if you are the only folks in the group. You can stroll the grounds unguided, but you cannot tour the buildings alone. The museum typically offers a holiday festivity in late November or early December. Living-history reenactments with costumed actors have been among past events; staged readings of holiday tales or visits from Saint Nicholas might occur. Check the website for these and other events of interest to families.

Talcott Mountain State Park (all ages)

Route 185; (860) 242-1158. Park open year-round dawn to dusk. Heublein Tower open mid-Apr to late Aug through Oct, Thurs through Sun, 10 a.m. to 5 p.m. In foliage season, the tower is open daily. Free.

If the excellent history lessons at the Phelps Tavern Museum overwhelm some in your party, refresh yourselves with a brisk hike. A popular family area because of the amazing Heublein Tower at the 1,000-foot summit of the Talcott Mountain Ridge, it has moderate trails, benches, picnic sites, and, on clear days, views of four states from the tower. Some, including Mark Twain, who used to walk this ridge, say it's the finest view in all of Connecticut. The park overlooks many of the fertile Farmington Valley farms and pretty towns like Avon. From Route 10 between Simsbury and Avon, you can't miss seeing the white 165-foot-tall tower built in 1914 by businessman Gilbert Heublein.

Once you're in the park, you hike the 1.5-mile King Philip's Trail to the tower and then climb up. The observation deck, at the top of several flights of stairs, provides a 50-mile view on clear days. A local history exhibit is also at the tower base, with interesting facts about the park and tower.

International Skating Center of Connecticut (ages 3 and up)

1375 Hopmeadow St. (Route 10); (860) 651-5400; www.isccskate.com. Public ice skating Mon through Fri from 11:45 a.m. to 1 p.m., Sat 1:30 to 2:45 p.m. and Sun from 2:30 to 3:45 p.m. Added sessions on some holidays or during school breaks. Visitors welcome daily 6 a.m. to midnight. $–$$.

You want to skate, and you'd love to learn from the example of an elite coaching staff. Come here to this world-class twin facility that offers an Olympic-size and an NHL-size rink. Both are linked to the Sk8ters Cafe, a restaurant and coffee shop that allow diners a view of both rinks. Two thousand seats allow spectators to watch figure skating and hockey events and practices. Small classes for beginners to pros are offered here, and

CT Department of **Lost Culture and History**

Northeast of Simsbury, the little town of **East Granby** is downright bucolic, and it's a pleasure merely to explore the gentle twists and hills of its rural roadways. Just a handful of miles from the Massachusetts border, its village center is a quiet place of refuge from the busy hub that grows in an ever-widening circle around Hartford. In the town's beautiful hills is also a National Historic Landmark and state archaeological preserve that may be closed for the very long foreseeable future, due in large part—well beyond the apparent and legitimate safety issues—to state budget cuts.

The Old New-Gate Prison and Copper Mine (115 Newgate Rd.; http://ct .gov/cct) is closed for a massive restoration (check the website for current information), but the completion of that important task promises to be long delayed. The first North American copper mine chartered by the British monarchy in 1707, New-Gate is also Connecticut's first prison, named after London's notorious New-Gate Prison. When copper mining ceased in the facility in 1773, the subterranean tunnels and chambers were designated as a perfect place to confine the burglars, horse thieves, and counterfeiters who had broken the laws of the English colonies. Soon, however, English sympathizers were imprisoned here as the American Patriots revolted against the monarchy and took New-Gate as their own. During the Revolution, George Washington sent captured Tories here along with American deserters. Just to make sure no one was having any fun underground, prisoners were forced to mine the tunnels and to make nails and shoes.

The facts and fictions of this site are remarkable, and the view from the prison grounds is one of the finest views in the state, especially during the glorious foliage season. Alas, you can no longer take tours of the prison ruins or explore the mine's subterranean tunnels. You can no longer picnic here, and the nature trail, designed long ago to demonstrate wildlife habitat–management practices, is no longer maintained by the DEP. If you care about this loss, do write your legislators. Otherwise, you may wait a long time to learn something here.

the instruction programs and scholarships bring young skaters from all over the world. Learn-to-Skate programs include special kids' classes for ages 3 and up. Skate rentals, purchases, and sharpening and repair services are all available to the public. Private birthday parties can be arranged.

Flamig Farm (ages 2 to 10)

**West Mountain Road; (860) 658-5070; www.flamigfarm.com. Open daily 9 a.m. to 5 p.m.,
weather permitting, primarily from Apr through Nov. Pony rides in warm weather, weekends only 11 a.m. to 3 p.m., $ for children up to 75 pounds. Other rides offered, weather
permitting. Zoo admission $ for folks over 1 and under 80.**

A petting zoo of farm animals is the big ticket at this farm most of the season. See Belgian
draft horses, miniature horses, llamas, pigs, goats, sheep, chickens, rabbits, turkeys,
geese, and ducks. Buy a cupful or a handful of grain to give the animals a snack, and visit
the barns, if you like.

Pony rides are given on weekends only; occasionally a draft horse is saddled as well
for larger riders. In pumpkin season, public hayrides to the pumpkin fields are given on
weekends only, on the half-hour from 11 a.m. to 4 p.m. Private horse-drawn rides and
tractor hayrides can be arranged in advance; sleigh rides can also be arranged when the
weather cooperates. Pony-ride birthday parties are also frequent; a covered pavilion is
available here for that use. Check the website for rates and dates for rides, parties, and
seasonal events. In summer, a Farm Adventure Camp attracts lots of local campers, and
in the fall, haunted hayrides and breakfasts with Santa are very popular. You can buy fresh
eggs and cut flowers at the farm store, and you can bring your own meal to the picnic
area. Visitors are welcome year-round, but activities are limited and staff may not be on
hand to answer questions in the ways they are in warm weather.

Where to Eat

Abigail's Grille and Wine Bar. 4 Hartford
Rd.; (860) 264-1580. For tasty Continental fare
in a newly restored and expanded historic
setting, come for dinner daily, lunch on weekdays, and Sunday brunch. A lighter-fare tavern menu ($$–$$$) and children's menu make
this easy for family budgets; a patio makes
warm-weather dining a delight. $$$–$$$$

Maple Tree Cafe. 781 Hopmeadow St.;
(860) 651-1297. For lunch and dinner daily,
choose soups, sandwiches, burgers, salads,
pastas, and seafood with an emphasis on
Italian favorites, plus typical American appe-
tizers. Children's menu. Patio tables in fair
weather. Live music on Friday and Saturday
evenings. $

Sakimura. 10 Wilcox St.; (860) 651-7929.
For a delicious and cultural food adventure,
try lunch or dinner at this excellent Japanese
establishment. A sushi/sashimi bar, more
than two dozen appetizer dishes, teriyaki,

tempura, and American favorites made
Japanese style are among the many choices.
Open daily. $–$$$

Where to Stay

The Simsbury Inn. 397 Hopmeadow St.;
(860) 651-5700. 100 "luxury rooms with a
country inn ambience" is how the inn's owners describe it. They're right. Indoor pool, 3
restaurants, fitness room, sauna, tennis, jogging paths, and continental breakfast make
this a special place for families. $$$$

Windsor

Six miles north of the state capital lies Windsor, which calls itself Connecticut's oldest town. In 1633 English adventurers from Plymouth Colony in Massachusetts camped at the confluence of the Connecticut and Farmington Rivers in a place the native inhabitants called Matianuck. Briefly named Dorchester by the newcomers, the town was renamed Windsor in 1637 and has enjoyed a prosperous history ever since, based on the varied enterprises of brick making, cigar tobacco farming, and the milling of woolens and paper. Now largely suburban in nature, this town on the western bank of the Connecticut River has a variety of attractions that will add to a family's appreciation of the state's north-central Heritage Valley.

In addition to the main attractions listed in the following paragraphs, Windsor offers a pleasant array of places and events families might enjoy. Summer concerts on Thursday evenings on the historic town green, a winter carnival, a clown day, and a just-for-fun dog show are the kinds of activities that characterize this family-oriented town. Other annual events include the Shad Derby Festival the third Saturday in May, a Yankee Doodle Fourth of July Celebration, and an early autumn Revolutionary War Encampment (see www.revolutionarywindsor.com). Walking and cycling on the Windsor Center River

History in the **Heritage Valley**

Windsor is proud of its history as the cradle of European settlement and development in the Connecticut River Valley, and it celebrates that through several museums and events. Most of these are located in or near the town's historic district, which centers roughly on the Broad Street town green and the Palisado Green, on or near Routes 75 and 159. The marvelous **Windsor Historical Society** (96 Palisado Ave. near the corner of North Meadow Road; 860-688-3813; www.windsorhistoricalsociety.org) has three galleries with changing art and artifact exhibitions and a hands-on history learning center that covers three centuries of life in Windsor. Here, for instance, you can try on colonial-style clothing, pretend to attend the one-room schoolhouse, or learn about hearth cooking. The society also operates the adjacent **1758 Strong House** and nearby **1765 Chaffee House.** The museum is open and tours of these homes are given year-round, Tues through Sat, from 10 a.m. to 4 p.m. ($). The **1780 Oliver Ellsworth Homestead** (778 Palisado Ave.; 860-688-8717; www.ctdar.org/oeh) re-creates the life of its namesake Revolutionary patriot and statesman through domestic furniture, implements, and ephemera. It is open for tours from noon to 4:30 p.m. May through Oct on Tues, Wed, and Sat; $, children under 12 are free.

Trail, ice-skating on the town green, and canoeing on the Farmington River are among the town's outdoor activities; indoors are museums that explore 300 years of history (see sidebar). Consider booking a room at a local hostelry and have an old-fashioned good time.

Northwest Park and Nature Center (all ages)

Luddy/Taylor Connecticut Valley Tobacco Museum (ages 8 and up)

Lang Road; park and nature center: (860) 285-1886; www.northwestpark.com; tobacco museum: (860) 285-1888; www.tobaccohistsoc.org. Park open daily year-round, dawn to dusk. Nature center open daily year-round, Mon through Sat 10 a.m. to 5 p.m.; Sun noon to 4 p.m. Tobacco museum open Mar to mid-Dec, Tues through Thurs and Sat noon to 4 p.m. Free admission to all.

Lovely Northwest Park has nearly 475 acres, 12 miles of trails, picnic areas and pavilions, community and demonstration gardens, a playground, and much more of appeal to visitors of all ages. Any time of year, you can see live-animal exhibits in the Animal Barn and Nature Center, and you can explore a wetland forest, a bog, a softwood forest, a hemlock forest, and a pond, among other habitats. In late winter, visit the maple-sugaring house; in summer, linger in the bird and butterfly gardens. Register for a guided walk, a family nature program, or a kids' camp, or come just to hike, bike, or picnic on your own. In snowy weather, come to snowshoe or cross-country ski; a rental center offers equipment ($$). An annual Country Fair offers games, races, hayrides, and entertainment especially for children 2 to 10. Call or check the website for dates. Throughout the academic year, come in the evening or on occasional afternoons on selected Saturdays for the Northwest Park Coffee House Concert series. All performances are suitable for families ($$$). Check the Northwest Park website for the current schedule.

At the Luddy/Taylor Connecticut Valley Tobacco Museum, located in the park, you can explore a restored tobacco-curing barn to gain a sense of the venerable history of tobacco farming in this valley. The world's finest cigar wrappers are still grown in this area, although the total acreage is reduced to 2,000 acres from a peak of 30,000 acres in 1921. Learn how the shade-leaf tobacco was grown and cured; see the authentic equipment stored in the barn; and peruse the historical displays in the museum building near the barn to gain an appreciation for the ways the tobacco industry contributed to the region's economy and even its ethnic culture.

Where to Eat

Bart's Deli and Restaurant. 85 Palisado Ave.; (860) 688-9035. Within the historic district not far from the center of town is this cozy and down-to-earth place right on the banks of the Farmington. Great breakfasts and, for lunch and early dinner, hearty sandwiches of all kinds, rings and dogs, burgers, and traditional American hot meals. Open daily year-round, typically at 7 a.m. (11 a.m. on Sun). Picnic tables by the river if you'd like to eat outdoors. $–$$

Dom's Broad Street Eatery. 330 Broad St.; (860) 298-9758. Try Dom's for cuisine similar to Bart's—hearty traditional American breakfasts, and generous sandwiches, soups, salads, and such for lunch. Open year-round from 7 a.m. to 2 p.m. on weekdays, from 6 a.m. on weekends, and breakfast only on Sun. $

Where to Stay

Residence Inn by Marriott. 100 Dunphy Lane; (860) 688-7474; www.residenceinn .com. 96 suites with fully equipped kitchens. Complimentary continental buffet breakfast; outdoor pool, whirlpool, sports court. Pets welcome. $$$$

Windsor Locks

Best known for its current role as the home of Bradley International Airport, Windsor Locks is on the Connecticut River about a dozen miles from downtown Hartford and has a large concentration of hotels, motels, and restaurants serving travelers. It also has one of the nation's best aviation museums.

New England Air Museum (all ages)

36 Perimeter Rd.; (860) 623-3305; www.neam.org. Open daily year-round, except New Year's Day, Christmas, and Thanksgiving, from 10 a.m. to 5 p.m. $$, children under 4 free. Birthday parties by prior arrangement ($$$$).

Right within sight of the runways at Bradley International Airport is the home of the largest collection of aircraft in the Northeast. From a 1909 wood-and-canvas Bleriot XI monoplane to modern jets, the museum includes more than 80 aircraft. Most are restored and housed in three hangars, transformed to museum-gallery quality and focused on military and civilian aviation history. Others in the outside yard can be viewed in seasonable weather. The evolution of humankind's mastery of gravity is chronicled at every turn, nowhere more evidently than in the aircraft themselves. The museum owns the oldest aeronautical artifact in the United States—a beautiful wicker balloon basket built by Silas Brooks of Plymouth, Connecticut, in 1870. From that vintage onward, the museum houses a 1912 Pusher, a Flying Boat, a B-25 bomber, a Grumman Hellcat and Wildcat, a Navy Blimp Car, a B-29 Superfortress, an F-4 Phantom, an F-14B Tomcat, and many other fully and partially restored aircraft. Excellent exhibits tell the story of flight from the drawings of Leonardo da Vinci to the space flights of NASA astronauts. Among the many intriguing displays are an outstanding Igor Sikorsky exhibit and a fascinating Apollo 13 rescue exhibit.

Parents of very young children may have to read or paraphrase some of the excellent information the museum provides. Nevertheless, the museum is exceptionally well suited to children, and, on weekends especially, museum personnel eagerly provide extra activities and assistance to curious kids. A kid-sized "airport" called KidsPort, designed for visitors 5 through 12, offers an exploration of aviation through touch-screen games, video clips, and music. Elsewhere are computer flight simulator games and kiosks that offer brief presentations on such topics as aerodynamics, milestones of flight, and women in aviation. In the Aviation Pioneer Theater, you can see films on flight, the space program, and other topics. On Open Cockpit Sundays aviation enthusiasts of all ages can climb inside certain aircraft. This opportunity is offered a few times annually, so check the website calendar for the schedule of these and such other special events as Space Expo and Women Take Flight.

As you will see, the museum is right off the road that rings Bradley airport, so if you pull over and sit there awhile, you will very likely enjoy the comings and goings of local and national aircraft.

Where to Eat

Skyline Restaurant. 106 Ella T. Grasso Turnpike (Route 75); (860) 623-9296. For good Italian food and views of the air traffic, ask for a window seat in the front atrium; you can't see the planes take off or land, but they are there in the sky. The children's menu includes chicken parm and ravioli along with typical tenders, dogs, and the like. Lunch and dinner from 11:30 a.m. daily except major holidays. $–$$

Where to Stay

Doubletree Hotel. 16 Ella T. Grasso Turnpike (Route 75); (860) 627-5171. 200 rooms, 2 suites, indoor pool, fitness room, restaurant. $$$–$$$$

Fairfield Inn by Marriott. 2 Loten Dr.; (860) 627-9333 or (800) 228-2800. 121 rooms and suites, indoor pool, continental breakfast. $$$–$$$$

Ramada Inn at Bradley. 5 Ella T. Grasso Turnpike (Route 75); (860) 623-9494 or (800) 2-RAMADA. 148 rooms, indoor/outdoor pool, restaurant, continental breakfast. $$$–$$$$

East Windsor

You'll need to cross the Connecticut River to get from Windsor Locks to East Windsor, a trip made easy if you drive across the Route 140 East bridge. Once the northernmost point that could be reached by steamboats before encountering the Connecticut's southernmost rapids, East Windsor became a busy freshwater port with a crowded warehouse area still known as Warehouse Point. Now an interesting mix of suburban and rural areas, East Windsor holds a few treasures for families who look past the fast-food joints and businesses that line the main thoroughfares close to I-91.

Connecticut Trolley Museum (all ages)

58 North Rd. (Route 140); (860) 627-6540; www.ct-trolley.org. Open June through Aug, 10 a.m. to 3:30 p.m. Mon and Wed through Fri; 10 a.m. to 4:30 p.m. on Sat; and noon to 4:30 p.m. on Sun. In Sept and until early Oct, open on the weekends only at the same hours. In Oct, open on the weekends plus Fri 10 a.m. to 3:30 p.m. and on Columbus Day for the Pumpkin Patch event. Also open Fri and Sat evenings (7 to 9:30 p.m.) for Rails to the Darkside in October, and Thurs through Sun evenings (5 to 9 p.m.) for the Winterfest Light Display in late November and through December 30. Closed Thanksgiving Day and Christmas. Check the website for details of this year's schedule. $–$$. Includes admission to the

adjacent fire museum. Festival admission slightly higher. Birthday parties and group outings can be arranged.

Enjoy the nostalgia of riding on real trolleys as they make 3.5-mile round-trip excursions through the East Windsor woodlands. The museum owns nearly 80 vintage trolleys collected from all over the world. Half are housed in storage barns; the remainder sit on the side of the tracks, waiting for restoration. Of the dozen or more restored trolleys, two to eight may be out on the tracks on any given day. The cars run every 20 minutes; your admission ticket buys you unlimited rides and self-guided tours of the visitor center, which houses several restored cars, a steam locomotive, a large model trolley collection, a library, a gift shop, and restrooms. Inside the center, see exhibits about the ways the electric trolley affected society and watch a short film about the history of trolleys and the railroad. On weekends only, the Trolley Stop Snack Shop offers simple fare, which you can enjoy in a dining car. You can also picnic if you've packed your own meal.

From early October to just before Halloween, come for special Pumpkin Patch days. Planned especially for children ages 3 to 10, these feature games, treats, prizes, and rides to a pumpkin "patch," where each rider chooses a pumpkin to decorate and take home. Older children may enjoy the evening (and pretty scary) Rails to the Darkside, also during October. In December, the Winterfest features decorated cars and a canopy of colorful lights along the track through the woods.

Connecticut Fire Museum (all ages)

58 North Rd.; (860) 623-4732; www.ctfiremuseum.org. Open June through Aug on weekends, noon to 4 p.m., and Mon and Wed through Fri from 10 a.m. to 4 p.m.; in Sept and Oct, weekends only, noon to 4 p.m. $–$$. Includes admission to adjacent trolley museum.

This museum next door to the Connecticut Trolley Museum houses an amazing collection of vintage firefighting vehicles and equipment. An original 1904 switchboard alarm system, which still operates, is preserved exactly as it would have been used in decades past. The main hall contains 21 trucks, from a turn-of-the-20th-century horse-drawn sleigh to a 1955 Zabek pumper. Other memorabilia, tools, and model fire trucks are also displayed. This museum is crowded, but if you love fire engines and you're here, it's worth a look.

Where to Eat

Maine Fish and Seafood Restaurant.
Bridge Street (Route 140); (860) 623-2281.
Seafood, sandwiches, burgers, and more.
Open for lunch and dinner daily. $–$$

Where to Stay

Clarion Inn & Suites. 161 Bridge St.; (860)
623-9411. 111 rooms, outdoor pool, patio,
gardens, whirlpool, steam bath, restaurant,
continental breakfast. $$

Holiday Inn Express–Bradley Airport.
260 Main St.; (860) 627-6585. 116 rooms,
continental hot breakfast, fitness room.
$$–$$$$

Manchester

First the summer camping ground of the Podunk Indians and later called "Silktown" because of its fabrics and paper mills, Manchester is now a mostly residential area just 9 miles to the east of Hartford. It seems that shopping mall developers like the open farmlands around Manchester, a fact that has forever altered the rural landscape outside of the historic town center. Visiting families may want to shop till they drop—or just drop in to one of Connecticut's children's museums and a few other attractions instead.

Lutz Children's Museum (ages 2 to 10)

247 South Main St.; (860) 643-0949; www.lutzmuseum.org. Open Tues through Fri 9 a.m. to 5 p.m., and Sat and Sun noon to 5 p.m. $.

Devoted to making interesting concepts in art, history, science, and nature accessible to children, the small and accessible Lutz offers hands-on experiences for children from toddlerhood to 10. Activities, experiments, and workshops lead to discoveries that are reinforced by the opportunity to participate. Live domestic, native, and exotic animals and do-touch exhibits on natural history and science engage both the youngest visitors and older siblings. A large playground on the grounds provides an outlet for energy. Another outdoor portion of the museum is the Oak Grove Nature Center on Oak Grove Street. Its nature trails are open daily from dawn to dusk at no charge.

The Fire Museum (all ages)

230 Pine St.; (860) 649-9436; www.thefiremuseum.org. Open mid-April through mid-November on Sat only, from noon to 4 p.m. or by special arrangement. $, children under 6 free.

If the trucks at the Connecticut Fire Museum in East Windsor weren't enough to please you, come to see more on the two spacious floors of this turn-of-the-20th-century firehouse. The collection includes hand-pulled, horse-drawn, steam-powered, and motorized trucks, along with other firefighting equipment such as buckets, hats, helmets, tools, and lanterns. The model and toy fire engines are very appealing.

Wickham Park (all ages)

1329 West Middle Turnpike; (860) 528-0856; www.wickhampark.org. Open early Apr through late Oct daily from 9:30 a.m. to dusk. Parking fee, $.

This former estate has a breathtaking spread of more than 10 acres of formal ornamental gardens—but that's far from all you will find here. The panoramic views of the woodlands, ponds, and brooks of the park's 250 acres provide incentive to play and picnic here, but the park's other features make it a destination attraction. Walking trails, three playgrounds, a walk-through aviary, a nature center, a log cabin (which is transformed into a superior Santa's workshop during the winter holidays), a snack bar, and wide-ranging sports facilities encourage day-tripping families to stop for a break from the museums. Younger visitors and visitors of all abilities will delight in the spectacular Sensory Garden, the largest of its kind in New England; sight scopes, information telephones, and a model train are among its appealing features. Older kids will love the 18-hole disc golf course that winds throughout the park; bring your own discs or buy or rent them here. If that is not enough, come to play softball, volleyball, tennis, or throw some horseshoes. Even without the two nearby museums, this special park is worth a drive from anywhere in the state.

Where to Eat

Romano's Macaroni Grill. 170 Slater St.; (860) 648-8819. Primarily Italian food plus steaks, chops, and chicken, for lunch and dinner from 11 a.m. daily. Kids' menu. Not exactly picturesque, but convenient, especially if you went to the mall. $–$$

Where to Stay

Courtyard Marriott Manchester. 225 Slater St.; (860) 533-8484. 87 rooms. 3 suites. $$–$$$$

Hampton Inn & Suites Manchester. 1432 Pleasant Valley Rd.; (860) 644-1732. 107 rooms, 1 suite. Fitness room; indoor pool; complimentary breakfast. $$–$$$$

Hartford

The hub of the county is, of course, the state's capital city of Hartford. Connecticut's oldest city, it holds a wealth of historical, cultural, and educational attractions. Founded in 1636 by Thomas Hooker and his Puritan followers, Hartford evolved from a peaceful agrarian community to a bustling industrial metropolis by 1900. The first city in the United States to be fully electrified, Hartford was by that time reputedly the wealthiest city in the nation. Well-established as the center of the insurance industry, it was also a center for the production of firearms, machine tools, typewriters, and bicycles.

Hartford's neighborhoods grow more diverse with each wave of immigrants, and the people within the city limits invested their talents in building a city of "firsts." Bushnell Park was the first public park in the United States to be conceived, built, and paid for by its citizens through popular vote. Elizabeth Park Rose Garden was the first municipal rose garden in the country. The Wadsworth Atheneum was the nation's first public art museum. These and other important fixtures of the city provide ample incentive to explore Hartford time and time again. This guide contains only the best sites for families. Pick up a Greater Hartford tourism pamphlet for thumbnail descriptions of all of Hartford's excellent museums, parks, and historic sites. To get around town, consider the **free** Hartford Star Shuttle, which operates about every 12 minutes, Mon through Fri from 7 a.m. to 11 p.m. and on Sat from 3 to 11 p.m. (see http://Hartford.com/shuttle_map.php).

Connecticut Science Center (all ages)

50 Columbus Blvd. and Phoenix Plaza at Adriaen's Landing; (860) 727-0457; www.ctscience center.org. Open Tues through Sun, 10 a.m. to 5 p.m. (last entry 4 p.m.); also open on Monday holidays and on Mon in July and Aug. Closed Thanksgiving and Christmas. $$$; children 2 and under, **free.** Extra charge for movie-science-center combo.

The flashiest attraction in Connecticut just may be this exceptional and amazingly interactive nonprofit science exploration space. Offering learning opportunities for visitors of all ages, its primary mission is to inspire children and awaken their creativity in all areas of science.

You'll see that the minute you enter Science Alley, the 130-foot-high central artery that leads into the center from both Columbus Boulevard and Phoenix Plaza, part of the dramatic revitalization of the Connecticut River waterfront district. Through nearly countless interactive activities, you'll learn about your mind and body, the physical world, and outer space. Bridges crossing Science Alley connect to such exhibit galleries as Forces in Motion, a gallery of physical science offering large-scale elements that magnify motion-related phenomena and accommodate multiple users who can compare efforts, strategies, and results. Learn how sailboats are moved by the wind; see how dropped objects change shape; explore robotics; hear, see, and feel the energy of sound and light; discover the patterns and behaviors of music. In the Sports Lab and the Picture of Health Gallery, use math and science to analyze your performance at games; uncover the mechanics and health benefits of physical activity, cardiovascular fitness, and mental fitness; and learn about DNA, genetic traits, stress, motivation, and choice-making. The Planet Earth and Exploring Space galleries include solar system exhibits about exploration for signs of life in our galaxy; the Galaxy and Beyond exhibits focus on remote exploration of the Milky Way and cosmic questions about the universe. The Invention Dimension gallery explores the process of invention and invites you to apply imagination and logic to solve physical puzzles and abstract riddles. In the earth sciences galleries, explore lessons on energy, ecology, weather, the environment, climate change, and the effects that life on earth have on the earth itself. When you need a break from all the action, take a seat in the 3-D Science Theater, which shows science and nature films suitable for the whole family. You may go home exhausted, but you'll feel great.

Old State House (ages 4 and up)

800 Main St.; (860) 522-6766; www.ctosh.org. Open Tues through Sat 10 a.m. to 5 p.m. Last tickets sold at 4 p.m. Closed major holidays. Special programs (free with admission) for children and families on Saturday in the Holcombe Education Center. $–$$; children under 6 are free.

Many tourists begin a trip to Hartford here. Having undergone a complete restoration, the Old State House is the perfect place in which families can orient themselves to the city and gain some perspective on its laudable history. Designed by Charles Bulfinch and constructed in 1796, on the site of the founding of the colony in 1636 by Thomas Hooker, the building is the oldest state house in the nation, established in service of the American people and their new Constitution.

The site on which George Washington greeted French General Rochambeau in 1780 when he arrived to assist the Patriot cause, the halls of the Old State House have also echoed with the footsteps of Lafayette, Andrew Jackson, and other principal players in American history. Both the *Amistad* and the Prudence Crandall trials took place here. If you are thinking that this must be, therefore, a dusty, stodgy relic that expects quiet awe from whispering students on class trips, you've made a terrible mistake.

This bright, sparkling, airy—and yes, entertaining—place is anything but stodgy. Despite its hallowed-halls reputation, it actually invites children to touch, to run, to cheer, to ask questions. Don't miss the colorful and interactive multimedia "History Is All around Us" exhibit, which tells the story of the city across six centuries. You can also see gallery exhibits (with an Acoustiguide audio tour option) of art and history, as well as portions of the collection of Steward's Museum, a re-creation of the state's first museum, founded by Joseph Steward, collector of everything extraordinary, impossible, and downright fraudulent. A smorgasbord of delights Barnumesque in nature, the museum has among its many "natural and other curiosities" a unicorn's horn, an elephant's molar, a whole Bengal tiger, and an ostrich egg, just to name a few.

Also here are public restrooms, public telephones, and a fabulous museum store that specializes in Connecticut-made crafts.

Wadsworth Atheneum   (ages 4 and up)

600 Main St.; (860) 278-2670; www.wadsworthatheneum.org. Open Wed through Fri 11 a.m. to 5 p.m.; Sat and Sun 10 a.m. to 5 p.m.; and on the first Thurs of each month 11 a.m. to 8 p.m. $–$$, children 12 and under free**. Discounted admission on First Thursdays from 5 to 8 p.m.;** free **on last Saturday of every month from 10 a.m. to 1 p.m.**

Just two blocks from the Old State House is the Wadsworth Atheneum, housing more than 45,000 works from ancient to modern times. The nation's oldest continuously operating public art museum, the atheneum has a well-deserved reputation as one of the finest museums of its kind in the United States, and it is soon to become even better when it completes its most current expansion and renovation projects in 2011. Visitors will soon enjoy improved signage and complete reinstallation of the museum's excellent permanent collection of 19th-century French and American Impressionist masters, major works from the Hudson River School, Old Master paintings, and American and European decorative arts. Many children especially enjoy the costume and textile gallery, the *Amistad* collection of African-American art, and a gallery of contemporary art.

Ask the folks at the Main Street info desk for a Family ArtPack, which makes the museum appealing to and manageable for kids. These colorful take-home guides have interactive ideas for exploring the galleries with young children.

The museum's cafeteria has a children's menu, the gift shop is exceptional, and the calendar of events includes films, workshops, concerts, and tours for families with young children. Family activities and gallery tours directed to children are often offered on First Thursdays and Last Saturdays; story hours are on the first and third Wednesday at 11 a.m. An annual festival of holiday trees is staged each December.

Bushnell Park and Carousel   (all ages)

Elm and Jewell Streets; Bushnell Park Foundation: (860) 232-6710; www.bushnellpark.org. Park open daily year-round, dawn to dusk; free**. Walking tours, noon to 1:30 p.m.; call for schedule. Carousel: (860) 585-5411; open 11 a.m. to 5 p.m Tues through Sun from May through Aug, and Thurs through Sun in Sept and Oct (closed in severe weather); $1 per ride; two-hour birthday parties by advance arrangement, $8 per child with unlimited rides.**

Just west of Hartford's Ancient Burying Ground Cemetery on Main Street, pass under the Soldiers and Sailors Memorial Arch on Jewell Street at the entrance to the park.

Spend some time exploring America's oldest public park, established in 1854. Landscaped as an arboretum, its plantings, monuments, fountains, and bridges are pointed out in the wonderful **free** pamphlet *Bushnell Park Tree Walks,* available in the Old State House, the capitol building, or from the DEP office at 165 Capitol Ave. An art gallery showing works by local artists is in the park's pump house, an actual working pump station for the city's flood control authority. Throughout the park are statues of famous Connecticut citizens, such as Israel Putnam, and monuments honoring veterans. The memorial arch, for instance, is dedicated to the 4,000 Hartford citizens who served in the Civil War. This huge sandstone arch depicts scenes from the war on its terra-cotta frieze. Guided walking tours of the park can be arranged (call the Bushnell Park Foundation or visit the website), but younger children especially will gladly skip the tour and head straight for the park's most popular feature: After you pass through the soldiers' arch, immediately look to your left and you'll find the Bushnell Park Carousel in a low brown pavilion with stained-glass windows encircling its upper walls.

Managed by the New England Carousel Museum in Bristol, this gorgeous 1914 carousel was hand carved by master craftsmen Stein and Goldstein; its band organ is a 1924 Wurlitzer. Charming murals, lit by 800 lights, portray the seasons of the year. Forty-eight exceptionally well-restored prancing horses on gleaming brass poles provide the best— and maybe the fastest—carousel ride in the state. Thirty-six of the steeds are jumpers, which go up and down; the rest are stationary. Two ornate chariots complete the set. Hold onto toddlers, parents, and don't be fooled by the slower warm-up of the first pass. You pay for each ride, so bring a pocketful of bills or buy a family pass for the whole season. You may want to ride this one more than once. Come back in late October for the Haunted Carousel festivities—or for the First Night celebrations on December 31.

State Capitol Building (ages 6 and up)

210 Capitol Ave.; (860) 240-0222; www.cga.state.ct.us/capitoltours. Free one-hour tours of the capitol and the Legislative Office Building year-round on weekdays (self-guided) on the quarter hours between 9:15 a.m. and 1:15 p.m. and on Sat (guided) from Apr through Oct between 10:15 a.m. and 2:15 p.m. In July and Aug, a 2:15 p.m. tour is added on weekdays. Closed on state holidays.

When you escape the enchanting music of the Wurlitzer, you might notice the gleaming gold dome of the state capitol building high on the hill to the right (or west) of the carousel. You can't miss it, actually. It's the icing on a rather overstated piece of cake, so to speak. Opened in 1879, the Connecticut State Capitol Building features architecture that has been the subject of much commentary. Words like "monstrosity" have been used to describe this remarkable structure, but few families will be offended by its departures from architectural purism. To a child, this behemoth is just grand.

Be sure to stop in the Capitol's main rotunda to see its magnificent dome. The first floor also includes several pieces of sculpture—some huge, some graceful, like the young Nathan Hale. A large collection of Civil War memorabilia in the west wing is

Hartford **Extras**

If you are on a whirlwind tour of Hartford, visit the above-described attractions first. If your schedule allows other pleasures, choose from among the following sites.

- **Connecticut Historical Society.** 1 Elizabeth St.; (860) 236-5621; www.chs .org. Beautiful facility with products, furnishings, artifacts, and portraits related to Connecticut history. Open noon to 5 p.m. Tues through Fri and 9 a.m. to 5 p.m. on Sat. Charmingly low-tech interactive exhibit called *Choice, Chance, and Change,* on immigration; and excellent hands-on and dress-up opportunities in *Tours and Detours through Early Connecticut,* which focuses on the colonial and Revolutionary periods. Nice book and gift shop; family events throughout year. $–$$.

- **Butler-McCook House and Garden and Main Street History Center.** 396 Main St.; (860) 522-1806; www.ctlandmarks.org. Open for tours April 1 through December 31. Through the words, experiences, and collections of the extraordinary Butler and McCook families, learn about the evolution of this part of the city from the days of the American Revolution to the 20th century. $.

- **Charter Oak Landing.** Riverfront Plaza; follow signs from Brainard Road exit off I-91; (860) 722-6505. Rescued from decay by an organization called Riverfront Recapture (860-293-0131; www.riverfront.org), the plaza has a playground, gazebo, benches, walkways, a boat launch, and activities from the arts to sports. It is now linked to both Constitution Plaza and Great River Park across the river. Riverside Park is also right nearby. Check the website for schedule of events, or just grab a picnic and have a good time. Free; events might charge a fee.

- **Travelers Tower.** 1 Tower Sq.; (860) 277-4208. If it's a clear day, this is a great place to have a look at the lay of the land and learn about Amelia, the tower's resident peregrine falcon. Elevator ride, then 70 stairs. Open year-round; free tours mid-May to late Oct. Check http://hartford.omaxfield .com/travelers.html.

- **Bushnell Memorial Hall.** 166 Capitol Ave.; (860) 246-6807. Designed in the 1930s by the architects of New York City's Radio City Music Hall, this National Historic Landmark has a year-round slate of top-billed performing arts, including a family matinee series. Home of Connecticut Opera, Hartford Ballet, Hartford Symphony. Promenade Gallery features works of area artists. Free 45-minute backstage tours available year-round by appointment. Call (860) 987-6000. $$–$$$$.

impressive; it includes uniforms, many former US flags, and the equipment of important personages.

On Saturday, tours are guided and begin at the Capitol Avenue entrance to the Capitol; on weekdays, you begin inside the west entrance of the Legislative Office Building, where you pick up a self-guided tour booklet. The tour includes visits to the public galleries of the assembly rooms, explanations of the functions of major offices, and information on how a bill becomes law.

Museum of Connecticut History (ages 8 and up)
231 Capitol Ave.; (860) 566-3056; www.museumofcthistory.org. Open Mon through Fri, 9 a.m. to 4 p.m.; Sat 9 a.m. to 2 p.m. Closed on state holidays. Free.

This beautiful collection is housed in the same magnificent building as the Connecticut Supreme Court and the Connecticut State Library, opposite the capitol building. Check out the library's incredible main reading room while you are here. The museum exhibits include aspects of Connecticut history from all periods, with examples of Connecticut products such as Colt firearms, clocks, hats, furniture, and more, with a focus on government, industrial, and military history. See the table on which Lincoln signed the Emancipation Proclamation. See the 1622 Royal Charter of the Colony of Connecticut and learn the Charter Oak story. Have a look at Freedom Trail quilts, which portray the important story of the state's African-American experience, and see the portraits of Connecticut's governors. Changing exhibitions, special tours, and events of interest to families are on the calendar. This museum is well worth a second day in the city if your kids are old enough to appreciate it.

Elizabeth Park and Rose Gardens (all ages)
Prospect and Asylum Avenues; (860) 722-6514 or (860) 231-9443; www.elizabethpark.org. Open daily year-round, dawn to dusk. Greenhouses open Mon through Fri, except holidays, from 8 a.m. to 3 p.m. Free.

The first municipal rose garden in the country, this beautiful park has 15,000 rose bushes of 800 varieties. With lanes, arbors, and gazebos that bring *The Secret Garden* to mind, the formal garden is most glorious in late spring and throughout summer. Truly a haven within the bustle of the city, Elizabeth Park's rock gardens, ornamental grasses, perennial and herb beds, and a trail through its forest of specimen trees make it a lovely spot to play.

Special events such as concerts, poetry readings, or storytellings are sometimes on the calendar here. In mid-June come to the park's gala celebration of peak rose season. Called Rose Weekend, the event features music, food, art, tours, and activities for the whole family.

The park extends across Prospect Avenue to acres of athletic fields and a children's play area with swings, tennis courts, and a picnic grove. The Elizabeth Park Overlook provides a panoramic view of the city as well as a gorgeous spot to watch the sun rise. Frisbee players, kite flyers, joggers, in-line skaters, bicyclers, and brides and grooms regularly inhabit this space in spring, summer, and fall. In winter you can sled on the huge hill near the overlook or skate (conditions permitting) on the pond. The Pond House Cafe (860-231-8823) is open from Tues through Sat for lunch and dinner from 11 a.m. or for brunch on weekends from 10 a.m. to 2 p.m.

Mark Twain House and Museum Center (ages 6 and up)

351 Farmington Ave., at Woodland Street; (860) 247-0998; www.marktwainhouse.org. Open Mon through Sat 9:30 a.m. to 5:30 p.m.; Sun noon to 5:30 p.m. Last tour 4:30 p.m. daily. Closed on Tue, Jan through Mar, and on major holidays. $$$, children under 6 free.

Next on a must-do tour of Hartford is the home of novelist Samuel Langhorne Clemens, who gained fame as Mark Twain. It is located on a property known as Nook Farm, once the site of a lively community of artists, writers, and other literate folk. Quite bucolic in the last decades of the 19th century, Nook Farm is now nearly eclipsed by the sprawl of Hartford and its suburb of West Hartford. Nevertheless, the homes and grounds give visitors a sense of the area's former air of gentility and simplicity.

Of course, simplicity is nowhere to be found in the Twain house. The Gilded Age with all its splendid cacophony of detail is apparent in every inch of this remarkable home. Guided tours here are among the most excellent tours we have taken in the state. You will hear marvelous tales of the family's life and a generous sampling of the owner's sardonic wit and wisdom. While living here from 1874 to 1891 with his wife, Olivia, and their three daughters, Clemens wrote *Tom Sawyer, Huckleberry Finn, The Prince and the Pauper, A Connecticut Yankee in King Arthur's Court,* and *Life on the Mississippi.*

The 19 rooms of the house are restored to reflect its appearance in 1881, when the house was redecorated by a guild of artisans including Louis Comfort Tiffany. The tour includes the family living quarters and Twain's private study (where he did much of his writing). Nearly half the decorations and furnishings in the house were owned by the family, including many photographs, a feature that gives the suggestion that Twain himself might appear in a doorway at any moment.

Before or after a tour, don't miss the magnificent three-story Museum Center with exhibit spaces, a lecture hall, classrooms, a museum store, and a 75-seat cafe with an outdoor terrace.

Harriet Beecher Stowe Center (ages 6 and up)

77 Forest Street at Farmington Ave.; (860) 522-9258; www.harrietbeecherstowecenter.org. Open Wed through Sat, 9:30 a.m. to 4:30 p.m.; Sun noon to 4:30 p.m. Open on Tues also from June through Oct. Closed major holidays. $$, children under 5 free.

Just across the lawn from the Twain House is the 1871 cottage built for Stowe and her family. The house is austere compared to its gaudy neighbor, but it is in itself a serenely beautiful Victorian dwelling that has been restored in every detail. The last residence of Stowe, whose *Uncle Tom's Cabin* can be said to have changed the course of US history, this house is furnished mostly with items belonging to the Stowe family. The kitchen is patterned after the model kitchen described by Stowe and her sister Catherine in their book *The American Woman's Home.* In this home, too, one fairly expects its owner to step into the room and continue the grand tour.

Docents present the center's renewed emphasis on family-friendly tours; in fact, a special children's tour offers reduced admission for adults. The house is filled with decorative artworks done by Stowe, an accomplished painter who often painted the flowers she grew in her gardens. Outside, the gardens have been replanted with exotic and native perennials that Stowe grew here before her death in 1896.

Tours include a visit to Stowe's niece's house on the corner of the Nook Farm property. The Katherine Seymour Day House contains Stowe's personal belongings and excellent exhibits that explain the effect of *Uncle Tom's Cabin* on the abolitionist movement and the Civil War. It also includes exhibits on 19th-century architecture, decorative arts, history, and literature. A research library on these subjects as well as social reform, the women's suffrage movement, and women's studies in general is open by appointment. Children are welcome to use the library, but a letter of recommendation from a teacher or librarian is necessary.

Tour tickets are purchased in the Carriage House Visitors Center, which has an introductory exhibit on the Beecher family as well as a gift shop. A few events designed for children are held annually; check the website for the schedule.

Where to Eat

Agave Grill. 100 Allyn St.; (860) 882-1557. Zesty, fresh, spicy Mexican-Caribbean food in a zippy place in the heart of downtown, not far from Bushnell Park. Excellent "guac" made right at your table. Lunch and dinner daily. $$–$$$

Black-Eyed Sally's. 350 Asylum St.; (860) 278-RIBS. Award-winning Cajun, creole, and barbecue—all the down-home Southern cooking you can eat. Come for gumbo, grits, greens, po' boy sandwiches, pulled pork, and chicken-fried steak. Absolutely delicious. The joint hops after 9 p.m. with the best open-mike blues jam anywhere around. Lunch and dinner on weekdays; dinner only on Saturday. $–$$$

In the city's South End is Franklin Avenue, also known as Hartford's Little Italy. Stroll the sidewalks between Elliot and Eaton Streets and search for your own favorite eatery among the espresso cafes, bakeries, and full-service restaurants. Our favorite is **Carbone's** (588 Franklin Ave.; 860-296-9646). Children very welcome among adult diners. $$$

Firebox Restaurant. 539 Broad St.; (860) 246-1222. Not far from the capitol building, this establishment in a vintage brick factory complex serves up locally produced foods with a flair for flavor and freshness. Pricey but delicious. No children's menu, but families will still be happy. Lunch on weekdays; dinner Mon through Sat. $$$–$$$$

Where to Stay

Crowne Plaza Hartford–Downtown. 50 Morgan St.; (860) 549-2400. 350 units, restaurant, fitness room, outdoor pool. $$$

Hilton Hartford Hotel. 315 Trumbull St. at the Civic Center; (860) 728-5151 or (800) 325-3535. 390 units including 6 suites, restaurant, fitness room, sauna, indoor pool. $$$$

Residence Inn by Marriott Hartford Downtown. 942 Main St., near Market Street; (860) 524-5550 or (800) 331-3131. 120 rooms, studios, and suites. In-room kitchens, complimentary hot breakfast buffet. Restaurant. $$$$

West Hartford

West Hartford sashays outward from the left of Hartford just as smoothly as Fred Astaire and with just as much debonair grace. In its upscale downtown less than 5 miles from downtown Hartford you'll find terrific shops and restaurants and a couple of attractions great for a family day trip. Peruse the boutiques, visit the Noah Webster House, spend some time at the Children's Museum, and have dinner at one of a zillion restaurants.

Noah Webster House/Museum of West Hartford History (ages 6 and up)

227 South Main St.; (860) 521-5362; www.noahwebsterhouse.org. Open for tours Thurs through Mon from 1 to 4 p.m. Last tour 3 p.m. Extended summer hours; closed major holidays. $–$$, children under 6 free.

The birthplace and childhood home of the author of the first American dictionary, Noah Webster House is one of the best colonial restorations in the state. An excellent short film introduces visitors to the admirable story of citizen Webster, and tours by costumed guides fill in the gaps of the tale. You'll see Webster's desk and clocks and original editions of his books, including his *Blue-Backed Speller* and the dictionary he spent nearly 27 years writing.

The house has an active calendar of family and children's events—genealogy workshops, open-hearth cooking, colonial dancing and games, and more. Children going into grades four, five, and six can participate in the Colonial Child Summer Camp, a week of activities typical of an 18th-century childhood.

The Children's Museum (ages 2 through 10)

950 Trout Brook Dr.; (860) 231-2824; www.thechildrensmuseumct.org. Open Tues through Sat 10 a.m. to 5 p.m. and Sun noon to 5 p.m. Also open Monday holidays, school vacations, and in July and Aug. Closed Easter, Thanksgiving, and Christmas. $$–$$$, children under 2 free. SciDome shows have additional fees.

One of the oldest children's museums in the state, this facility has a brand-new name and renewed focus on igniting preschool and toddler curiosity through science and nature. All changing and permanent exhibits are interactive, allowing children and adults to discover a range of scientific facts or truths and to conduct experiments that reinforce those findings.

In the Idea Zone, learn about gears and motion, race a car on the LEGO racetrack, or walk through a kaleidoscope. In the toddler play space, Critter Crossing, explore nature-themed discovery centers. At Kids' Corner, explore concepts of sound, light, touch—and bubbles; and study earth science in the Excavation Station. Programs suitable for the whole family are shown in the Travelers SciDome at Gengras Planetarium, featuring a digital projection system. Explore the sun, stars, and galaxy, or see laser light shows that accompany environmental or mythical narratives. Outside, a wildlife sanctuary includes a collection of 80 birds, reptiles, and mammals from around the world. And, of course, you can still walk into a full-scale model of Connecticut's state animal, the sperm whale.

Where to Eat

A. C. Petersen Farms Restaurant. 240 Park Rd.; (860) 233-8483. Open for breakfast, lunch, and dinner from 7 a.m. to 11 p.m., this renovated landmark in WH Center is still old-fashioned at heart. Traditional American meals and good ice cream, perfect for families. $–$$

The Elbow Room. 986 Farmington Ave.; (860) 236-6195. This cheery place has great nooks and the best mac and cheese on the planet. Eat up on the roof in warm weather. So fun. Open daily from 11 a.m. for lunch and dinner. $$–$$$

Elements Bistro. 1128 New Britain Ave. in Elmwood section; (860) 233-8125. This chic, contemporary neighborhood bistro and bar is way more than workable for kids and delicious for mom and dad. Patio in warm season. Open from 11:30 a.m. Mon through Sat for lunch and dinner. $$–$$$

Where to Stay

West Hartford Inn. 900 Farmington Ave.; (860) 236-3221. 50 units, exercise room, restaurant, continental breakfast. $$$

Farmington

From West Hartford take Route 4 south to the pristinely restored 17th-, 18th-, and 19th-century homes that line the main street of affluent and elegant Farmington. From these homes to the prestigious Miss Porter's School to the upscale shops and restaurants, Farmington presents the polished side of Hartford County. Having played a principal role in the *Amistad* story, Farmington also was an important station on the Underground Railroad, contributing to its importance in the history of the state and the nation. You can arrange a guided Freedom Trail tour ($) of the nine Farmington sites associated with the Africans of the *Amistad* by calling the Farmington Historical Society (860-678-1645; www.farmington historicalsociety-ct.org). On these walks, you can visit the places where the Africans lived and studied and see the hall where abolitionists met. You can see the gravesite of a freed *Amistad* survivor who later lost his life in Farmington, and see the homes and churches of citizens who spoke out against slavery and in support of the *Amistad* group.

Hill-Stead Museum (ages 8 and up)

35 Mountain Rd.; (860) 677-9064 or (860) 677-4787. Grounds open daily 7:30 a.m. to 5:30 p.m. House open Tues through Sun 10 a.m. to 4 p.m. One-hour guided tour; last tour at 3 p.m. $–$$, children under 6 **free.**

This colonial revival home may not seem like a place to come with small, squirmy folk who'd rather be chasing the butterflies on the gorgeous front lawn of this 150-acre country estate. It is, however, a fine place to come if you and the children would like to see the magnificent artworks that hang in the mansion designed by Stanford White and owner Theodate Pope Riddle, herself an architect. The house is beyond reproach in its taste and gentility as well as its elegant design, and its outstanding art collection is unparalleled

The *Amistad* Story

From Havana, Cuba, on June 28, 1839, the Spanish ship *Amistad* set sail with 53 Africans who had been taken from their homeland to be sold as slaves. On their way to another part of Cuba for what they knew would be a lifetime of enslavement and hard labor, the captives, led by Sengbe Pieh, seized control of the ship and forced its owners to set a course for Africa. Under cover of night, however, the navigators charted a northward course, hoping to reach an American slave state before their plot was discovered. Instead, the boat sailed into Long Island Sound, where it was apprehended by the U.S. Navy and taken into custody in New Haven. A two-year trial in which the Africans were defended by John Quincy Adams centered on the question of whether the captives were to be considered slave or free. Eventually declared free, the *Amistad* Africans were sent to Farmington to live while funds were raised to return them to the area in Africa now called Sierra Leone. Thirty-seven survivors from the original group set sail for home as free people again in November 1841, reaching their home shores in January 1842. Nine sites linked to the case and to the lives of the Africans during the waiting period remain in Farmington. The First Church of Christ Congregational in Farmington has maintained its connection to the enslaved Africans of the *Amistad* through ongoing support of the people of Sierra Leone, especially during its recent brutal civil wars. In December 2007 the re-created vessel *Amistad* (see *Amistad* entry in the New Haven section) sailed to Sierra Leone to celebrate the rebuilding of the Hope Primary Day School in Freetown, funded in large part by donations from the church.

by other house museums. Cassatt, Degas, Manet, Monet, and other French and American Impressionists are on the walls. School tours are common here, and tour guides are warmly welcoming and comfortable with youngsters. On the first Sunday of each month, you can come any time after noon to stroll through at a pace that feels right for your family; guides are on hand in every room to answer questions. Be sure to visit the Orientation Gallery to watch an introductory video, and, by all means, explore the wonderfully restored sunken garden and walk the wooded and wild-flowered paths.

Stanley-Whitman House (ages 6 and up)
37 High St.; (860) 677-9222; www.stanleywhitman.org. Open May through Oct, Wed through Sun, noon to 4 p.m. and on Sat and Sun at the same times from Nov through Apr. $.

Amazingly well-curated and impeccably restored, this 1720 house brings the colonial period alive again. Tours include a peek behind the scenes through window-like panels that offer a look at early-18th-century construction methods. Among the other inside points of interest are a gift shop and an exhibit of archaeological artifacts and discoveries. Outside is a kitchen herb garden. Check the website for details of family history hikes, toddler programs, ghost walks, a colonial fair, cooking demonstrations, and a holiday candlelight tour.

Day-Lewis Museum (ages 6 and up)

158 Main St. (rear); (860) 677-2754. Open Wed 2 to 4 p.m., Mar through Nov, except in Aug. Call ahead to be sure of hours. $.

This small museum, owned by Yale University, is in a colonial post-and-beam house on a piece of property discovered to be the site of human habitation, as well as a trading place, as early as 10,000 years ago. The Native American artifacts unearthed at the site during an archaeological dig are on display here. Arranged by date in four display cases, these objects span several centuries, from the pre-contact era to the European contact period. Recently renovated extensively, this property also includes Yale's renowned noncirculating research library of English 18th-century literature.

Winding Trails Recreation Association (all ages)

50 Winding Trails Dr., off Route 4; (860) 678-9582; www.windingtrails.org. Open daily 9 a.m. to 6 p.m., weather permitting. Daily fees for day-users; family memberships to year-round recreation options. All fees posted each season on website. Ski rentals, ice-skating, sledding, and guided walks at daily rates, also on website.

Since 1972, this pretty 350-acre property has been the site of a 20-kilometer trail system for cross-country skiers— but it is also much more than that. For sure, its ski trails are clearly mapped and carefully groomed, and snowshoeing and back-country trails are also on the property. But this nonprofit outdoor recreation area also has an 8-acre natural ice rink on its picturesque Walton Pond; a self-guided interpretive nature trail through its woodlands and past brooks and other spring-fed ponds; a summer day camp; naturalist-guided Saturday Night Walks and Sunday Family Walks; summertime swimming, boating, and fishing on 100-acre Dunning Pond; all kinds of boat rentals, ball fields, and sports courts; a climbing tower and zip line; and even overnight tent camping for members.

In winter, do come to enjoy a healthy day in the crisp air. Cross-country ski instruction is offered to beginners on both weekends and weekdays. Rental skis are available, as are wooden toddler sleds, and you can purchase skis, waxes—even gloves and hats—in the retail shop. In the Winding Trails Lodge, warm your toes by the fireplace and wrap cold fingers around warm mugs of cocoa, or remain outside at tables near the snow-draped pines. And then, come back in the summertime.

Where to Eat

Joey Garlic's. 372 Scott Swamp Rd.; (860) 678-7231. Totally Italian in every way, from antipasto to pizza to zuppa, plus freshly ground burgers, fries, and awesome real-deal milkshakes in two dozen incredible ice cream flavors. Open daily for lunch and dinner. $–$$

The Silo Restaurant. 330 Main St.; (860) 677-0149. Children will like the pleasing (mostly Italian) choices at this family-owned casually fine dining establishment that caters to a loyal grandma-and-grandpa kind of crowd. Barn-sided dining rooms with a silo in the middle. Open for lunch on weekdays; dinner Mon through Sat. $$–$$$

Where to Stay

Centennial Inn Hotel and Apartments. 5 Spring Lane; (860) 677-4647; www.centennialinn.com. 56 hotel suites, outdoor pool, and fitness room on 12 acres (with a brook); getaway packages for families. Suites include kitchen, living room, and 1-2 bedrooms. Continental breakfast. Pets welcome. $$$$

The Farmington Inn. 827 Farmington Ave.; (860) 677-2821 or (800) 648-9804. 72 units, with 13 suites, restaurant, passes to health club, continental breakfast. $$$$

Hartford Marriott Hotel–Farmington. 15 Farm Springs Rd.; (860) 678-1000. 381 units, restaurant, fitness room, indoor and outdoor pools, tennis, game room, jogging trail. $$$$

New Britain/Kensington

Ten miles southeast of Hartford is the small city of New Britain, once nicknamed "Hardware City" with an ethnic population that included every major European nation and most of the minor ones. The steady pace at the Stanley tool works has slowed in recent years, and the immigrant groups have mixed and changed, but the city is much the same—a modest metropolis with a low-key reputation that keeps it well out of the limelight. It has some special treasures, though, inside its city limits and in nearby Kensington. Less than 5 miles southeast of downtown New Britain on Route 372, the small town of Kensington is home to Hungerford Park and the Youth Museum's nature center.

New Britain Youth Museum (ages 2 to 12)

30 High St.; (860) 225-3020; www.newbritainyouthmuseum.org. Open Tues 10 a.m. to 5 p.m., with a storytime/activity program at 10 a.m.; Wed through Fri noon to 5 p.m.; Sat 10 a.m. to 4 p.m., with a craft/activity program at 2 p.m. Free.

The New Britain Youth Museum is not new—in fact, it's well past its half-century mark—it's not big, either, or slick, sleek, or sophisticated. Some days it's downright sleepy, and on some days just a few activities take place in its exhibit rooms and play areas. Still, this little wonder is a two-thumbs-up terrific place for kids, offering very creative exhibitions and some of the best and least expensive children's workshops offered anywhere.

With an extensive permanent collection of dolls and toys and a continuing focus on historical and cultural artifacts of childhood, this charming and playful learning museum has a terrific puppet theater area, a dinosaur room, and an outdoor play area. It also has a

Walnut Hill Park

The New Britain Museum of American Art overlooks **Walnut Hill Park,** designed by Frederick Law Olmsted, who also designed New York City's Central Park. Its sweeping lawns and towering oak trees make it a perfect place to play or picnic. A children's playground, playing fields, and bicycle paths make the park a family destination. A free summer music festival at the Miller Bandshell is held in July and August on Monday and Wednesday at 7:30 p.m. An annual American Arts and Crafts Fair in mid-September includes admission to the nearby museum ($$).

sister attraction housing the museum's natural history exhibits at Hungerford Park in Kensington; see the separate entry.

New Britain Museum of American Art (all ages)

56 Lexington St.; (860) 229-0257; www.nbmaa.org. Open year-round, Tues, Wed, and Fri 11 a.m. to 5 p.m.; Thurs 11 a.m. to 8 p.m.; Sat 10 a.m. to 5 p.m.; Sun noon to 5 p.m. Closed Mon and holidays. Cafe on the Park is open Tues through Sat 11:30 a.m. to 3:30 p.m. and Sun noon to 3:30 p.m. $$, children under 12 free. Saturday from 10 a.m. to noon is free for everyone.

If you have never taken your children to an art museum, begin here. Perfect for families because of its manageable size—even with its stunning 43,000-square-foot wing—this institution is in every way a gem. The museum's 5,000 holdings from the early 18th century to the present include some of the greatest treasures of American art. Gilbert Stuart, Asher Durand, Thomas Cole, Frederic Church, Winslow Homer, Maxfield Parrish, John Singer Sargent, Mary Cassatt, Childe Hassam, Georgia O'Keeffe, N. C. Wyeth, Andrew Wyeth, Norman Rockwell, and Thomas Hart Benton are just some of the artists represented here. Ask for their terrific Children's Guide, and inquire about audio tours designed for children, which may be available when you visit. The museum offers a full slate of educational programs in the contiguous early-20th-century mansion built by William Hart, founder of the Stanley Works tool company. In that space, you'll find Art Lab, created for children ages 3 to 12, with hands-on art activities that youngsters can complete independently. Among the possible features here are computer stations with art games, a costume rack that interprets clothing portrayed in the collection, puzzles, collage and sculpture opportunities, and music and poetry explorations. The Art Studio, an additional space, offers drop-in children's art classes, workshops, and exceptionally well-planned hands-on art birthday parties. Check the NBMAA calendar online for information on the Art Start program for preschoolers (Tues in July/Aug; Sat in Sept through June; $; drop-ins welcome) and the Art Adventures and Art Explorers programs for children ages 6 to 8; all are excellent introductions to making art. As if all that were not enough, the museum also offers a gift shop and a cafe, which overlooks the lovely Walnut Hill Park.

Copernican Space Science Observatory
and Planetarium (ages 8 and up)

1615 Stanley St., Central Connecticut State University; (860) 832-3399 or (860) 832-2950; www.ccsu.edu/astronomy/. Planetarium shows year-round on the first and third Saturday of the month at 8 p.m. Closed on state holidays. Free.

Located at the top of Copernicus Hall at CCSU, this observatory boasts one of the largest public telescopes in the United States. Special programs on a variety of fascinating themes related to the stars and space science are offered throughout the year for both children and adults. Weather permitting, planetarium shows are followed by a session in the observatory. Exhibits on flight and the American space program are adjacent to the observatory and planetarium.

New Britain Youth Museum
at Hungerford Park (ages 2 to 10)

191 Farmington Ave. (Route 372); (860) 827-9064; www.newbritainyouthmuseum.org. Trails open dawn to dusk, free of charge. Open Tues through Sat 10 a.m. to 4:30 p.m. Live-animal programs on Sat at 11 a.m., 1:30 p.m., and 3:30 p.m. Closed Sun and Mon. Exhibit hall admission, $, children under 2 free.

Located on 27 acres of wooded park, swamp, pond, and wetland habitats, the New Britain Youth Museum at Hungerford Park represents the natural history collection of the museum. Housed in a restored 1920s show-horse stable, its stimulating and detailed exhibits change by the season or by the year; check the website for the latest installations.

A weather station, aquariums, terrariums, and an iguana rain forest habitat complete with waterfall are also indoors. Outside the main exhibit hall are wonderful gardens, designed as sensory experiences for visitors, who are welcome to taste, feel, look, smell, and touch the plants.

Among the animals you might see here are a pig, goat, steer, sheep, turkeys, ducks, and geese in the Hungerford Barnyard and lizards, turtles, snakes, and a leopard tortoise in the Exotic Animal Room. A trail system, a pond with observation stations, and a picnic area are also part of the complex. Check the website for their frequent children's programs and family events.

Where to Eat

Fatherland. 450 South Main St.; (860) 224-3345. Delicious, authentic Polish food in a low-key setting friendly to families. Excellent house-made soups, pierogies, stuffed cabbage, and perfect potato pancakes, including sweet potato ones. Half-size servings for kids. Open for lunch and dinner daily. $

Where to Stay

La Quinta Inn and Suites. 65 Columbus Blvd.; (860) 348-1463. 135 rooms, with 4 suites; complimentary full breakfast; restaurant. $$

Glastonbury/Rocky Hill

If farms and rivers and their accompanying flora and fauna appeal to your family, then the ancient and affluent town of Glastonbury, which hugs the Connecticut River in a lovely way, is a place you might want to spend some time. Glastonbury is brimming with some of Connecticut's richest farmland and ripest orchards, so no better place exists in the state for a true farm-to-table experience for your children. Find your way to Routes 3, 17, or 2 southeast of Hartford and grab a copy of a CT Farm map or check the farm listings on the Visitors page of www.glasct.org. Three favorites, easily found in quick succession, are **Rose's Berry Farm** at 295 Matson Hill Rd.; **Sleepy Bee Lavender Farm** at 424 Matson Hill Rd.; and **Belltown Hill Orchards** at 483 Matson Hill Rd. No matter when you come, be sure to return for the **Apple Harvest Festival,** a joyous three-day event held annually in October. If your children are attracted to dinosaur research, they'll love Rocky Hill, about 8 miles south of Hartford off I-91. The hills and valleys west of the Connecticut River are relatively new, you see. The area commonly called "Rockie Hill" in its colonial days was far different 185 million years ago. Then it was a bona fide Jurassic Park—a wide mudflat on the edge of a broad, shallow lake that filled a basin carved by glaciers a few million years before that. The lake was densely populated with vegetation, fish, and reptiles of a roughly crocodilian description. The dinosaurs roaming nearby liked the menu, so they stayed until their luck ran out in the next ecological disaster.

Now only their tracks remain, a fact discovered during excavations in the 1960s for a modern ecological disaster called an office building. Bulldozer operator Ed McCarthy recognized something unusual about the ground he was clearing, and soon the place was crawling with paleontologists. Now families are the most frequent pilgrims to this ancient site.

Ferry 'Cross **the River**

Another way to examine the ecosystem of the Connecticut River is aboard the *Hollister III*, the latest boat in the 350-year-old ferry service that crosses from Rocky Hill to Glastonbury. The original ferry service dates from 1655, when local families used long poles to push along a small raft. Later, a horse on a treadmill in the center of the craft supplied the power for crossings, and, in 1876, steam power made the job faster and easier, at least on the horse. Now a diesel towboat leads an open flatboat. Four minutes from one side to the other, the ferry is accessible from the Rocky Hill Landing on Route 160 off Silas Deane Highway or from Glastonbury Landing on Route 160 off Route 17. It runs May 1 through October 31, weekdays from 7 a.m. to 6:45 p.m. and weekends from 10:30 a.m. to 5 p.m. You pay $1 per person to walk on (or $3 per vehicle); pay a bit more for ice cream at the Pilot House at the riverside in Rocky Hill.

Connecticut Audubon Society Center at Glastonbury (all ages) ⊗ ⊛

1361 Main St., Glastonbury; (860) 633-8402; www.ctaudubon.org/centers/glastonbury. Open Tues through Fri 1 to 5 p.m., Sat 10 a.m. to 5 p.m.; Sun usually 1 to 4 p.m. (but call ahead). Closed major holidays. Free, except for $1 for Discovery Room in nature center.

Located near the Connecticut River, this facility focuses on the unique natural and cultural history of New England's largest waterway. Hands-on exhibits in the center's Discovery Room promote awareness of the river ecosystem, and children will gain a sense of the place and the importance of its preservation through a diorama of the river's Great Meadow and a number of live-animal displays featuring the creatures of this diverse and fragile habitat. Outdoors are gardens, bird stations, and picnic areas. The 48-acre Earle Park adjacent to this center has forest trails near and around Tom's Pond and the meadows and bluffs overlooking Holland Brook. Environmental programs, workshops, and hikes are on the full calendar of events throughout the year. A nature shop and bookstore provide materials for continuing education at home and in the field.

Dinosaur State Park (all ages) ⊗ ⊞ ⊛

400 West St., Rocky Hill; (860) 529-8423 or (860) 529-5816; www.dinosaurstatepark.org. Exhibit center open Tues through Sun 9 a.m. to 4:30 p.m. year-round, except holidays. $, children under 6 free. Casting area open daily (except holidays) May 1 to Oct 31 from 9 a.m. to 3:30 p.m. at no charge. Park open daily year-round (except holidays) from 9 a.m. to 4:30 p.m. at no charge.

Many of the 2,000 Jurassic-period tracks uncovered have been recovered to preserve them, but about 500 are exposed to public view in this amazing park. A giant geodesic dome protects the mostly three-toed impressions from the elements. A walkway around the tracks provides a good view, and a full-scale reproduction of the sort of dinosaur most likely to have made the tracks stands in a running pose on the platform above the pit. The exhibit center also has exhibits on geology, history, and dinosaurs, and two murals show how the region may have looked in the Triassic and Jurassic periods. An auditorium shows related films on weekends and during school vacations.

In the warm months, visitors are invited to make plaster casts of some of the tracks in the outdoor casting area. Signs provide the instructions, but you must provide the supplies necessary to complete the project. Bring a quarter-cup of vegetable oil, 10 pounds of plaster of paris, a five-gallon plastic container, and clean-up rags and paper towels. If you decide to do this, you have to be finished by 3:30 p.m.

Outside the dome there is no evidence (except in the casting area) of prehistoric animal life, but the park offers 60 acres of nature preserve with more than 2 miles of hiking trails and a picnic area. The Dinosaur Park Arboretum is home to more than 250 species of conifers, plus gingkoes, redwoods, magnolias, and other plants that originated in prehistoric times.

Where to Eat

Max Amore. 140 Glastonbury Blvd. in the Somerset Square Shopping Area; (860)

659-2819. Come for excellent pizza with creative toppings and innovative pasta dishes, seafood, poultry, and vegetarian choices. Children's menu. Lunch and dinner daily, plus Sunday brunch. $$

Min Ghung Asian Bistro. 39 New London Turnpike, #311; (860) 659-2568. Open daily for lunch and dinner, this is a do-not-miss kind of place, perfect for palate-pleasing plate-sharing for the whole family. Excellent, fun, delicious. Sushi and Korean specialties. $–$$$

Rose's Berry Farm. 295 Matson Hill Rd., South Glastonbury; (860) 633-7467. On Sundays in season, have breakfast on Rose's deck overlooking the picking fields of strawberries, blueberries, raspberries, pumpkins, mums, and Christmas trees. You can also pick fruit for a home-cooked breakfast or buy fresh-baked muffins, pies, cider, and picnic goodies. $

Where to Stay

Connecticut River Valley Inn. 2195 Main St., Glastonbury; (860) 633-7374;

ctrivervalleyinn.com. Open year-round, this spacious and gracious 1740 B&B run by cheerful owners welcomes families whenever possible. Book a room, a floor, or the whole house. Beautiful grounds and gardens near the riverfront. Wonderful breakfasts. $$$$

Hartford Marriott Rocky Hill. 100 Capital Blvd., Rocky Hill; (860) 257-6000 or (800) 228-9290. 250 rooms and suites, restaurant, fitness room, whirlpool, indoor pool. $$

Udderly Woolly Acres B&B. 581 Thompson St., Glastonbury; (860) 633-4503. Open year-round, this certified-organic working farm offers families a 2-room suite that includes a sitting room and a spacious bedroom with 2 twin beds, 1 child-size trundle bed, and a rollaway bed upon request. Private entrance and bath, small refrigerator, and hearty breakfast make this a cozy place for families. $$$

Wethersfield

Preserved a mere 5 miles south of the modern hub of Hartford, the historical center of Wethersfield is in itself a miniature museum. The first permanent settlement in the colony and the most northerly trading post on the Connecticut River, the town has the largest authentic historic district in the state. Its pretty Main and Broad Streets are chock-full of 17th- and 18th-century homes that reflect Wethersfield's past, and children may enjoy the fantasy that they have stepped back in time here. When you go, be sure to stop at the ever-handsome historical buildings of **Comstock, Ferre & Co.** (263 Main St.; 860-571-6590; call for hours of operation), which has reopened under new ownership and management. In business since 1820 in this spot, this landmark enterprise is famed as the longest continually operating seed company in the United States. Explore its indoor and outdoor areas for all kinds of plants, natural food products, handcrafts, and antiques. Most important, come here for open-pollinated, pure, non-GMO seeds—and great advice on how to start your own home garden.

The Wethersfield Historical Society (ages 6 and up)
150 Main St.; (860) 529-7656. Old Academy and Cultural Center open Mon through Sat 10 a.m. to 4 p.m. and Sun 1 to 4 p.m. The Francis and Hurlbut-Dunham Houses are open

mid-May through mid-Oct, Sat 10 a.m. to 4 p.m. and Sun 1 to 4 p.m. Cove Warehouse open mid-May to mid-Oct, at those same times. $, children under 16 free.

The Wethersfield Historical Society owns and maintains five historic buildings, four of which are open to the public. The 1790 Hurlbut-Dunham House at 212 Main St. is an elegant late-Georgian brick beauty updated in the mid-1800s in the Italianate style. The Cove Warehouse, at the end of Main Street at Cove Park on the river, is the only warehouse to have survived the flood of 1692 that created the cove; it has exhibits on local maritime industry and history. A research archive and a library of local and state history, genealogy, and architecture are in the 1804 Old Academy. A museum shop, exhibits on Wethersfield's history, and a gallery of changing exhibitions are housed in the Keeney Memorial Cultural Center (860-529-7161) at 200 Main.

Webb-Deane-Stevens Museum (ages 6 and up)

211 Main St.; (860) 529-0612; www.webb-deane-stevens.org. Open for tours May 1 to Oct 31, Wed through Mon, 10 a.m. to 4 p.m. (last full tour at 3 p.m.; 30-minute highlights tour at 3:30 p.m.) and Sun 1 to 4 p.m. and weekends only in Apr and Nov. Holiday tours daily in Dec (weekdays 10 a.m. to 4 p.m.; Sat 10 a.m. to 8 p.m.; Sun 1 to 4 p.m.). Closed Jan 1 to Mar 31. One-hour three-house tour ($$); 20-minute Buttolph-Williams House tour ($); Highlights tour ($). Family rates are offered; children under 5 free.

This wonderful museum is composed of three 18th-century homes, each restored and furnished to provide a glimpse into distinct periods of American life. Each house, respectively, offers a look at the family lifestyle of a merchant, a diplomat, and a tradesman spanning the years from 1690 to 1840. A lovely children's bedroom is arranged to reflect the lifestyles of the five children who grew up in the house in the 1830s. A doll and toy collection displayed in cases is charming. The herb and flower gardens behind the three houses are extraordinary. Check the website for children's programming and special events.

Buttolph-Williams House (ages 6 and up)

249 Broad St.; (860) 529-0460 or (860) 529-0612. Open from May 1 to October 31 from 10 a.m. to 4 p.m., Wed through Mon. $ ($$ if you include the Webb-Deane-Stevens Museum).

This beauty reflects the medieval architecture of an early-18th-century "mansion" house. Furnished to provide a sense of an affluent family within a Puritan community, the 1710–20 house is the site of many fine family events, workshops, and celebrations.

Eleanor Buck Wolf Nature Center (all ages)

156 Prospect St.; (860) 529-3075. Open Tues through Sat, 10 a.m. to 5 p.m. First Thursday programs (registration required) from 4:30 to 6:30 p.m. Free.

This environmental education center at the entrance to Mill Woods Park offers science and outdoor explorations especially for children in grades kindergarten through six. Live native mammals, reptiles, and birds are here, along with hands-on science displays, a wildlife and botanical library, and a gift shop. Trails link the center to the 110-acre Wintergreen Woods Park, which is also a nice place for day-tripping families to rest, relax, and explore.

Where to Eat

Vito's. 673 Silas Deane Hwy.; (860) 563-3333. This Wethersfield classic provides pizza, pasta, pesto, and a Marsala sauce second to none. Lunch and dinner daily from 11 a.m. (noon on Sun). $–$$

Where to Stay

Best Western Camelot. 1330 Silas Deane Hwy.; (860) 563-2311. 110 units, whirlpool, fitness room, sauna, extensive continental breakfast. $$$

Motel 6. 1341 Silas Deane Hwy.; (860) 563-5900. 145 units, clean and basic for families. $

General Information

Central Regional Tourism District. River Valley/Connecticut. One Constitution Plaza, 2nd floor, Hartford 06103; (860) 787-9640; (800) 793-4480; www.enjoycentralct.com.

Greater Hartford Convention and Visitors Bureau. 31 Pratt St., 4th floor, Hartford 06103; (860) 293-2365; www.enjoyhartford .com.

Farmington Valley Visitors Association. 33 East Main St., Avon 06001; (860) 676-8878; (800) 4-WELCOME; www.farmington valleyvisit.com.

New Haven County
Urban Culture and Country Adventure

Shaped sort of like a five-point star, this county reaches widely from its historic center in New Haven. The small cities of Meriden and Waterbury in the north are balanced by suburban towns and rural villages to the east and west. Sliced into three parts by the Quinnipiac and Naugatuck Rivers, the county is usually perceived more along those divisions than as a whole.

New Haven is most definitely the cultural center of the county, a situation made difficult by the unfortunate struggle to overcome the public perception that the city might be a dangerous place. In fact, New Haven has much to offer and little to fear. Areas of interest to tourists are well cared for, well lit, and well protected. Both in and outside of its cities, New Haven County is a great place for families.

TopPicks for fun in New Haven County

1. **Connecticut Audubon Coastal Center and Silver Sands State Park**
2. **Yale Peabody Museum of Natural History**
3. **Eli Whitney Museum**
4. **Freedom Schooner *Amistad* at Long Wharf**
5. **Thimble Islands cruises**
6. **Lake Quonnipaug and Dudley Farm**
7. **Hammonasset State Park and Meigs Point Nature Center**
8. **Lake Quassapaug and Quassy Amusement Park**
9. **Barker Character, Comic, and Cartoon Museum**
10. **CoCo Key Water Resort**

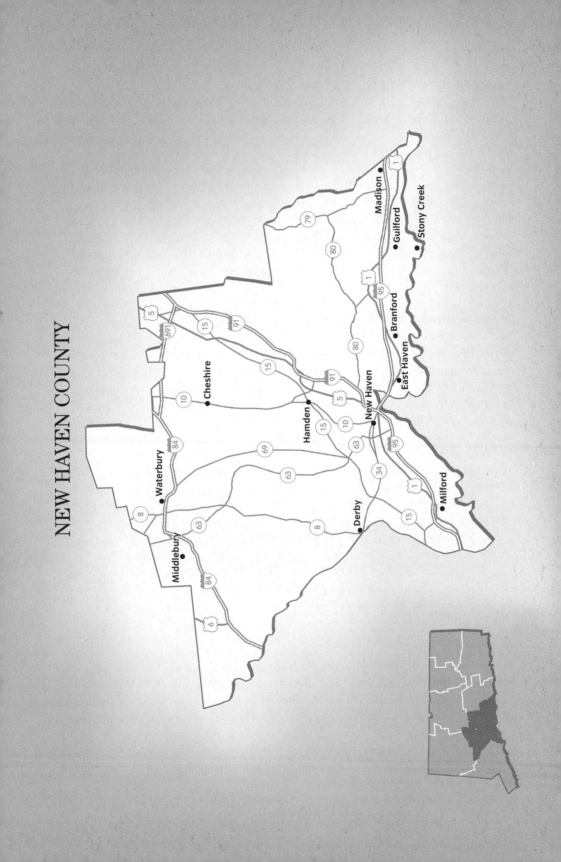

NEW HAVEN COUNTY

Clogged Arteries in Greater New Haven

The largest roads through and into New Haven are I-95 (running east–west but labeled north–south) and I-91 (running north–south and actually labeled north–south). Both are often jammed with cars during rush hours, though I-91 tends to run a little more smoothly than I-95. From roughly 7 to 9 a.m. and again from 3:30 to 6:30 p.m., drivers are likely to encounter slow-moving traffic on both roads. Families may want to stay put at those hours. Linger at home, in the parks, or at the museums for an extra hour. You are unlikely to get anywhere quickly by trying to exit the highway to find alternate routes, but if you must, try Route 1 (an option only for the insane), Route 80 (a viable option but also likely to be crowded with commuters if the interstate is backed up), or Route 34. Route 10 will take you north or south between I-95 and Route 15 (called the Wilbur Cross Parkway in this county and the Merritt Parkway in Fairfield County); this is an option for skirting the I-95/I-91 interchange.

Major Routes throughout New Haven County

The Wilbur Cross Parkway (Route 15) sweeps diagonally on a northeast–southwest course through the county, from Milford in the south to Meriden in the north. Traffic can become heavy on this road at rush hour or on summer weekends, but it rarely is so heavily congested that the flow nearly stops. Route 8 runs north–south through the western part of the county, from Derby to Waterbury, then on up to Litchfield County. Often crowded at rush hour in its Fairfield County portion, it is rarely crowded in New Haven County once the northbound traffic passes Ansonia. I-84 passes in an arc right across the northernmost part of the county from Southbury through the northern part of Cheshire. In Cheshire the road splits; I-84 continues to New Britain and Hartford, and I-691 connects to Meriden and I-91.

If you prefer slower or quieter suburban and rural routes, you can travel north–south on Route 69 all the way from the Wilbur Cross Parkway in northern New Haven through Waterbury and on to Hartford County, Route 63 from the Wilbur Cross through Naugatuck and on to Litchfield County, or Route 10 from I-95 or the Wilbur Cross through Cheshire and on to Hartford County. To travel east–west, pretty Route 68 will link Route 8 to Route 15 and on to Durham in Middlesex County. Route 80 meets I-91 in New Haven and travels east–west across North Haven, North Branford, and the northern parts of Guilford and Madison and onward to Middlesex County.

Milford

This community on the western border of the county is Connecticut's sixth-oldest town, settled in 1639 by families from New Haven and Wethersfield. It now has enough citizens to qualify it as a small city, but its pretty green, duck ponds, beaches, and residential neighborhoods have helped it retain the charm of a New England shore town. Although busier than most, especially along the Boston Post Road, where few signs of charm are at all apparent, it still draws families to its downtown arts-and-crafts shows, its summer concerts at the gazebo on the green, its coastal attractions, and its famed Oyster Festival.

Connecticut Audubon Coastal Center (all ages)

One Milford Point Rd., off Seaview Avenue; (203) 878-7440; www.ctaudubon.org/visit/milford
.htm. Open year-round. Outdoor areas open dawn to dusk at no charge. Center open Tues
through Sat 10 a.m. to 4 p.m. and Sun noon to 4 p.m. Suggested donation, $.

This pristine habitat, composed mostly of salt marshes that border the Sound and the
mouth of the Housatonic River, provides families the opportunity to see one of the last
surviving unaltered coastal properties in Connecticut. Just a few of the sanctuary's 800
acres of marshland and shore are passable to foot traffic, but these reveal the treasures of
the rich ecosystem that flourishes here. A pathway provides access to the area's beach,
a serene place for enjoying native flora and fauna. Observation platforms help you gain
a better view of the shore birds and other wildlife. This is not a park, so no picnic areas
or trash receptacles are provided. Simply stroll peacefully through the habitat and learn
about this fragile environment through the signage, the guided walks, and the exhibits in
the coastal environment education center.

   Inside, you can see a 300-gallon saltwater tank with tide-pool specimens native to
the area. You can also see a diamondback terrapin, an endangered creature that inhabits
the tidal estuaries. Though this one cannot be returned to the seashore, she serves as a
reminder of the beautiful life forms we all have a responsibility to protect. Birthday parties
that include beach walks and other nature fun can be arranged here. Check the website
for summer camp programs, craft workshops, and family activities.

Historic Wharf Lane Complex (ages 6 and up)

34 High St.; (203) 874-2664; http://milfordhistoricalsociety.angelfire.com. Open Memorial
Day through Columbus Day, Sat and Sun 1 to 4 p.m. Free.

Revisit the past through a visit to the three historic houses maintained by the Milford Historical Society. Featuring the 1700 Eells-Stow House, the 1780 Clark Stockade House, and

Milford **Oyster Festival**

Slap on the sunscreen and load your wallet with cash for the irresistible fun
at this annual celebration of the gustatory delights of the homely but delicious oyster and other pure pleasures of summer on the shore. The third
Saturday of August (and the previous Friday evening) is the usual date of the
Milford Oyster Festival, which brings tens of thousands of visitors to the harbor, the green, and Fowler Field on New Haven Avenue for an arts-and-crafts
show, a classic car show, children's activities, a canoe race, a moonlight
music dance party, and a food court featuring oysters, of course. The action
starts on Fri at 5 p.m. and begins again at 10 a.m. on Sat. Admission is free,
but food, crafts, and boat rides cost at least a little something. Call (203) 878-
5363 or check www.milfordoysterfestival.org for more information.

Milford Beaches

In addition to the passive recreation possible on the beach at the coastal center, Milford offers families a chance to enjoy its public beaches for fun of a more active nature. The State of Connecticut also owns a stretch of shoreline in Milford, and visitors are welcome at its as-yet-undeveloped beach. For further information on town beaches, call the Milford Parks and Recreation Department (203-783-3280) or check Milford's website (www.ci.milford.ct.us).

- **Gulf Beach.** Gulf Street. Visitor per-vehicle parking fee ($) from Memorial Day through Labor Day. Concession, restrooms, lifeguards, bird watching/fishing pier.

- **Walnut Beach.** Corner of East Broadway and Viscount Drive. Small pavilion, restrooms, picnic tables, lifeguards. Open view of Charles Island; convenient location adjacent to Silver Sands State Park and close to Milford Point CAS Coastal Center. Open daily July 1 through mid-August. Weekends only earlier and later in the season. Per-vehicle parking fee ($) or free street parking.

- **Silver Sands State Park.** Silver Sands Park Way, off Mayflower Avenue. Department of Environmental Protection (860-485-0226; www.ct.gov/dep). Approximately 300 acres of shoreline and marshland. Lifeguards, portable toilets, boardwalk across top of beach and into salt marsh; picnic area with tables and barbecue grills. Bring drinking water, picnic foods and beverages, and trash bags. Free.

the circa 1785 Bryan-Downes House, the complex has been curated to portray three centuries of life in New England through the furnishings, artifacts, and tours given in the trio of homes. One of the homes contains the Claude C. Coffin collection of Native American artifacts, touted as one of the finest archaeological records ever gathered in Connecticut. Period flower and herb gardens and a small country store add a touch of authenticity to the site.

Where to Eat

Cafe Atlantique. 33 River St.; (203) 882-1602. This corner bistro is a great place for sandwiches, soups, salads, and baked goods for breakfast, lunch, and light dinner. Open at 7 a.m. Mon through Fri, at 8 a.m. on Sat, and at 9 a.m. on Sun. Live music on weekend evenings. $–$$

The Olive Tree. 2009 Bridgeport Ave.; (203) 878-4517. Great falafel made from scratch in this small Middle Eastern–Mediterranean deli with two tiny eat-in tables. Take out your excellent wraps, pitas, salads, baba ghanoush, and baklava, and eat on the green. Open Mon through Sat 9:30 a.m. to 8 p.m. $

Where to Stay

Fairfield Inn by Marriott. 111 Schoolhouse Rd.; (203) 877-8588. 104 rooms, outdoor pool, fitness room, continental breakfast. $$–$$$

Hampton Inn-Milford. 129 Plains Rd.; (203) 874-4400 or (800) HAMPTON. 148 rooms, fitness room, continental breakfast. $$

Howard Johnson Hotel. 1052 Boston Post Rd.; (203) 878-4611 or (800) I-GO-HOJO. 100 units with 3 suites, sauna, whirlpool, indoor pool, miniature golf. $$

SpringHill Suites Milford. 50 Rowe Ave.; (203) 283-0200 or (866) 324-3357. 124 suites, indoor pool, whirlpool, fitness room, complimentary buffet breakfast. $$$

New Haven

Once the site of a Native American village called Quinnipiac, which means "long water land," New Haven was renamed by English settlers who established a colony here in 1640. Since its earliest days an important center of industry, education, and culture, New Haven remains one of the most vital cities in the state. A treasure chest of attractions and historic sites appealing to every generation of visitors, the city takes pride in its firsts—fact and folklore support evidence of America's first football, Frisbees, burgers, dogs, pizza, and even lollipops being birthed right here in New Haven.

This chapter contains the best family attractions in the city, but by no means does it attempt to consider all the possibilities your family may enjoy. Be certain to call the Greater New Haven Convention and Visitors Bureau (203-777-8550 or 800-332-7829) to ask for its terrific guides to the city and its 'burbs. The visitors guide is also on the website www.visitnewhaven.com. You can also check the website www.infonewhaven.com for listings of events scheduled at New Haven's universities, museums, galleries, parks, and theaters. New Haven is a not-to-be-missed city.

West Rock Ridge State Park

Wintergreen Avenue; (203) 789-7498. Open year-round daily for walk-in visitors, 8 a.m. to sunset. South Overlook Drive to summit open to vehicles Memorial Day through last weekend in October. No restrooms.

If the layout of the city mystifies you, you might want to start a tour of New Haven high above the urban clamor. Overlooking the entire city (and the Sound and other parts of Connecticut on a clear day), West Rock is one of two ridges of basalt forced skyward through volcanic action 200 million years ago. The state park runs along the top of the western ridge; its recreational areas include hiking trails, a picnic area, and a fishing and boating pond called Lake Wintergreen (for car-top vessels only, such as canoes and kayaks).

A scenic drive traverses parts of the park. Its southern portion is open to motor vehicles on a seasonal basis (see boldface information above). The northern section is closed to vehicles but open to hikers, cyclists, and skiers year-round. Leashed pets are welcome on the trails. Folks in cars wishing to hike when the scenic drive is closed can park at the nature center on Wintergreen Avenue or at Lake Wintergreen. The park entrance is about 200 feet south of the nature center entrance, also on Wintergreen Avenue.

The park's blue-blazed main trail, called **Regicides Trail,** is accessible at the top of the ridge via the scenic drive or you can walk in off-season from the nature center (see following paragraphs). This 6.3-mile trail begins near the summit at Judges Cave and follows the crest of the West Rock Ridge range northward, ending at its junction with the Quinnipiac Trail in Hamden. The trail offers beautiful views of the harbor and leads through scenic woodlands, as you might expect. The most infamous site on the trail is **Judges Cave,** where in 1661 John Dixwell, Edward Whalley, and William Goffe hid from bounty hunters hoping to claim the £100 reward for their capture as traitors against the Crown, having signed the warrant for the execution of Charles I many years earlier.

West Rock Nature Center (all ages)

1020 Wintergreen Ave.; (203) 946-8016; www.cityofnewhaven.com. Open year-round Mon through Fri 10 a.m. to 4 p.m. Closed holidays. Free.

Listed on the state's register of historic places, this 43-acre parcel of upland woods and fields is believed to be the first urban nature center in the nation. Owned and operated by the city, this separate area just north of the entrance to West Rock Ridge State Park on Wintergreen Avenue hosts a great variety of ranger-led, nature-related interpretive programs and guided walks. At the visitor center is a backyard-birding area, displays on pond life and aquatics, and exhibits on local wildlife and nocturnal denizens of the woodlands. The Nature House includes live reptiles, amphibians, and insects. Short nature trails take you past the ravine, a small waterfall, and so on. The center also has a picnic shelter and restrooms. Come in the wintertime with your sleds and toboggans.

East Rock Park (all ages)

Enter from East Rock Road in New Haven or Davis Road in Hamden; playground, environmental education center, and ranger station in College Woods at corner of Cold Spring and Orange Street; (203) 946-6086; www.cityofnewhaven.com. Park open daily year-round, sunrise to sunset. Summit Road open daily April 1 to Oct 31, 8 a.m. to sunset, and at the same time on Fri and weekends only Nov 1 through Mar. Two other roads are closed to vehicles but open to cyclists, in-line skaters, and walkers. Hiking trails are closed to mountain bikes. Free.

The twin of West Rock, East Rock is on the other side of the city, recognizable by its matching sandstone and traprock cliffs. Its 425-acre park is city-owned and is most well known for its spectacular views of the city and harbor from its summit. The towering Soldiers and Sailors monument here honors New Haven veterans, and the Compass Rose identifies New Haven points of interest within sight. Use the long-range binoculars to get your bearings on the city below, or rest on the benches at the scenic overlook as you enjoy the scene. A grassy area with barbecue grills is perfect for picnics here. The Trowbridge Environmental Center contains displays about local wildlife and plant life. Guided

Yale University Visitor Information
and Walking Tours

Whether you're in a consumer-minded mood or not, Yale is a wonderful university to tour. See the Gothic splendor of the Sterling Memorial Library (where you can peruse newspapers in dozens of languages). Slip into the dimly lit galleries of the Beinecke Rare Book and Manuscript Library (where you can see a Gutenberg Bible, among other treasures). Walk through Phelps Gate, listen to the bells in Harkness Tower, and stop at the statue of Yale grad Nathan Hale outside the 1750 Connecticut Hall (the oldest building in New Haven and the last remaining structure from Yale's Old Brick Row), where Hale, Noah Webster, and William Howard Taft perfected their studies.

You can join a **free** one-hour guided walking tour on Sat and Sun at 1:30 p.m. and on Mon through Fri at 10:30 a.m. and 2 p.m. (no tours on Thanksgiving Day or December 22 through January 1). It leaves from the Yale Visitor Information Center (203-432-2300) at 149 Elm St., across from the north side of the New Haven green. No reservations or tickets are necessary. You can also pick up a self-guided tour pamphlet from the visitor center and explore campus on your own.

nature walks, workshops, and talks appropriate for families and children are on the schedule at this center. Visitors can also walk 10 miles of hiking trails, including the 1,000-foot, 285-step cliffside ascent called the Giant Steps Trail. A bird sanctuary, a self-guided nature trail, playing fields, picnic pavilions, playgrounds, an ice-skating rink, a basketball court, and opportunities for sledding, fishing, and kite flying are also located within park boundaries. Stop at the Trowbridge Center for a map.

Connecticut Children's Museum (ages 3 to 10)

At corner of Orange and Wall Streets; (203) 562-5437; www.ctchildrensmuseum.org. Open most Fridays and Saturdays, noon to 5 p.m. Call ahead or check the website for calendar of closings. $$; children under 3 are free.

This educational play center/museum is housed in the Children's Building, not far from the city green and the arts district of Audubon Street. Although public visiting hours are limited, this stimulating play space is well worth a visit and is especially cheerful on wet, too-hot, or too-cold weekends when little spirits get dampened by the weather.

Exhibit areas are carefully shaped to engage the eight intelligences as described by Howard Gardner and others. In the musical intelligence room, for instance, you will find children "Making Music" everywhere. Varied learning stations offer a piano, a saxophone, a guitar, wind chime components, an ocean drum, and a steel drum and pipe drum made from found objects. In the bodily/kinesthetic room, mirrors reflect faces, and children explore emotions in English, Spanish, and American Sign Language. Sculptures portray favorite literary characters, and children can "act" with props and costumes on a stage with spotlights.

In the mathematical room, a maze wall with movable slats allows kids to create pathways for rolling balls; a gear wall has inviting gears and cranks; and tangrams, mosaics, and fraction games are available for quiet problem-solving.

Other areas exercise spatial intelligence; and young naturalists will love an ant farm, an observation hive with thousands of live bees, and a sitting space of hexagonal honeycombs where visitors can just "nest" awhile. Magnifying glasses help young naturalists examine the ant farm and other earthly wonders. There's even a "great, green room" complete with a bunny in a bed and a little red house.

On Saturday at 2 p.m., artists and educators engage children with dramatic readings of favorite books. The aim is to engage young readers in a hands-on book experience through creative interpretation of the story. You can't go wrong here with children ages 3 to 7; you might even have trouble getting many 10-year-olds to go home.

Yale University Art Gallery (ages 4 and up)

1111 Chapel St. at York Street; (203) 432-0600; http://artgallery.yale.edu. Open Tues through Sat 10 a.m. to 5 p.m. and Sun 1 to 5 p.m.; 8 p.m. closing on Thurs. Closed major holidays. Free; donation suggested.

Founded in 1832, the oldest university art museum in the United States has undergone a restoration that has uncovered the original design of its renowned architect, Louis Kahn. Engaging for children, especially because the scene changes markedly from gallery to gallery, it provides families with an excellent overview of the history of art from ancient to modern times. Among the ancient treasures are many from Egypt, elsewhere in the Middle East and Africa, the Pacific islands, and the Far East. The American paintings and decorative arts are exquisite; O'Keeffe, Kandinsky, and Pollack are among the 20th-century notables; earlier works from the Hudson River School and the American Impressionist colonies also abound. The European collection includes van Gogh, Manet, Monet, and Picasso, among other greats. The sculpture garden provides an intriguing outdoor respite.

The museum hosts wonderful changing exhibitions, plus tours, programs, and concerts designed to appeal to families.

Yale Center for British Art (ages 4 and up)

1080 Chapel St. at High Street; (203) 432-2800; http://ycba.yale.edu. Open Tues through Sat 10 a.m. to 5 p.m., Sun noon to 5 p.m. Closed major holidays. Free.

Home to the largest collection of British art outside Great Britain, the center exhibits paintings, drawings, prints, rare books, decorative arts, and sculpture from the Elizabethan period to the present. Works by Stubbs, Hogarth, Turner, Constable, Blake, Lear, and Reynolds are among the treasures here. Aligned with a research institute, a reference library and photographic archive, and a paper conservation laboratory, the museum has a serene and serious aura, but families are most welcome here. You should aim to enjoy at least some of the collection, even if only for a brief visit with young children.

Carillon Concerts at **Harkness Tower**

If you are in New Haven in summertime on Friday night at 7, grab a blanket and a picnic dinner and head to Harkness Tower, near the Old Campus
between Chapel and Elm Streets. Settle yourselves in the courtyard of Saybrook College, on Elm Street near the corner of High Street, and relax awhile
and listen to the incredible music of the carillon. Students of the art as well
as international artists play here several times each summer for about an
hour. Don't pack anything crunchy in your picnic and make sure you close
your eyes for the full and unforgettable effect of the glorious classical pieces
on each concert's program. For a schedule of these **free** performances, call
the **Yale Events Hotline** (203-432-9100), the **Yale Guild of Carillonneurs** (203-
432-2309), or check the website www.yale.edu/carillon/summer. In case of
rain, the concerts are held at Phelps Hall at 344 College St. Please leave pets
at home.

The museum's **free** lectures and symposia are best suited to adults and students,
but children are welcome to gallery tours, concerts, and films. Programs especially for
children occasionally appear on its calendar of events. The monthly Sunday afternoon
concerts are especially wonderful and, like the tours and films, are offered at no charge.
The museum gift shop is exceptional —a great place to shop for the holidays or special
occasions.

The Yale Collection of Musical Instruments (ages 8 and up)
15 Hillhouse Ave., between Trumbull and Grove Streets; (203) 432-0822. Open from Sept
through June, Tues through Fri 1 to 4 p.m.; Sun 1 to 5 p.m. Suggested donation, $. Concerts
($$–$$$) Sun at 3 p.m. in the second floor gallery. Check the website for the concert sched-
ule and to reserve a ticket.

If you have a little someone who really loves music, this awe-inspiring collection is well
worth a visit. More than 850 European and American instruments from the 16th to 20th
centuries are on display, and an annual concert series is offered from September through
March.

Yale Peabody Museum of Natural History (all ages)
170 Whitney Ave.; (203) 432-5050; www.peabody.yale.edu. Open year-round daily, Mon
through Sat 10 a.m. to 5 p.m. and Sun noon to 5 p.m. $–$$, children under 3 **free;** admis-
sion **free** to all on Thurs from 2 to 5 p.m.

Last in the Yale neighborhood is one of the most popular family destinations in the state.
Everybody has probably already been here, but for those people who have not, just think
dinosaurs, dinosaurs, dinosaurs, plus fossils, birds, insects, seashells, rocks, shrunken
heads, minerals, meteorites, mummies, mastodons, mammals, and much, much more. A

Historic New Haven **Walking Tours**

The **New Haven Museum** (114 Whitney Ave.; 203-562-4183) has designed a walking tour of New Haven's historic buildings, parks, monuments, and cultural sites. It's mostly adult-friendly, but it won't hurt to have the brochure tucked in your pocket on a self-guided walk with the family. See the 18-acre green that was planned in 1638 for the citizen's common use. See its three historic churches, its Bennett Memorial Drinking Fountain, and its World War I Memorial Flagpole. Check out the finest sites of Yale University, then wander through Grove Street Cemetery if you'd care to see the graves of Noah Webster, Eli Whitney, Roger Sherman, Lyman Beecher, Timothy Dwight, Charles Goodyear, or Walter Camp. Walk past the mansions of Hillhouse Avenue on your way to the Peabody Museum, then stop at the New Haven Museum, the New Haven City Hall, and the *Amistad* Memorial.

two-story life-size statue of the dinosaur *Torosaurus latus* sits outside the museum amidst plants of the Cretaceous period. Excellent wildlife and cultural dioramas from many habitats and periods include studies of Neolithic, Pacific, Mesoamerican, ancient Egyptian, and Connecticut Native American peoples. A Discovery Room for young visitors meets the need to touch, feel, and smell interesting natural objects. Changing exhibitions and tons of special events, classes, workshops, and hands-on activities are offered throughout the year.

The New Haven Museum (ages 6 and up)

114 Whitney Ave.; (203) 562-4183; www.newhavenmuseum.org. Open Tues to Fri 10 a.m. to 5 p.m. and Sat noon to 5 p.m. Closed major holidays. $; children under 6 free.

This beautiful building designed expressly as the museum of the Colony of New Haven is alone worth a visit—a colonial revival masterpiece built in 1930 in the late Georgian style, it has a most lovely skylit rotunda, marble staircases, an alluring ballroom, and magnificent moldings at every doorway. Kids may not appreciate the architecture, but they may enjoy the exhibits focusing on the inventions and industries begun in New Haven County. See Eli Whitney's cotton gin, Charles Goodyear's rubber inkwell, an organ made by the New Haven Organ Company, and an original Mysto Magic Erector Set. Enjoy a marvelous three-story dollhouse with a bevy of silent inhabitants and a thousand other details of decoration. Be sure to linger at the exhibit on Sengbe Pieh and the *Amistad*. Along with these are maps, ships' models, and other wonderfully curated, often interactive changing exhibitions.

Amistad Memorial and the Freedom Schooner *Amistad* at Long Wharf Pier (ages 4 and up)

The memorial is located in the plaza at 165 Church St. at the New Haven City Hall. Accessible year-round and around the clock free of charge. The Freedom Schooner *Amistad* is berthed, when she is not sailing as an educational ambassador to other ports, at Long Wharf Pier off Long Wharf Drive. For a schedule of *Amistad* homeport tours and voyages, call *Amistad* America at (203) 495-1839 or visit the website (www.amistadamerica.net), an excellent source of facts about the *Amistad* incident and the construction of this historic replica. Tours, $–$$; sails, $$$$. Note: *Amistad* sustained damage to her bowsprit recently and is being repaired at Mystic Seaport, where deck tours during this time are weekdays 1 to 3 p.m. and weekends 2 to 4 p.m.

Lessons of courage, honor, and justice are to be learned at the base of the marvelous bronze sculpture outside New Haven's City Hall and aboard the re-creation of the *Amistad* itself at Long Wharf Pier. Created by Kentucky artist Ed Hamilton, the *Amistad* Memorial reminds visitors of the bravery of Sengbe Pieh and the commitment of his American supporters to take a moral stand against the outrage of slavery and the illegal capture of free Africans from their homelands.

The story of the *Amistad* Africans started in the seas off Havana, Cuba, in 1839, when 53 Mendi captives seized control of the merchant ship *La Amistad,* which was taking them closer and closer to the unspeakable ordeal of a lifetime of slavery. Days under sail on an eastward course toward Africa were compromised by the slavers' alteration of the course toward the northern United States by night. Eventually apprehended by the U.S. Navy as the ship met the waters of Long Island Sound, the slavers accused their captives of piracy, and the Africans were taken into custody and held in the New Haven jailhouse, then on a site opposite the present city hall. Here the captives awaited trial, as abolitionists and attorneys and former president John Quincy Adams joined the battle to restore the Africans' freedom.

Connecticut **Freedom Trail**

From monuments such as the *Amistad* Memorial to Underground Railroad sites to notable birthplaces, gravesites, and museum exhibits, the Connecticut Freedom Trail traces the historic importance and contributions of Connecticut's African Americans and their supporters in the abolition of slavery and the movement toward freedom and equality for African Americans. An excellent pamphlet providing a map and details about 60 sites throughout the state is available at tourism information centers, tourism district offices, and the **Connecticut Historical Commission** (59 South Prospect St., Hartford 06106; 860-566-3005). You can also visit the website www.ctfreedomtrail.ct.gov.

Theater and Music in New Haven

The arts flourish in New Haven, and you can check the websites of these groups and theaters to find the best performances for families.

- **New Haven Symphony Orchestra.** 33 Whitney Ave.; box office: (203) 776-1444 or (800) 292-NHSO; www.newhavensymphony.com. The fourth-oldest orchestra in the United States, this symphony offers an October to June concert season in beautiful Woolsey Hall at the corner of College and Grove, plus a free summer series on the green. Its annual Holiday Pops! Concert is a joyous collaboration of orchestra and choruses singing traditional carols, gospel, and even reggae tunes.

- **Shubert Performing Arts Center.** 247 College St.; (203) 562-5666; www .shubert.com. This refurbished theater offers Broadway shows, ballet, opera, modern dance, comedy, and more in a full season from September through May. Many shows are suitable for or aimed at families; some are offered at prices as low as $10 per ticket.

- **Long Wharf Theatre.** 222 Sargent Dr.; box office: (203) 787-4282; www.long wharf.org. Renowned for excellence and intimacy, this award-winning theater has two stages; check for affordable Kids on the Wharf plays and other productions suitable for the family. Summer camps for teens and middle-schoolers; workshops for kids 6–9.

The heroic acts of the group's leader, Sengbe Pieh, also known as Joseph Cinque, are celebrated on the 14-foot, three-sided bronze sculpture that stands near the site of the jailhouse where the kidnapped Mendi Africans were imprisoned. Although the morally laudable and eventually triumphant teamwork of the principal players in this incident did not lead directly or immediately to the release of other captive Africans, it did contribute greatly to the abolitionist movement and inspired the courage of countless other Africans who sought, fought for, and won their own freedom. This monument reminds all visitors of the importance of pursuing justice, freedom, and equality for all people against all odds. A tour of the re-creation of the schooner itself (usually in port from April through October) is a moving, eye-opening experience that makes the reality of the Mendi ordeal all the clearer. When the schooner is in port, it also does three-hour public sails on Fri and Sat from 5 to 8 p.m.; reservations are necessary.

Lighthouse Point Park and Carousel (all ages)

2 Lighthouse Rd., off Woodward Avenue, from I-95 exit 50 northbound, or exit 51, Frontage Road, southbound; follow the signs down Townsend Avenue to Lighthouse Road and the park; park manager: (203) 946-8005; ranger station: (203) 946-8790; http://cityofnewhaven

- **New Haven Folk.** www.ctfolk.com. These traditional and contemporary folk artists sponsor acoustic concerts and workshops featuring national and regional touring artists and local performers. They also produce the wonderful Connecticut Folk Festival and Green Expo each September. Check the website for dates of this and their concert series.

- **Music on the Green.** Presented by New Haven Office of Cultural Affairs; concert hotline: (203) 946-7821; www.infonewhaven.com. Free summer concerts in July and August on selected Saturday evenings. Bring a picnic or buy dinner at the food booths set up at the edge of the green. Dance in the twilight with music all around you.

- **International Festival of Arts and Ideas.** (203) 498-1212 or (888) ART-IDEA; www.artidea.org. Performers come from nearly every continent to raise our awareness and our spirits in an outpouring of artistic energy that spans five days in late June each year. Of the scores of indoor and outdoor performances staged on or near the green and on the Yale Campus, many are free, others require paid tickets. See classical and modern dance; hear stories, plays, opera, folk, salsa, reggae, jazz, and classical artists; participate in art activities, dances, or mask and puppet pageants.

.com. Park open daily 7 a.m. to 7 p.m., free of charge except from Memorial Day to Labor Day, when out-of-town vehicles pay a day-use fee ($$). Carousel operates weekends and holidays only from Memorial Day to Labor Day, from noon to 4 p.m. Private rentals available.

New Haven is not often characterized as a city on the sea, but it is a major working port in New England, and some of the best the city has to offer is by the shore or on the Sound. Although it is not known for its fine beaches, the city does have a great seaside park and swimming area.

Now popular mostly with city residents and bird watchers, Lighthouse Point Park was once the enormously popular last stop on the New Haven trolley line. In those olden days the park had bathhouses, boat rides, and baseball games, with such legends as Babe Ruth and Ty Cobb playing here on Sunday afternoons in the Roaring Twenties. Nearly destroyed in the hurricane of 1938, the park later was home to a small amusement park.

Today only one of its famed rides remains. Housed in a New Haven landmark building listed on the National Register of Historic Places is the Lighthouse Point Carousel, an astonishingly well-restored treasure and a joy to ride. Assembled around 1911 from new and used parts, this sparkling beauty carved mostly by masters Looff and Carmel has 72 figures mounted in 20 ranks on a 60-foot platform. Jumping horses that slide on gleaming brass poles stand four abreast, alternating with the steadfast steeds, which stand shoulder to shoulder in rows of three. With these are a beautifully saddled camel and twin dragon chariots, the latter carved by Charles Illions. For 50 cents per ride, you can hop on any one of these gorgeously painted Coney Island–style mounts, with names like Wild Wind, Sweet Sue, City Lights, Sea Dreamer, and Sundance. The beveled mirrors at the center of the ride reflect the glimmer of hundreds of twinkling light bulbs; the refurbished antique murals on the rounding board at the top of the carousel depict scenes from the history of New Haven; the air-driven Stinson Band Organ makes heavenly music. Group reservations are accepted—what a great place to party.

The 82-acre park also has the pre–Civil War Five Mile Point Lighthouse and a great little nature center at the East Shore Ranger Station. When Ranger Terry is here, you may learn something about natural history, marine ecology, and maritime history at a program. Lighthouse tours are among the programs on the calendar.

The park's alcohol-free beach is clean and safe; a first-aid station, a snack bar, changing rooms and showers, a playground, several swing sets, and a picnic grove are here. A splash park with 10 fountain displays provides cool fun for visitors of all ages. A public boat launch, a fishing pier, volleyball nets, a nature trail, and several excellent bird-watching areas in the bird sanctuary are also here. Hawk-watching during the annual migration, from late August through November, brings birders from all over the state.

A holiday display called the **UI Fantasy of Lights** (info line: 203-777-2000) is staged each year at the park (5 to 10: 00 p.m. daily November 15 through December 31). Cruise the park's roadways past 60 colorful oversized symbols of Christmas joy. Fees ($$ per car or minivan) benefit Easter Seals rehabilitation programs. Through your car radio, you will hear a musical program timed for the ride through this animated spectacle.

Fort Nathan Hale and Black Rock Fort (ages 6 and up)

Woodward Avenue; (203) 787-8790; www.fort-nathan-hale.org. Open daily Memorial Day to Labor Day from 10 a.m. to 4 p.m. Free.

After you leave Lighthouse Point, you might want to make a historical pit stop as you travel north again on Townsend Avenue. Take a left on Fort Hale Park Road to visit two of New Haven's oldest historic sites. Black Rock Fort was built in 1776 by order of the Connecticut Colony to protect the Port of New Haven from the British. Unfortunately, by the time the British arrived in 1779, only 19 defenders remained at the fort; they were swiftly captured by the enemy, which then marched on to New Haven.

Fort Nathan Hale was built near the same site in the early 1800s as the British and Americans prepared again to fight. This time, during the War of 1812, the defenders successfully repelled the British invaders. Rebuilt in 1863 with new ramparts, bunkers, a drawbridge, and 18 guns, the fort was prepared for Civil War action, but it never came.

Now you can make a self-guided tour of both sites. The drawbridge, its moat, the ramparts, bunkers, and other fortifications either still exist or have been restored. It's a neat site with terrific views of the harbor, but it's very low-key. In addition to the remains of the forts, there is a handsome statue of the young Nathan Hale, a colorful flag display, and some signage and self-guided tour brochures at the information booth at the entrance to the site.

Schooner Sound Learning Cruises (ages 4 and up)

60 South Water St.; (203) 865-1737; www.schoonersoundlearning.org. Late May through Sept. Private charters, plus public sails. Among the latter, the best for families are Educational Sea Adventures, Pirate Sails, and Sunset Cruises. Other specialty cruises are offered as well; check the website calendar and call to inquire about suitability for children. Cruises leave from the Long Wharf. $$$$.

If you want to see New Haven from the Sound and get a history and ecology lesson and a great boat ride to boot, call this tour operator during the warm months. Weather

Other New Haven **Parks**

New Haven has a variety of small parks that are notable for special reasons. Check http://cityofnewhaven.com for details about each park's hours of operation and special events.

- **Edgerton Park.** On Whitney Avenue and Cliff Street near the Hamden line; enter observatory area at 75 Cliff St.; (203) 777-1886; http://edgertonpark.org. Listed on the National Register of Historic Places; 22-acre property originally owned by Eli Whitney and later the site of the Edgerton mansion. Crosby Conservatory of tropical plants with a simulated rain-forest path. Greenbrier Greenhouse with culinary herbs and seasonal plants for sale year-round, plus a children's corner with modestly priced plants. Outdoor flower gardens and magnificent trees, walking, biking, and cross-country skiing paths, picnicking areas, community garden center; seasonal fairs and concerts.

- **Edgewood Park.** 720 Edgewood Ave. between Whalley Avenue and Chapel Street; (203) 946-8028. 120 acres with nature walkways, playground, ranger station with wildlife displays, duck pond, tennis and basketball courts, playing fields, Holocaust memorial, and Spanish-American War monument.

- **Wooster Square Green.** On Chapel Street between Academy and Wooster Place; www.nhpt.org/Historic_District_Pages/woostersquare.html. Near New Haven's Little Italy is a historic district of some of New Haven's prettiest architecture designed in the early 1800s around a central square named for New Haven's Revolutionary War hero David Wooster. Have a look at the monument to Christopher Columbus, sit on benches under flowering cherry trees, and breathe deeply—the aromas of olive oil, garlic, and spicy tomato sauces will remind you that you are steps from the city's finest Italian restaurants and the world's best pizza and pastries.

permitting, they'll take you out on chartered half-day, full-day, and sunset sails aboard the *Quinnipiack,* a 91-foot gaff-rigged wooden schooner. On the public sails, the lively crew offers entertaining and educational stories about the history of New Haven, the ecology of the Sound, and the cultures that affected the present ecosystem. Sea Adventures offers hands-on activities about marine science; Pirate Sails include costumed reenactors. On both chartered and public cruises, passengers are welcome to bring picnics and beverages; some specialty public cruises include food and/or beverages as part of the cruise package. Inquire also about the birthday parties and the excellent weeklong summer day camps for children ages 4 through grade 12.

Where to Eat

Bella's Cafe. 896 Whalley Ave.; (203) 387-7107. Best place in town for breakfast and brunch. Oh, and lunch. Yum, lunch. Tues through Sun until 3 p.m. $

Claire's Corner Copia Cafe. Corner of College and Chapel Streets; (203) 562-3888. Close to the green, Claire's offers flavorful vegetarian main dishes, soups, sandwiches, quesadillas, and baked goods. Takeout or tables with a semi-self-service, casual flair. Open for breakfast, lunch, and dinner daily 8 a.m. to 10 p.m. $

Kitchen Zinc. 966 Chapel St.; (203) 772-3002. A great place for families who like pizza. Funky modern design that's urban/industrial in flavor and casual in spirit. Open Mon through Sat from 5 p.m. $–$$

Kudeta. 27 Temple St.; (203) 562-8844. Dramatic decor; tiny jewels of appetizers and zesty trans-Asian, Chinese, and Thai dishes. Family-size tables with spinner in the middle make sharing fun and easy. Lunch and dinner daily from 11:30 a.m. $$–$$$

Louis' Lunch. 263 Crown St.; (203) 562-5507. Opened by Louie Lassen in 1895, this landmark luncheon stand now has a place on the National Register. The first hamburger in America was made here in 1900. Fresh-daily burgers and cheeseburgers are served on toast in adult- and child-size portions; tuna salad is added to the menu on Friday. Open Tues and Wed 11 a.m. to 4 p.m.; Thurs through Sat 11 a.m. to 2 or 3 a.m. Closed Sun and sometimes Mon and the entire month of Aug. $

New Haven's Little Italy–Wooster Street. Whether it's pizza, pasta, or pastries you crave, a walk down Wooster Street will be sure to satisfy. Worth the wait in line, both **Pepe's Pizzeria Napoletana** (157 Wooster St.; 203-865-5762; $–$$) and **Sally's Pizzeria** (237 Wooster St.; 203-624-5271; $) offer up coal-fired brick-oven thin-crust pizza to die for. Pepe's is closed on Tues and Sally's on Mon. For pasta, try **Consiglio's** (165 Wooster St.; 203-865-4489; $$–$$$). It looks fancy, but they love children. For a small treat, go to **Libby's Italian Pastry Shop** (139 Wooster St.; 203-772-0380; $) for the best cannolis and rice and ricotta pie for miles around.

Where to Stay

Courtyard by Marriott at Yale. 30 Whalley Ave.; (203) 777-6221. 207 units, breakfast cafe, fitness room. $$$

La Quinta Inn & Suites. 400 Sargent Dr.; (203) 562-1111 or (800) 753-3757. 152 units, including 35 suites, outdoor pool, fitness room, sauna, hot buffet breakfast. $$–$$$

New Haven Premiere Hotel & Suites. 3 Long Wharf Dr.; (203) 777-5337. 112 suites with kitchens, fitness room, outdoor pool and hot tub, hot buffet breakfast. $$$$

East Haven

This shoreline community is a bustling outgrowth of New Haven's sprawl, seen mostly by travelers passing along I-95 through the shopping areas on Frontage Road. If it weren't for the seemingly endless construction on or near the Lake Saltonstall Bridge, few travelers would slow down along this route to see what the town has to offer. Those who exit the highway in East Haven will find one of Connecticut's most popular family attractions.

Shore Line Trolley Museum (all ages)

17 River St.; (203) 467-6927; www.bera.org. Open Memorial Day to Labor Day 10 a.m. to 5 p.m. Also in Apr on Sun only, and in May on Sat and Sun at the same hours. Weekend tours, Sept through Dec; check website for special events schedule. First trolley leaves at 10:30 a.m.; last one leaves at 4:30 p.m. $–$$; children under 2 free.

The efforts of the Branford Electric Railway Association have kept alive and well one of Connecticut's oldest tourist attractions—the oldest continually operating trolley line in the United States. Nearly 100 classic trolley cars are stored on the grounds and in the car barns of the property. Admission buys you unlimited 3-mile round-trip rides on beautifully restored cars, plus guided or self-guided tours of the museum's display areas, which include interactive and audio-video exhibits on the history of the technology and the local lines. The trolley rides are great fun, especially for young children, and special themed rides offered throughout the year focus the appeal. Among these are Haunted Isle and Pumpkin Patch days in October, and Night Lights rides and Santa on the Trolley days in late November and December.

You can picnic on the grounds, but there is no food concession or snack bar. You can also arrange birthday parties and special charters at a group discount if booked in advance.

Branford/Stony Creek

One of the most relaxing family excursions in the state centers in and around Branford's Stony Creek, as quintessential a quaint New England fishing village as can be found in these parts. Only Stonington, in New London County, transports one more thoroughly to the nautical past.

Less than 10 miles from New Haven, Stony Creek has a long and lively history, complete with tales of pirate treasure and other romances of the sea and heart. Once home to farmers, fishers, and quarriers, the village is now famed for its quiet Yankee charm and its sprinkling of pink granite islands just offshore—the Thimbles.

In fact, the village's principal industry, if one can call it that, is the Thimble Islands sightseeing tour business. Two enterprising captains have updated the centuries-old trade of ferrying livestock, groceries, visitors, and even the occasional piano from the town dock to the islands. Now, from mid-May through Columbus Day, landlubbers can board ship to enjoy the sea breeze and scenery while listening to the colorful tales of the islands' past and present.

To reach the Stony Creek Dock, take I-95 to exit 56, and go south on Leetes Island Road for two miles. At the stop sign, go straight on Thimble Island Road, and follow the signs to the dock.

Shoreline **Greenway**

Families who love the outdoors are sure to appreciate the **Shoreline Green-way Trail,** a multiuse recreational footpath that is being built, one section at a time, from Lighthouse Point in New Haven to Hammonasset State Park in Madison. Hugging as closely as possible to the coastal environment, it will eventually snake 25 miles through the four shoreline towns of East Haven, Branford, Guilford, and Madison. When the work is finished, the trail will connect parks, railroad stations, village centers, and other existing trails. Designed for nonmotorized recreation, the Greenway will be suitable for walkers, hikers, bicyclists, runners, and cross-country skiers. Approximately 10 feet wide and made of hard-packed crushed stone, the improved sections of the trail are accessible to outdoor enthusiasts of all ages, from senior citizens to babes in strollers, and, in some sections, may be accessible to in-line skaters and folks in wheelchairs.

An improved section in Branford—just about 2,500 linear feet—lies parallel to Birch Road, going from the west side of Young Park to the east end of the Branford Day Care Center's Nature Classroom (at 16 Birch Rd.). To reach it from the Branford Green, travel east on Main Street and turn right on Montowese Street, which is Route 146. Turn left onto Pine Orchard Road and then left onto Birch Road.

Another section, as yet unimproved but perfect for hikers, is the old Trolley Trail, also in Branford. It winds about 1 mile through the tidal salt marshes and woodlands between Pine Orchard and Stony Creek, offering up-close-and-personal experiences of the estuary habitat and its wildlife, as well as views of Branford Harbor and the Thimble Islands. A 480-foot-long footbridge in the footprint of the historic trolley track connects to a nature walk from which visitors can see a seasonal variety of shorebirds, mammals, and invertebrates nesting, feeding, and wading in the creek and marsh areas. To reach this trail portion, take I-95 to Leetes Island Road at exit 56. Follow that road south to Thimble Islands Road, then take a right on West Point Road to the parking lot.

A third section, about 1 mile long, has been cleared in Madison. For Greenway news and developments, check the website at http://shorelinegreenway trail.org.

Volsunga IV (all ages)

Stony Creek Dock; (203) 488-9978 at the dock; (203) 481-3345 for reservations and information; www.thimbleislands.com. Cruises every hour on the hour, weather permitting, from 11 a.m. to 4 p.m. daily (except some Mondays) July 1 to day before Labor Day. From mid-May through June and from Labor Day through Columbus Day, fewer cruises daily and no operation on Monday of several weeks at either end of the season. Check the website for current schedule. $–$$. Groups of more than 12 should make reservations. Two-hour evening charters ($375 for 30 people) are also available.

From Captain Kidd to General Tom Thumb, the stories told by Stony Creek native Captain Bob Milne aboard the *Volsunga IV* are exceeded in quality only by his sure navigation of the reefs surrounding the 23 inhabited islands of the total 365. Milne's 40-foot vessel is rated for 49 passengers.

All seats are great seats for parents and kids alike on its single deck, and Captain Bob's easygoing manner makes for terrific storytelling, easily heard over the *Volsunga IV*'s sound system (the engine is soundproofed). Along with views of the islands' 95 homes, which range from a palatial Spanish mansion to Victorian cottages to a veritable aerie on stilts, you will enjoy the sights of human and winged islanders—kids wearing life jackets in their yards, teens diving from rocks, and seabirds to spare.

Sea Mist II (all ages)

Stony Creek Dock; (203) 488-8905; www.thimbleislandscruise.com. In May and Sept (including Memorial Day and Labor Day) 45-minute cruises depart Fri through Sun at 10:15 a.m. and 12:15, 2:15, and 4:15 p.m. In July and Aug cruises depart Wed through Mon on every quarter hour from 10:15 a.m. to 4:15 p.m. In Oct cruises depart on Sat and Sun at 12:15 and 2:15 p.m.; $–$$. Two-hour charters available ($450 for up to 34 people). Reservations suggested for large groups. Public seal watches at noon on weekends only in March and April; two hours; $$$.

Captain Mike Infantino Jr. offers a similar ride on his similar boat, a 45-foot vessel that carries 46 passengers. The navigation is just as sure, the stories are an entertaining mix of myth and fact, and the views of the sea, the birds, the islands, and the islanders are basically identical. All passengers are seated comfortably and can easily hear both the stories and the sounds of the sea. Chartered seal and bird watches can also be planned for groups of 10 or more. Call for details. Bird watches are arranged year-round; seal watches are typically December through mid-April.

Stony Creek Village (all ages)

On your ride down to the water, you may notice Stony Creek's other attractions. Browse in the small array of shops between the railroad bridge and the dock, or rest or play awhile in the village park, which has a children's playground. Stony Creek Market (203-488-0145) is great for breakfast, lunch, dinner (some nights), soft drinks, and picnic fare, and Creekers at Stony Creek Marine and Cuisine (203-481-2836) offers drinks, deli, snacks, and summertime-only lunch and dinner under a tent at the waterside. When your appetite is satisfied, stroll the rest of the village. When you return to your car, you can reach the Branford town green by following Route 146 to its end and continuing straight into the center of town.

Around the green are many stores and restaurants, and to its west are the beautiful landmark Blackstone Library and the historic Harrison House museum.

Where to Eat

Darbar India. 1070 Main St.; (203) 481-8994. Delicious traditional favorites; all-you-can-eat buffet ($) Fri through Sun noon to 3 p.m. Lunch and dinner daily. $$

La Cuisine Market and Cafe. 750 East Main St.; (203) 488-7100. This bright and immaculate eat-here or take-out establishment offers cheerful table service for hearty and healthful breakfast and lunch, plus lunch and dinner to go, and delicious baked goods. Cafe open 8 a.m. to 3 p.m. Tues through Sun; market open 8 a.m. to 6 p.m. Tues through Fri and to 3 p.m. on weekends. $–$$

Lenny's Indian Head Inn. 205 South Montowese St.; (203) 488-1500. A menu of New England seafood is epitomized in Lenny's Famous Shore Dinner of clam chowder, cherrystones, sweet corn on the cob, lobster, steamers, and watermelon. Steaks, burgers, fries and rings, and a children's menu served in the casual ambience of worn wood floors and wooden booths makes this a happy, noisy place. Open daily for lunch and dinner, indoors or out. $$

Stony Creek Market. 178 Thimble Island Rd.; (203) 488-0145. For breakfast (8 to 11 a.m.) and lunch (11 a.m. to 3 p.m.), come here for front-deck views of the harbor. On Thursday through Sunday evenings in summer only, the market doubles as Stony Creek Pizza. $

Where to Stay

Holiday Inn Express. 309 East Main St.; (203) 488-4035. Clean, basic rooms with indoor pool and complimentary continental breakfast. $$$–$$$$

Guilford

Just 15 miles east of New Haven, Guilford feels like a country town, and one of the most exceptional colonial greens in New England is in its center. Lying south of the Boston Post Road, as you drive toward the Sound, its 12 acres are crisscrossed by walkways and dotted with benches that make this a popular site to relax and to play. Shops, restaurants, churches, galleries, and beautiful colonial, federal, and Victorian homes surround this classically lovely spot. Bring the kids here to bicycle or to skate, to listen to a summer concert or a Shakespearean play, or to browse at one of the frequent fairs or festivals held on the site. Afterward, leave the green to explore other parts of Guilford. Walk or cross-country ski on the wooded trails through an old quarry site or an ancient farm. Stroll, snooze, or sift for forgotten treasures on the beach. Visit one of the four historical homes representing lifeways of the 17th, 18th, and 19th centuries. In every season, Guilford is a shoreline gem.

Guilford **Craft Expo**

Surely the most magical of all the events held on the green, this fabulous three-day festival, well past its fiftieth year, celebrates American handcrafts created by 170 juried artists from all corners of the nation. Displayed under huge, cheerfully lit tents, the pieces demonstrate an astonishing array of talent in every medium. Basketry, weaving, jewelry, toys, clothing, candles, leather goods, sculpture, pottery, paper crafts, glass, musical instruments, furniture—you name it, it's here.

The **Guilford Art Center** tent features hands-on activities and demonstrations by crafters who practice their arts at the center. Storytellers, face painters, and other live performers help make the event a happy experience for all visitors. A food concession sells unremarkable fast-food fare, so you may want to pack a picnic to enjoy under the trees.

The tents are lit from noon to 9 p.m. on Thurs and Fri and from 10 a.m. to 7 p.m. on Sat in the middle week of July. A perfectly lovely and inspiring way to spend a summer afternoon, the expo is also a great opportunity for exposing children to the creative arts. Who knows? You may have a budding artist in your clan. Call (203) 453-5947 for more information. $$, members and children under 12 free.

Guilford Art Center (ages 3 and up)

411 Church St. (Route 77), north of Route 1 and approximately 200 yards north of the I-95 overpass; (203) 453-5947; www.guilfordartcenter.org. Studios open year-round for classes and visitors; call for schedule and course catalog. Gallery and shop open year-round Mon through Sat 10 a.m. to 5 p.m. Extended hours for annual Holiday Exhibition in December. Closed major holidays. Free.

Composed of a shop, a gallery, and a school, the Art Center was founded in 1962 by the local artists who organized the first of its remarkable annual expositions (see sidebar). Still a home away from home for many of those artists, the center has pottery, weaving, painting, and metalsmithing studios, plus multiuse classrooms for instruction in basketry, beading, fiber arts, glass arts, and blacksmithing. Visiting artists also travel here to offer workshops for adults and children. A bounty of talented role models offers instruction, guidance, and encouragement as young artists tease from their own minds and fingers the wondrous creations born in these studios. The Mill Gallery hosts small expositions throughout the year, and the shop sells the works of as many as 300 artisans. Craft birthday parties and scouting activities are also offered here.

Henry Whitfield State Museum (ages 6 and up)

248 Old Whitfield St., at the corner of Stone House Lane; (203) 453-2457 or (860) 566-3005; www.whitfieldmuseum.com. Open for mostly self-guided tours, Wed through Sun May 1 to October 31 10 a.m. to 4 p.m. and for groups year-round by appointment. $, children under 6 free.

This historic home is the oldest stone house in New England and the oldest house in Connecticut. Built in 1639 by Reverend Henry Whitfield, the post-medieval house has stone walls 3 feet thick and is the last remaining of four such houses strategically placed in Guilford as strongholds for the citizens during threat of war. No record confirms that the house was ever in fact used for this purpose.

Now restored more as a museum than a period house, the structure contains an outstanding collection of furniture, housekeeping implements, textiles, weapons, and other important Connecticut pieces. The entire house, including the attic, is open to the public, as are the gardens and lawns. Among the large collections displayed in the attic, you can see the 1726 Ebenezer Parmelee steeple clock, the first wooden-works tower clock made in the colonies. In the separate visitor center is a reference library, an exhibit gallery with excellent changing displays, and a charming gift shop, which reopens for a week in late December for holiday shopping.

Special educational and entertaining programming for families is planned throughout the public season. Check the website for a calendar of these inventive and interactive events. Among the best are the Puritans at Play day of old-fashioned games, annually in June on the state's Open House Day; the Holidaze exhibit with costumed interpreters and period foods in late November; and the Firelight Festival in December with luminaria, chestnut-roasting over an open outdoor fire, and other winter activities and refreshments.

Hyland House (ages 6 and up)

84 Boston St., which leads east from the south side of the green; (203) 453-9477; www .hylandhouse.com. Open early June to early Sept daily except Mon 10 a.m. to 4:30 p.m. and weekends Labor Day to Columbus Day. Suggested donation: $, children under 12 free.

This red overhung saltbox frame house was originally the home of the Hyland family. One of the Hyland daughters married Ebenezer Parmelee of clock-making fame; it was through their efforts that the house was expanded from its original two-rooms-over-two size. Though the house was built in 1660, the museum's focus is on the 50 to 75 years before the Revolution. Especially in the house's wonderful kitchen in the lean-to addition at the back of the house, visitors step into the 18th century here, and tour guides, in tune with the interests of children of every age level, make the house come alive with scores of facts and stories. The architectural details and the collections in this house are among the finest in the state. Gorgeous paneling, wide-board floors, walk-in fireplaces, and artifacts of every sort are abundant. Outside, the flower and herb garden is lovely in summer and fall.

The house is the site of the Historic Foodways Festival on the last full weekend in September. Hearthside cooking and other activities are among the special events designed for families.

Thomas Griswold House (ages 6 and up)
171 Boston St.; (203) 453-3176 or (203) 453-4666; www.thomasgriswoldhouse.com. Open June through Sept Tues through Sun 11 a.m. to 4 p.m.; Oct, weekends only at same hours. $, children under 12 free.

Greatly restored by the Guilford Keeping Society, this 1774 saltbox home has a large number of important architectural details, including an original Guilford cupboard and a 10-foot-wide fireplace. This house also includes period rooms set with furnishings and implements in positions of use. Samplers, coverlets, costumes, dolls, and toys are among the treasures here.

Special events such as twilight tours, an antiques show, or reenactments are sometimes offered. Check the website's calendar of events. On these special days the museum's blacksmith shop and barn are usually open.

Westwoods Trails (all ages)
Trail entrance on Sam Hill Road near junction with Route 146; (203) 453-8068; www.west woodstrails.org. Open year-round dawn to dusk. Trail map available at Guilford town hall, library, police station, and Parks and Recreation Department at 32 Church St. Guilford Land Conservation Trust (P.O. Box 200, Guilford 06437) can also provide copies. Free.

For those of you who are fatigued with art and history, a walk in the woods may be the answer to your prayers. Head, therefore, to Guilford's Westwoods Trails, located less than a mile from the green in an open area of more than 1,000 acres. Forty miles of very pretty trails lace through forest and marshland.

Take Route 146 west from the green to Sam Hill Road and park in the small lot right near that corner. Follow the white-blazed trail from that point and connect with the other trails that lead to waterfalls, rock cliffs, colonial caves, an Indian cave, rock carvings, and vistas of the Sound and lake. The "G" Trail connects the Westwoods Trails to the Stony Creek Quarry Preserve; here you can see the remains of old quarrying operations.

Jacobs Beach (all ages)
Seaside Avenue off Whitfield Street; Guilford Parks and Recreation: (203) 453-8068. Park and playground area open year-round 8:30 a.m. to 9 p.m. Swimming allowed only when lifeguards are present, Memorial Day to Labor Day, Mon through Sat 9 a.m. to 5 p.m. and Sun 11 a.m. to 5 p.m. Out-of-town visitors pay a day-use parking fee ($$ per vehicle), Memorial Day through Labor Day.

Hikers and bikers may want a refreshing swim or at least a cool wind through their hair after some trail exercise. Head down to the Sound for a rest on the sand at Jacobs Beach.

Comb the beach for treasures swept in on the tide, play on the playground, listen to the rustling marsh reeds. You can swim if the lifeguards are on duty, but you can use the beach and volleyball court even if the guards are off duty. Restrooms and a pavilion with picnic tables and nearby grills are also here. The beach is relatively small, but it's a pretty spot, and out-of-towners are more than welcome. Season passes cost families $50.

Lake Quonnipaug (all ages)

Route 77 in North Guilford, about 3 miles north of Route 80. Open Memorial Day through Labor Day; gated during remainder of year. Mon through Sat 9:30 a.m. to 7:30 p.m., Sun 11 a.m. to 7:30 p.m. Purchase per-vehicle day tickets at the lake ($$) or a season pass ($50), which allows unlimited visits. Passes can be purchased only at the Guilford Parks and Recreation Department (32 Church St.; 203-453-8068).

If freshwater swimming is pleasing to you, head north to Lake Quonnipaug for salt-free water play, boating, fishing, and picnicking. This pretty lake is in a rural area dotted with barns, pastures, stone walls, and fences—the perfect setting for a New England day trip.

A good-size beach and grassy area are open to the public. Bathrooms with two outdoor showers are also provided. Small car-top boats such as inflatables, canoes, kayaks, sailboards, or tubes may be launched from the grassy area, but no snorkeling or scuba diving is allowed. A state-owned public boat launch ramp is at the north end of the lake, outside of the Guilford property.

Dudley Farm (all ages)

2351 Durham Rd. (Route 77), north of Route 80; www.dudleyfarm.com. Open May through Oct, Fri and Sat, 10 a.m. to 1 p.m. and Sun, noon to 3 p.m. (but call ahead); also by appointment. Farmers' market June through Oct on each Sat from 9 a.m. to 12:30 p.m.; winter market in Munger Barn on only the first Sat of Feb through May. Grounds, trails, and market are free; house tour, $; children under 16 free.

Settled in the arms of nature, the house, barns, and remnant structures at this peaceful 10-acre farm site are the legacy of the Dudley family, who tilled the soil and tended animals through two centuries in Guilford. Now the Dudley Foundation has as its mission the preservation of the farm and its structures and the restoration of its meadows, fields, and flower gardens. Through this process, the foundation hopes to inspire present generations to recognize their own connection to the soil.

You can tour the 17-room 1840s farmhouse, with rooms restored to their appearance in 1900, and you can see an enormous U-shaped barn that evolved through two centuries of farm life. Also here are the Munger Barn (with a small display of Native American artifacts), a sugarhouse, an herb garden and flower gardens, a vegetable field, beehives, and animal enclosures sheltering oxen, sheep, chickens, and geese. A visit here may rekindle in both children and adults an appreciation for the natural environment and an attitude of stewardship toward the earth—or you may just want to see the animals and take a hike. A 2-mile loop trail through 95 acres of woodland traces the path of 18th-century wagon roads.

The farm is most lively on Saturday mornings in the summer, when the market offers the farm's own produce as well as that of other local farmers and crafters. Choose some

Anne Conover **Nature Trail**

The **National Audubon Society** offers a 2-mile trail through the 200-acre Guilford Salt Meadows Sanctuary near the East River. Open dawn to dusk year-round, the sanctuary and the trailhead are accessible from Meadowlands Road off Clapboard Hill Road, not far from exit 59 (Goose Lane), on the north side of I-95. Secondary-growth forest and meadow-, river-, and tidal marshland are habitats for herring and eels, eastern box turtles, salt marsh sparrows and osprey, and many other birds and beasts of the Eastern Woodlands. The easy trail is beautiful in all seasons. A kiosk at the parking area provides trail guides. Admission is free. For more information, check the website www.audubon.org/local/sanctuary/guilford.

fruits, vegetables, flowers, honey, and baked goods, then see what the farm staff might be doing in the house, the barns, or on the grounds. Depending on the weather and season, you may see, or even participate in, demonstrations of varied old-time and traditional housekeeping skills and farm and barn chores. On the first Saturday of each month, musicians play acoustic instruments under the trees.

Special events include an Arbor Day celebration, May Day festivities, and a Farm Day. The foundation produces an occasional newsletter to let folks know what's happening at the farm; call to ask for a copy or check the website for news of markets and events.

Where to Eat

It's So Rich. 23 Water St.; (203) 453-1160. This wee place sells Durham's famous super-premium 80 Licks ice cream, plus soups and salads and such in the cooler seasons. Opens at noon Mon through Sat; closing varies with the day and season. $

Little Stone House Cafe. 514 Whitfield St.; (203) 458-9800. Practically in the water, this family-friendly cafe offers gourmet-quality soups, sandwiches, paninis, wraps, lobster gazpacho, and the best BLT wrap on the planet. Eat outside on the patio or at a few tables inside. Open 11 a.m. to 8 p.m., May through Sept, Tues through Sun. Live music on Thursday evenings and weekend afternoons. $–$$

The Place. 901 Boston Post Rd.; (203) 453-9276. Seasonal dining in the rough at one of Connecticut's most unique eateries. Outside under tents, sit on rough-hewn seats at picnic tables and eat charcoal-grilled steak, pit-roasted corn on the cob, and fresh seafood. Open from late Apr through Oct on Mon though Thurs from 5 to 10 p.m., Sat from 1 to 11 p.m., and Sun from noon to 10 p.m. $$

Som Siam. 63R Whitfield St.; (203) 458-0228. In the rear of Whitfield Alley, directly across from the town green, this little place graciously serves delicious Thai favorites in a pretty, thimble-size setting warmly welcoming to families. Open for lunch Tues through Sun and dinner daily. $–$$

Where to Stay

Comfort Inn. 300 Boston Post Rd.; (203) 453-5600. 45 clean, basic rooms in newer 100 percent nonsmoking facility with complimentary continental breakfast with scrambled eggs and hot waffles; fridge and microwave in rooms. $$–$$$

Madison

Inarguably one of the prettiest towns on the New Haven County shoreline, Madison was one of Connecticut's earliest settlements. Once called East Guilford and connected geographically and politically to the town of Guilford, it was incorporated as a separate town in 1826. In previous centuries a fishing and shipbuilding center and later a seaside resort area, Madison is now primarily a comfortable residential suburb whose population increases sizably in the summertime because of its beautiful beaches. In fact, Connecticut's longest stretch of public beach is located here at the most popular state-owned park.

Hammonasset State Park and
Meigs Point Nature Center (all ages)

Off the Boston Post Road, exit 62 off I-95; (203) 245-2785. Open daily year-round, 8 a.m. to sunset; most planned activities held in summer. Nature Center open Tues through Sun, 10 a.m. to 5 p.m. in season and until 4 p.m. in the off-season. Daily per-vehicle admission fee ($$–$$$) Memorial Day to Labor Day. From mid-Apr to Memorial Day and from Labor Day through mid-Oct, admission is charged on weekends only. All weekdays are free after Labor Day and until the Friday before Memorial Day. In season, reduced entrance fee after 4 p.m.; free after 6:30 p.m. Season pass ($$$$) allows unlimited visits. Campsites, $ nightly.

Enormously popular, this alcohol-free park offers a 2-mile beach with four bathhouses, several picnic shelters, a 550-site campground, playing fields, a cheery year-round nature center, walking trails, a bike path, and sun, sand, rocks, and salty spray in abundance. Come here, then, to camp, swim, fish off the jetty, scuba dive, picnic, play ball, hike, sailboard, or boat (car-top vessels only have access here) on Long Island Sound.

You can also learn lots about the coastal environment and its many denizens at the **Meigs Point Nature Center** (203-245-8743), a modest but active facility with several fresh- and saltwater aquariums, a marine touch tank, a few well-executed dioramas, and a variety of live amphibians and reptiles. Outside, the Willard Island walking trail winds out through the salt meadow and onto the island, once farmed in colonial times and now home to the mammals and birds of the marshlands. See the nesting sites of the ospreys that soar overhead in spring, summer, and fall.

Throughout the year Ranger Russ and the nature center volunteer staff provide walks, slide presentations, and craft workshops for families. The Junior Naturalist program for children 9 to 12 and the Outdoor Explorer program for 6- to 8-year-olds include such free activities as fishing, crabbing, tidal pool exploration, and bird and bat house building. Held midweek in July and August, the program is open to drop-in visitors.

The windswept seaside campground is extremely popular in the summertime. The sites are almost all open, so if you like the hills and woods, you are in the wrong park. Bring a metal tub or fire ring (or rent one here); there are no grills or fire pits, and campfires are permitted only in metal containers. Campfire programs, bingo, movies, and a small children's playground are part of what you'll enjoy here. Bring bikes and in-line skates—the campground has excellent lanes for both sports.

Allis-Bushnell House (ages 6 and up)

853 Boston Post Rd,; (203) 245-4567; www.madisoncthistorical.org. Open on occasion for special events or for guided tours year-round by appointment. Free; donations gratefully accepted.

Owned by the Madison Historical Society, the 1785 Allis-Bushnell House is notable for its unusual corner fireplaces and cupboards, its exceptional collection of tools and fishing and farming equipment in its annex, and its 18th-century-style herb garden in the lovely rear yard. The birthplace and childhood home of Cornelius Bushnell, a founder of the Union Pacific Railway and chief financier of the Civil War ironclad ship, the USS *Monitor*, this house museum also has a collection of fascinating memorabilia regarding that famed vessel and Madison's maritime history.

Special guided tours by a costumed interpreter of Cornelius's mother, Chloe Bushnell, are offered to school groups; call to arrange visits or see the website for more information. During the summer months, parts of the collection are moved to the historic Lee's Academy (see next entry) for special themed exhibitions.

Downtown **Madison**

Families weary of the sun and sea may enjoy a stroll through Madison's shops, galleries, cafes, and restaurants, most of which are independent establishments in vintage homes and historic commercial buildings centered mostly on Wall Street, the Boston Post Road, and Samson Rock Road in the village center.

Choose some great summer reading at **R. J. Julia Booksellers** (once voted the best independent bookstore in the nation; 768 Boston Post Rd., 203-245-3959; www.rjjulia.com); see a movie at the **Madison Art Cinemas** (761 Boston Post Rd.; 203-245-3456; www.madisonartcinemas.com); and be sure to have a cup or a cone at **Ashley's Ice Cream** (724 Boston Post Rd.; 203-245-1113). Savvy kids will ask for a scoop of gelato at **Savvy Tea Gourmet** (28 Durham Rd.; 203-318-8666; www.savvyteagourmet.com), where parents may enjoy a cup of the very best teas to be had anywhere.

Lee's Academy (ages 8 and up)

14 Meeting House Lane, on the green in Madison; (203) 245-4567; www.madisoncthistorical .org. Open Sat from early June through late Aug, 11 a.m. to 4 p.m. $.

Now the headquarters, library, and exhibition gallery of the Madison Historical Society, Lee's Academy was used as a schoolhouse from 1821 to 1922. Its first students, who came from local families as well as from out of town and state, studied mathematics, English, Greek, and Latin. Moved five times in its long history, the structure is built of native timber and topped with a bell tower and a bell that its benefactor Captain Frederick Lee salvaged from a sunken revenue cutter. Used for many civic and community purposes after its tenure as a schoolhouse, the building now hosts the summer exhibitions of the Madison Historical Society. Suitable for adults and children 8 and older, recent exhibitions have included one on the history of the schoolhouse itself and another on the construction and opening of the Connecticut Turnpike; in summer 2011, an exhibit on Madison's role in the Civil War is slated to open here. On the adjacent green, an annual MHS family event in late October features a Ghost Walk and Pumpkin Blaze ($). Meet five ghostly figures who tell the chilling tales of their lives (and their demise), then enter your own carved jack-o'-lantern in a contest ($) and participate in a Grand Illumination as evening falls (see website for details).

Deacon John Grave House (ages 6 and up)

581 Boston Post Rd.; (203) 245-4798. Open for tours mid-June through Labor Day on Fri, 3 to 6 p.m. or by appointment throughout the year. $, children under 6 free.

Just a block east of the green in Madison, surrounded by stately period homes and its classically New England white Congregational church, is one of Connecticut's oldest homes, on a pretty parcel known in the past as Tuxis Farm. Occupied for more than 300 years by descendants of its original owner, Deacon John Grave, the house is a fine example of 17th- and 18th-century architecture, easily seen through the fine restoration work that has taken place here.

Adapted for use in the past as an ordinary, a school, a wartime infirmary and weapons depot, and even a courtroom, the house also was home to 10 children at one time—and that was before its 18th-century additions were added! Come here to imagine the life of a farming family in pre-Revolutionary days, see the secret staircase that led to a hidden room used for storing arms during the French and Indian War, hear the ghost stories associated with the house, and sample open-hearth cooking done on special events days. A local farmers' market is offered on Friday evenings in summertime.

Where to Eat

Friends and Company. 11 Boston Post Rd.; (203) 245-0654. Both casual and refined, this riverside establishment is a longtime local favorite for healthful and often locally grown seasonal meals. Dinner daily from 4:30 p.m.; Sunday brunch 11 a.m. to 2 p.m. Children's menu; half portions. $$–$$$

Lenny and Joe's Fish Tale. 1301 Boston Post Rd.; (203) 245-7289. Serving the shoreline since 1979, this classic seafood shack-plus upholds a long tradition of fresh fish, chowder, award-winning lobster rolls, shrimp, scallops, and more. Eat inside, daily year-round, or outside, March through Nov. From mid-May to mid-September, they serve terrific ice cream and operate a tyke-size carousel ($) in an outdoor pavilion. If it's too busy here, cross the street and order similar and tasty meals at the cheerful seafood shack, **The Clam Castle** (1324 Boston Post Rd.; 203-245-4911), which offers outdoor tables, a small inside dining area, delicious onion rings, and affordable lobster rolls, along with all the shore classics. $–$$

Red Tomato Pizzeria. 37 Boston Post Rd.; (203) 245-6948. From 3 p.m. Tues through Sun, order out or eat in at this cheery eatery that makes excellent thin-crust New Haven–style pizza $–$$

Zhang's. 44 Boston Post Rd.; (203) 245-3300. Open daily for lunch and dinner, this sit-down or take-out restaurant with a Far Eastern flair offers tasty Chinese and Japanese fare. $–$$

Where to Stay

Beech Tree Cottages. 1187 Boston Post Rd.; (203) 245-2676. In summertime, this 3-acre enclave just steps from Hammonasset Beach offers bedroom-and-bath guest houses, plus more ample cottages with bath and kitchen facilities, large enough for a small family. Clean, simply furnished, and well-equipped; queen beds in every cottage. Friendly hosts; lovely grounds with rope swing, volleyball net, barbecues, walkways. Guest houses, $$$ nightly; cottages, $$$$ nightly; weekly rates available.

The Madison Beach Hotel. 94 West Wharf Rd.; (203) 245-1404; www.madisonbeach hotel.com. Directly on the water, this brand-new-in-spring-2011 full-service hotel offers a rare and wonderful Connecticut lodging treat: a private beach and unbeatable views of the Sound. Each of the 32 roomy nonsmoking luxury units has a balcony. Parents may enjoy the day spa, and guests 12 and older are welcome in the fitness area. Families can rent bikes and kayaks and can dine inside or out on the open-air decks of two restaurants: The Wharf for casual dining and Tides on the Sound for finer fare. Open year-round. Save the airfare; make this your family's summertime—or anytime—resort. $$$$

Scranton Seahorse Inn. 818 Boston Post Rd.; (203) 245-0550; www.scrantonseahorse inn.com. Children of all ages are warmly welcomed at this lovingly restored bed-and-breakfast establishment in the historic downtown village district, close to beach and state park. Chef-owned and operated, so do come for the full multi-course breakfasts. Bring your own portable baby bed for wee ones. $$$$

Hamden

The most conspicuous feature of Hamden (north of New Haven) is in fact one of the most conspicuous features of all of Connecticut. Best viewed from a distance for the fullest impact, the rounded hills of Sleeping Giant State Park look exactly like a figure in repose, its head toward the west, its chest and body stretching eastward. (A great view is possible from I-91.) Hamden is also famous for its notable early citizen, inventor Eli Whitney.

Sleeping Giant State Park (all ages)

200 Mount Carmel Ave. off Route 10; ranger station: (203) 789-7498. For a schedule of guided walks, call (203) 272-7841 or check www.sgpa.org. Open year-round daily, 8 a.m. to sunset. Parking fee ($$) on weekends and holidays (usually April 15 to November 1).

Up close, the park is a great outdoor recreation area. Just off Route 10 a few miles north of Hamden's business center, its 1,500 acres of rolling woodland are traversed by hikers and cross-country skiers on 32 miles of trails. You can fish for trout in Mill River or you can hike the Tower Trail, an easy walk on a wide gravel path to the top of the ridge. At the top is a four-story stone building completed in 1939 as a WPA project. Go inside and walk up its ramps (not wheelchair-accessible) for scenic views of the area. The park also offers a pine-canopied picnic grove with tables, an open-air picnic shelter, drinking water, restrooms, and grills.

A booklet available at the park entrance booth explains the 40-point self-guided nature trail, which may take you about an hour. You may also take a guided trail walk, usually scheduled on Sunday at 1:30 p.m. in the spring and fall.

Eli Whitney Museum (ages 4 and up)

915 Whitney Avenue (Route 10); (203) 777-1833; www.eliwhitney.org. Open year-round; Memorial Day to Labor Day, 11 a.m. to 4 p.m. daily. During remainder of year, open noon to 5 p.m. Wed through Fri, 11 a.m. to 4 p.m. Sat, and noon to 5 p.m. Sun. Closed Thanksgiving, Christmas, and New Year's Day. Fee for workshop projects.

Back down Route 10 toward the center of town is the Eli Whitney Museum. Not at all another historic home, this experimental learning workshop "collects, interprets, and teaches experiments that are at the root of design and invention." It happens to center on the remaining and restored buildings of Whitneyville, a factory complex founded by Eli Whitney in the 19th century, but it is entirely a hands-on place for inquiring young minds. On the site is a covered bridge, a wonderful outdoor Water Learning Lab (open May through Oct, weather permitting), and exhibits and project stations inside the restored armory and gun factory.

The exhibits in the armory focus on the scientific principles Whitney used in his inventions, including interchangeable gun parts and the cotton gin. A fascinating one-third-scale model of the factory village once centered in this neighborhood is also here.

Especially busy in summers and during school vacations, the museum hosts many child-focused special events and activities. Some of these, especially the daylong and weeklong projects, require advance registration. Walk-in visitors, however, can also participate in experiments and building projects. An extensive summer camp program offers excellent workshops and classes by registration only. During the winter holidays, a marvelous toy train exhibition has been an annual event; call to inquire if it will happen again this year.

Brooksvale Park (all ages)

524 Brooksvale Ave.; (203) 287-2669 or Hamden Parks and Recreation: (203) 287-2579; www .brooksvale.org. Open daily dawn to dusk. Free.

Take a left turn off Route 10 going north to reach Brooksvale Park, a 190-acre recreation area that families flock to for hiking, picnicking, softball, basketball, and good old relaxing in the outdoors. A domestic animal barnyard with such creatures as peacocks, a horse, oxen, rabbits, geese, and ducks is there for the delight of young visitors. Weather permitting, you can also enjoy ice-skating, cross-country skiing, and sledding here, and a maple-sugaring shack operates in late winter.

This popular park is a great place to stop if you are using the Farmington Canal Linear Park, which spans nearly 6 miles between Hamden and Cheshire. Brooksvale Park is directly adjacent to the linear walkway and happens to be nearly midway between the southernmost and northernmost end points, so it is a wonderful place for families to lace on their skates or have a rest before or after beginning a trek along the canal.

Farmington Canal Linear Park (all ages)

Park at Todd Street across from Sleeping Giant Golf Course or at Brooksvale Park on Brooksvale Avenue. Open year-round from dawn to dusk. Free.

This recreational greenway lies along the abandoned rail route that previously ran along the old Farmington Canal from Northampton, Massachusetts, to New Haven. Measuring a total of 83 miles, the canal required a 10-foot towpath, a depth of 4 feet, a width of 36 feet, and 25 locks to control the flow of water. All this was constructed using only manpower, horsepower, and simple tools like scoops and dregs. Twenty years later, the canal system was outmoded—replaced by the swifter and less expensive railroad in 1848.

Today the Farmington Canal Heritage Greenway offers a wonderful reuse of land through some of the county's prettiest woodlands, both here and in Cheshire (see details later in this chapter). The two sections provide 11 miles of paved and soft-shoulder pathway suitable for walkers, bikers, bladers, joggers, and cross-country skiers. Picnicking is possible along the route on benches made from stone taken from Sleeping Giant State Park. You can also linger at **Brooksvale Park** in Hamden or **Lock 12 Historical Park** in Cheshire. This is a great place for a simple family outing on a nice day.

Where to Eat

Aunt Chilada's Mexican Eatery. 3931 Whitney Ave.; (203) 230-4640. Near Sleeping Giant and one of the entrances to the Linear Park, this cheerful establishment invites kids to eat free (one child per parent) on Sunday from 4 to 8 p.m. Magician and prizes on that night draw in crowds of families. On Tuesday it's $2 taco night—a good deal for children—or choose salads, enchiladas, fajitas, and more from the regular menu. Open daily for lunch and dinner year-round. $–$$

Wentworth Old-Fashioned Ice Cream. 3697 Whitney Ave. (Route 10); (203) 281-7429. Fifty flavors, 24 toppings, egg creams, root beer floats, fresh-squeezed lemonade, coffees, and baked goods are served up by friendly faces in this cheerfully painted parlor. Open daily year-round, 10 a.m. to 10 p.m. Sun through Thurs and until 11 p.m. on Fri and Sat in summer; in spring, fall, and winter, they close earlier, depending on weather and business. $

Where to Stay

Clarion Hotel & Suites. 2260 Whitney Ave.; (203) 288-3831. 103 units with suites; indoor pool; fitness room; on-site diner and coffee shop. $$$

Days Inn. 3400 Whitney Ave.; (203) 288-2505. 34 basic units with one or two beds. $$

Cheshire

Centered near the junction of Routes 10 and 70 toward the north of the county, Cheshire was founded in 1690 by families who made their living as farmers, a fact that still influences this eclectic suburb. Close to New Haven, Meriden, Hartford, and Waterbury, Cheshire is a bedroom community for those cities, but it is also a region of nurseries, orchards, dairy and tree farms, and even a vineyard.

Bishop Farm (all ages)

500 South Meriden Rd.; (203) 272-8243. Fully open June through Dec, 9:30 a.m. to 5:30 p.m. daily. Extended hours on fall Saturdays. Closed January 1 through late March, then gradual reopening as season progresses. Free.

Right on Route 70, Bishop Farm represents the work of five generations. In business since 1805, Bishop grows and sells six varieties of apples, ten of peaches, four of pears, and five of plums, plus blueberries and raspberries. Some of these crops are pick-your-own; call for information and remember that the level of activity varies with the weather and the season. During most autumns, more than 70,000 pounds of pumpkins leave their fields. Fall is also a perfect time for walking the trails through the orchards, watching the press squeeze fresh cider and juice, and relaxing near the pond while you enjoy an apple cider doughnut.

In the snack bar, you can purchase apple crisp, baked goods, gourmet coffees, and soft drinks, or cruise for take-home treats in the gift shop. A Christmas Shop is open in season, and Christmas trees are for sale from Thanksgiving through December 24.

Barker Character, Comic, and Cartoon Museum (all ages)

1188 Highland Ave.; (203) 699-3822 or (800) 995-5372; www.barkermuseum.com. Wed through Sat noon to 4 p.m. Closed on major holidays. Self-guided group tours for ages 8 and older by appointment only. Wheelchair accessible on first floor only. $; children under 2, free.

Want to just smile and smile and smile some more, Mom and Dad, Granddad and Gran? Herb and Gloria Barker, who own Barker's Animation Art Gallery here, share their private collection of vintage Disney characters, cartoons, comics, advertising characters, TV westerns, and all the toys and gewgaws that have been manufactured in association with them. The oldest such item dates to 1873.

This 5-acre complex also includes the huge Barker Animation Art Gallery, but it is in the museum and on its grounds that visiting baby boomers will begin to grin. Remember Lone Ranger cereal box rings, Dennis the Menace sling shots, Popeye Pez dispensers, and Little Orphan Annie decoder badges? You name it, it's here.

Among the 80,000 objects are toys, trinkets, lunchboxes, and other memorabilia of the art and industry of cartooning. This is the place to learn the complete stories of Betty Boop, Raggedy Ann and Andy, Sylvester, the Simpsons, Star Wars, the Hulk, and hundreds of other characters. Inside its own building, a cartoon theater plays cartoon movies from the 1930s to 1950s on a big screen (summertime only). You'll learn some of the fascinating details of the art and history of many classic films and characters. Make a visit to this happy place and be inspired to take up collecting—or animation—yourself.

Farmington Canal Linear Park (all ages)

Parking areas at Cornwall Avenue and at Lock 12 at 487 North Brooksvale Rd.; Cheshire Parks and Recreation Department: (203) 272-2743. Open daily dawn to dusk. Free.

Cheshire has joined hundreds of other communities across the United States in reclaiming for both recreational and historic preservation purposes the valuable land of abandoned railroad lines and canal routes. Thus far, the town maintains a 2.84-mile section that ends at the Hamden town line. The Hamden section to the south picks up where this one leaves off (see earlier in this chapter), and eventually the trail will reach New Haven Harbor.

This ribbon of land was once on the property of the Farmington Canal, built in 1828 and extending from New Haven Harbor to Northampton, Massachusetts. The longest canal in New England, it was later replaced by a railroad along the same corridor. Now a 12-foot-wide pathway has replaced the railway, and the picturesque canal flows beside it (when rain and snowmelt permit). Visitors can stop at the park-within-the-park at Lock 12 of the canal. Engineered by Henry Farnum under the direction of James Hillhouse and Eli Whitney, the canal was an astonishing feat for that period. The Lock 12 site includes the lockkeeper's house, a small museum, a helicoidal bridge, and a picnic area. On the first Sunday of the month (in warm weather) from noon to 2 p.m., a Cheshire Historical Society guide (203-272-0701) is typically available to explain the history of the site and the technology of the locks. (The wooded pathway is used by joggers, walkers, in-line skaters, and cyclists in the summertime, and whenever there is snow, the section from North Brooksvale Road south to Mount Sanford Road in Hamden is left unplowed for cross-country skiers. Mostly paved with asphalt, the path has a stone dust shoulder perfect for joggers. No skateboarding is permitted.

Where to Eat

Bagelicious Bagels. 945 South Main St.; (203) 250-9339. This casual eatery is open daily year-round for breakfast and lunch, 7 a.m. to 3 p.m. Fresh bagels, nice sandwiches, salads, and freshly made soups. $

Blackie's. 2200 Waterbury Rd.; (203) 699-1819. In business since 1928, this famed roadside stand transports you right back to, well, let's say the summer of '64. Hummel dogs are boiled in cottonseed oil and then grilled; you can top yours with their renowned hot green-pepper relish. Burgers, chips, and shakes as well. Open Sat through Thurs 11 a.m. to 8 p.m. Closed Fri. $

Vespucci's. 150 Main St.; (203) 271-9143. Just past the library, this restaurant offers mostly old-world Italian cuisine and pizza, with a children's menu that also adds American kid-favorites. Tues through Sun for lunch and dinner. $$

Where to Stay

Red Carpet Inn & Suites. 1106 South Main St. (Route 10); (203) 272-3244. 25 basic units with microwave and fridge in clean, nicely landscaped setting. $$

Waterbury

Known for nearly two centuries as one of the nation's most industrial cities, Waterbury is also one of Connecticut's best embodiments of the term "melting pot." For three centuries its citizenry has been among the most diverse of all Connecticut populations, as wave after wave of immigrants has come here in search of the American dream.

Though their toil in the factories and mills of Waterbury was often far from idyllic, many of these workers would say their dream did come true. This success is evident in the thriving, busy neighborhoods, the beautiful early-20th-century architecture, and a rich variety of cultural entities and entertainment and educational opportunities.

Mattatuck Museum (ages 4 and up)

144 West Main St.; (203) 753-0381; www.mattatuckmuseum.org. Open Tues through Sat 10 a.m. to 5 p.m., Sun noon to 5 p.m. Closed on major holidays. $, children under 16 free.

Excellent for families wishing to expand their appreciation for the unique contributions the little state of Connecticut has made to American culture, the exceptional Mattatuck Museum shows off its valuable collection in an innovative facility on the Waterbury green. Designed to enhance the "museum experience" for children, this engaging museum is the only one in Connecticut that has selected the works in its art galleries entirely from American masters who have been associated with Connecticut. This exclusivity allows visitors to celebrate both Connecticut artists and Connecticut themes through the work of John Trumbull, Frederic Church, Maurice Prendergast, Alexander Calder, and others. You will also learn of the amazing number of products that originated in the industries of Waterbury and other towns of western Connecticut. Clocks, watches, cameras, tableware, rubber products, and furniture made the Naugatuck Valley one of the most productive areas of the nation during and after the Industrial Revolution. Visit the Button Museum here, where 10,000 buttons, many made in Waterbury, are on display. Fine arts of the 19th and 20th centuries, decorative arts, and furniture are part of the permanent collection, but the period settings are among the best exhibits in the state for children. In the Brass Roots history exhibit, you can examine a re-created 17th-century house frame, you can wander through a 19th-century boardinghouse re-creation that has the voices of immigrants telling their stories, and you can explore a 19th-century brass mill while listening to the voices of workers describing their workdays in the factory. You'll learn what a colonial house looked like, you'll discover the pastimes of wealthy Victorians, and you'll even find out what role a saloon may have played in the lives of the workers who populated this busy industrial city at the end of the 19th century. One of the best permanent exhibits is the fascinating story of the African-American captive named Fortune, who lived in Waterbury during the 1700s with other free and enslaved Africans.

This complex also includes a museum store, a café, a courtyard garden, a performance center, and studio art classroom. Special festivals, performances, children's workshops, and lectures are listed on the website calendar. Be sure to look at the online exhibits that provide excellent educational materials related to museum themes and collections.

Timexpo: The Timex Museum (ages 6 and up)
175 Union St.; (203) 755-TIME; www.timexpo.com. Open Tues through Sat, 10 a.m. to 5 p.m. Watch and gift store open until 7 p.m. $$.

It's about time (well, someone had to say it): This unusual small museum at the Brass Mill Commons mall has developed into a legitimate educational attraction in recent years, offering a history not just of the Timex watch-making company and its heritage of time-related innovations dating back to 1854 but of the history of timepieces and timekeeping in general and Waterbury-made clocks and watches in particular. Kids can discover the history of the Timex Mickey Mouse watch, and they can learn about the important role of the Waterbury Clock Company in making wristwatches for the US armed forces during World War I. They can walk through a time tunnel, participate in the Tools of Time presentation, and, for an additional charge, can even make and decorate a working clock that can go home with your family. And that's not all: Due to an interest in archaeology and the skills and beliefs of ancient cultures, the family who founded the museum has also included an excellent exhibit about ocean travel and the life and journeys of Norwegian explorer Thor Heyerdahl; kids can learn about his journey across the Pacific in his raft *Kon-Tiki* as well as what he discovered about the mysteries of Easter Island and ancient mound-making cultures. A watch and gift store are here as well, but your family may simply be pleased with its take-home clock or the paper wristwatches your kids may make. Keep an eye on your little ones, though—they may be inspired to build a boat and take to the high seas.

CoCo Key Water Resort (ages 2 and up)
3580 East Main St.; (866) 754-6963; www.cocokeywaterresort.com. Hours vary by day and season; check website calendar. Day and annual passes and room-and-resort package deals are available. Birthday and other private parties can be arranged. Important notes: Purchase of day passes online is the *only* guarantee that you and each member of your party can gain admission to the water resort for a single day's use. Do not come to the water resort to buy a day pass without an online reservation/purchase. Also note that you

must bring your own towels from home. Picnic foods and drinks (with the exception of baby formula in glass-free containers) are not permitted in the water resort. A snack bar and a Pizza Hut Express are here for dining options. The hotel offers additional restaurants outside the resort area. Lifeguards are on duty at all times, but parents are strongly advised to provide USCGA-approved life vests for all non-swimmers or weak swimmers. Some life vests are available for use at the park, at no additional charge, on a first-come/first-served basis. Children who wear diapers must use swim diapers, which are available here for a nominal charge. Users of the body slide must be 42 inches tall; users of the tube slide must be 48 inches tall. $$$; children under 2 are free.

Developed on the theory that just about anything involving water is fun, one of Connecticut's most popular attractions is this 55,000-square-foot indoor water park at Waterbury's Holiday Inn. It's largely designed for package deals, wherein you book a hotel room and stay a while, but families can also come here just for the day to splash and slide and scream—all of which are near-guarantees of family fun, minus the sand and the sunburn. An "adventure river" takes tube riders through Coconut Grove; Parrot's Perch features interactive activities for young swimmers; the Shark Slam, Pelican Plunge, and Barracuda Blast are body-and-raft waterslides that ensure a thrill every moment; and the Coral Reef

Cultural Arts in Waterbury

Waterbury and nearby Thomaston also offer other excellent opportunities for family fun. All of the following groups have reputations for presenting arts performances of the highest caliber for audiences of all ages. Single tickets for productions at all these venues range from $–$$$ for children to $$$–$$$$ for adults. Subscription rates available at most.

- **The Brass City Ballet;** (203) 573-9419. This celebrated company offers performances throughout the year.

- **The Waterbury Symphony Orchestra;** (203) 574-4283. Full season of symphony concerts, special pops concerts, and a Discovery series especially for families. Children's tickets for the last are $5.

- **The Palace Theater;** (203) 755-4700; www.palacetheaterct.org. Spectacularly restored—really, you must see this—theater built in 1921 by Thomas Lamb in Renaissance Revival style. See touring companies of major Broadway shows plus concerts, comedians, and family entertainment and educational productions.

- **The Seven Angels Theatre;** (203) 757-4676; www.sevenangelstheatre.org. Awarded several Connecticut Critic Circle Awards for direction, acting, and design, this Equity venue stages a year-round professional series of Broadway-quality musicals, plays, children's theater, and cabaret concerts.

Cavern is an activity pool with changing displays in its coral-reef backdrop. For quieter, gentler fun, swim the indoor/outdoor passage to the Palm Grotto whirlpool spa, where wearied parents and offspring are likely to wander when the kids are tuckered out. When your skin gets too pruney or your lips too blue, the Key Quest Arcade provides 75 games and activities; admission requires an extra ticket ($$$$), unless it's bundled into a package deal. The whole watery extravaganza is bright, clean, and climate-controlled to a balmy but comfortable 84 degrees. In summer, you'll be glad you came; in winter, you'll be gladder.

Where to Eat

Diorio Restaurant. 231 Bank St.; (203) 754-5111. Excellent Italian fare is served at this elegant Waterbury landmark. High-backed booths and an etched-glass mirror across the back of the bar add to the old-time charm. Lunch and dinner Mon through Fri, dinner only on Sat. $$$

Domenic's and Vinnie's Apizza. 505 Wolcott St.; (203) 753-1989. North of New Haven's Wooster Street, there's no finer place for pizza than this one. More than 30 years' practice makes perfect pies. Open Wed through Sun, late afternoon through evening. $

San Marino Ristorante. 111-23 Thomaston Ave.; (203) 755-1148. More traditional Italian favorites in a friendly ambiance easy for families to enjoy. Chicken, steaks, chops, seafood, home-style pastas, house-made desserts. Seasonal patio; children's menu. Open daily for lunch and dinner. $$

Where to Stay

Courtyard by Marriott. 63 Grand St.; (203) 596-1000. 200 units, including 11 suites, 2 restaurants, fitness room, sauna, Jacuzzi, indoor pool. $$$

Holiday Inn Waterbury. 3580 East Main St.; (866) 754-6963, (203) 706-1000, or (800) HOLIDAY. 284 units; fitness room; racquetball courts; indoor pool for guests of the hotel only, in addition to the on-site water resort; restaurants, lounge; kids eat **free.** $$$–$$$$

Middlebury

Way out in the middle of the hills that begin the rise toward Litchfield County and the Berkshires is the pretty community of Middlebury, about 6 miles southwest of Waterbury. And right in the middle of Middlebury is one of the state's most popular family amusement parks.

Quassy Amusement Park (all ages)

Route 64; (800) FOR-PARK or (203) 758-2913; www.quassy.com. Open nearly daily Memorial Day through Labor Day and on Apr, May, Sept, and Oct weekends. Check the website for current pricing and hours of operation. Parking fee ($$ per vehicle). Regular admission,

$$$ for an all-rides/all-day pass. After 5 p.m. on Fri, all rides are just $.50 each; Saturday night carload specials, 5 to 10 p.m.; after 5 p.m. any day, a rides pass is $$. Season passes available.

Located on the shores of Lake Quassapaug, Quassy Amusement Park is a sort of old-fashioned affair similar to the Savin Rock park old-timers may remember in West Haven. Not quite as sophisticated as other New England amusement centers, such as Connecticut's Lake Compounce or Massachusetts's Six Flags New England, Quassy is newly refurbished and a whole lot of fun for families, especially those with young children.

Twenty-four rides, an 18-hole miniature golf course, a narrow-gauge miniature railway, paddleboats, a petting zoo, a lakeside entertainment theater, and a swimming and picnic area at the lake make this a happy place for a family outing. You can ride the carousel (a fiberglass repro of the original), two roller coasters, bumper cars, and all kinds of carnival-style rides. At the Saturation Station near Lake Quassy's beach, you can find 30 ways to get wet. The Big Flush water coaster offers a wild rubber-raft ride down its 400-foot twisting tube of rushing whitewater. The Frog Hopper is a vertical thrill designed for kids 2 to 13, and the Titanic invites you to climb its catwalk and then slide 45 feet down its deck to a soft landing. In 2011 a 1,200-foot-long coaster is due for unveiling; it works with the natural topography of the park and crosses the railway twice, promising thrills for both sets of riders.

Along with these features are arcades, games of chance and skill, and a special area for children under 5. The park's concessions sell typical American fare, such as hot dogs and barbecued chicken. Check the website for dates of concerts, ethnic festivals, and fireworks.

Where to Eat

Vinnie's Pizza. 504 Middlebury Rd. (Route 64); (203) 758-8846. Tasty pies are the rule here, with the only exceptions being soda, beer, and wine. Clean, comfortable, and great for families leaving Quassy. Open Wed through Sun 3:30 until 8 or 9 p.m. (on Fri and Sat). After pizza, stop next door for ice cream at Johnny's Dairy Bar. $

Derby

One of the oldest towns of the Naugatuck Valley, Derby has been characterized largely by the development of manufacturing since the Industrial Revolution. Luckily, a small portion of its lush woodlands, once the hunting grounds of the Paugussett Indians, has been preserved for future generations. To reach Derby from New Haven, take Route 34 10 miles west.

Osbornedale State Park/Kellogg Environmental Center/ Osborne Homestead Museum (all ages) ⊗ 🕊 🎿 🏛

Park at Chatfield Street; Kellogg Center and Homestead Museum at 500 Hawthorne Ave.; park office: (203) 735-4311; Homestead Museum: (203) 922-7832; Kellogg Center: (203) 734-2513. State park open year-round 8 a.m. to dusk daily. Homestead Museum open late Apr through Dec 15; Thurs and Fri 10 a.m. to 3 p.m.; Sat 10 a.m. to 4 p.m.; Sun noon to 4 p.m. Environmental Center open year-round Tues through Sat 9 a.m. to 4:30 p.m. Free.

This pretty property lies in the hills just north of the confluence of the Housatonic and Naugatuck Rivers. Once the site of a silver mine and a spring water operation, the 400-acre park was for many years a famed breeding farm for prize-winning Osbornedale Holstein cows owned by Frances and Waldo Kellogg.

Activities at the park include hiking and fishing in the summer and skating and cross-country skiing in the winter. However, most activities here center on the Kellogg Environmental Center and the Osborne Homestead Museum, located on property adjacent to the park. The nationally registered 1850 colonial revival homestead is the former residence of Frances Eliza Osborne Kellogg, who willed Osbornedale Park to the state of Connecticut. The house and its formal rose and rock gardens are open for tours (Apr through Dec) that focus on the history of its first occupants and the fine art and antiques collection that they amassed here. Please consider offering a small donation if you take one of their hour-long tours. At other times of the year, the grounds of the mansion can be explored daily from 8:30 a.m. to 3:30 p.m.

The Kellogg Environmental Center is a natural science and environmental education facility that includes a solar exhibit area, a water study area, a nature store, a solar greenhouse, and classrooms and labs. Talks, walks, slide presentations, and activity workshops are offered here on a drop-in and registration basis.

General Information

Central Regional Tourism District: River Valley/Connecticut, One Constitution Plaza, 2nd Floor, Hartford 06103; (860) 787-9640 or (800) 793-4480; www.enjoycentralct.com.

Greater New Haven Convention and Visitors Bureau. 59 Elm St., New Haven 06510; (203) 777-8550 or (800) 332-STAY; www.newhavencvb.org.

Western CT Convention and Visitors Bureau. P.O. Box 968, Litchfield, CT 06759; (860) 567-4506 or (800) 663-1273; www.litchfieldhills.com or www.visitwesternct.com.

Middlesex County

Riverside Villages and Shoreline Towns

I f you were to stand on the bare, windblown summit of Great Hill in the Meshomasic Forest, you would be easily convinced that Middlesex is the most beautiful county in Connecticut. On a clear day, the water of Long Island Sound glimmers far to the south. Four hundred feet below you, Great Hill Pond laps at the forest. And out of the north curls the broad ribbon of the Connecticut River on its way to the sea. The small country charms of the northern counties are eclipsed by this spectacular vista that reveals the best-kept secret of the region. From sea to river to vernal ponds, Middlesex County is a land shaped by water.

Also shaped by the sea and the river have been the lives of the inhabitants of these shores. Many of the attractions families visit in these parts are closely linked to the culture

TopPicks for fun in Middlesex County

1. **Connecticut River Museum**

2. **Essex Steam Train and Riverboat Ride**

3. **Gillette Castle State Park**

4. **RiverQuest Expeditions**

5. **Devil's Hopyard State Park**

6. **Brownstone Exploration and Discovery Park**

7. **Kidcity Children's Museum**

8. **Durham Fair**

9. **Air Line Trail**

MIDDLESEX COUNTY

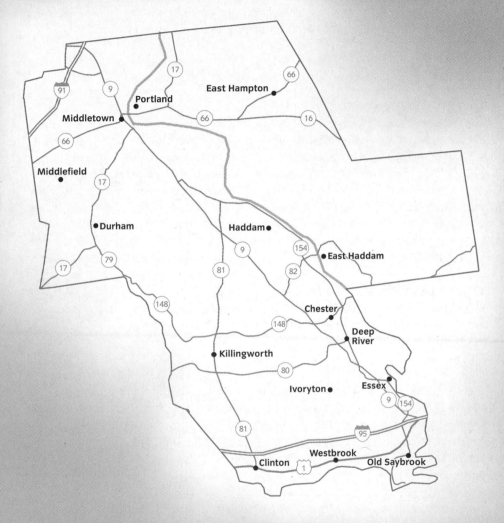

and industries that developed in response to the geography. Come to Middlesex for salt-water taffy, seafood of every sort, steamboat rides, covered bridges, and riverside rendez-vous. Enjoy the bounty of its forests and farms—the water has nourished these well, and the riches they yield are jewels in Connecticut's crown.

Essex

North of Old Saybrook on Route 9 or 154, Essex must fall on nearly everyone's list of favorite Connecticut towns. Honored in the past by the accolade "best small town in America," Essex is most certainly a New England gem, especially at the height of summer and in the stillness of winter. Elegant, gracious, and welcoming to families, Essex is another of Connecticut's windows to the past. Three-masted schooners, whale-oil lamps, scrimshaw, taverns with steaming bowls of chowder, sailors and captains and patient wives waiting at the widow's walks—these are the stuff of Essex's past.

Today, Essex offers a reminder of all that. Its concentration of 18th- and 19th-century homes on narrow village lanes, its wharf and marinas, its shops and restaurants—all are evocative of earlier centuries when Essex was one of the busiest ports on the Connecticut River.

Connecticut River Museum (ages 4 and up)
67 Main St. at Steamboat Dock; (860) 767-8269; www.ctrivermuseum.org. Open year-round, Tues through Sun 10 a.m. to 5 p.m. (4 p.m. in winter). Closed on Mon and major holidays. $–$$, children under 6 free.

This small, top-notch museum in a restored 1878 dock house presents the history of the Connecticut River from its geology to its inhabitants, from its industries to the cultures that developed in the area because of the river. Among the artifacts and displays are scale models of the river's most famous warships, steamboats, and pleasure crafts as well as shipbuilding tools, marine art, and archaeological treasures unearthed in the area. One gallery focuses on the first submarine, the *American Turtle,* represented by a working replica. Another tells the tale of the Evolution of the River, with a focus on the economic and environmental importance of the waterway. A children's discovery trail makes this exhibit especially accessible to the youngest visitors.

In temperate weather, you may enjoy the long tidal river itself aboard the schooner *Mary E.* The afternoon excursion departs daily at 1:30 p.m. and 3:30 p.m. for a 1.5-hour cruise ($$$$ adults/$$$ children under 12) on the Connecticut, or bring a picnic supper aboard for a 2-hour sunset cruise ($$$$ all ages), daily at 6 p.m. All cruises are subject to weather, but if you've made a reservation (highly recommended), they'll call you with cancellation information; call or e-mail crm@ctrivermuseum.org with your name, cruise date, and phone number.

On summer weekends, hands-on activities are often planned especially for families. These workshops may have an extra fee. At winter holiday time, an annual exhibit incorporating magnificent model train layouts crafted by Connecticut artist Steven Cryan opens on Thanksgiving weekend.

Ivoryton

Officially a section of the town of Essex, this little village just a few miles east of Route 153 gained its name from its production of ivory products, in particular piano keys, in the 19th century. First settled in the mid-17th century, Ivoryton maintains an interest in preserving the traditions of the early colonials that comes as no surprise in its museum celebrating one of the colonies' oldest traditions. The **Museum of Fife and Drum** (62 North Main St.; 860-399-6519 or 860-767-2237; donation; children under 13 free) is dedicated to the history and development of parade music, with a special emphasis on the traditional fife and drum corps that are called ancients. See the uniforms, parade and performance gear, musical instruments, music, and photographs of corps from all over the nation and Europe. Learn about the history of fifing and drumming from the Middle Ages through modern times. Usually open June 30 through Labor Day weekend, on weekends from 1 to 5 p.m.(except for the third weekend of July and the fourth weekend in Aug), the museum offers evening performances featuring two corps per night on selected Tuesdays at 7:30 p.m. in July and August.

Ivoryton also boasts a regional reputation in the arts because of its venerable theater at the village center. The **Ivoryton Playhouse** (103 Main St.; 860-767-8348; www.ivorytonplayhouse.org), which since 1930 has been home to some of Connecticut's best repertory and summer-stock theater companies. In addition to its year-round professional slate of comedies, dramas, and musicals, for adult and general audiences, it also hosts a terrific summer series of productions perfect for children 2 to 10. Among these are fairy tales, magic shows, and puppet theaters. Staged in July and August, the performances are at 11 a.m. (and sometimes also at 1 p.m.); all seats are $12.

Essex Steam Train and Riverboat Ride (all ages)

Valley Railroad, 1 Railroad Ave., off Route 154; (860) 767-0103 or (800) 377-3987; www.essexsteamtrain.com. Open early May through Dec, plus special combination rides throughout the year (riverboat combos only in warm season). Check the website for special events and schedule. $$–$$$$, parlor car extra, children under 3 free.

One of Connecticut's most popular family tourist activities is offered by the Valley Railroad Company. On a typical daily run, vintage steam locomotives and railcars take passengers on a 12-mile, one-hour, round-trip ride from Essex to Deep River. At Deep River Landing, in warm weather, you can opt to board the triple-decker riverboat for a one-hour cruise upriver, past Gillette Castle to the East Haddam Bridge and then back downriver. The total trip takes about two and a half hours if you take the boat ride. Each segment of the ride

The Parade of **Lighted Ships**

Early in December (or, rarely, in late November) the Connecticut River Museum sponsors a charming festivity that draws many visitors eager to experience the magic of Essex in winter. Called **Trees in the Rigging,** this free festival features a lantern-lit community caroling march, led by the Cappella Cantorum and the Ancient Mariners' Fife and Drum Corps, and a parade of lighted ships on the river. Beginning at the Essex Town Hall at 4 p.m. on Sunday of the selected weekend, carolers make their way down West Avenue and Main Street to the waterfront park at historic Steamboat Dock to see the colorfully lit garlands and nautical flags on scores of participating boats. Santa himself arrives on the dock by tugboat, and children can greet him and warm themselves with hot mulled cider at the museum.

includes an entertaining narration about the railroad and the steamship lines. The sights and sounds of the river and countryside—and the trains—are wonderful. Bells, whistles, and the clackety-clack of the railroad track are accompanied by shouts of blue-capped conductors calling, "All aboard!"

At the train yard you can visit the station (which offers exhibits and children's activities), the car barns, and the gift shop. A stationary grill car called the Trackside Cafe ($) offers hot dogs, deli sandwiches, salads, and soft drinks. For a special dining experience, book tickets for the Essex Clipper Dinner Train. Feast aboard a 1920s dining car, with a two-hour excursion through the river valley (May through Oct). Thomas the Tank Engine is an occasional visitor here. Other special events include an Easter Eggspress, a Trick or Treat Special, a Santa Special, and a North Pole Express (see website for dates).

Where to Eat

Crow's Nest Gourmet Deli. 35 Pratt St. in Brewers Dauntless Shipyard; (860) 767-3288. This year-round dine-in, take-out, or out-on-the-deck eatery is the only restaurant overlooking the water in Essex. Breakfast and lunch daily 7 a.m. to 4 p.m. mid-June to Labor Day (3 p.m. closing in spring and fall); closed on Tues from Columbus Day to Memorial Day. Omelets, pancakes, sandwiches, lobster, chicken, ribs, chowders, and fresh-made bakery treats. $–$$

Griswold Inn. 36 Main St.; (860) 767-1776. Stop here for a meat pie in winter near one of the fireplaces or in summer for fresh seafood. See the moving mural of the steamboat on the Connecticut River. "Young Sailors" menu, plus Sunday Hunt Breakfast (10 a.m. to 2 p.m.) is half-price for kids 7 to 12 and free for kids 6 and under. $$–$$$

Oliver's Tavern. 124 Westbrook Rd.; (860) 767-2633. Good American fare (steaks, seafood, specialty sandwiches, chowder) in a warm, friendly setting. Lunch and dinner daily from 11 a.m. Closed Thanksgiving and the evening of December 24. $–$$

Where to Stay

Griswold Inn (same address and phone; www.griswoldinn.com) is also a very fine hostelry, offering 30 rooms and suites and even a charming guest cottage. Beautiful maritime and river artworks, fireplaces, private baths, and continental breakfast served in the library for all guests make this a cozy place for families. $$$–$$$$

Deep River/Chester

These two small towns are two of the most charming country villages in the state, although neither is exactly the family entertainment center of its county. Still, there are some excellent opportunities in both places for families.

Chester is quiet, quaint, and tiny. Located on Route 148 and surrounded by the Cockaponset State Forest, Chester was founded in 1692 as Pattaquonk Quarter, the fourth parish of Saybrook. An independent town by 1836, it seems content to remain in that century. Its winding lanes lined with historic buildings are unblemished by purveyors of fast food, slushy red soft drinks, or other atrocities of modern civilization. In Chester you will find lovely shops, great restaurants, and serenity.

Chester's **Norma Terris Theater** (www.goodspeed.org) offers the premieres of new musicals on its stage, and its famed **Connecticut River Artisan's Cooperative** (5 West Main St.; 860-526-5575) showcases the creative output of more than 20 visual artists who offer their work for sale here. Chester's downtown is, of course, primarily a retail center, but it is, in my opinion, one of the most charming and idiosyncratic in the state. So if you would like your children to see a thriving New England village that doesn't include glaring evidence of the corporatization of retail America, come here and enjoy the adventurous and serendipitous nature of independent emporiums. You might venture here also for annual events such as the Chester Fair (late August), the Lobster Festival (September), the Winter Carnival (mid-February), or the Holiday Stroll (mid-December).

When I first heard the name Deep River as a child on a family day trip to Gillette Castle, I thought Tom Sawyer must live in this town. Somewhere he sits dangling his feet in the water, chewing on a piece of straw and watching the steamboats pass by.

Forty years later, Deep River is not much different than it was the first time I saw it. Centered on the main thoroughfare of Route 154, it is a quiet town that still has the look and feel of a town of the 1950s. Famed in the more-distant past as a steamboat port accepting cargo and passengers to its docks, Deep River was once at the heart of the ivory trade that gave neighboring Ivoryton its name and supported the piano factories that you can still see in Deep River along Route 154. In the late 1800s, three-quarters of the ivory taken from Zanzibar was shipped to Deep River. Today piano keys are long forgotten as the principal product of the area, and the tourists arrive mostly just to savor its quaint aspects.

Chester Museum at the Mill

9 West Main St. (Route 154), Chester; (860) 526-5781; www.chesterhistoricalsociety.org. $; children under 12 free.

For charming lessons on the cultural history of a New England village, come to this very pretty place for a view of community life. Two floors of exhibits open a window on the area's natural resources and the ingenuity and resourcefulness of Chester's farmers, millers, craftspersons, and artists throughout the centuries. Open weekends only, June through Oct, Sat 10 a.m. to 4 p.m.; Sun 11 a.m. to 2 p.m.

Canfield-Meadow Woods Nature Preserve (all ages)

Access from the east side of 377 South Main Street, Deep River, just south of the Sunoco station. Open daily year-round, dawn to dusk. Free.

Three hundred acres of woodlands, wetlands, ridges, and valleys are the habitats and terrains in this preserve. Open for passive recreation such as hiking and wildlife watching, the preserve has an easy 3.5-mile trail; maps are usually at the trailhead.

Where to Eat

Main Street Sweet Shoppe. 162 Main St., Deep River; (860) 526-9012. Get in line for bliss: excellent chocolates, super-rich ice cream, hot cocoa, espresso, in a delightful pink-and-chocolate setting. Open Wed through Sun noon to 6 p.m. in late fall and winter; longer hours in summer and warmer months. $

Deep River Muster of **Ancient Fife and Drum Corps**

Held every third Saturday in July, this must-see family-style event may be the only one of its kind—or at least the largest. A gathering of up to 70 separate corps from all over the nation and overseas, this famed muster includes a colorful parade up the main street (Route 154) of Deep River. Chairs and blankets line the parade route long before you hear the first salute. Authentic uniforms, unforgettable music, and even bagpipers, pirates, Uncle Sam, and Dan'l Boone are part of the show.

After the parade, which can easily last two hours, walk to Devitt Field (at the bottom of the parade route), where the corps meet for food, drink, and special performances. Buy fifes, drums, music, tricornered hats, and related items in the tents lining the perimeter of the field. The parade and admission to the field are free, but parking will cost you ($) in one of the many "lots" set up on the front lawns of the townsfolk. For information, call (860) 767-2237.

Simon's Marketplace. 17 Main St., Chester; (860) 526-8984. Very popular sandwiches, savory and sweet crepes, and exceptional scones are the mainstay at this eat-in market/general store. Open daily year-round from 8 a.m. $

The Wheatmarket. 4 Water St., Chester; (860) 526-9347. These friendly folks serve delicious, out-of-the-ordinary sandwiches, soups, cheeses, and breads. Vegetarians will find food they can eat here, thank goodness. Open Mon through Fri 9 a.m. to 6 p.m. and until 4 p.m. on Sat. $

The Whistle Stop Cafe. 108 Main St., Deep River; (860) 526-4122. You can't get any more small-town charming than this. Owner Hedy Watrous, continuing the business her grandfather started in 1928, offers children's specials at every meal. Breakfast is served all day, beginning at 7:30 a.m. Lunch begins at 11 a.m. and ends at 2 p.m., when the cafe closes. Eat inside or outside. Open Thurs through Mon. $–$$

East Haddam/Haddam

Though it is famed as the home of Connecticut's castle and its riverside opera house, the town of East Haddam is also a rural enclave that few visitors explore past the sight and sound of the river. In actual fact, the town spreads far eastward for several miles where Middlesex County pushes itself squarely into the western boundaries of New London County. Adventurous families who love the woodlands as much as the water should spend an extra day near East Haddam just to be sure they've seen all its wonders. Take Route 9 or Route 154 to Route 82 to reach its center.

In the town of Haddam, the Connecticut River beckons to visitors, this time from the west bank. In this town, too, the boundaries far exceed the visitor's concept of the few structures that hug close to the river. The town actually goes westward all the way to the Durham town line, but it is near the water that the action for families centers. Luckily a historic and remarkable bridge links both towns, and if you have the patience for the openings and closings of the swing bridge (which most kids do), you'll have fun making the crossings from place to place.

Gillette Castle State Park (ages 3 and up)

67 River Rd., East Haddam; (860) 526-2336. Park open daily year-round, 8 a.m. to sunset; no entrance fee is charged. Castle open 10 a.m. to 5 p.m. daily from the Saturday of Memorial Day weekend through Columbus Day. Note: Last castle tour tickets are sold at 4:30 p.m. $, children 5 and under free.

Few Connecticut guidebooks can resist mentioning the medieval-looking wonder perched on a bluff called the Seventh Sister, high above the eastern bank of the Connecticut River. Recent restorations to this splendid fieldstone fortress have ensured that many more generations of visitors can enjoy this enchanting structure, toured by 100,000 visitors each year.

Completed in 1919 as the retirement home of the eccentric actor William Gillette (famed for his stage portrayal of Sherlock Holmes in the early part of the 20th century), the house was built to his exact specifications. The turrets, terraces, archways, and fountains found outside are awesome enough, but the interior will make you gape.

The 24 rooms contain gorgeous stonework, extraordinary hand-carved woodwork, and many of Gillette's original furnishings and possessions. A separate visitor center includes a gift shop, a picnic deck with tables, and restrooms. (A food concession operates in the summer season in another building.) The visitor center houses exhibits on Gillette's life and career, along with a portion of the castle's incredible collection of Holmes-related memorabilia. Here, too, is one of the restored electric engines from Gillette's train that used to loop the property; it is on display along with a passenger car from the original assortment of cars that Gillette used to take such guests as Albert Einstein and Calvin Coolidge on tours around his estate.

Only on the weekends (10 a.m. to 4 p.m.) between Thanksgiving and the week before Christmas, the castle has an annual Victorian Holiday Celebration that features special decorations, musical performances, and other entertainments. Have a cup of hot cider at the bonfire outside (no charge) or come inside for a tour ($). Call ahead to be sure this tradition has continued.

The castle grounds are part of the nearly 200-acre Gillette Castle State Park, with breathtaking views of the river and valley. You will see some of the same views painted by Connecticut artists in earlier times; look for the Viewpoints signage of the Connecticut Art Trail. Three miles of trails allow you to explore safely; many spots are perfect for picnicking, napping, or playing knights and ladies.

Nathan Hale **Schoolhouse**

So-called because the Connecticut patriot taught here, at the age of 18, for six months in 1773 and 1774, this one-room building is at the rear of St. Stephen's Church property on Route 149, just north of the opera house. Exhibits under development here tell the story of our state hero. A Yale graduate, he taught in New London the year after he taught here and later joined George Washington's revolutionary forces in New York City, where he was hung by the British for treason against the Crown. Maintained by the Connecticut Sons of the American Revolution, this small museum is open on weekends and holidays from noon to 4 p.m. in the summertime only. The exact address is 29 Main St., East Haddam; for more information, call (860) 873-3399. $.

Devil's Hopyard State Park (all ages)

Route 82 to Mount Parnassus Road to 366 Hopyard Rd., East Haddam; (860) 873-8566. Open year-round from 8 a.m. to sunset. Free entrance to park; camping fee, $. Picnic shelter, tables, pedestal cooking grills, pit toilets. Camping season, April 20 through September 30; call ahead to be sure the campsites are open.

Beautiful in all seasons, the moderate trails through the heavily wooded terrain of this lovely park are wonderful for families. Views of the countryside are especially breathtaking in the fall, but the 60-foot cascades of Chapman Falls are most impressive in the spring. Look for the potholes in the rocks at the base of the falls. Legend says that these formations were made by the hot hooves of the devil as he hopped from ledge to ledge so as not to get wet.

Leave your own footprints on the paths that lead to the many scenic overlooks of the pretty Eightmile River, which threads itself through the woods and farms in the area. Stay overnight (if you dare) in one of the 21 wooded campsites with drinking water and outhouses. You can call for reservations or try your luck at the first-come, first-served game. You can also fish from the streams and picnic wherever you like. A large picnic area with tables is provided near the parking area, but in our opinion the best spots for picnicking are actually at the trailside overlooks. Choose the one that pleases you most. Leave well before dark if you believe the stories that this wood is haunted by the devil and the ancient hags of Haddam.

Goodspeed Opera House (ages 6 and up)

Goodspeed Landing on Route 82, East Haddam; box office: (860) 873-8668; tours: (860) 873-8664; www.goodspeed.org.

Perched on the eastern riverbank, the state's best-known opera house, a fully restored Second Empire confection built in 1876, presents a three-show season of hit musical productions from April through December. Mostly revivals of Broadway favorites from the 1920s through the 1960s, the shows in this intimate theater are great family entertainment. Except for the very youngest children, who might have trouble staying settled through these full-length performances, bring the whole family if you can afford the moderately priced (compared to Broadway) tickets.

Real theater buffs may enjoy the 30-minute tours of the opera house offered in season on Saturday and Monday; call for specific times and reservations ($). You'll see all the inner workings, and you'll hear great stories of the Goodspeed's illustrious past.

Thankful Arnold House (ages 8 and up)

Hayden Hill Road, Haddam; (860) 345-2400; www.haddamhistory.org. Open year-round, 9 a.m. to 3 p.m. Wed, 2 to 8 p.m. Thurs, and noon to 3 p.m. Fri; plus 1 to 4 p.m. Sun from Memorial Day through Columbus Day. Also open by appointment. $.

If you are spending a weekend in the area, you might enjoy a tour of this historic house museum, built between 1794 and 1810. It is one of the 13 historic sites on the Connecticut Women's Heritage Trail. Visitors can hear the story of the Widow Arnold, her daughter, and her granddaughter, all of whom were heads of the household for three successive

Clip-Clop through **the Countryside**

No outing in Connecticut may be more enchanting than a horse-drawn hay
or sleigh ride, and **Allegra Farm,** deep in the woodlands of East Haddam, has
a collection of 60-plus vehicles that can help you make a day-in-the-country
dream come true. Home to the largest authentic livery stable in the state, the
farm is located on beautiful Lake Hayward on the border of Colchester. The
forest paths, agricultural fields, and dirt lanes in this part of the planet make
a perfect setting for a journey down a time-warped road. John Allegra or one
of his staff will be more than happy to hitch a team to a wagon, a surrey, a
carriage, a caleche, a sleigh, or even—gulp—a hearse and take you for a ride.
Allegra Farm is also home to the **Horse-Drawn Carriage and Sleigh Museum
of New England,** which means you can visit here if you just want to see the
vehicles (and the horses). You must call ahead for an appointment, but you'd
be welcome nearly any day of the year. You can even arrange for a lesson in
carriage driving. Sleigh and carriage rides can be pricey for many budgets,
but some vehicles here carry multiple revelers, so that can bring the price-
per-person down to a reasonable splurge. Leaves will crunch or snow will fly,
and you'll be bundled safely under a toasty lap rug, out in the arms of Nature.
Could be worth every penny for an unforgettable birthday or holiday treat.
The farm/museum is located at 69 Town Rd. in East Haddam (but punch in
Colchester if you're trying to use GPS to get here). Call (860) 680-5149 or
(860) 537-8861 for reservations. For more information, check the website at
www.allegrafarm.com.

generations. Local history programs, walking tours, and hands-on workshops are often on
the calendar of events; children are given special attention on house tours. A lovely garden is out back, and from time to time a special event (such as a fall family apple festival) is
hosted on the grounds.

Haddam Meadows State Park (all ages)

**Route 154, about a mile south of Route 82 in Haddam; (860) 663-2030; www.ct.gov/dep.
Open year-round from 8 a.m. to sunset. No parking fee or individual day-use fee. Pets must
be leashed.**

Used for agricultural fields in colonial days, the Haddam Meadows floodplain also served
as a common pastureland for the livestock of Haddam's first European settlers. Now 175
acres of parkland have replaced those fields of hay and grain. Very peaceful and low-key
in nearly every season, this park offers a sweeping view of the river from its broad lawns
and picnic areas. Fishing is allowed, and you can launch a boat right into the river from
the state boat-launch ramp. Picnics and field games are among the prime activities (bring

a Frisbee, for sure), and on rare occasions a festival or other special event occurs, but life is typically quiet in these parts, and you can happily eat, read, nap, and watch the Little League kids take a swing at the ball. You might wade a bit at the boat launch, but swimming is prohibited, and the park offers no beach area or lifeguards.

RiverQuest **Expeditions** (all ages)

Eagle Landing State Park, directly off Bridge Road (Route 82), Haddam; (860) 662-0577; www.ctriverexpeditions.org. $$$$; on warm-weather cruises, children under 2 are free.

If anyone in your party is in the mood for a little "expotition," check out the excursions on *RiverQuest,* leaving from the west bank of the Connecticut River, just south of the swing bridge. The narrated cruises on the twin-hulled, 54-foot *RiverQuest* reveal the many reasons the Connecticut is a designated National Heritage River, also declared "one of the last great places" by the Nature Conservancy. Learn about its abundant wildlife and the natural and cultural history of the river itself. These 90-minute warm-weather adventures are offered once daily at 1:30 p.m., Wed through Mon. Reservations are not required but are strongly encouraged. Arrive at the dock 10 minutes in advance of the stated departure time, and be sure to check the website for weather-related changes. In the cooler months of spring and early November, the cruise schedule is more limited; check the website or call ahead to be sure of sailing times. In February and March, the fully enclosed cabin is heated for naturalist-guided eagle cruises to see resident eagles as well as seasonal visitors. (These cold-weather cruises are strictly limited to folks aged 9 and older.) More than 100 bald eagles now make their winter home on Connecticut's largest waterways, including this river, so although sightings are not guaranteed, they are not at all unusual. Many

The Greatest **of Ease**

If you're looking for a summer adventure that may offer something completely different (and wonderful) for your child's athletic and personal development, you might consider **Om-FLY,** a marvelous pro-joy, anti-fear circus arts camp in East Haddam. Each August, on the Sanctuary at Shepardfields (a 40-acre nonprofit land preserve and environmental education center at 59 Bogel Rd.), the Om-FLY eco-circus day program ($$$$) is a holistic, integrative approach to fitness and strength and the importance of play. Taught by movement artist and Circus Minimus ringmaster Jen Taylor, it includes circus yoga, trapeze skills, acrobatics, and other imaginative exercises and games. Each of the two two-week sessions (8:30 a.m. to 3 p.m. each day) culminates in a remarkable life-affirming student performance called Cirque de Sphere. It is open to children and young adults (ages 7 to 14) of all abilities. For more information, call program director Jen Taylor at (860) 575-1166 or visit www .om-fly.org. To learn more about circus yoga, visit www.circusyoga.com.

Ferry to **the Castle**

If you're headed to or from Gillette Castle or you need to cross the river for any other reason, catch a ride on the **Chester–Hadlyme ferry** (860-443-3856), which docks at the end of Route 148. The ride takes about four minutes. The flatboat *Selden III* begins each day's labor on the east bank at the village of Hadlyme at 7 a.m. Mon through Fri and at 10:30 a.m. on weekends; the last ride of the day leaves from the west side at Chester at 6:45 p.m. on weekdays and at 5 p.m. on weekends. Running daily (with the exception of Thanksgiving Day) from April 1 through November, the Chester–Hadlyme ferry service is one of the oldest in the country; it's been in continuous operation since 1769. $.

other birds inhabit this beautiful stretch of river as well, and the scenery along the banks makes for fine viewing, too. Bring snacks, a thermos of hot cocoa, and binoculars and cameras.

Some spring cruises focus on the nesting and migrations of ospreys; in autumn, everyone is looking at the foliage. The warm-weather schedule also includes two-hour sunset cruises, but these dinnertime trips are designed for adults (who may bring alcoholic beverages in their picnics) and are strictly limited to passengers over the age of 12.

In September, awesome 3.5-hour tree swallow cruises are offered on selected evenings, but they too are limited to passengers aged 8 and older.

Where to Eat

The Blue Oar River Bank Grille. 16 Snyder Rd., off Route 154 in the Midway Marina, Haddam; (203) 345-2994. For a casual meal outdoors on picnic tables or on the veranda inside, come to this sailor's secret, 1 mile north of the swing bridge. The views are beautiful, the chowder is great, and sandwich specials or grilled dinners will please both yachters and landlubbers. Open mid-May through mid-Oct, for lunch and dinner, Tues through Sun, 11:30 a.m. to 9 p.m. $–$$

The Cooking Company. 1610 Saybrook Rd. at Swing Bridge Market Place, Haddam, near junction of Routes 82 and 154; (860) 345-8008. Open from 10 a.m. daily except Sun, this gourmet deli/bakery/coffeehouse has excellent hot or cold sandwiches, wraps, salads, soups, and desserts. Eat in or take out. $

Gelston House. 8 Main St., East Haddam; (860) 873-1411. For a river view that's pretty much incomparable, come to this lovely historic setting. For special occasions, dine inside, which is fancier. In the warmer months, dine outside on the much more casual patio ($$). Main dining room open year-round; lunch, Tues through Fri; dinner, Tues through Sun; brunch on weekends, 11 a.m. to 3 p.m. Pre-theater prix-fixe dinner in main dining room. $$$–$$$$

Hadlyme Country Store. Near the corner of Routes 82 and 148 (called Ferry Road after the intersection) on the eastern bank in Hadlyme; (860) 526-3188. Open daily 6:30 a.m. to 6 p.m. (4 p.m. on Sun), this little store is run by cheerful folks who sell great picnic/hiking food and supplies—sandwiches, salads, baked goods, ice cream, even charcoal and marshmallows. $

La Vita Gustosa. 9 Main St., East Haddam; (860) 873-8999. Across from the opera house, this cheery family-owned place offers reasonably priced, home-cooked Italian favorites, plus pizzas, paninis, and a "bambini" menu for the kids. Lunch and dinner year-round from 11:30 a.m., Tues through Sun. $$

Me and McGee. 40 Saybrook Rd. (Route 154), on the western bank, in Higganum; (860) 345-3777. The great food and good company at this friendly eatery keep the locals coming back. Excellent breakfast omelets, home-style soups, fish and chips, and Mom-made bakery treats and breads. Open 6 a.m. to 2 p.m. every day except Sun. $–$$

Where to Stay

The Bishopsgate Inn. Just steps from Goodspeed Landing on Route 82; (860) 873-1411. Children are more than welcome in this polished, six-guest-room inn. A lovely suite with a sauna will meet all your family's needs. Fireplace rooms, private baths, cozy common areas, and generous breakfasts. Bring your own portable crib. $$$–$$$$

Sunrise Resort. Route 151; (860) 873-8681. Open May through October, this family resort/campground on the Salmon River has 200 guest units, 30 campsites, an outdoor pool, a restaurant, playground, tennis, volleyball, shuffleboard and bocce courts, paddleboats, rowboats, and canoes. Nightly and weekly rates. $$–$$$

Wolf's Den Family Campground. 256 Town St. (Route 82); (860) 873-9681. Tent and RV sites for 209 campers. Swimming, fishing, and hiking nearby. Tennis on the property. Game room, laundry facilities, toilets, showers. Nightly and weekly rates. $$

Portland/East Hampton

Nestled against the Connecticut River on one side and the Meshomasic State Forest on the other, the town of Portland has been famed in state history for its incredible brownstone quarries. In operation from the 1600s right up to the present day and now designated as National Historic Landmarks, these quarries are undergoing a tremendous evolution in the 21st century. In two of the quarries, all Connecticut families will benefit from the efforts of three enterprising brothers who have the support of the Portland community in their spectacular new recreation site.

Not far to the east, near the shores of Lake Pocotopaug, is the center of East Hampton, the town in which I took my first childhood family vacation, saw my first snapping turtle, and learned both how to canoe and how to capsize a canoe. Whoops! Outdoor fun like that is still yours for the asking in these parts. The town of East Hampton also includes the villages of Cobalt, Haddam Neck, and Middle Haddam, which make the historic East Hampton town center near the lake seem like a metropolis. East Hampton was once famed in Connecticut's history as "Belltown, USA." From 1808 onward through a great deal of the 20th century, a whole lot of bells were manufactured here. Only one of at least 30 bell-making firms remains today (and its bells are made overseas). Just yards from the lakefront is another historic industry: The famed T. N. Dickinson witch hazel products are created here at American Distilling and Manufacturing, which processes raw witch hazel and extracts, purifies, distills, and bottles the therapeutic skin-care and pharmaceutical properties of this native Connecticut plant. Sadly, no public tours are offered at either the distillery or the empty bell factories, but the quarries, lake, and trails of this quintessentially New England area should ring the bells of your whole clan.

Brownstone Exploration and Discovery Park (all ages)

161 Brownstone Ave.; (860) 342-0668; www.brownstonepark.com. Seasonal limitations on some activities; canoeing, kayaking, and diving are permitted year-round. Hours vary by season; check the website for the full schedule. General day passes and Adventure Sports Passes, $$$; season passes for individuals and families, $$$$. Children under 3 free. Portland residents pay half the daily rate; proof of residency required. All park visitors must register at the main gate, complete a liability waiver (which is kept on file for the season), and pay admission. Scuba divers not accompanied by an instructor must present a valid certification card from a recognized agency to dive. Solo diving is not permitted. Zip line users must weigh more than 70 pounds and less than 250 pounds. Cliff jumpers must be over 18. All water-based activities require use of personal flotation vests, which are provided. Scuba equipment rentals available with advance notice. Canoe, kayak, water bikes, and water ball rentals available.

Simply unbelievably wonderful, this extraordinary outdoor recreation park on the eastern bank of the Connecticut River may well become the state's most popular attraction as it evolves throughout its five-year development plan. In two of the nation's few brownstone quarries, three Connecticut brothers have devised more fun for more people in less time than even seems possible. In operation from 1660, the sandstone quarries—now designated National Historic Landmarks—continue to yield the softly colored building material known the world over as brownstone. Quarrying operations are active, however, at just one of the three "holes" in Portland. In the other two, a fabulous recreation facility has taken shape in just a few years.

Remarkably well tucked into an industrial zone just north of the Portland Bridge, the park is among the most surprisingly beautiful sites in the state, both within the quarries themselves and in the many nearby acres of parkland above the river. The latter, owned by the Town of Portland, offers expansive vistas of the river and is open to hikers and bikers, dawn to dusk, year-round. The quarries are, quite simply, stunning. They have been one of the nation's premier sources of brownstone, and during the mid- to late 19th century, 1,500 quarriers, 500 oxen, and at least one locomotive cut, dragged, and toted the stone to quarry schooners that carried it to New York City and elsewhere for use in residences, public buildings, and monuments. The floods and hurricanes of the 1930s put an end to all that. One day in that era, the Connecticut River overflowed its banks, and two of the quarries filled to the brim with water in 14 minutes. Fed by natural springs that opened under the weight of all that water, the quarries—60 to 90 feet deep from the water line down and with sheared cliffs up to 100 feet above the water line—remain flooded to this day, with nearly pure, crystal-clear freshwater. Due to the efforts, imagination, and ingenuity of the Hayes brothers and their many supporters, you can now swim, slide from the Aqua Tower, scuba dive, kayak, canoe, and ride a water bike in the quarry, with those magnificent cliffs rising all around you. You can rock climb and rappel. You can zip line, cliff jump, or tower climb. Arrange for lessons in just about any of the above, or just picnic, wander, and soak up the excitement. Have a birthday party, boost your self-esteem, or master a challenging obstacle course. You can even rent a private floating party barge complete with a canopy and picnic table and a canoe to get your guests out to it!

In future years, you may visit museum exhibits and explore the learning center to discover the site's geological and natural history. The staff is highly trained and certified in safety, first aid, and CPR. Lifeguards are everywhere; personal flotation devices are required and provided for water sports; helmets and harnesses are a must for rock climbing. Safety rules are clear and strictly enforced. Hidden under the water are carefully mapped scuba stations, complete with underwater training platforms at varying depths; divers can learn and practice scuba skills with the park's certified instructors. A gift shop provides souvenirs and water activity gear; a concession provides light meals, snacks, and beverages. Restrooms and changing rooms are newly expanded. You've got to see this to believe it. It's gorgeous; it's historic; it's fun.

Happiest Paddler (ages 4 and up)

70 North Main St., East Hampton; (860) 267-1764. Boat rentals are primarily Apr through Oct. West Shore Marine is open year-round but closes for seasonal transitions. Call ahead to be sure they are in operation. Reservations are recommended during the summer. $$–$$$$.

At West Shore Marine, you will find the friendly folks at Happiest Paddler, who rent canoes, kayaks, and other vessels you might take out on the peaceful waters of pretty

The Bridge of **Middlesex County**

Over on Route 16, almost at the New London County line between East Hampton and Colchester, is the **Comstock Covered Bridge,** believed to be the oldest of the three remaining authentic covered bridges in Connecticut. Constructed in William Howe's covered-timber truss style, patented in 1840 and used often for highway and railroad bridges, this bridge served travelers on the main road from Colchester to Middletown. It's open only to pedestrians now. Built in 1873 and placed on the National Register of Historic Places in 1976, the two-span bridge has an overall length of 110 feet, which includes a rare 30-foot pony truss span on its east side. Artists, photographers, and those who would like to fish in the Salmon River frequent the area, as do visitors who just want to enjoy a quiet, cool refuge on a sunny day. If you happen to be nearby, stop and have a walk across this pretty remnant of the past.

Lake Pocotopaug. Call ahead for the current scoop on their vessels, rates, and regulations. Ask too about the sunset cruises they offer in conjunction with the folks at Angelico's Lake House Restaurant, just up the road. In past seasons, they have offered one-hour cruises at 5:30 and 6:30 p.m. on Wednesday and Sunday, weather permitting. Hors d'oeuvres are served aboard the boat, then you debark for dinner at the Lake House. Not a bad outing for the kids or for Mom and Dad. Be sure to call for both reservations (required) and for this year's rates.

Sears Park (all ages)

62 North Main St., on Lake Pocotopaug; East Hampton Parks and Recreation Department: 20 East High St.; (860) 267-6020. Open year-round, dawn to dusk. May 15 to Labor Day, open only to residents; early Sept through May 14, free to nonresidents. Alcoholic beverages are prohibited.

This town-owned park offers a sandy swimming area, a boat launch, a pavilion, and other recreational facilities only to residents during the summer months (May 15 to Labor Day), but nonresidents are welcome to swim, picnic on its wide lawns, or play on its playscape during the rest of the year at no charge. It is one of the few public access areas to Lake Pocotopaug, which is one of the state's largest inland bodies of water.

Hurd State Park (all ages)

South of East Hampton center, on Route 151, in Cobalt section; (860) 526-2336; www.ct .gov/dep. Free day-use; overnight camping fee ($).

Hurd State Park is another of the excellent facilities the State of Connecticut maintains for public use. Like other state parks, it is typically beautiful, clean, safe, and fun. It's special, however, because of its location overlooking the Connecticut River and because of its pretty Hurd Brook Gorge. Its 884 acres offer a variety of recreational activities, including rock climbing, snowmobiling, cross-country skiing, freshwater fishing, and hiking. The Split Rock trail takes you to some magnificent views of the river.

Most important, Hurd offers campsites for youth groups and boaters. Many folks camp and canoe from here to Gillette Castle or to Selden Neck State Park, a 528-acre island downriver toward Lyme. Accessible only by boat, those parks also have primitive riverside campsites available from May through September. The state provides toilets and drinking water at Hurd; drinking water, outhouses, and fireplaces are at Selden Neck.

Air Line Trail (all ages)

East Hampton trailhead off Smith Street, at Cranberry Meadow parking area; East Hampton Parks and Recreation: (860) 267-6020; www.easthamptonct.org/pdf/park/airline_trail.pdf or CT DEP site, www.ct.gov/dep. Open year-round, dawn to dusk, for nonmotorized (except for wheelchairs) recreation. Pets must be leashed. Free.

This multipurpose greenway trail wends its way in a 22-plus-mile corridor carved by the former Air Line Railroad, which by 1873 ran from New Haven to Willimantic and from those points onward to other rail lines that connected New York and Boston. The railroad, which fell into decline by the 20th century, crossed the Connecticut River and cut across prime farmland and woodland tracts. In 1996 the Department of Environmental Protection proposed its rehabilitation as a recreational linear park, formed through the cooperative effort of the DEP, funds provided through the National Recreational Trails Act, and the four towns of East Hampton, Colchester, Lebanon, and Hebron, through which the trail runs.

Great Hill **Overlook**

You might recall from the intro to this chapter a mention of Great Hill in the Meshomasic State Forest. It is from the Cobalt section of East Hampton that you will reach it. From the intersection of Routes 151 and 66 in Cobalt, drive north 0.8 mile on Depot Hill Road (which is a continuation from Route 151). Turn right at the Y intersection onto Gadpouch Road, which becomes gravel. The trail starts on the left, 0.4 mile from that Y intersection. Park at the trailhead, which is the southern terminus of the southern section of the Shenipsit Trail system, marked by blue blazes. From the trailhead on Gadpouch Road, take the path through a section populated by tall tulip trees; cross a small brook before you ascend a steep section to a plateau and then another short, steep climb to the Great Hill Ridge. So far, you've hiked about 0.4 mile. Continue along to reach the white-blazed Lookout Trail on your left. Follow that for 100 yards to see the view of the river and the pond. The trail goes on from there, but if you retrace your steps to your car from this point, you will have had a hike of just under 1 mile. It's relatively steep in sections, but it's a short distance for a spectacular view. Be sure to wear proper footgear.

Before you attempt this or longer sections of the trail, you might want to call the **Connecticut Forest and Park Association** at (860) 346-2372. They can confirm the trail's condition or refer you to the volunteer trail manager. The CFPA, by the way, are the dedicated folks who produce the wonderful *Connecticut Walk Book*, which actually has two volumes—one for the eastern part of the state and one for the west. These excellent guides to the state's blue-blazed hiking trails are the most accurate guides to state trails that are open for nonmotorized recreation. Seven hundred miles of such trails lace through the uplands, shore lands, and fertile river valleys, through state parks and forests, for sure, but also across privately held lands. The GIS maps in each *Connecticut Walk Book* are backed up by the carefully updated website www.ctwoodlands.org, on which you can check for any trail closings, openings, or improvements. You can also order the books on the website. The oldest private nonprofit environmental organization in the state, the CFPA works tirelessly for all of Connecticut's citizens. They like nothing more than seeing families exploring the natural heritage of the Eastern Woodlands.

Hiking, bicycling, cross-country skiing, and horseback riding are the most common activities. It's a great place both to observe plant and animal life in the Eastern Woodlands and to gain a sense of its human history. Hemlock forest, marshlands, waterfalls, cranberry bogs, ponds, rivers, historic railroad sites, viaducts, and bridges—including the Comstock covered span—are part of its beauty. Bring your own picnic and beverages as well as a trash bag to pack out. Pick up a trail guide and map at the trailhead. In time, this greenway is likely to be linked to the East Coast Greenway, which will connect cities from the Canadian border to Florida.

Where to Eat

Angelico's Lake House Restaurant. 81 North Main St.; (860) 267-1276. Right across the road from the lake, this restaurant is one of the fancier places to eat in the area but not too formal for families. Quite casual, actually, it features live entertainment and sunset cruise/dinner packages in season. A kids' menu includes every kind of comfort from smoothies and mac and cheese to a "kid kut" prime rib. Lunch and dinner daily; Sunday brunch buffet (10 a.m. to 2 p.m.) is **free** for kids under age 5.

Portland Restaurant. 188 Main St., Portland; (860) 342-2636. Straightforward in both name and presentation, this old-fashioned, hometown-style place is clean, no-fuss, and affordable, in a 19th-century brick building with high ceilings, black-and-white floor tiles, and dartboards. Italian fare, pizza, subs, daily specials, desserts. Lunch and dinner Mon through Sat from 9 a.m., even though the only "breakfast" dish might be a BLT or an egg-and-cheese sandwich. $

Rossini's Italian Restaurant. 62 West High St., East Hampton; (860) 267-1106. Every employee in this made-for-families restaurant is gracious and warmly welcoming. Delicious Italian favorites—pastas, pizzas, seafood, salads, soups, and more. Tues through Sun from 10 a.m. $$

Where to Stay

Markham Meadows Campground. 7 Markham Rd., off Route 16, in East Hampton; (860) 267-9738. Seasonal, weekly, and nightly spaces in 100-acre family-owned campground. Fishing, swimming, boat rentals, entertainment; all necessary hook-ups for outdoor lodging. Bring your own tent or camper. Open April through mid-October. $

Riverdale Motel. 1503 Portland-Cobalt Rd. (Route 66), Portland; (860) 342-3498; http://riverdale-motel.com. Family-owned since 1928, this complex includes a 47-room motel built in 1989. Simple, clean rooms with refrigerators; 4 units have equipped kitchenettes; smoking and nonsmoking units. Children 16 and under, **free;** complimentary morning coffee and pastry. $–$$

Middletown

This small city, once the largest and busiest port on the whole Connecticut River, is now best known as the home of Wesleyan University, one of the nation's finest centers of higher education. The city's interesting history and architecture and its position on the river have led entrepreneurs to capitalize on the tourist business that may help to revive the formerly sleepy atmosphere of the refurbished downtown area. Shops and restaurants of every description now line several blocks of Main Street, and the new hotel in the old armory makes it easy to explore for a weekend. These efforts as well as some traditional favorite events and sites make Middletown a good destination for families looking for fun in one of Connecticut's funkiest small cities.

Kidcity Children's Museum (ages 1 to 8)

119 Washington St.; (860) 347-0495; www.kidcitymuseum.com. Open Sun through Tues 11 a.m. to 5 p.m. and Wed through Sat 9 a.m. to 5 p.m. $$, babies under age 1 free. Annual family memberships available; birthday parties can be arranged.

The brainchild of Wesleyan alumna and Middletown mom Jennifer Alexander, Kidcity is devoted to integrated learning and play experiences for young children. Dedicated to the idea that parents and kids who play together will also learn together and reach out to others together, this innovative attraction continually reinvents itself in 13,500 square feet of play space in two linked buildings. Designed to entertain and challenge the intellects and energies of children ages 1 to 8, Kidcity always has something new to offer in its hive of interactivity. Your kids might choose to explore a sailing ship, a farm room, a diner, a market, a bagel shop, a push-button streetlight, a post office, a wooden train layout, or a laundry nook. On a clipper ship that recalls the days of Middletown's heyday as a shipping port, kids can hoist the sail, steer the vessel, walk the plank, and otherwise romanticize the olden days of wooden sailing vessels.

When the kids tire of that fun, they can rumble around Cornfield farmyard and climb an Apple Tree House. Other play spaces include a construction zone, a schoolroom with a giant chalkboard, an old-fashioned farm kitchen with a vintage fridge, and a farmhouse market garden where they can plant carrots. Visual and musical thinkers will appreciate the video production theater and instruments from around the planet; bookworms will love the Reading Room, a re-creation of Arrietty's library from Mary Norton's beloved classic, *The Borrowers.*

Be sure to come a few times annually, just to absorb all the creative energy here. You won't be disappointed.

Oddfellows Playhouse Youth Theater (ages 4 and up)

128 Washington St. (Route 66); (860) 347-6143; www.oddfellows.org. Year-round. Tickets in advance or at door; $–$$.

The state's oldest theater dedicated to works performed by and for children, Oddfellows was started in 1975 by Wesleyan students. Now privately run, the renovated theater with a colorful marquee on its refurbished redbrick building on one of Middletown's main drags is spurred by the efforts of many Wesleyan folks. With a mission to provide educational, multicultural entertainment for all students, including disadvantaged and minority children, the theater stages high-quality productions enhanced by the direction of professionals who come from all over the country to direct the young actors in its Teen Repertory company. The annual—and amazing—Children's Circus, held outdoors at 6 p.m. on the

Friday of the first full week of August, features Middletown schoolchildren ages 8 to 14, who learn circus skills in a five-week summer camp. (Inquire too about the Connecticut School of Circus Arts, a collaboration between Oddfellows, ArtFarm, and Matica Arts; it meets here and teaches kids ages 12 to 20 such circus skills as juggling, acrobatics, stilting, and riding a unicycle.) All other plays are open to student actors from out of town, and all productions are open to the public. As many as two shows per month run throughout the school year; summer productions vary in number.

The Wesleyan Potters (ages 6 and up)

350 South Main St. (Route 17); (860) 344-0039; www.wesleyanpotters.com. Open year-round. Gallery/shop: Wed through Fri from 10 a.m. to 6 p.m., Sat from 10 a.m. to 4 p.m., and Sun from noon to 4 p.m. Studios: Check website for class schedule. Free.

One of Connecticut's finest craft centers, this prestigious studio was inspired by the work of a Wesleyan professor who began a pottery class for Middletown residents in 1948. Now housed in 9,000 square feet of studio and gallery space, this cooperative includes

ArtFarm: Theater. Simple Living. **Activism.**

These three concepts compose the umbrella philosophy of one of Connecticut's most dynamic performance arts organizations. Currently offering theater workshops for children, youth, and adults from Middletown specifically and the lower Connecticut River Valley in general, ArtFarm is the brainchild of Marcella Trowbridge and Dic Wheeler, both formerly associated with Oddfellows Playhouse. In the past few years they've developed a theater company with a social mission as well as an artistic and educational vision. They aim to purchase a river valley farm or other open space as a future permanent home with performance spaces, theater workshops, retreat possibilities, and even some sustainable organic gardens. For now they offer a Shakespeare in the Grove production each summer on the campus of Middlesex Community College at 100 Training Hill Rd. in Middletown. Performances, offered at 7 p.m. for several days in mid-July, are preceded by an EcoFestival that begins at 4 p.m. The festival features musicians, circus performers, and interactive Shakespearean theater activities along with local organic farmers, crafters, artisan bakers, green vendors, and environmental organizations with exhibits related to conservation and sustainable agriculture. Shakespeare in the Grove and the ArtFarm EcoFestival are offered at no charge, but along with your picnic basket and blanket, you might consider bringing along a donation. The suggested amount is $10 per person, but these free-will folks will accept whatever you can afford. For more information, call (860) 346-4390 or visit the website www.art-farm.org.

100 potters, weavers, basket makers, and jewelry artists. They also teach a year-round schedule of classes and workshops, all of which are available to the public. The frequency of these classes nearly ensures that a visit here by a family could include observation of teachers and new crafters at work. Your interest is welcomed; just check the website to see when particular classes are offered; when you arrive, stop in the office to ask someone to escort you to a spot from which you can observe without disrupting the class. Sometimes the studios can be as quiet as a tomb; other times there is plenty of activity and lots to see. Call ahead to arrange a guided tour of the pottery and weaving studios (860-347-5925). Come in late November through mid-December to enjoy the wares at the annual exhibit and sale.

Where to Eat

It's Only Natural. 386 Main St.; (860) 346-9210. ION is perfect for families who crave the delicious and fresh taste and texture of vegan and vegetarian entrees, soups, and sandwiches. Open daily 11 a.m. to 9 p.m. $

Javapalooza. 330 Main St.; (860) 346-5282. A fine stop for breakfast, lunch, or light dinner fare, this café offers crepes, sandwiches, salads, teas, smoothies, coffees, and sweets, daily from 7:30 a.m. on weekdays and 8 a.m. on weekends. Live music on Saturday nights. $

Sweet Harmony Café & Bakery. 158 Broad St.; (860) 344-9646. From 11 a.m. each day, this lovely, intimate bake shop, with fine cakes and other confections, also offers tables and outdoor seating for soups, salads, sandwiches, quiches, and teas. $–$$

Tuscany Grill. 120 College St.; (860) 346-7096. In an old opera house with high ceilings, enjoy fresh sauces over perfect pastas; well-seasoned soups; thin-crust brick-oven pizza; innovative salads. Lunch and dinner Mon through Sat; dinner only on Sun. $$

Typhoon. 360 Main St.; (860) 344-9667. This reasonably priced establishment is owned by an energetic woman who cheerfully welcomes everyone. After your Thai, Vietnamese, or Chinese specialties, you'll get American-style treats with your bill. Lunch and dinner, Mon through Sat. $–$$

Vecchittos. 323 DeKoven Dr.; (860) 346-2637. The place to go on a hot summer night, this classic seasonal stand offers lemon, raspberry, chocolate, watermelon, banana, you-name-the-flavor of Italian ice, from noon till 9:30 p.m. from Memorial Day until the crowds go away sometime after Labor Day. $

Where to Stay

The Inn at Middletown. 70 Main St.; (860) 854-6300; www.innatmiddletown.com. Once the city's National Guard Armory, this restored landmark is now a lovely 100-room inn. 12 two-room junior suites equipped with microwave and refrigerator; cribs available at no charge. Heated indoor pool; fitness room; 100-seat Tavern at the Armory, specializing in traditional New England cuisine with seasonal favorites. Three meals daily (dinner, $$$–$$$$); children's menu. $$$–$$$$

Middlefield

I mean no disrespect at all when I say that Middlefield is very aptly named. Situated north of Durham close to the New Haven County line, it is an area of fields and farms, the pretty Coginchaug River, and parts of the Cockaponsett State Forest. Along with these features are two attractions particularly suited to families.

Lyman Orchards (all ages)

At the junction of Routes 147 and 157; (860) 349-1793; http://lymanorchards.com. Open daily; seasonal hours; call for schedule.

A huge family-owned operation since 1741, this bucolic extravaganza includes apple and peach orchards, strawberry and pumpkin fields, raspberry and blueberry patches, a sunflower maze and a corn maze, and the Apple Barrel Farm Store. A grand destination in every season, the farm is very popular with families wanting to pick their own produce and see the countryside.

Many festival-style events are planned throughout the year, mostly in celebration of various harvests. Food tastings, barbecues, hayrides, and other festivities are planned on those days. The Apple Barrel store is filled daily to the brim with fresh produce and baked goods, cheeses, maple products, fudge, freshly pressed apple cider, and take-out sandwiches, soups, and wraps. Come anytime to enjoy the ducks on the pond and the fresh air and sunshine.

Wadsworth Falls State Park (all ages)

Route 157; (860) 566-2304. Open daily year-round 8 a.m. to sunset. Day-use charge on weekends only from Memorial Day to Labor Day. $.

This state park has hiking trails and picnic areas, but its special attractions are a swimming area, which is available for ice-skating in the winter, and a beautiful waterfall with an overlook. One of the prettiest cascades in the state, Wadsworth Falls is a great place to spend a country afternoon. The swimming area and the falls are distinctly separate. Ask rangers or follow trails to the falls. You can also visit this 285-acre park to cross-country ski in winter and fish in the streams in summer.

Durham

Durham has some of the prettiest farmland in the county. Centered on Route 17 just south of Middletown, this quiet rural and residential town is admired for its farms and its charming historical Main Street of vintage homes and (mostly) independent businesses. It also has an intriguing new ice cream factory, but nothing can beat its incomparable country fair.

Durham Fair (all ages)

Durham Fairgrounds, 24 Town House Rd., off Route 17; (860) 349-9495. Third weekend in Sept, beginning at 9 a.m. on Fri. $$–$$$, children 10 and under free. Off-site parking fee ($); free shuttle bus to off-site parking at high school and other lots.

The fairgrounds are hardly noticeable most of the year as you drive past the green, but for three days annually, the joint is hoppin'. Like all country fairs, the Durham Fair celebrates the culture and traditions of Connecticut agriculture through hundreds of exhibits, demonstrations, and food and craft booths.

The largest agricultural fair currently held in Connecticut, it displays sheep, llamas, cattle, draft animals of major proportions, and every other barn and farm animal you can name. Look at the quilts, pies, fruits, and flowers. Ride the Ferris wheel and go through the Fun House. Eat candied apples; hot cashews; delicious chili, chicken, and chowder; and strawberry-topped Belgian waffles. Wander through the farm museum; buy something pretty at the crafts show. A terrific section for the youngest fairgoers includes kiddie rides and special programs for tots.

Over the aroma of fried everything rise the sounds of country music, announcements of contest winners, and screams from the midway. If your family has sleek, sophisticated city ways, put them aside for a day and come to the fair for a down-home good time. The ballet can wait, and your kids really ought to see the oxen and draft horses. They are a tribute to biodiversity, evolution, or Supreme Intelligence. Whatever your belief system, you have to be amazed at these creatures.

80 Licks Ice Cream Factory (all ages)

27-F Parsons Rd.; (860) 349-1190; www.80Licks.com. Call for current tour ($) information and for birthday party arrangements ($$$$).

If you love both rock 'n' roll and ice cream, you're going to be very happy in Durham. Jill and Johnny, the cheery and hardworking owners of this ice-cream factory, manufacture super-premium treats here. Most of the dozens of flavors have deliciously inventive rock 'n' roll names (Oreo Speedwagon, Vanilla Nice, Judas Peach, and the Almond Brothers, of course), and rock 'n' roll memorabilia decorate the plant's walls. Come here for a guided 30-minute tour of the operation: learn how they invent the flavors they add to the Guida's Dairy ice cream base; see how the machinery blends ingredients; sample the ice creams, gelatos, sherbet, sorbet, and Italian ices that emerge from their batch freezer—or have a birthday party here! Details are on their website. If you need Another Brick in the Walnut, you know where to come.

Where to Eat

Perk on Main. 6 Main St.; (860) 349-5335. This friendly establishment is a best bet year-round for breakfast, lunch, and take-out dinners Sat through Wed 6:30 a.m. to 4 p.m. and until 8 p.m. on Thurs and Fri. Creative omelets, sandwiches, burritos, crepes, quesadillas, house-made soups, salads, and smoothies. $–$$

Killingworth

Nearly completely residential and rural in nature, this hilly town south of Durham (take Route 79) supports a few small farms and nurseries and is usually missed altogether by tourists. Nevertheless, it has a popular site perfect for a day in the eastern woods, complete with pretty trails, a miniature covered bridge, and an ol' swimmin' hole.

Chatfield Hollow State Park (all ages)

Route 80, about 1.5 miles west of the rotary at the junction of Route 81; (860) 663-2030; www.ct.gov/dep. Open year-round daily 8 a.m. to sunset. Day-use vehicle charge Memorial Day to Labor Day, $$.

The hills in these parts are deeply etched reminders of the glaciers that passed this way thousands of years past; those icy masses carved out nooks and crannies well worth exploring in this pretty park. Crisscrossed by several miles of well-marked hiking trails that present a merely moderate challenge even to small children, the park also has a pond for swimming and fishing in the summer months and ice-skating, if the weather permits, in the winter. The pond's water is the color of iced tea, but don't let that stop you from plunging in. The clear, clean water is just tinged with the natural colors of the minerals loosed from the soil in the pond's basin.

Changing facilities, rustic flush toilets, and a picnic shelter provide a few comforts, but there are no showers and no concession. A privately owned mobile lunch truck is here all day most weekends in summertime.

Where to Eat

Cooking Company Killingworth. 187 Killingworth Turnpike (Route 81); (860) 663-3111. Sister store to the similarly named eatery in Haddam, the Cooking Company offers excellent soups, salads, sandwiches, and baked goods. Mon through Fri 10 a.m. to 7 p.m.; Sat 10 a.m. to 6 p.m.; closed Sun. $

Old Saybrook/Westbrook/Clinton

These three towns compose Middlesex County's trio of Long Island Sound shoreline towns. Easy to group together because of their geography, they are also similar in other quintessentially Connecticut shoreline ways. Heavy with salt and briny mud smells of the sea and shore and marsh, the air here carries the sounds of screeching gulls, slapping rigging, lonesome train whistles, and bellowing foghorns.

These are the towns where you eat crab cakes and clam strips and play real mini-golf with windmills and lighthouses. Where you stroll along seawalls, have double-dip ice cream cones, and skip stones off the jetty. Where you walk barefoot, break out in freckles, and let the sun bleach your hair. These are the towns of summer.

Very, very few true "suck-'em-in" tourist attractions are here (unless you count the Stay and Play (175-2 Elm St., or 175-2 Research Parkway if you're getting here by GPS; 860-395-4446) indoor play space, but that's mostly for local and nearby families with young children), but you can wander for hours along the shore roads that splinter south from the Boston Post Road. Also known as Route 1, footpath of the Pequot Indians and stomping grounds of the beach bums of Connecticut, this road is richer than a sea captain's treasure chest. Seafood shacks, antiques shops, ice cream parlors, and all those sort of half-rundown Cape Cod-y kinds of emporiums are designed to make you put on your browsing shoes.

Begin a tour in Old Saybrook, taking Route 154 south, bearing left on Main Street and continuing basically straight on College Street (both of which are actually still Route 154) toward the water.

Saybrook Point Park
and Saybrook Monument Park (all ages)

Follow College Street (Route 154) to its end at Saybrook Point; Old Saybrook Parks Department: (860) 395-3152. Both park sites open dawn to dusk daily year-round. Free.

Proceeding down Route 154 you will find Saybrook Point Park and a few satellite sites. Stop for a while in the big parking lot to your left as you approach the dead end in the roadway here, and walk to the seawall along the park's edge. It is here that nature provided the Connecticut River Valley her first big break. Down here near the mouth of the river, a sandbar prevents huge oceangoing vessels from entering the river. Thanks to the sandbar, which makes the Connecticut the largest river in America without a port, the river has stayed healthier than many others, and her towns have retained many of their old-time characteristics.

At this popular destination for day-trippers, miniature golfers, and anglers, you will find great fishing spots on the seawall, long-range binoculars to help you get a better view of the boats and lighthouse, and benches and picnic tables that encourage you to linger here. From the paved walkway you can see the breakwater that protects the harbor, and you can watch the boats and gulls and swans. You can pick up a bite to eat at the **Dock & Dine Restaurant** (860-388-4665), and you can play 18 holes at the **Saybrook Point Mini-Golf Course** (203-388-2407). Affordable and well maintained, it provides picnic tables, lights, and bug zappers for your comfort.

When you've seen the sights at Saybrook Point, explore the **Saybrook Monument Park** just half a block up the street, with its own small parking lot. Storyboards there describe its historic remains and artifacts from Saybrook Plantation's early days; a lovely short boardwalk provides an observation area of the tidal marshlands and its bird life. When you've soaked up the sights, get back in the car and follow Route 154 across the causeway and all the way around the peninsula (you'll turn sharply to the left immediately after you leave the Point parking lot). Enjoy the water views as you drive, then, when you arrive back at Route 1, turn left and drive toward Westbrook.

If you're hungry for lunch, stop in Old Saybrook for a sandwich that'll put you on cloud nine, head west a bit for the best pizza made anywhere between Providence and New Haven, or hold out until you reach the seafood king in Westbrook. See the end of this section for descriptions of all three restaurants. No matter which you choose, head for the beach when you're done.

West Beach (all ages)

Seaside Avenue; (860) 399-3095; www.westbrookct.us. Open 8 a.m. to 10 p.m. Restrooms, concession, showers in season. Nonresidents pay a day-use per-vehicle parking fee ($$$$) from late June through Labor Day, from 9 a.m. to 5 p.m.

After you eat, drive along the Boston Post Road and turn south onto Seaside Avenue in Westbrook. Highlighted by one of the prettiest views of the water and the offshore islands, this drive also takes you to what might very well be the best public beach in the tri-town area. Nonresidents are welcome to use the beach year-round; once school gets out (usually the third week in June), a daily per-vehicle parking fee goes into effect. Space in the parking lot is limited, so arrive early in the day if you are coming from some distance and would like to be sure there is room for you. **Free** parking on the nearby side streets is mostly prohibited. You can spend the day on the sand or stroll the long seawalk past the cottages that line the roadway across from the shoreline. This very clean beach is great for young children. Its swimming area has an extraordinarily sandy bottom that slopes very gradually toward deeper water.

When you leave the beach area, continue toward Clinton by driving west on Route 1. Except for its pretty beach and views of the water from its various beach roads and marinas, no attractions set it apart as a place for families. Still, you may while away a summer afternoon with some time at the beach, a stop at a restaurant or an ice cream emporium. Come on Thursday evenings in summer to the gazebo at the historic Pierson School for the outdoor concert series. Programs generally begin about 6:30 p.m.

Clinton Town Beach (all ages)

At the foot of Waterside Lane off Route 1; (860) 669-6901. Open year-round. Concession and restrooms in season only. Day-use per-vehicle parking fee ($$$) for nonresidents payable at the gatehouse from 9 a.m. to 3 p.m. only, from Memorial Day weekend through Labor Day weekend.

Visiting families are welcome at this small crescent-shape beach. Cross the wooden bridge at the foot of the narrow, pretty road that leads past some lovely old houses and enter the beach area. A children's playground, restrooms, and a snack bar that provides simple summer beach fare are here. This is a nice, quiet beach perfect for families with young children. Sometimes they show open-air movies in the evening—great fun!

Clinton Town Marina and Cedar Island Marina (all ages)

Riverside Drive, Clinton.

Ending a tour of the beach towns at this little slice of the shoreline in Clinton might be the perfect close to your day, especially if you visit near sunset. It may be a bonus if you

Keeping Things **Uniform**

If the beach holds no interest for you, you might care to stop in Westbrook at the **Company of Military Historians Museum** at Westbrook Place on North Main Street. The nation's largest collection of American military uniforms is here, as are completely restored and operable military vehicles from World War II and other late-20th-century conflicts. Open year-round, 8 a.m. to 3:30 p.m. Tues through Fri and by appointment. Call (860) 399-9460. **Free.**

are also hungry for dinner. Take Grove Street south from Route 1 at the weathered blue and gold sign that lists the harbor sites. This quiet, residential avenue reaches the water about ½ mile down, ending at a point where the Bluefin Charters leave the harbor for sport-fishing trips and the freshest lobster for miles around comes into harbor at the Lobster Landing, a refreshingly ramshackle establishment that offers excellent hot lobster rolls you can eat on the Landing's very casual deck, especially if the sunset entices you to linger awhile. You can also step on the brakes just a bit before you reach the doors of that quintessential shanty, and take the right turn onto Riverside Drive instead. There you'll find the Clinton Town Dock and Marina, with a public boat launch and a seasonal seafood shack, the Galley Grille. It serves up the best—maybe the only—bluefish nuggets in the state, along with hefty haddock sandwiches and other great seaside fare, from 7:30 a.m. to sometime after the sun goes down in summer.

At the waterside, a row of benches along a small stretch of walkway provides a front-row seat on the colorful spectacle the sun may be painting on the sky as it drops into the Sound to the west of Cedar Island. The view here may not be exactly glamorous, but if you can't see the beauty in the palette above you as the boats return to their moorings, then you've definitely left your rose-colored glasses at home. If you savor such scenes, you can even let the kids play in the sand awhile at teeny-tiny Esposito Beach, immediately to the west of the main parking lot. It's just a pier-side patch of sand, with no lifeguard (you wouldn't want to swim here anyway; this waterway is also leeward of the gasoline dock), but it can make for a good place for the kids to construct a quick castle while the folks crack open some steamers.

You can also head to Aqua, the seafood restaurant tucked within the parking area of the private Cedar Island Marina. Ask for a table at the windows inside or eat out on their deck. The folks at Cedar Island Marina don't mind if you sit on their benches or stroll their walkways, too. The private areas for their members are clearly marked (by a gate you'd need to swipe a card to get through), so just use your common sense and enjoy the wee stretch of walkway where you can see the locals exercising their dogs or pushing their baby strollers. No matter what portions of this little enclave you choose to enjoy, you've probably had a full day by now. Wait till the stars come out, brush the sand from your toes, and head on home to brush the salt air out of your hair. You'll come back, I'd guess.

The Pink **Sleigh**

Last in Middlesex County is a little bit of magic before you head home. Best seen in the twilight when the air is crisp and your breath rises steamily from your throat is a haven of peace and beauty for anyone who delights in the wonder of Christmas. Housed in an old barn, this store is truly charming—a place where every small child will suck in his or her breath in awe of all its glitter and gold. Dazzling displays of every color and material fill the rustic two-story barn, which is in itself beautiful. Stepping into this place on a crisp autumn afternoon just as twilight falls is like stepping into an elfin workshop hidden in the hills. Halloween and harvest decorations are here as well, at 512 Essex Rd. (Route 153) in Westbrook, ½ mile north of I-95 (860-399-6926). Open from early July until Christmas Eve, Tues through Sat, 10 a.m. to 5 p.m., Sun 11 a.m. to 4 p.m., and Mon from November 1 to December 24. Extended hours in Dec on Thurs, Fri, and Sat, when closing is typically at 8 p.m.

Where to Eat

Alforno Brick Oven Pizzeria and Ristorante. 1654 Boston Post Rd., Old Saybrook; (860) 399-4166. For the shoreline's best pizza, come here for thin, crisp crust, fresh toppings, and excellent sauce. Great salads and pasta, too. If you can wait for a table, you won't be disappointed. $$

Aqua Restaurant. 34 Riverside Dr., Clinton; (860) 664-3788. This shoreside classic at Cedar Island Marina offers great views, a friendly ambience for families, and adult-friendly seafood. There's no better place to watch the sailboats return to the marina. Open daily for lunch and dinner, except closed Mon and Tues from Columbus Day through Apr. $–$$$

Bill's Seafood Restaurant. Route 1 in Westbrook; (860) 399-7224. If seafood wins the toss of the coin, stop near the singing steel bridge, and slip into Bill's. The food is good, prices are reasonable, and the setting is picturesque. Watch swallows swoop and chatter; look for ospreys nesting above the tidal marsh; feed the ducks that hang out near the riverside deck; feast on chowder, steamers, clam strips, and more. The place hums most nights with live jazz, Dixieland, rock 'n' roll, and old-time banjo played by locally famed combos. $–$$

Cloud Nine Deli Cafe. 256 Boston Post Rd., Old Saybrook; (860) 388-9999. Healthful breakfast, lunches, and take-out dinners in a simple, sunny setting, come here year-round, Mon through Fri 8 a.m. to 3 p.m. and Sat 9 to 3 p.m. Closed Sun. $

Edd's Place. 478 Boston Post Rd., Westbrook; (860) 399-9498. For breakfast, lunch, and casual dinner or takeout, Edd's is terrific for soups, sandwiches, paninis, lasagna, pies, and muffins, at outdoor tables at the riverside or in a heated gazebo; open daily mostly year-round, 9 a.m. to 8 p.m., weather permitting. $

Paperback Cafe. 210 Main St., Old Saybrook; (860) 388-9718. Diner-style menu; live music on Sunday afternoons. Outside seating in warm weather. Breakfast and lunch daily, 7 a.m. to 4 p.m. $–$$

Where to Stay

Comfort Inn. 100 Essex Rd., Old Saybrook; (860) 395-1414. 121 units; sauna, indoor pool, fitness room; complimentary continental breakfast. $$–$$$

Days Inn. 1430 Boston Post Rd., Old Saybrook; (860) 388-3453 or (800) 329-7466. 48 units with refrigerator; complimentary beach passes and continental breakfast. $$–$$$$

Econolodge Inn & Suites. 1750 Boston Post Rd., Old Saybrook; (860) 399-7973. 45 renovated units, plus family suite with kitchenette; outdoor pool, beach passes. Nicely kept and popular with families. $$–$$$

Water's Edge Inn and Resort. 1525 Boston Post Rd., Westbrook; (860) 399-5901 or (800) 222-5901. Fifteen acres on the Sound, 100 luxury units with private beach, terraced lawns and gardens, tennis, indoor and outdoor pools, fitness room, spa, water-views public restaurant, entertainment, and activities for the kids. Year-round. $$$$

Westbrook Inn B&B. 976 Boston Post Rd., Westbrook; (860) 399-4777. This Victorian beauty has 9 rooms, 1 suite, and a two-bedroom cottage perfect for families. On the river with a dock and fishing; three minutes to beach, full breakfast on the wrap-around porch in fair weather. Gear available for boating, biking, and fishing. $$$$

General Information

Central Regional Tourism District. River Valley/Connecticut. One Constitution Plaza, 2nd floor, Hartford 06103; (860) 787-9640; (800) 793-4480; www.enjoycentralct.com.

Tourism Information Center. I-95 northbound in Westbrook. Staffed in summer months; maps, vacation guides, brochures.

Tolland County
Simple Dreams and Country Comforts

The hills of northeastern Connecticut have magic in them. As with Washington Irving's Catskills, something within these knolls has defied the physical laws governing the passage of time. The traveler is transported centuries backward just by being here. The magic of Tolland County lies not in what one does here. This is not a place well known for action. Rather, its magic lies partly in the sweet relief of having nothing to do here. It is, simply, a nice place just to wander.

Families looking for the quieter pleasures of life in New England will find much to please them here. The museums are smaller and have fewer buttons to press, but they are no less excellent than their showy counterparts in the city. The activities have fewer moving parts and use little or no fossil fuel, but they'll invigorate the body, feed the soul, and leave time for the mind to restore itself.

Begin a circular tour of this county by starting in Coventry; its center is on Route 31, most easily reached from Route 44 to the north or Route 6 to the south.

TopPicks for fun in Tolland County

1. **Nathan Hale Homestead**
2. **Coventry Regional Farmers' Market**
3. **Mansfield Drive-in Theatre and Marketplace**
4. **Connecticut Archaeology Center events**
5. **Ballard Institute and Museum of Puppetry**

TOLLAND COUNTY

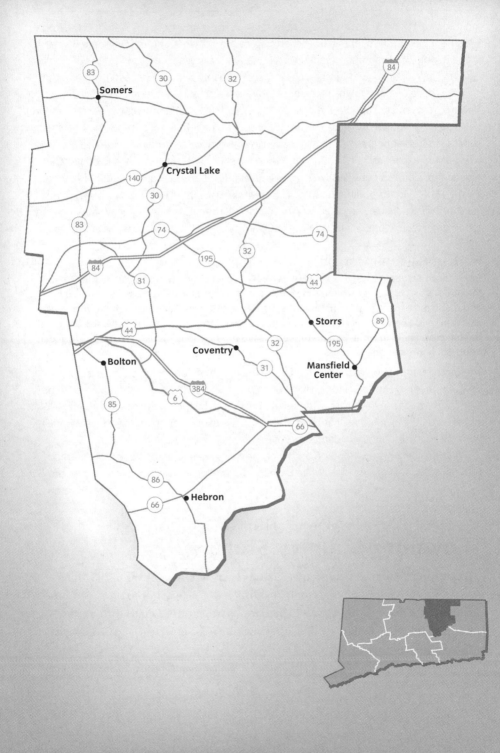

Coventry

Incorporated in 1712, Coventry describes itself as the gateway to the state's Quiet Corner, which is a fair appraisal of this truly charming country town. Centered on Route 31 neatly in the middle of the southern end of the county, its rolling, second-growth woodlands are laced by mile upon mile of twisting country road, beautiful in every season.

Like those of many towns in the area, Coventry's chief temptations are its scenic byways, farm stands, antiques shops, and inns. The slick stuff of the city is not to be found here. Still, Coventry provides a few attractions and a healthful trio of regular and annual events that will appeal to any family that enjoys history or nature. In the future, look for word of the expanded public hours of one of the state's newest history museums: The Museum of Connecticut Glass (www.glassmuseum.org) is under development in the John Turner House on North River Road, which is within Coventry's National Historical Glass Factory District. Plans are under way for the installation of a glass furnace that will demonstrate early techniques of glassmaking in Coventry and at other glassworks in the state.

Nathan Hale Homestead (ages 6 and up)

2299 South St.; (860) 742-6917 or (860) 247-8996; www.ctlandmarks.org. Open for tours Memorial Day weekend through October 31. In May, tours are Sat from noon to 4 p.m. and Sun from 11 to 4 p.m. From June through Aug, tours are Wed through Sat from noon to 4 p.m. and Sun from 11 a.m. to 4 p.m. In Sept and Oct, tours are Fri and Sat from noon to 4:00 p.m. and Sun from 11 a.m. to 4 p.m. Also open Monday holidays. Tours every half hour. $; children under 6 free.

The most famous spot in Coventry might be the home of Connecticut's state hero, Nathan Hale. On the fringe of the Nathan Hale State Forest off Route 31, the Nathan Hale Homestead is perhaps the most stately of Revolutionary-era historic homes in the country. Its situation on the property is a fitting memorial to the proud young man who lost his life in the service of his country in September 1776.

Nathan spent his boyhood on this lovely property, raised here in apparent harmony with his nine surviving siblings. While Nathan was serving in the Continental Army, the

Coventry Visitor Center and
Coventry Country Store

Day-tripping families may stop at the **Coventry Visitor Center** (1195 Main St.; 860-742-1085) in the old brick post office in the heart of town. Open year-round on weekends only from 10 a.m. to 2 p.m., it offers maps, brochures, and assistance from knowledgeable volunteers. Be sure to visit the **Coventry Country Store** at 1140 Main St. (860-742-5336). Open 10 a.m. to 5 p.m. Wed through Sun, it's chockfull of antiques, local crafts and comestibles, and old-fashioned penny candy.

The Story of a **Hero**

At just 21 years of age, the young Nathan Hale, a graduate of the class of 1773 at Yale and a teacher by profession, set out on the most dangerous mission known to his generation. Acting under the principles of freedom that drove the Patriot cause, Nathan, now a captain in the rebel army, walked on foot in the disguise of a poor schoolmaster to infiltrate the British encampment at New York City and bring the plans of the enemy back to General Washington. Apprehended within sight of the smoke from the American campfires, Nathan was relieved of the secrets he had written on a parchment hidden in his boot and was hanged from the gallows without a trial for the crime of treason against the Crown.

Legend tells us that it was on this occasion, facing his death, that Nathan Hale uttered his most famous words: "I only regret that I have but one life to lose for my country." His body was left hanging for three days as a warning to other traitors and was buried in an unknown, unmarked grave in Artillery Field, now underneath the pavement near New York City's Sixty-sixth Street and Third Avenue. Back home in Coventry, years later, his father erected a headstone in his memory graven with these words: HE RESIGNED HIS LIFE A SACRIFICE TO HIS COUNTRY'S LIBERTY.

house currently standing on the property was rebuilt to add space to the original smaller house in which the 10 brothers and sisters had been raised. Sometime after the death of the first Mrs. Hale (I presume from exhaustion), Nathan's father, Deacon Richard Hale, married the second Mrs. Hale, a widow with seven children of her own. Clearly there was just cause for building a new homestead that represented not only breathing space but the prosperity that Nathan's father had achieved.

The homestead tour begins with an excellent short film shown in the small 18th-century barn, which also serves as the gift shop, to the left of the drive at the left of the house. The house includes many Hale furnishings and belongings. See Nathan's musket, his shoe buckles, the trunk he left with his friend Asher Wright when he left on his mission, and the Bible he received as a gift on his 17th birthday. The tours are among the best we have heard for children in the state—filled with detail but quick and not above the heads of young listeners. You may even see a costumed character cooking at the open hearth, making soap, or toiling in the period herb and vegetable garden. Hands-on activities are typically incorporated for children, and, on Sundays in summer, these **free** programs are often coordinated with the themes of the on-site Coventry Regional Farmers' Market (see sidebar); if you are here on one of those Saturdays, you are in for an extra treat. On selected market days, craft classes are also offered for an additional fee ($$–$$$); these may include rug-making, doll-making, basketry, or other old-time arts.

Rural and **Herbal Pleasures**

Part of the rural culture and agrarian legacy of the state's Quiet Corner is reflected in its agricultural fairs, farms, and farmers' markets. Coventry is home to some of the best opportunities for celebrating the gifts of the earth. If you do nothing else in Tolland County this year, you must come to the award-winning and wonderful **Coventry Regional Farmers' Market** (www .coventryfarmersmarket.com), which runs from June through October on Sunday from 11 a.m. to 2 p.m. on the grounds of the Nathan Hale Homestead. If you like locally grown produce and regional crafts, don't miss this exceptional market. Chock-full of every kind of deliciousness plus special demonstrations and live music, it is Connecticut's largest and most diverse farmers' market and one of the very best outdoor markets in all of New England. Nearly 50 vendors offer all manner of farm-grown and handcrafted products. Leave your picnic at home and buy everything here. Each Sunday a different theme is featured; check the market website to see what's happening and what activities are planned for the celebration. Compare those listings with the events being offered by the Homestead staff, and, undoubtedly, all members of the family will find something to love here. It is well worth the long ride to the countryside, even if you are coming from afar.

If you would like to visit some of the nearby farmers themselves, you might begin at **Topmost Herb Farm** (244 North School Rd.; 860-742-8239; www.topmostherbfarm.com), owned and operated by Carole Miller. On the land her grandfather farmed since 1915, she grows medicinal and culinary herbs and heirloom tomatoes according to organic standards. The display gardens and the greenhouse on her lovely 20-acre property are open from May

Check the website calendar for listings of the many special events offered annually. In early June Nathan's birthday is celebrated with cake and a performance by the Nathan Hale Ancient Fife and Drum Corps. On the first Sunday in June, an Antiques Festival draws 100 or more exhibitors; in late July a Revolutionary War encampment takes over the grounds for a full weekend of camp-life reenactments and a multi-corps fife and drum muster. An October walking tour called I Spy History focuses on the homestead as well as the forest and other nearby historic sites. In November, come for Thanksgiving-related hearth-cooked treats or come for a full farmhouse meal from soup to dessert.

An exceptional Colonial Life weeklong day camp for children involves kids in colonial games, crafts, weaving, cooking, clothes making, plant study, and the opportunity to roleplay a Hale historical character. Call well in advance of summer to register.

through Sept, Thurs through Sat from 9 a.m. to 5 p.m. On the first Saturday in June (9 a.m. to 4 p.m.), Topmost (or another nearby farm) hosts the **Connecticut Herb Association's HerbFest** ($$), with workshops, demonstrations, craft and herb vendors, food vendors, a bake sale, and children's activities. Check www.ctherb.org for information on this year's event. You can also go to **Taste! Organic Connecticut** ($), a celebration of local organic agriculture at Manchester Community College on the first Sunday after Labor Day from 10 a.m. to 4 p.m. Sponsored by the Northeast Organic Farming Association and the Willimantic Food Co-Op, this event offers fresh produce and plants, honey, maple syrup, crafts, and herbal products, along with workshops, music, and children's events. For more information, visit www.ctnofa.org or call (203) 888-5146.

The folks at **Edmondson's Farm** (2627 Boston Turnpike, which is Route 44; 860-742-6124; www.edmondsonsfarm.com) also welcome families to ride their hay wagons in September and October, when they are open daily from 9 a.m. to 6 p.m. Take a tractor-driven ride ($) guided by Mrs. Pumpkin through the woods and back to the farm stand. Buy a pumpkin, a bushel of crisp apples, or some mums. Veggies and herbs are all available seasonally, and Christmas trees and trimmings come out around Thanksgiving.

Patriot's Park (all ages)

Lake Street (Route 275 becomes Lake Street at the Route 31 junction); (860) 742-4068. Open 8 a.m. to dusk year-round; fees in summer only. Nonresident day-use in the summer, $ per vehicle on Mon through Fri and $$ on weekends. If you have more than five occupants in your car, pay a bit more ($) for each extra person over the age of 5. Concession in summer only; lifeguards from May 1 through September 30.

This 17-acre park with trails linked to the 57-acre Patriot's Forest trail system offers a public beach on 373-acre Lake Wambungaug, also known as Coventry Lake. A picnic pavilion and snack hut, a children's playscape, open fields, a performance pavilion, and restrooms are all here for public use. In winter, weather permitting, enjoy the ice-skating pond with a warming hut; bring your own skates.

History **Lessons**

Families with history buffs among them might like to check out Coventry's **Brick School House** on Merrow Road. Built from 1823 to 1825, it served as a one-room district school until 1953. Now restored and furnished with 19th-century artifacts, it's open on Sunday afternoons from mid-May to mid-October. The **Strong-Porter House** at 2382 South St., just down the road from the Hale Homestead, includes local artifacts and memorabilia about the Hales, their relatives the Strongs, and the Porters. The property includes carriage sheds, a barn, and a carpenter's shop. It is open Saturday and Sunday afternoons from mid-May to mid-October. Both **free.** For more information, visit www.coventrychistoricalsociety.org.

Where to Eat

Bidwell Tavern. 1260 Main St. (Route 31); (860) 742-6978. Famous for its chicken wings, this classic 1820s tavern is a local favorite that deserves its reputation for good steaks, burgers, ribs, and seafood. Lunch and dinner daily year-round except Thanksgiving and Christmas. $–$$

Lake View Restaurant. 50 Lake St.; (860) 498-0500; www.coventrylakeview.com. For most of its long history, this casual establishment was a rough-and-ready bar—but not anymore. Renovated under new ownership, it now is a family-friendly restaurant (and bar) with a 2,500-square-foot deck overlooking Coventry Lake. An extensive menu of American and Italian favorites suits the families and boaters who come for lunch and dinner daily.

Live music Thursday through Sunday nights. $$–$$$

Where to Stay

Special Joys Bed and Breakfast. 41 North River Rd.; (860) 742-6359. This pink-towered B&B offers families (with children over the age of 6) a private balcony, private entrance, and dining room, plus 2 immaculate guest rooms with private baths. Glassed-in conservatory with fountain; extensive gardens; full country-style breakfast. Special Joys Doll and Toy Shop offers dolls, dollhouses, doll clothes and accessories (open year-round Thurs through Sun, 11 a.m. to 4 p.m.). If you are not a guest at the bed-and-breakfast, call ahead to confirm the shop hours. $$–$$$

Hebron/Bolton

The trouble with Tolland County is that it's so rural that its towns are sort of rambling affairs without boundaries that are crystal-clear to the traveler. The boundaries exist, of course, but to find Point A in Town A, it might actually be easier to travel to Point A from Town B. And so on.

If you were to leave Coventry, for example, to find Gay City State Park (which is, from a north–south perspective, halfway between Hebron and Bolton), it would be absurd to travel to either Hebron or Bolton proper. You'd go to Andover first, and then on through the countryside to the park. It's a curious Yankee phenomenon that even your GPS may not have yet figured out, but a local inhabitant would likely smile wryly at your gadget and say something along the lines of, "W'aall, it found us, so you cain't be too far off." And then you're on your own again.

The fact of the matter is that Gay City State Park is in Hebron, but even the state campground guide explains its position as 3 miles south of Bolton on Route 85. I say it's 4 miles west of Andover at the junction of Routes 31 and 85. The bottom line is that it's actually easy to find and very worthwhile no matter how you get there.

Gay City State Park (all ages)
Entrance on Route 85 in Hebron; (860) 295-9523. Open year-round 8 a.m. to sunset. Parking fee on weekends and holidays, $$.

Adjoining the vast acreage of the Meshomasic State Forest, this 1,569-acre park centers on the remains of an 18th-century mill village settled in 1796 by a religious sect led first by one Elijah Andrus and later by a man named John Gay. Quite successful and nearly self-sustaining, the community had, at its peak, a population of 25 families and a handful of thriving mills that produced lumber, woolens, and paper, among other goods. For nearly 80 years, the industrious citizens of Gay City managed to overcome their various hardships, but by 1879 the struggle to sustain themselves became overwhelming. In that year, the last of their mills burned to the ground, and the citizens abandoned the settlement. Soon the fields lay fallow, the silent ruins were home to wild dogs, and nature removed nearly every trace of human habitation. Now only some tumbling foundations, some cellar holes, a few gravestones, and the ruins of an old aqueduct remain.

Leave your car at a parking area near the pond and pick up a trail map in the wooden box near the trailhead. Ten trails lace through the park, but the easiest ones for children are those with the greatest concentration of historic spots. The park offers swimming, fishing, hiking, and picnicking in warm weather. In winter, you can ice-skate and cross-country ski. The state provides picnic tables, drinking water, and flush toilets, and leashed pets are permitted.

Maple **Madness**

Hebron is home to five of Connecticut's sugarhouses, and, since 1990, the whole town celebrates their industriousness and deliciousness on the second weekend in March at the annual **Hebron Maple Festival.** You can take self-guided tours of the operating sugarhouses and learn how maple sugar and syrup are produced, and you can also come for the dog-sled racing, old-fashioned games, pony rides, quilt and craft show, and spun maple sugar candy—yum. Visit www.hebronmaplefest.com for a brochure and schedule.

Fish Family Farm Creamery and Dairy (all ages)

20 Dimock Lane, Bolton; (860) 646-9745. Open Mon through Sat, year-round, from 8 a.m. to 6 p.m. Walking around is free, but they charge for the ice cream.

After a full day of hiking and swimming, there's no better place to replace some calories than at another of Connecticut's finest ice cream emporiums. Now you can go to Bolton (you see, you didn't miss anything at all arriving at Gay City through Andover), straight north on Route 85. This dairy is one of the very few operations in Connecticut that milks, pasteurizes, and bottles its own milk, and its enterprising owners also make fabulous ice cream.

Visitors are welcome to take a self-guided tour around the farm as long as the path taken is safe and doesn't endanger anyone, but do pay attention to any signage. You can explore the dairy barn and pet any of the adorable wee calves who might be here when you come. The Jersey cows are milked here every day, and the best viewing place of the bottling plant is through a glass window in the farm store where you buy their ice cream. Be here around 3:30 p.m. if you'd like to see the milking process; bottling is usually done between 6 a.m. and noon on Monday and sometimes Tuesday. They make ice cream on Monday, too. You can arrange for a birthday party here, and these and other groups can make appointments for a one-hour guided barn tour as well. The store also sells the Fish family's own fresh eggs, cream, milk, butter, and cottage cheese; best of all, though, is their ice cream—you won't get it any closer to the source anywhere in the state.

Where to Eat

Bolton Pizza and Family Restaurant. 270 West St. (Route 85); (860) 643-1014. Famed for its spinach pies and calzones, this eatery offers Greek pizza and Italian favorites at great prices for families. Open Tues through Sun, except closed in Aug. $–$$

Georgina's. 275 Boston Turnpike (at junction of Routes 6 and 44); (860) 647-0345. Tuscan/Mediterranean fare in a sparkling clean, family-friendly restaurant/banquet facility with an enormous menu and affordable prices. $–$$$

Somers

Way up north in Tolland County just a stone's throw from the Massachusetts border is the small town of Somers, pronounced like the season. Once the home of the Scantic Indians and later settled by colonists who made use of the Scantic River to power grist and woolen mills, it remains a quiet community with rural charm.

If you have been lingering in the south of the county, make your way up Route 85 to the center of Vernon at Route 85's junction with Route 30. Take a right on Route 30, also called Hartford Turnpike, and go to the second light to the shopping center called 30 Plaza. Stop at **Rein's New York Style Deli** (435 Hartford Turnpike; 860-875-1344;

open year-round daily except December 25) in the shopping center and buy some wonderful take-out sandwiches, kosher pickles, German potato salad, and whatever other picnic fixings you may need for a day in the country. Then go northward on Route 83 to Somers.

Shallowbrook Equestrian Center (ages 4 and up)

247 Hall Hill Rd. (Route 186); (860) 749-0749; www.shallowbrook.com. Open year-round; call for seasonal hours, events, and information on lessons.

Those of you who love horses probably already know about this place; it's the largest family-owned complex of its kind in the United States, it has the largest indoor polo arena in the nation, and it enjoys a national reputation as one of the country's best riding schools. Indoor and outdoor riding rings, a hunt course, indoor and outdoor polo courses, 40 hours a week of scheduled riding lessons for all levels and ages of riders, facilities for carriage shows, rodeos, and gymkhana competitions, and much more keep participants and spectators alike arriving for the year-round special events on this beautiful 50-acre site. Among the most popular visitor programs here are the Equestrian Experience birthday parties, which offer a barn tour, lessons on pony care, grooming, and safety tips, and a pony or horse ride around one of their rings; you supply the cake and party goods—and they clean up! Whether you come to watch the pageantry or the sportsmanship or to develop your own skills, you will find much to occupy the family at Shallowbrook.

Soapstone Mountain (all ages)

Soapstone Mountain Road. Open year-round dawn to dusk unless closed due to weather conditions. Free.

If you want to save those sandwiches just a little bit longer, take Route 190 east from its junction with Route 83. Drive 1.2 miles to Gulf Road. Take a right on Gulf Road and drive 2 miles to the entrance of the Shenipsit State Forest. Pass the parking area and turn west onto Soapstone Mountain Road, which will twist upward to a beautiful vista just under a mile from Gulf Road. Stop at the overlook, then drive onward to a picnic area near the top of the mountain. Park here and enjoy your lunch. If the state forest trails are open when you visit, walk to the nearby weather-relay station and take the short trail to the wooden fire tower beyond it.

Retrace your route to Gulf Road and take a right onto it so you're going south toward **Crystal Lake,** which is just a few miles away at the junction of Routes 140 and 30. If you have the equipment, stop at Crystal Lake's public boat launch and public fishing area and see if you can land some trout. Crystal Lake Brook, which runs parallel to Route 30, is a major trout stream, stocked in early spring and open from the third Saturday in April through March 1 of the following year. If the fish aren't biting, go east on Route 140 to Stafford Springs, and hook a right onto Route 32 toward Mansfield.

Mansfield

If you don't have a firm grip on the township concept, you'll have a great chance to process it fully in Mansfield. Composed of several village centers and a large university, it lies roughly between Routes 44 and 6 at the north and south and is crisscrossed by Routes 195, 275, 32, and 89.

I mention this because even if you have driven for miles you will know that you are still in Mansfield if you are between any two of these points, a fact that can become very important since the village names are Mansfield Depot, Mansfield Center, and Mansfield Four Corners. Plus Eagleville, Spring Hill, and Storrs (the home of the University of Connecticut and the name by which most out-of-towners refer to Mansfield). For the purposes of this book, we are going to group the university-related attractions under the town heading of Storrs, just a few pages onward.

A day in Mansfield can include all four of the following attractions if you plan well: the Mansfield Drive-in Theater, the Gurleyville Grist Mill, the Mansfield Hollow Dam and State Park, and the Mansfield Marketplace, which is held at the drive-in.

Mansfield Hollow Dam and State Park (all ages)
Just about a mile east of Mansfield Center near the junction of Routes 195 and 89; (860) 455-9057. Open year-round from sunrise to sunset. Free.

Created to protect the land around the 550-acre reservoir made by the damming of the Natchaug River by the Army Corps of Engineers, the park includes more than 2,300 acres of open space perfect for hiking, picnicking, cross-country skiing, and bird or wildlife watching.

Among the amenities are a field-sports area, a picnic grove (with some pretty tall pines, tables, fire pits, restrooms, and seasonal water fountains), horseshoe pits, an interpretive nature trail, and miles of other hiking trails. Trash containers are not provided, so be prepared. The park is an alcohol-free facility, so leave the wine and beer out of your picnic fixings.

Unfortunately, because the lake is a public water supply, you can't swim here, but you can bring in your fossil fuel–burning powerboat at the public boat launch. As they say in New York, go figure. You can also fish here. I guess the fish don't mind the petrochemicals.

Follow the signs to the 1952 Mansfield Hollow Dam (you can walk to it along the top of the dike that runs through the first part of the park or you can drive to it on the roads). The dam is a fairly impressive structure, unless you've already seen Hoover, of course, and it overlooks the lake, the river, and Kirby mill, a stone structure dating from 1882.

Gurleyville Grist Mill (ages 5 and up)
Stone Mill Road; (860) 429-9023; www.joshuaslandtrust.org or www.mansfieldhistory.org. Open late May through mid-October on Sun from 1 to 5 p.m. Free.

If historic structures or industrial history intrigue you, head up Route 195, take a right onto Gurleyville Road, and follow the signs to the mill. A mill site since the 1720s, this small stone building is the state's only remaining gristmill. Dating from 1830, it contains its original 19th-century machinery, and from the lower level, you see the huge waterwheel and the original mill race. A marvelous working model of the mill is on the main level, complete with pulleys, gears, conveying devices, and grindstones. In the shed addition of the nearby miller's house (the birthplace and home of Governor Wilbur Cross) is a museum of Mansfield history and the mill; it is also open for self-guided tours at the same time the mill is open.

You may want to explore the surrounding area, where Michael's Preserve, a large meadow, stretches out along the river. The riverside is a lovely place to stop for a picnic lunch—or you may even want to slide a kayak into the cool water. The nearby Nipmuck Trail follows the pretty twists of the Fenton River, on which the mill is situated. To hike, park near the bridge that crosses the river and look for the blue blazes that lead northwest close to the west bank. The trail is 39 miles long, but you can enjoy a short section right here near the mill. Walk about a quarter-mile to where the trail crosses Gurleyville Road, then retrace your steps to your car or continue up to Route 44 (about another mile) and then return to your car.

Mansfield Drive-In Theatre and Marketplace (all ages)

228 Stafford Rd., which is at the junction of Routes 31 and 32; drive-in: (860) 423-4441; www.mansfielddrivein.com; marketplace: (860) 456-2578; www.mansfieldmarketplace.com. Drive-in open every Fri through Sun evening from mid-April through May and in Sept, and every night in June, July, and Aug; $–$$. Wednesday night is Family Night; special per carload price. Opens at 7:10 p.m. Marketplace open 8 a.m. to 3 p.m. on Sun from March 15 until Thanksgiving. Rain or shine. Free. Small parking fee.

For fun in a time warp, come for one of the first-run films playing on the big screen. If you were a child of the 1950s or '60s, you probably know how this works: The kids get into pajamas just before dark and pile into the Ford Country Squire, and the whole family cheerfully heads off to the drive-in to watch wholesome, family values–type movies under the stars.

If it's really warm, the kids spread a blanket on the roof of the car and pile on top, hoping to get a good view of anything interesting going on in the next car. There's lots of giggling involved and lots of popcorn, and when there's too much noise on the roof, Dad says something like "June, can you make those kids settle down?" and Mom says something like "Oh, Ward, they're just high-spirited," and everybody starts giggling again.

This drive-in is one of two remaining open in Connecticut and the only one east of the Connecticut River. The three screens offer "family" films, but call to be sure you share their opinion of appropriate films for your children. Often there are double features, with the earlier film being most oriented toward younger audiences. A full-service snack bar prepares dogs and burgers and such and hawks typical theater treats. Depending on your comfort level here, you can send the kids to play on the on-site playground. Restrooms complete the package.

Return here on Sunday from mid-March until Thanksgiving to check out the goods at the largest indoor/outdoor weekly flea market in eastern Connecticut. Don't be concerned that children won't have fun here. Of the 200 or so dealers who sell here regularly, a large percentage sell toys, crafts, candy, baseball cards, dolls, sporting goods, books, and other goods of appeal to families. Breakfast and lunch are offered for sale at the snack bar.

Storrs

Not surprisingly, the University of Connecticut provides several resources for family activities on its main campus at Storrs. If you enter the university near the information booth at the main entrance on Route 195, you can pick up campus maps and inquire about guided and self-guided tours of the campus. In addition to the attractions detailed below, you can visit the Kellogg Dairy Barn exhibits at the School of Agriculture daily from 10 a.m. to 4 p.m. and ask for the self-guided walking tour of the campus trees, which is actually pretty amazing. Planted with trees from all temperate parts of the world, the campus itself has achieved arboretum status, and its School of Horticulture maintains beautiful themed gardens, including one planted in the school colors. Be sure to visit the Little Stone House, which is constructed from stone taken from every town in the state of Connecticut and has an interior wall with a specimen stone from every state in the union. The Geology Park is made from stone taken from every working quarry in Connecticut and includes a set of Connecticut dinosaur footprints.

UConn Greenhouses and Animal Barns

At 75 North Eagleville Rd., behind the Torrey Life Sciences Building, are the University of Connecticut Department of Ecology and Evolutionary Biology's greenhouses, which house the most diverse collection of plants between New York and Boston. Nearly 4,000 species thrive here, including cacti, succulents, bromeliads, and more than 500 species of orchids. The facility is open to the public for **free** from 8 a.m. until 4 p.m. Mon through Fri; it is closed on weekends and state holidays. Check the website for further information: http://florawww.eeb.uconn.edu/visiting.html. This may be the closest you come to a rain forest—it's lush, humid, and lovely.

UConn's animal barns are also open to the public for **free** self-guided tours. The barns are located on Horsebarn Hill Road and are open daily year-round from 10 a.m. to 4 p.m. (plus an hour or two later in summertime). You may see cattle, horses, and sheep; you may have even more fun if you pick up a copy of a brochure called *Follow the Animal Trail: A Children's Guide to the Animals at UConn Storrs*. The brochure is available at the UConn Visitor Center, at the Dairy Barn, and in the barns.

Connecticut Archaeology Center (all ages)

2019 Hillside Rd., University of Connecticut, off Route 195; (860) 486-4460; www.cac.uconn .edu. Open Wed through Fri 10 a.m. to 4 p.m. Closed Sat through Tues. Free; donations appreciated. Check the website for the calendar of special events, workshops, and activities. The center is in the building to the right of the UConn Co-op. Parking on weekdays is available in the garage behind the Co-op for a fee; on weekends free parking is permitted in the lots and on the streets as well.

The Connecticut State Museum of Natural History at UConn and the Office of State Archaeology have created both a partnership and a venue for their considerable collections and resources. The Connecticut Archaeology Center has a wonderful permanent exhibit called *Human's Nature: Looking Closer at the Relationships Between People and the Environment.* One of the finest natural history collections in the state is kept here and is displayed, in part, in this exhibit exploring the effects of the land on its inhabitants and the impact of the people upon the land. Geology, ethnobotany, archaeology, and climatology are among the sciences explored here in several "story stations" and multimedia presentations.

A full slate of activities includes family programs, nature walks, science workshops, field trips, Sunday lectures by scientists and scholars, and guided tours. Children entering grades one through five, accompanied by an adult, may particularly enjoy the free Fridays at the Museum programs offered monthly (second or third Friday) from 1 to 3 p.m.

William Benton Museum of Art (ages 8 and up)

University of Connecticut, 245 Glenbrook Rd.; (860) 486-4520; www.thebenton.org. Open year-round Tues through Fri 10 a.m. to 4:30 p.m., Sat and Sun 1 to 4:30 p.m. Closed during exhibit changings or some academic breaks. Free.

Housed in a building now on the National Register of Historic Places, this museum's galleries are devoted to changing exhibitions and displays from the university's 5,500-piece permanent collection of American and European art.

The small size of the museum makes it a wonderful place in which to introduce young children to fine art, and the museum's exhibitions are of the highest caliber, often focusing on art from many cultures beyond the scope of its own collection. Check the website: summer exhibitions often have a special family focus. Cafe Muse provides a convenient place to eat and relax; the museum gift shop is also excellent.

Ballard Institute and Museum of Puppetry (all ages)

6 Bourne Place, in Willimantic Cottage on the UConn Depot Campus, which is on Weaver Road off Route 44; (860) 486-0339; www.bimp.uconn.edu. Open Apr through Nov Fri, Sat, and Sun from noon to 5 p.m. Free; suggested donation, $.

This unique museum grew out of one of the Benton Museum's most impressive exhibitions of one of the university's most important collections. Named for professor emeritus Frank Ballard and dedicated to preserving and displaying the Ballard puppets as well as the puppets of other student, state, national, and international puppeteers, the museum also has as its purpose the aim to educate the public and promote the puppet arts.

Showcasing a collection of thousands of puppets from around the world, the institute and museum celebrate the wondrous art form of puppetry through changing exhibitions of marionettes, glove puppets, rod puppets, shadow puppets, and the props, paraphernalia, and publicity materials associated with puppet productions. Two exhibit galleries are open to visitors, as is an intriguing gift shop.

The University of Connecticut is the only university in the nation with a degree program in puppetry arts. At the helm of that tradition for more than 30 years was Frank Ballard, directing the work of the latest generation of puppet creators. Ballard's own stories are inspirational tributes to the generous support he received from childhood onward as he carved out his life in the arts. He made his first puppet at the age of 5. Inspire your own kids—bring them to this must-see museum and be sure to visit its hands-on puppet stage, where you too can be a puppeteer.

Throughout the year, student puppeteers as well as renowned international performers offer puppet productions for families as well as adults. Contact the Department of Dramatic Arts at the university for ticket information and a schedule.

Jorgensen Center for the Performing Arts (ages 4 and up)

2132 Hillside Rd. at UConn; (860) 486-4226; www.jorgensen.uconn.edu. Oct through May. Also Connecticut Repertory Theatre, (860) 486-3969. Check the website to select performances suited to your family's interests. Single tickets ($$$) and subscription series are available; you can also design your own series. Children, $$.

This 2,630-seat contemporary theater offers top-drawer entertainment in the form of musicals, comedies, Broadway classics, dance, opera, and drama. The full season of productions features professional touring companies as well as nationally and internationally known soloists and symphonies. Nearly all the productions are appropriate for the whole family.

The Jorgensen Children's Series offers several productions each academic season, featuring favorite tales such as *Sleeping Beauty* or the *Wizard of Oz*. Recommended for children ages 5 through 11, these Sunday performances are at 1 and 3 p.m.

Where to Eat

You can eat on campus in the student union during the academic sessions in the coffee shop and cafe-style eateries or at the Blue Oak Cafe in the Nathan Hale Inn (open year-round for breakfast, lunch, and dinner). You can also try one of these local favorites:

Altnaveigh Inn. 957 Storrs Rd.; (860) 429-4490. For something a bit more elegant, try this inn for finer Continental fare at lunch (Tues through Fri; $$–$$$) and dinner (Tues through Sat; $$$–$$$$); children's menu.

Angellino's Restaurant. 135 Storrs Rd. (Route 195); (860) 450-7071. You just can't go wrong here. Pizza, great pasta, quick service, lots of families. Lunch and dinner daily year-round. $–$$

Mansfield General Store. 534 Storrs Rd. (Route 195), Mansfield Center; (860) 450-0597. Open daily year-round, with breakfast, lunch, and dinners to eat in or take out, plus baked goods, ice cream, picnic goods, penny candy, and gifts and groceries of all kinds. $

UConn Dairy Bar. 3636 Horsebarn Rd. Extension, UConn School of Agriculture, just north of Gurleyville Road on Route 195; (860) 486-2634. Eat dessert first: that is, sensational ice cream made from scratch year-round. Creative flavors invented daily by students. Mon through Fri, 10:30 a.m. to 5 p.m., Sat and Sun, noon to 5 p.m. Longer hours in summertime. Closed major holidays. $

Where to Stay

Best Western/Regent Inn. 123 Storrs Rd. (Route 195) in Mansfield Center; (860) 423-8451. Near UConn, 88 rooms with two double beds, indoor pool, fitness room. Continental breakfast. $$–$$$

Nathan Hale Inn. 855 Bolton Rd.; (860) 427-7888. This inn and conference center offers 100 guest rooms and 18 suites right on the UConn campus. Restaurant, indoor pool, fitness room. $$$$

General Information

River Valley/Connecticut covers 46 towns of the Central Regional Tourism District, including some towns in Tolland County and other areas of the Connecticut River Valley. For maps and brochures and information on attractions, dining, and accommodations, visit One Constitution Plaza, 2nd floor, Hartford 06103; (860) 787-9640; (800) 793-4480; www.enjoycentralct.com.

Mystic Country/Connecticut covers 42 towns in the Eastern Regional Tourism District, including parts of Tolland County. Call (860) 536-8822, or visit 27 Coogan Blvd., Building 3A, Mystic CT 06355; www.mystic .org for visitor's guide, maps, calendars of events.

Windham County
River Valleys and Rural Byways

I don't know in what year some clever copy writer labeled Windham County the "Quiet Corner," but the name has stuck so thoroughly that you might think it is the region's official name. Though parts of Tolland County share the name, at least in the state tourism materials, it is here in Windham that the full impact of the term hits the traveler. It's quiet here.

Although a portion of the county is sliced by I-395, which leads travelers toward Worcester, Boston, and points beyond, the area is little altered by the traffic. In fact, the whole 25-town region along the Quiet Corner's two major rivers has been designated the Quinebaug and Shetucket Rivers Valley National Heritage Corridor in recognition of its status as one of the last unspoiled and undeveloped areas in the Northeast. In keeping with that honor and spirit, the proprietors of the region's museums, shops, and inns have deliberately and successfully maintained the county's old-fashioned ambience, partly to please those very travelers who seek its peaceful thoroughfares.

TopPicks for fun in Windham County

1. **Fort Hill Farms and Corn Maze**
2. **Quaddick State Park**
3. **Mashamoquet Brook State Park**
4. **Creamery Brook Bison**
5. **Prudence Crandall Museum**
6. **Roseland Cottage**
7. **Valley View Riding Stables**

WINDHAM COUNTY

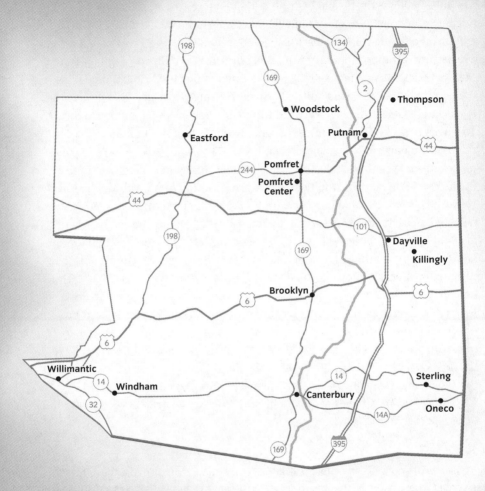

The Last **Green Valley**

The hills, valleys, rivers, and historic mill villages of the northeast corner of Connecticut constitute part of one of America's national heritage corridors, established by the National Park Service but managed by 25 towns and many private organizations that lie within this portion of Windham County. (Ten Massachusetts towns manage the Massachusetts portion.) Called the Quinebaug and Shetucket Rivers Valley National Heritage Corridor, this thousand-square-mile area extends northward from Norwich in New London County to 10 towns in south-central Massachusetts. Notable for its tranquility, its pristine natural environments, and its historical importance as one of the birthplaces of the American Industrial Revolution, the region is much admired for its recreational opportunities and its preservation of natural and historic resources. Most of the important attractions within the corridor have been selected as destinations deserving treatment in this guide, but many others also could have been included had space permitted. For a complete understanding of this heritage corridor and its attractions, call the **Quinebaug and Shetucket Rivers Valley National Heritage Corridor** at (860) 963-7226. You can also check the website www.tlgv.org. From the website, you can download (or call to ask for) such publications as the National Park Service brochure and map titled *The Last Green Valley; The Green and Growing Guide to the Agricultural Treasures of the Q&SRVNHC;* the *Walking Guide to the Q&SRVNHC;* the *Walking Weekend Guide,* and three "Ventures" tour maps to the Green and Growing places, the Villages, and the Wild.

You can also call the **Eastern Regional Tourism District** at (860) 536-8822 or check the website www. mystic.org.

Call it what you will—some folks call it the "Last Green Valley" amidst the sprawl that has spread from Boston all the way to D.C.—I just call it beautiful. Families looking for fun in Windham County are going to find mostly simple pleasures. Kick back, take your shoes off, sit a spell. Get ready to use your senses. This is the place to explore, to take a deep breath, to listen to the brooks, the breeze, and the birds. It's the place to contemplate how this land—all of this land, this whole now–United States—must have looked before 1636, when the European settlers came.

Dayville/Killingly

Beginning right in the heart of the county, take a ride up I-395 to Dayville, a barely there village on the western side of the highway in the larger town of Killingly. An excursion here will draw you into the sort of down-home, laid-back, unhurried action typical of the county.

Valley View Riding Stables (ages 3 and up)

91 Lake Rd.; (860) 617-4425 or (860) 779-9855; www.valleyviewridingstables. Open daily year-round, for group and private lessons, rides, and parties.

Get on your jeans and some sturdy shoes and head up the trail to Dayville for a day of fun and learning in the great outdoors. On the belief that children are very nice people, owner Amy Lyons has created some great opportunities for families with children ages 3 and up to enjoy the pretty terrain of her 250-acre former dairy farm-cum-full-service equestrian facility. Valley View has indoor and outdoor arenas, trails, and 75 acres of pasture, which means that there is both room and opportunity for families to learn how to ride or just have a chance to be with the horses and other creatures who live in this welcoming space. Riding lessons are provided for all ages and skill levels, with special emphasis on beginning or timid riders. Pony rides and pony birthday parties are very popular here, and, with some advance notice, Amy can also help you arrange a guided trail ride for your family, as long as it's paired with a 30-minute riding lesson that you all have before you take to the trails on her gently rolling property. No prior experience or special equipment is necessary; helmets and anything else you might need are provided. In late October (call for this

Bikin' the **Backroads**

In Danielson—another of the villages of Killingly—there's a soft-spoken, laid-back, and generous fellow named Don Dauphinais, owner of **Danielson Adventure Sports** (21 Furnace St., Danielson; 860-774-6010; open Mon through Sat year-round). He'll help your family create a blue-highways or off-road biking itinerary in the Northeast Corner that will get you closely in touch with the great outdoors. He has 10 or more on- and off-road routes already mapped, and he can hand you a hard copy of those routes at no charge. You tell him how far you want to go, how much time you have, and how strenuous you want the route to be for your clan. Or, from April through October, for families with kids 12 and older, he can take you out on a guided ride ($$$$)— and all you have to do is follow him. He can take you through Old Furnace State Park or across the West Thompson Dam, for instance—or visit his website at www.bikect.com and click on Links to see some other great spots you might visit. Guided or not, you must bring your own bikes and helmets. You'll be in good hands—Don has biked solo cross-country and is a World Cup racer and bike mechanic.

If for some reason you'd rather get wet, try http://paddlekillingly.webs.com to get to folks who will get you and yours into a boat and onto the water.

year's date), you can come for the **free** Halloween Open House Day—an extravaganza of pony rides, hay rides, a kids' costume contest, a costumed horse show, plus face painting, pumpkin picking and painting, and games. If you live nearby, your kids can also come for weeklong sessions of horsemanship day camp, which includes riding lessons as well as horse care and handling lessons. No matter how you choose to participate here, you'll be matched with very safe beginner mounts, perfect for youngsters and first timers. It's also fine with Amy if you just drop by to enjoy a look at the farm and its many creatures—so if you are curious about horses, farmyard animals, and New England farmlands, come here.

Where to Eat

Mozzarella's Italian Grill. 460 Hartford Pike, Route 101; (860) 774-3434. Delicious prime rib, steaks, grilled chicken, pastas, salads, soups, finger foods, and home-style specials in a casually contemporary dining room of a quaint country house. In warm weather, dine on the patio near a water garden. Lunch and dinner from 11 a.m. until 11 p.m. on Fri and Sat, until 9 p.m. on Sun and Mon, and until 10 p.m. Tues through Thurs. Kids' meals, $1.99 on Wed, Sat, and Sun. $–$$

Zip's Diner. Junction of Routes 101 and 12; (860) 774-6335. Authentic stainless steel and spinning counter stools are here in this classic 1954 O'Mahoney diner. Nothing's changed here in 50 years, folks, and that's a good thing. Open daily from 6 a.m. to 9 p.m. $–$$

Where to Stay

Comfort Inn and Suites. 16 Tracy Rd., off exit 94, I-395; (860) 779-3200. 78 rooms and suites, indoor pool, fitness room, complimentary continental breakfast. $$$$

Thompson

Some people think that Connecticut's most northeastern town of Thompson has the quintessential village of the Quiet Corner. Tiny and serene, it is lined with houses, churches, inns, and merchants that still seem almost eerily reminiscent of the 18th century. Were the town managers to outlaw automobile traffic, this village that grew alongside the stagecoach route to Boston and Providence would be surreal indeed. A stroll along the main avenue (Route 193) of town is pleasant for parents and patient children, but the real family values in Thompson lie off the main thoroughfare.

Fort Hill Farms and Gardens (all ages)

260 Quaddick Rd.; (860) 923-3439; www.forthillfarms.com. Fort Hills Farms (which includes the A-Maze-ing Corn Maze Adventure, Quintessential Gardens, Lavender Labyrinths, Fort Hill Creamery, and Fort Hill Mining) is open daily from 9 a.m. to 9 p.m. (or dusk), weather permitting. The Creamery itself is open 11:30 a.m. to about 9 p.m. Garden tours ($$$), May through Oct. Corn Maze Adventure ($$) open mid-Aug through mid-Nov. Call for dates and prices for Fort Hill Mining Company and berry picking (in season).

Ten thousand visitors come to tiny Thompson each summer to tour the state's most a-maze-ing cornfield. On 8 acres of her 1,200-acre dairy farm, Kristin Orr dreams up, plans, plants, and cuts an astonishing educational themed Corn Maze Adventure each year. One theme was Revolutionary history; another was Rivers of the United States, and, in 2010, the theme was The Farmer's Cow-Lick, named for the ice cream of the Farmer's Cow milk cooperative to which the farm belongs. Each year, Kristin creates the signage and the four-page game sheet of clues, questions, and activities that help visitors navigate through all the stations within this immaculate maze. "That there is one maze of beauty," wrote one young visitor after a walk through this splendidly "corn-fusing" agricultural wonder. Kristin loves those fan letters, and she's had many, as word of her exceptional maze has spread around New England and beyond. Scout troops, school groups, sports teams, and a ton of families have toured her maze and her pristine farmland, in cultivation since 1889. This is no Halloween-style free-for-all romp; it's a well-organized, mind-opening education in agriculture and whatever the year's theme may be.

Kristin is a high-energy gal, and she's also created Quintessential Gardens and Lavender Labyrinths, where thousands of organic lavender plants thrive under her care. Children's tours of the farm's 70 organically grown display gardens are also offered from May through August; call to arrange one for your family. You can also come here to pan for gems and fossils at Fort Hill Mining Company, or if you just have good, safe food on your family menu for the day, come here to pick and purchase your own organic blueberries and currants—grown with no pesticides anywhere. Tours of the dairy can also be arranged, or you can just visit the Calf Barn and discover whatever other animals might be around the barnyard. Four hundred Holstein, Jersey, and Guernsey cows and calves are on the property, and half of those are milked each day to contribute to the milk cooperative. This is a truly beautiful piece of sacred ground, as Kristin believes, and her philosophy, shared by her husband and children, is to ensure that it remains a pristine center for global well-being. Some folks drive miles in winter just to see the lighted message of peace that Kristin and her family create each December in their fields. It's a farm sanctuary, for sure, and visitors are lucky that the Orrs have opened it up for sharing.

Quaddick State Park (all ages)

East Putnam Road off Route 44; (860) 928-9200. Open year-round from 8 a.m. to sunset. Free, except parking fee ($$) on weekends and holidays from Memorial Day through Labor Day. No lifeguards.

Unless you've had your fill of simple pleasures, you'll find Quaddick a great place to spend an afternoon. Located on East Putnam Road off Route 44, the land and the lake were once the summer camp and fishing ground of the Nipmuck Indians. Later it was the Thompson town farm, where elderly citizens spent their dotage in peaceful contemplation. It's a fair bit noisier now, being one of the most popular state parks in the county.

The 466-acre reservoir and sandy beach are the source of most of the activity. You can swim, fish, water-ski, Jet Ski, and sail or canoe here in the summertime. Those delights are made easier with such facilities as changing houses, restrooms, drinking fountains, a boat launch ramp, a picnic pavilion, and a food concession. You can also hike through 116 acres on well-marked woodland trails or play ball or horseshoes on the sports fields. In winter you can ice-skate or ice-fish on the reservoir as long as the weather permits. Cross-country skiing is not possible on the trails, but you can hike or snowshoe if the spirit moves you to take the kids out for a brisk walk in the crisp air.

Where to Eat

L. B.'s Family Restaurant. 860 Riverside Ave.; (860) 923-1899. If you are looking for something very unfussy but down-home—a place where the locals go—try this diner-style favorite in business for nearly 20 years. Open for three meals daily from 6 a.m., except breakfast only from 7 a.m. to 1 p.m. on Sun. $

For other choices, it's necessary and best to head to Putnam.

Where to Stay

Corttis Inn. 235 Corttis Rd., North Grosvenordale; (860) 935-5652. Some folks might call this house spacious, but it's enormous. Inside, you'll be back in the 18th century among period furnishings, having hot cocoa near the kitchen fire or savoring delicious blackberry jam on freshly baked muffins. Outside, you can skate on the pond, bicycle the country lanes, hike, or cross-country ski on trails through 900—yes, 900—acres of this private property. Comfortable rooms with private bath and private entrance. $$

Lord Thompson Manor. Route 200, exit 99 off I-395, in Thompson; (860) 923-3886; www .lordthompsonmanor.com. Set off from the main thoroughfare, this 36-acre estate, once a horse farm, is often booked for weddings or family reunions. On occasion, however, you may rent a room nightly here or at its sister bed-and-breakfast inn (and spa), the **Cottage House,** a historic tavern on the Thompson green. Due to summer weddings, weekend availability may be better in the off-season. $$$$

Woodstock

Of all the Windham County towns, Woodstock may be the most gentrified, the most artsy, the most sophisticated. It is lovely, to be sure, and one can't blame the tourists for flocking here for the array of treats in store at every turn in the road.

Composed of several villages named North Woodstock, South Woodstock, and so on, the town center most noted for its picturesque qualities is Woodstock proper, a tasteful and sedate community located on beautiful Route 169. Atop the hill, its pretty town common beckons to the traveler with an eye for tranquil spaces. A leisurely stroll through Woodstock Center will reveal many lovely places in which to browse, buy country treasures, or pick up something tasty to eat.

Roseland Cottage (ages 4 and up)
556 Route 169; (860) 928-4074; www.historicnewengland.org/visit/homes/roseland.htm.
Open June 1 through Oct 15, including July 4 and Columbus Day, Wed through Sun 11 a.m.
to 5 p.m., with tours on the hour until 4 p.m. Check website for current calendar of special
events and to register/buy tickets. $–$$.

If you allow the children to wander awhile on the common, it shouldn't take them long to
find Roseland Cottage just across the road. A candy-colored pink confection of a house,
it is a most surprising attraction that may provide at least an afternoon's worth of entertainment. Built in 1846 in the newly fashionable Gothic revival style, this magnificently
restored estate was the summer retreat of Henry C. Bowen, native to Woodstock but long
and successfully a New York dry-goods dealer.

Though he made and lost several fortunes in his lifetime, Bowen never lost his sense
of stewardship and philanthropy. Founder of churches, abolitionist and supporter of the
Union cause in the Civil War, advocate of the beautification of common property, and a
lifetime teetotaler, Bowen also liked nothing better than celebrations. Roseland Cottage
was the site of lawn parties, bowling contests in the indoor alley, and Fourth of July festivities that made all others look dull in comparison.

The special festival days held here are an appropriate tribute to its former owner. The
most popular events for families are the Fourth of July festivities, which include joyous
activities the Bowen family might have enjoyed decades ago, and the Civil War Encampment that spans a weekend in late August. At the latter event, which is **free** (unless you
decide to take a house tour), children can interact with Union and Confederate reenactors,
learning how to load a cannon, do codes and ciphers, march in a drill formation, and use
signal flags. Skirmishes between the artillerymen and soldiers, cooking and other camp-
like demonstrations, and musical performances are all part of the event. Also here in summertime—and also **free**—are two or three Twilight Lawn Concerts, very popular with
families. The Fall Festival of Fine Arts and Crafts, held on the weekend after Columbus Day,

The Woodstock **Fair**

Held from 9 a.m. to 9 p.m. on Labor Day weekend, this fair (860-928-3246;
www.woodstockfair.com) is one of the 10 largest and one of the five oldest country fairs in the state. Each year since 1858 it has offered oxen pulls,
horse shows, wood-chopping exhibitions, and hundreds of displays of pre-
mium livestock, prizewinning pies, gigantic vegetables, creative handiwork,
and much more. These days you'll also find a midway, go-kart races, tons of
food, and practically continuous stage entertainment to enhance your enjoyment of everything else. As many as 200,000 other fairgoers will be here with
you at this four-day festivity that begins on Friday and rocks steady through
Monday. $$, kids 10 and under **free.**

features tours, a food court, clowns and jugglers, and a juried show of nearly 200 artisans. On the first weekend in December, the house is open at no charge during Woodstock's Winter Festival.

Even on ordinary days, you can take tours of the luxurious "cottage," which retains most of its original furnishings, and you can wander the labyrinthine pathways of the 21 formal gardens, and explore such summer leisure activities as hoop rolling, graces, bilboquet, or playing marbles or jacks. The staff serves pink lemonade every day, and families are encouraged to bring picnics and eat on the lawn. Regular tours focus on details of special interest to young people whenever a guide sees a child among the visitors, and hands-on history activities in the visitor center entertain children waiting for a tour.

Where to Eat

Java Jive. 283 Route 169; (860) 963-1241. This gourmet espresso cafe has an artsy, urban feel and a down-to-earth motivation: Its profits are donated to Third World children in need of clean water and healthy food. Coffees, smoothies, pastries, confections, and healthy breakfast and lunch. Open 6 a.m. to 3 p.m. Mon through Fri, 7:30 a.m. to 4 p.m. Sat, and 8 a.m. to noon on Sun. $

Mrs. Bridge's Pantry. 292 Somers Turnpike (Route 169) in South Woodstock, across from the Woodstock Fairgrounds; (860) 963-7040. Four acres of picnic grounds, a charming gift shop, and outdoor table service on a wide deck make this a great place to stop and smell the roses. Teas, cocoa, and traditional British favorites such as scones with clotted cream and jam, meat pies, salmon cakes, and tea sandwiches are the focus. Open Wed through Mon year-round from 10 a.m. to 6 p.m. $

Stoggy Hollow General Store and Restaurant. 492 Route 198, Woodstock Valley; (860) 974-2889. This old-time roadside establishment offers omelets, homemade soups, grilled sandwiches, burgers, chicken pot pie, pizza, pasta, seafood, and fresh breads, muffins, turnovers, and pies. Open year-round, 7 a.m. to 8 p.m., with shorter hours on Sunday and in winter. Eat on the deck in warm weather; shop in the general store for locally made goodies. $

Sweet Evalina's. 688 Route 169; (860) 928-4029. If you love local independents as much as we do, definitely come to "Evy's" for seasonally grown, locally sourced favorites at breakfast, lunch, or early dinner. They do pizza Thursday through Sunday evenings, but they are open every day of the week from 7 a.m. (8 on Sunday) to 8ish p.m. $–$$

Where to Stay

Beaver Pond B&B. 68 Cutler Hill Rd., Woodstock; (860) 974-3312. 2 guest rooms with a shared bath make this a nice place for families who want a private getaway. Truly congenial hosts serve you a full country breakfast, then you can explore the options for hiking, fishing, and boating right on their 23-acre property. $$

The Inn at Woodstock Hill. 94 Plaine Hill Rd., South Woodstock; (860) 928-0528; www.woodstockhill.net. This former Bowen Mansion has a wonderful cottage with 3 rooms, plus 18 rooms with private baths in the main inn. Every inch of the 14-acre property is beautiful; the elegant atmosphere is enhanced by the friendly staff. Continental breakfast for guests; lunch, dinner, and Sunday brunch available in the restaurant, which enjoys its own major reputation. $$$$

The Mansion at Bald Hill. 29 Plaine Hill Rd., South Woodstock; (860) 974-3456; www .mansionatbaldhill.com. Like the inn above, this one is beyond gorgeous and mostly accommodates adults in need of quiet and romance, but, if you enjoy both beauty and fine dining, do come if you wish with the children—or better yet, book a room for your anniversary. Six exquisite rooms with private baths; notable restaurant; complimentary gourmet breakfast. $$$$

Pomfret/Pomfret Center/Putnam

First settled in about 1700, Pomfret was known in the 1890s as the "other Newport" as visitors from New York City began summering in these pretty woods and building three-story cottages to help them rough it here. Just 5 miles south of Woodstock on Route 169, it is home now to private secondary schoolers, several pretty inns and B&Bs, a great herb garden, a handful of antiques stores, and a new vineyard. Among its best attractions are the famed Wolf Den Trail in its state park and its early mill historic site, but be sure to stop also at the Connecticut Audubon Center at Pomfret if you treasure the outdoors. When you're ready to wander, head toward Putnam on Route 44 East. You should be at the center of downtown in less than 10 minutes unless you stop along the way. Besides the attractions you may want to see there, you'll find some great shops and galleries and a good number of eateries. Be sure to stop at Wonderland Books (120 Main St.; 860-963-2600), chockfull of everything readable, plus tons of toys and gifts to boot. Peek into the gallery and studios at Sawmill Pottery (112 Main St., #14; 860-963-7807)—or sign up ahead of time for a class. All proceeds from their sales are donated to charity. Pop into the Sochor Gallery at Arts & Framing (112 Main St.; 860-963-0105) to see, well, Big Bird—in the artwork of Caroll Spinney, who played that famed character as well as Oscar the Grouch on *Sesame Street*. If you have time to linger, walk the 1.1-mile River Mills Heritage Trail, which traces the Quinebaug River and links six historic mills, roughly between Pomfret Street and Providence Street.

Mashamoquet Brook State Park (all ages)

147 Wolf Den Dr., at the junction of Routes 44 and 101; park office: (860) 928-6121; http://ct .gov/DEP. Open year-round daily from 8 a.m. to sunset for day visitors. Free, except for parking fee ($$) only on weekends and holidays between Apr 15 and Oct 15. Camping reservations recommended especially for weekends and long stays; vacancies filled on first-come, first-served basis. Campsites, $.

Nearly 1,000 acres are the combined area of the three sections that compose this large park: Wolf Den, Saptree Run, and Mashamoquet Brook. Seven miles of great trails link the areas and make this one of Connecticut's most popular state parks. In addition to hiking, fishing, and picnicking, Wolf Den offers camping, and Mashamoquet Brook offers swimming and camping. Wolf Den has 35 open sites with a flush toilet and drinking water from April 15 through October 15. Mashamoquet Brook has 20 wooded sites with a composting toilet and pump water.

The most famous of park attractions are the Table Rock and Indian Chair stone formations and the nearby Putnam Wolf Den Trail, accessible from Wolf Den Drive. From the park's second parking area, a 4-mile loop trail leads past the campground to the Wolf Den area. Call for the schedule of guided walks if you'd like to get the full story of Israel and the Wolf, or ask a ranger for a self-guided tour map. After you've seen the site of this sinister encounter, check out the natural formations of Indian Chair and Table Rock, just a little farther along the Wolf Den Trail, which also crosses Mashamoquet Brook and then returns to the parking area.

Brayton Grist Mill and
the Marcy Blacksmith Shop Museum (ages 6 and up)

At the entrance to Mashamoquet Brook State Park on Route 44. Open weekends from late May through Sept from 2 to 5 p.m. Free.

Maintained by the Pomfret Historical Society, Billy Brayton's four-story gristmill is the state's finest example of a one-man, water-powered mill operation of the 1890s. The equipment for generating power to grind grain and shell corn survives in the exact locations where Brayton used them. The turbine, the millstone, and a corn sheller are among the items you'll learn about on a tour of the museum.

An exhibit of handcrafted tools represents the labor of the Marcy family blacksmiths, who plied their trade from 1817 to 1946 in an area known as Marcy Hollow at the side of Mashamoquet Brook. Orin Marcy opened the shop in 1830, using a water-powered

Israel and **the Wolf**

General Israel Putnam became famous for more than just his role in the Revolution and his famed ride against the British down the 100 stone steps of his Greenwich hillside homestead. You see, he spent his young manhood in these parts, successfully pursuing the dual careers of innkeeper and farmer.

Legend has it that for several years young Israel and his neighbors were bothered by the killing instincts of a lone wolf that occasionally made a meal of the local livestock. One night in 1742 the wolf awakened Israel's protective instincts by making off with more than just a few of Israel's sheep. Israel vowed to bring down the killer and assembled a ragtag army of neighbors to help him do it. For days Israel, his neighbors, and their hounds tracked the wolf, finally finding her lair in the face of a high cliff. In went the hounds braying and barking, and out they came again, yelping and mewling. None of them would re-enter the cave.

Israel himself decided to go in after the beast. After a few almost comic attempts to apprehend the criminal, Israel was finally successful. He shot her and dragged her out by the ears. Some say she was the last wolf to live in Connecticut. Today you can hike to her den via the Mashamoquet State Park's Wolf Den Trail.

bellows and trip-hammer. A collection of tools made by the blacksmiths includes some used in the manufacture of wheels and horseshoes. In fact, Orin's son, Darius, earned first prize for his horseshoes at the Chicago World's Fair in 1893.

Connecticut Audubon Center at Pomfret (all ages)

189 Pomfret St. (Route 169); (860) 928-4948; www.ctaudubon.org/visit/pomfret.htm. Open year-round; sanctuary open daily dawn to dusk; center open Wed through Sat, noon to 4 p.m. Free.

Folks who like birds and butterflies are going to love the Bafflin Sanctuary, a pristine refuge of nearly 700 acres of grassland and second-growth woodland that attracts many hard-to-find species year-round and seasonally. The trails in this beautiful area of meadows, forest, streams, and reclaimed farmland offer many opportunities to enjoy the Quiet Corner's uniquely preserved habitats. Owls, hawks, songbirds, ducks, and wildflowers are abundant, and you may join a scheduled field walk or take to the easy trails on your own. (Socks and water-resistant footgear are a great idea here.)

Changing natural history exhibits are inside the center, along with a classroom for after-school and weekend workshops perfect for families. Preregistration is either required or strongly suggested.

Gertrude Chandler Warner Boxcar Museum (ages 8 to 12)

South Main St. and Union Square, Putnam; (860) 963-0092. Open May through Oct on weekends from 11 a.m. to 3 p.m. Donation.

If you or your children are fans of the children's book series called *The Boxcar Children*, come to Putnam and find the little red boxcar that houses a museum dedicated to the author of those books. Gertrude Chandler Warner grew up in these parts, taught Putnam's first graders for 30-plus years, and penned the 18 or more books about the adventures of Henry, Jessie, Violet, and Benny Alden right here in Putnam. The little museum is arranged inside a boxcar with a likeness of her workplace, using her grandfather's actual desk, where she wrote as a child.

Where to Eat

85 Main. 85 Main S., Putnam; (860) 928-1660. New American cuisine at lunch and dinner daily in a casual setting in the old Union Station with fine-dining-quality ingredients, raw bar, children's menu. Perfect, really, for families. $$–$$$$

Vanilla Bean Cafe. 450 Deerfield Rd. at the junction of Route 97 with Routes 169 and 44; (860) 928-1562; www.vanillabeancafe .com. Ideal for families, this cafe offers a huge breakfast/brunch on weekends and breakfast muffins and sandwiches the rest of the week.

Lunch and dinner could be chili, quiches, stews, sandwiches, or soups. Check the website for the Saturday-night entertainment lineup. Except for major holidays, it's open from 7 a.m. to 3 p.m. on Mon and Tues, to 8 p.m. on Wed, Thurs, and Sun, and to 9 p.m. on Fri and Sat. $

Where to Stay

Feather Hill Bed and Breakfast. 151 Mashamoquet Rd., Pomfret; (866) 963-0522; www.featherhillbedandbreakfast.com. 5

spacious rooms and a suite, with private baths, in the main house (welcoming children 10 and older). Separate cottage, with bath and fireplace, that sleeps four can be rented by families with younger children. Full gourmet breakfast. $$$$

Eastford

West of Pomfret, taking Route 244 west from the center or going south on 169, then west on Route 44, take a side trip to Eastford, which is on Route 198. There's no doubt that Natchaug State Forest is the single biggest entity around here, and that's basically all that families might want to explore—at least after they stock up on all the wonderful agricultural goods produced in these parts by some of Connecticut's finest growers.

Buell's Orchard (all ages)

108 Crystal Pond Rd., off Route 198, 2 miles north of Phoenixville, via Westford Rd.; (860) 974-1150; www.buellsorchard.com. Open Mon though Sat, 8 a.m. to 5 p.m. and Sun, 1 to 5 p.m. in Sept and Oct (closed the first Sun of Sept). In Nov and Dec, Mon through Fri, 8 a.m. to 4 p.m. and Sat, 8 a.m. to 3 p.m. (closed Sun).

If you'd like to pack some snacks for a day of hiking, start at Buell's, following the signs to the 100-acre farm from the center of Eastford on Route 198. Beginning with strawberries in June, and going forward to apples in the fall, you can pick your own fruit in season. They also sell their pears, peaches, pumpkins, Vermont cheese, maple syrup, and cider. After Labor Day, you can sink your teeth into one of Buell's Famous Caramel Apples. Come Columbus Day weekend for the annual Fall Festival and the opening of the pick-your-own pumpkin patch. Hayrides and **free** cider and doughnuts are part of the hoopla.

Natchaug State Forest (all ages)

Note: Usual entrance is 4 miles south of Phoenixville on Route 198, but the bridge there is under repair and is closed indefinitely; to enter the forest, use the secondary entrance off Pilfershire Road; for picnicking and fishing along the river, continue to use parking areas off Route 198. Park supervisor's office: (860) 928-6121; www.ct.gov/dep. **Free.**

Certainly the largest of the treasures families will find in Eastford, this forest has a name that means "land between the rivers," a reference to its position at the junction of the Still and Bigelow Rivers. Bounded by Routes 44, 6, 198, and 97, it lies adjacent to the beautiful Natchaug River, formed by the confluence of the two smaller rivers. Its 13,000 pristine acres offer elbow room to thousands of outdoor enthusiasts who use it for camping, fishing, picnicking, hiking, snowmobiling, cross-country skiing, and horseback riding.

Picnic sites overlook the river, and anglers of all ages enjoy the trout fishing allowed here from the third week in April to March 1. Besides its trails and picnic area, the State Forest Service provides outhouses and drinking water to day visitors as well as overnight visitors. Backpackers and horseback campers must pack in all supplies and register with the rangers. Silvermine Horse Camp offers 15 **free** sites used by families with their own or rented horses.

Canoeing on the Natchaug is very popular. If you own a canoe, launch it just south of the junction of Routes 198 and 44 in Phoenixville, off General Lyons Road. A 7-mile run through a mix of flat water and quick water takes you past several dams and bridges to the take-out at England Road Bridge. This stretch is great for beginners; experienced canoeists might want to continue another 5.5 miles through several sets of rapids down to Mansfield Hollow State Park.

Town Line Sugarhouse (all ages)

96 Weeks Rd.; (860) 974-1618. Open Fri, Sat, and Sun during the last two weeks in Mar (but call ahead to confirm), from 10 a.m. to 4 p.m. Free visits; maple sugar for sale.

Steve Broderick, forester, conservationist, and manager of the **Goodwin Conservation Center** (also very worth a visit; see www.ct.gov/dep) in nearby Hampton, owns this little maple sugarhouse in Eastford. He's a terrifically knowledgeable fellow in terms of these lovely Eastern Woodlands and lots more, and he really knows how to explain the sugaring process. He taps 250 to 300 sugar maple trees on this property and boils it all down for you to taste, purchase, and, for a taste of ye olde New England, to drizzle over some good vanilla ice cream when you get home. Typically maple-sugar season in Connecticut is in the neighborhood of the last two weeks or so in March, depending on the weather.

Family Camping on the **Natchaug River**

The state forest campground offers the basic necessities for primitive camping, but some families may enjoy the amenities offered by two private campgrounds on the Natchaug. **Charlie Brown Campground** (860-974-0142 or 877-974-0142; www.charliebrowncampground.com) at 98 Chaplin Rd. (Route 198) has 123 grassy sites for tenters and RVers, plus laundry, restrooms, showers, covered camping pavilions, a camp store, a recreation hall with entertainment and planned activities, plus on-site opportunities for hiking, swimming, tubing, and fishing. **Peppertree Camping** (860-974-1439) on Route 198 has 50 wooded tent and RV sites along the river; it's a great place to launch canoes or tubes or to fish in the stocked river. It also has restrooms, showers, a laundry, and a store—but no rec hall or entertainment. Make your own fun here. At both camps, site rates, $; weekly rates available.

Where to Eat

Midway Restaurant & Pizza. 174 Ashford Center Rd., Ashford; (860) 429-1932. Authentic Greek specialties, pizzas, salads in family-owned, family-friendly casual setting Open daily from 10 a.m. $–$$

Still River Cafe. At North Ashford Farm, 134 Union Rd. (Route 171), Eastford; (860) 974-9988. Distinctly other than ordinary, this special-occasion restaurant offers gourmet-quality, truly locally grown (on this 27-acre farm) meals of particular note. Stunning—and pricey—but casual in mood. Dress nicely; bring good manners and a good appetite. You won't be disappointed. Dinner, Fri and Sat; lunch, Sun. Reservations encouraged. $$$$

Brooklyn

Windham County contains one of the top 10 scenic highways in the United States, selected for that distinction by Scenic America, an environmental organization that works, in part, to identify and protect scenic American roads. In 1996 the National Department of Transportation designated the road a National Scenic Byway. Historically known as the Norwich–Woodstock Turnpike, the 32-mile section of Route 169 that lies between Lisbon (in New London County) and Woodstock is just about as pretty as pretty can get. Part of that route goes through Brooklyn, a quaint village with beautiful New England churches and a monument to Revolutionary War hero General Israel Putnam in its center. In a building very close to the equestrian statue, at 25 Canterbury Rd., you'll find the **Brooklyn Historical Society** (860-774-7728), which has much more to tell you in its spiffy exhibits about ol' Put.

Creamery Brook Bison (ages 2 to 12)

19 Purvis Rd.; (860) 779-0837; www.creamerybrookbison.net. Public wagon tours, July to Sept, Sat at 1:30 p.m. (no reservations necessary), $$; children under 3 free. Families and larger groups can prearrange guided tours, ice-cream and butter-making activities, and wagon ride combinations. Check website for other special seasonal events. Store open Apr through Oct, Mon through Fri, 2 to 6 p.m. and Sat, 10 a.m. to 2 p.m.; Nov to Mar, Wed through Fri, 2 to 6 p.m. and weekends, 10 a.m. to 2 p.m.

Committed to educating the public about buffalo and dairy farming, this hundred-acre farm is the home of 70 buffalo who roam its pastures and woodlands. Visit here year-round simply to see the bison (early evening, around 6, is the best viewing time, when the herd leaves the woods and comes down toward the open field), or come on Saturday from July through September for a wagon ride out into those cool woods to see the herd. Along with Holstein and Jersey cows and the adult bison, you will more than likely see bison calves. Learn about bison history, habitats, habits, and myths; browse in the store for bison-related booty; see the wildflower maze; and visit the petting area.

You can also arrange a guided tour ($$$$) of the farm or an ice-cream-making outing in which you help make hand-cranked ice cream and butter. Birthday parties with a wagon tour and ice-cream-making activity can also be arranged. If you don't have time for a whole party, just gather at the ice cream shop, open in summer from 2 to 9 p.m. Be sure to check the website for other special events, including an ice-cream social in mid-summer and pumpkin-patch visits in October.

Brooklyn Fair (all ages)

Route 169, Brooklyn Fairgrounds; (860) 779-0012; www.brooklynfair.org. Fourth weekend in Aug, Thurs 4 to 10 p.m., Fri and Sat 8 a.m. to 10 p.m., and Sun 8 a.m. to 6 p.m. $$, children 12 and under free. Parking, $.

Every year in late August, Brooklyn's population soars as visitors from all over come to the oldest continuously active agricultural fair in the United States. Held for four days the weekend before Labor Day, it is perhaps the best country fair in the state. Here's a partial list of what's in store for you: Oxen pull. Draft horse show. Skillet toss. Dog show. Circus. Midway. Pony pull. Cattle parade. Christmas tree show. Bingo. Barbecue. Tractor pull. Country dancing. Beekeeping exhibit. Children's games and contests. Art show. Stage entertainment for adults and children. Although the agricultural events are all free, you'll need a wad of currency for a day or evening here. That is, unless you and the kids don't eat any food, buy any crafts or gadgets, or ride any rides.

Allen Hill Farm (all ages)

542 Allen Hill Rd., off Route 6; (860) 774-7064; www.allenhillfarm.com. Open in Nov and until Dec 24 from 10 a.m. to dusk Mon through Fri, and from 8 a.m. to dusk on the weekends. $.

Owners Charles Langevin, Robert Langevin, and Roland Gibeault welcome visitors to their choose-and-cut hundred-acre tree farm, which may just be among the prettiest such enterprises in the whole state of Connecticut. You board one of their hay wagons, and they take you to their fields, where the views are just spectacular. They give you a saw, you choose, you cut, they wrap, and you go home with a perfect Christmas tree, in the form of a Canaan, Douglas, Balsam, or Fraser fir, a blue or white spruce, or a white pine. Browse in the gift shop for locally made crafts, wreaths, and tree stands; sample complimentary cookies and hot mulled cider; visit with Santa and Mrs. Claus on weekends in December. If Christmas is important on your family calendar, Allen Hill is the kind of place you'll be happy to see.

Where to Eat

Hank's Restaurant. 416 Providence Rd. (Route 6); (860) 774-6071. Since 1972, this Brooklyn fixture has been serving up burgers, steaks, salads, soups, seafood, and pasta. A children's menu has typical favorites. Open for lunch and dinner from 11 a.m. Mon through Sat and from noon on Sun. $

Canterbury

Famed for its own architectural style and for Crandall Academy, founded in 1832 by Prudence Crandall, Canterbury is an almost completely rural town that appears nearly the same as it did a century ago. Six miles south of Brooklyn on Route 169, its pretty Congregational Church on the Green was built in the 1960s as a replica of the original one built

The Story of the **State Heroine**

In the summer of 1831, 28-year-old Prudence Crandall was asked by a group of Canterbury citizens to establish a private academy in which she would teach local children. Crandall purchased a large house on the Canterbury green and opened her academy in January 1832. All went well for several months. Crandall had the full support of the parents, who paid her $25 per quarter to teach their children reading, writing, arithmetic, grammar, geography, history, philosophy, chemistry, and astronomy.

Then, in the fall of 1832, Crandall accepted a new student. Sarah Harris, 20 years old, was black. Disapproval was immediate, and several families withdrew their children from the academy. Criticism was so harsh that Crandall dismissed the remaining students and reopened the school several months later as an academy for the instruction of "young ladies and little misses of color."

The first such school in all of New England, the academy added classes in French, drawing, painting, and piano. Outrage followed the earlier criticism as Crandall made it clear that no distinctions were to be made in the education of white and black children. In May 1833, Crandall was arrested and jailed for breaking the Connecticut General Assembly's new "Black Law," which prohibited the instruction of any "colored persons who are not inhabitants of this State."

Though her case was dismissed in July, Crandall and her students suffered greatly at the hands of the citizens of the Canterbury area. The house was pelted with rocks and eggs. An attempt was made to set it afire, and its windows were broken in an angry attack in September of 1834. Only then, fearing the physical safety of her students, did Crandall close the school.

Crandall and her husband left Canterbury and settled in Illinois, where they remained until his death in 1874. Crandall bought property in Kansas with her brother and lived there until her death in 1890 at the age of 87. She taught throughout her life.

in 1804, and its public library resides in the building that was the Canterbury district's one-room schoolhouse until the 1940s. Enjoy the beauty and learn from the history you'll discover in quiet Canterbury.

Prudence Crandall Museum (ages 8 and up)

1 South Canterbury Rd., at the junction of Routes 169 and 14; (860) 546-7800; www.ct.gov/ cct. Open seasonally at variable hours each year, dependent on state funding; call or check the website for current dates and hours, and do not hesitate to call year-round for an appointment. $$, children under 5 free.

Site of the first New England academy for African-American girls, the Crandall Academy is now called the Prudence Crandall Museum. A National Historic Landmark, the 1805 structure is one of several houses in Canterbury with the distinctive "Canterbury style." Basically conforming to the Federal style, the house has twin chimneys and an elaborate two-story entrance ornamentation with a Palladian window on the second floor above the front doorway.

Far more famous than its architecture is the house's history and its mistress, Prudence Crandall. The story of Prudence's courage and the dignity of her students is told in tours of the museum. Exhibits explore topics such as local history, African-American history, the abolitionist movement, and women's rights. The museum also includes three period rooms, a gift shop, and a research library.

Families might especially enjoy Prudence Crandall Day, typically held on the Saturday of Labor Day weekend. This special festivity offers 19th-century children's games, craft demonstrations, musical entertainment, and refreshments and crafts for sale. On the first Saturday in November from 1 to 4 p.m., the museum usually hosts an annual Tea with Prudence Crandall. Local living-history performer Donna Dufresne portrays Prudence in a 45-minute dramatic monologue and then interacts with the guests, who share tea and refreshments after the presentation. When the event is offered, advance registration is required.

Sterling/Oneco

If you enjoy taking the road less traveled, you might venture off I-395 and find the township of Sterling and its village of Oneco off exit 88. Here Windham County feels like a slice of life not so much from the 1850s but from the 1950s. If a time warp back to simpler days and pleasures seems appealing, wander here awhile and enjoy the country breezes and cool woods.

River Bend Campground and Mining Company (all ages)

41 Pond St. (Route 14A), Oneco; (860) 564-3440; www.riverbendcamp.com. Open mid-Apr through Columbus Day daily from 9 a.m. to 5 p.m. Day visitors should call ahead in the off-season before Memorial Day and after Labor Day. Mining rates, $$ for children; accompanying adults free. Gemstone panning, $$. Canoe rentals, $$–$$$$. Mini-golf, $. Paddleboats and aquacycles, $$ per hour. Campsites and cabin rentals, $–$$; weekly and seasonal rates available.

This family campground, amusement center, and gem mine is an award-winning compromise between the Great Outdoors and Great Adventure. Located on the beautiful Moosup River and a 35-acre pond, this center offers 160 campsites, some with rental cabins, trailers, and campers. You can rent a canoe, tour the live reptile exhibit or the indoor wildlife exhibit with diorama-style re-creations of life in the North American woodlands, or pan for gems and minerals in the outdoor sluice. A kiddie train, aquacycles, paddleboats, kayaks, horseshoes, mini-golf, basketball, sand volleyball, a moon bounce, outdoor movies, bingo, and other interactive areas, activities, and special events keep this place hopping. Luckily, there's plenty of room for deciding whether you want to be in or out of the nearly continuous action.

Sterling Park Campground (all ages)

177 Gibson Hill Rd., Sterling; (860) 564-8777; www.sterlingcampground.com. Open mid-Apr through mid-Oct. $, weekly rates available.

The owners of this KOA campground are proud of their commitment to providing wholesome family fun on their landscaped hills. With a staff of friendly faces, they offer guests two heated pools (one just for kiddies), a rec hall, a children's playspace, mini-golf, a full-service snack shack (which also offers three meals a day to non-camping visitors), a camp store, sports courts, and 160 pretty wooded or open campsites. You can arrive with your own camper or tent (electrical and water hookups are available) or rent their cabin or trailer. Hot showers and a laundry facility keep you comfortable throughout your stay.

Family movie nights, square dances, bingo games, hayrides, Kids' Olympics, and Christmas in July with a visit from Santa are among the events on the busy calendar. If you'd rather have quieter fun, you can fish in the 2-acre stocked pond.

Hill Towns and **Mill Villages**

The first textile mill in Windham County was built in 1806 by Smith Wilkinson on the Quinebaug near present-day Putnam. It was a small cotton mill that depended on the fluctuating level of the river to drive its wheels and turbines. Soon the technology developed to control the water through the use of reservoirs, dams, and canals. It was only a matter of time before every town and village on the rivers had a textile mill. Thousands of immigrants poured into the region to work in the mills and make their homes in the towns. The Quinebaug Mill, built in Killingly in 1852, was one of the largest. It had 61,340 spindles and 1,656 looms, and produced 28 miles of cloth each day.

On the website of the Last Green Valley (www. tlgv.org), you'll find an excellent self-guided driving- or cycling-tour brochure, from which I have borrowed the title of this sidebar; it provides a comprehensive look at the history hidden in these hills and of the principal mill sites remaining along Route 169).

Ekonk Hill **Turkey Farm**

Gobblers are just too darn funny to leave out of a family fun guide, so do get yourselves one way or another to Sterling for a look at the hundreds of free-range birds who live on this very lively and lovely farm (227 Ekonk Hill Rd., Moosup; 860-564-0248; www.ekonkhillturkeyfarm.com). Come too for its astonishing corn maze, open in September and October ($$; free for children under 5); it has an annual theme, and your admission fee also includes access to the barnyard, the pumpkin patch, and hayrides. While you are here, don't miss the farm's Brown Cow Café (open nearly daily year-round, for house-made ice cream, soft drinks, sandwiches, and the amazing Gobbler Sundae, which does not involve ice cream); its Milkhouse Bakery (open daily year-round for muffins, pies, cookies, cider doughnuts, and breads); and its Goose 'n Gobbler Shop (open nearly daily year-round; check the website for schedule) for eggs, pasture-raised poultry, pot pies, dairy products, honey, maple syrup, and much more, all locally grown and lovingly made in eastern Connecticut.

As if all this were not enough, the folks here decided a long time ago to set it all to music, at least once annually. Each year on the second weekend in June is the **Sterling Bluegrass Festival,** with foot-stomping, toe-tapping, knee-rocking music—the kind with banjos and guitars, mandolins and fiddles all singing sweetly in the great outdoors. A laid-back three-day affair that draws a moderate crowd, it features regional and local musicians. Call the campground for information, tickets, or camping reservations. For the festival, you're welcome whether or not you're campers.

Willimantic/Windham

Windham County has a sort of a little toe that pops westward from the lowest portion of its boundary with Tolland County. It is here in the toe that you'll find the small city of Willimantic and its sibling village of Windham. Situated on the banks of the Shetucket River, Willimantic has a history that is tied firmly to the textile mills that dominated three centuries of Connecticut industry.

In fact, the history of many Windham County towns would have been totally altered were it not for the textile mills built along the Quinebaug and Shetucket Rivers in the 18th and 19th centuries. Today in Willimantic, families can visit one of these sites to learn more about life in Connecticut's mill villages.

Windham Textile and History Museum (ages 6 and up)

157 Union at Main Street, Route 66; (860) 456-2178; www.millmuseum.org. Open year-round on Fri, Sat, and Sun from 10 a.m. to 4 p.m. and by appointment. Guided tours, Sun 2 p.m. Closed major holidays. $.

One of the most fascinating small museums in the state, the Windham Textile and History Museum examines the daily lives and culture of the people who labored in the mills, especially during the period from 1870 to 1920. It also explores the stories of those who developed the technology and collected the money earned from the labor of immigrants at the height of the Industrial Revolution. Through its creative exhibits, the museum provides an excellent overview of the cultural and economic changes brought about by both the development and demise of the Connecticut textile industry.

Located in two buildings of the former Willimantic Linen Company, the museum has an authenticity unsurpassed by any other re-creations in the region. Dugan Mill houses exhibits that bring the visitor right into the late 19th and early 20th centuries, when tens of thousands of workers labored under difficult conditions and for very low pay. The exhibits include re-creations of an 1880s mill shop floor, equipped with a carding machine, a spinning frame, a loom, and a textile printer. At one end of the shop is the overseer's office, from which the workers were carefully monitored.

The museum's main building houses the Company Store, a re-creation of the very shop that on this site once served employees' needs. It now doubles as the museum gift shop. A laborers' tenement, a mill agent's mansion from the Victorian era, and the 1877 Dunham Hall Library (a reading room open to visitors) are also housed here.

Connecticut Eastern **Railroad Museum**

Train enthusiasts may enjoy knowing that the Connecticut Eastern Chapter of the National Railway Historical Society is building a railroad museum in Willimantic, with hopes of eventually creating an entire railroad village, off Bridge Street, on the site of the Columbia Junction Freight Yard. A turntable, a roundhouse, a freight house, a section house, an operator's shanty, and other village buildings have been restored or constructed or are currently under construction here, and track has been repaired or laid to allow passengers to ride on the restored trains in the chapter's growing collection. Children are welcome to try a replica pump car along a section of track, and special excursions on the Providence and Worcester Railroad are planned. Open from May through Oct on weekends from 10 a.m. to 4 p.m., the museum is a work in progress. Admission $; children 7 and under free. Call ahead (860-456-9999) or check the website (www.cteastrrmuseum.org) to see what has developed here recently. The address is 55 Bridge St. (Route 32).

Special educational and social programs such as teas, sewing or needlework workshops, storytelling, and holiday events are scheduled regularly throughout the year for families, children, and adults. Check the website for the schedule.

Where to Eat

Willimantic Brewery and Main Street Cafe. 967 Main St., Willimantic; (860) 423-6777. The dining room inside a historic post office is a dramatic setting for kid-friendly pub fare. Lunch and dinner, Tues through Sun from 11:30 a.m. to 9 p.m. $–$$

Willimantic Food Co-Op. 91 Valley St., Willimantic; (860) 456-3611. Open daily from 9 a.m. (10 a.m. on Sun) for awesome baked goods, produce, soups, sandwiches, cheeses, salads, and more, either for take-out or to eat here in a small café area. $

General Information

Quinebaug and Shetucket Rivers Valley National Heritage Corridor Inc. (860) 963-7226; www.tlgv.org. From the website, download visitor guides, maps, and driving and cycling routes.

Mystic Country/Connecticut covers the Eastern Regional Tourism District, including Windham County. Call (800) TO-ENJOY or (860) 536-8822 or visit 27 Coogan Blvd., Building 3A, Mystic; www.mysticcountry.com; for brochures, maps, calendars of events, and information on attractions, dining, and accommodations.

Connecticut Department of Agriculture. 165 Capitol Ave., Hartford 06106; (860) 566-4845; www.ct.gov/doag. Produces map and pamphlets on pick-your-own farms, agricultural tours, farm activities, sugarhouses, and Christmas tree farms. See also www.ctfarms.uconn.edu.

Connecticut Department of Environmental Protection. Office of State Parks and Recreation, 165 Capitol Ave., Hartford 06106; Eastern District: (860) 295-9523. Publishes booklet describing state parks and state forests, with day-use and camping information for each site.

New London County

Coastal Voyages and Country Sojourns

The southeastern portion of Connecticut defies characterization. First, the county comprises a wide variety of habitats, so to speak. The hills and forests of its northern region are distinctly different from the meadows and marshes of its southern border along the Sound. Second, the population of the two areas is equally disparate. The peaceable hills to the north are much like Windham County in the state's so-called Quiet Corner, while the bustling towns of the shoreline reflect their long history of industry and commerce.

Both areas provide an abundance of attractions and activities for families. From fine art gallery to lighthouse museum, from woodland trail to fishing pier, with every level of sophistication and simplicity, New London's sights are as diverse as the county.

TopPicks for fun in New London County

1. **Mystic Aquarium and Institute for Exploration**

2. **Terra Firma Farm**

3. **Mystic Seaport Museum**

4. **Project Oceanology**

5. ***Sunbeam Express* Cruises**

6. **Historic Ship *Nautilus* Memorial and Submarine Force Museum**

7. **Florence Griswold Museum**

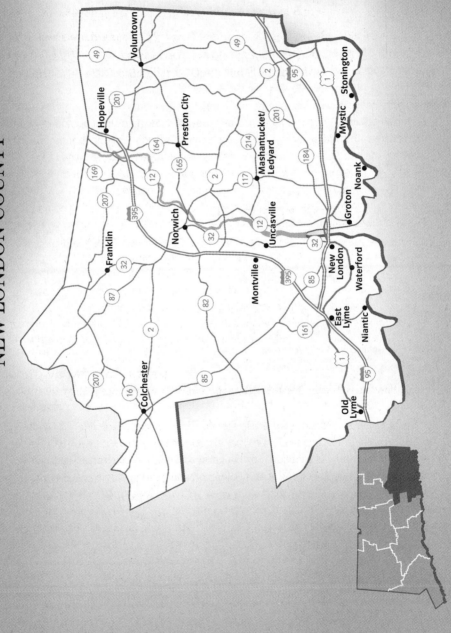

NEW LONDON COUNTY

Colchester

At the crossroads of Routes 11, 2, 16, and 85, Colchester is typical of the northern communities of New London County. Elegant houses surround its green; small shops, a few restaurants, and pretty public buildings provide the hub of a structure that is primarily rural in nature. Don't let it fool you that Colchester calls its main drag "Broadway." This really is a country town.

Day Pond State Park (all ages)

Route 149; (860) 295-9523. Free admission, except for day-use vehicle charge ($$) on weekends and holidays. Open daily, 8 a.m. to sunset.

That country flavor is clearly apparent out at Day Pond. In fact, though the dirt road to the park is clearly marked now, the first time we visited here the sign was a paper plate nailed to a tree. Ain't no fancy city stuff here! Originally constructed by a pioneering family named Day, the pond is an antique mill pond, the water of which once turned an overshot

Country Day-Tripping

With a little planning, a good night's sleep, and a hearty breakfast packed in a picnic basket, you can tour the next four towns right smartly if you get an early start. Pick a weekend in late summer or early fall and have a brisk morning walk to the Salmon River from Day Pond in Colchester. Eat breakfast on the covered bridge, return to the pond, herd everyone back into the car, and head south on Route 149 and then east on Route 16 and grab an ice cream at **Harry's** (104 Broadway [Route 85]; 860-537-2410). Ice Cream for lunch is a great way to make your kids think that maybe you're still a lot of fun or maybe just half crazy so they'd better behave in case you do something really reckless. While you still have the kids raising their eyebrows in the backseat, take Route 16 northeastward until you can hang a right on Route 207. Travel that road to Lebanon and the junction with Route 87. Here's the perfect place to stop for a remedial dose of Revolutionary War history. This medicine goes down easy at the wonderful **Lebanon Historical Society Museum and Visitor Center** (856 Trumbull Hwy; 860-642-6579; open Wed through Sat, year-round noon to 4 p.m.), just north of Route 207. Take a left on Route 87 and travel just a smidgen up the road. You'll pass the town's remarkable mile-long green—the same green seen by George Washington, the Marquis de Lafayette, French general Rochambeau, General Israel Putnam, colonial governor Jonathan Trumbull, and other principal players in the Patriot cause. A hands-on history room in the museum, which waterwheel that powered the up-and-down saw of the family's sawmill. Now empty of all signs of industry, the pond is stocked regularly with trout and is popular with fishers, swimmers, and skaters. No boating is allowed on the 7-acre pond, which is also a spawning ground for migratory salmon.

As is typical at these parks, the state has provided telephones, restrooms, picnic tables, a large picnic shelter with fireplaces, and drinking water for your comfort. A small nature trail across from the parking areas has a 14-point trail guide booklet that contains maps of the whole park and its various trails. Call the number above to obtain that guide in advance of your visit, or if you're here on the weekend, ask the parking attendant for a copy.

A loop trail that begins at Day Pond is an easy walk for families; it connects with a trail through the Salmon River Forest to the Comstock Bridge on the Salmon River. If there is a ranger around on the day you visit, ask for a map to these trails or come equipped with the wonderful *Connecticut Walk Book,* published in two volumes (East and West) by the Connecticut Forest and Park Association (860-346-2372; $24.95). You should also be able to find the trailhead yourselves by walking along Day Pond Road. The views of the Salmon

has been designed with children in mind, explains it all. In addition to this family-centered museum, you can visit Governor Trumbull's house and the War Office, where Council of Safety meetings ensured the provisioning of the Continental Army. Taken all together, these Lebanon landmarks compose one of the nation's best Revolutionary War sites. When you have had your fill of history, continue on Route 207 to North Franklin and the Blue Slope Farm & Country Museum. Chances are, things could be sleepy here, unless you choose its festival weekend in October—or you made a phone call in advance to arrange a guided tour or a wagon ride here). Have a quick stop to see the cows and goats, anyway, and then continue on Route 207 to Route 138 to Route 201 to reach Hopeville Pond State Park. Take out the fishing gear you packed along with the picnic goods, and throw a line and rest awhile until the trout start jumpin'. Pack up around 3 p.m. or so and continue on to Pachaug, where the cool woods in the late afternoon are just what you'll want to see. Skip the long hike—just drive up to near the top of Mount Misery and catch the breeze and the beauty of late afternoon. Now sweep southward on Route 165 and have a casual dinner at **Village Pizza** (353 Route 165; 860-887-1930) in Preston. When you can't eat another slice, mosey on up Route 164 and put up your feet at the Roseledge B&B, where a feather bed for you, a full-size trundle for the kids, and a fireplace at your feet await you. Zzzzzz . . .

River are beautiful; the trail actually hugs the river before reaching the 1873 covered bridge. The 4-mile combination of the two trails makes for a great day hike. Pack a lunch and eat at or on the bridge. Bring along a few night crawlers and a couple of poles and hooks, and you'll have the makings of a perfect country day.

Where to Eat

Harry's Place. 104 Broadway (Route 85); (860) 537-2410. On Route 85 back near the center of town is about as classic a roadside stand as ever stood on an American highway. Open only from April 15 usually through October, Harry's Place has been called "the ultimate burger joint" by the *Hartford Courant*. No waistline-trimming foods are served here—just burgers dripping with "juice," excellent onion rings, french fries, dogs, and sauerkraut. Wash these down with soft drinks and shakes while you sit at the picnic tables near the road. Harry's Place has been "proud to serve" since 1918, so maybe there's a secret to longevity in this greasy gastronomy. Check it out, daily from 11 a.m. to 9:45 p.m. (10 p.m. at the ice cream window). $

Franklin

With great affection I have to say that this little town is out in the middle of nowhere, a comment I can make safely because I know that most of its inhabitants like it just fine that way. There's not a lot here to make families jump in the car to get out this way, but one interesting site and a few events might make you tie in a visit with other plans elsewhere. Take Route 32 from Route 2 to reach the village. To reach Blue Slope Farm & Country Museum, take Route 2 to Exit 23 and follow the signs.

Blue Slope Farm & Country Museum (all ages)

138 Blue Hill Rd.; (860) 642–6413; www.blueslope.com. Open year-round by prior arrange-ment for school, scout, senior, and other groups. Open to the public year-round for sleigh and wagon rides ($$$$) by prior arrangement; for family square dances and campfire sing-alongs (both $ per person or $$$ per family) in summertime; and for a two-day festival ($–$$, children under 4 free) in Oct. See website events calendar for all dates. Families and other groups can inquire about guided farm tours by appointment.

Once a fairly sleepy place where a herd of happy Holsteins quietly grazed, this lovely 380-acre farm has more animals than ever and more events than ever for visiting families. Sandy and Ernie Staebner are good-hearted, energetic people who have revitalized some truly fun old-fashioned ways of life in the country that all kids will love to share. On select summer evenings, they throw open their barn doors for square dances (certain Fridays at 7:30 p.m.; all ages; no experience necessary) and family campfires (certain Thursdays at 7 p.m.), where folks circle up for mallow roasts, sing-alongs, stories, and lemonade. And just like always, each October, they pull out all the stops and invite the crowds in for a weekend of activities and wagon tours designed to let folks in on the bountiful history of farming and crafting that once flourished in these parts. On this weekend the place is truly steeped in history as volunteers, many dressed in period clothing, demonstrate the skills that farmers and crafters used throughout New England in centuries past. Spinning, weaving, stone splitting, mowing, quilting, basketry, broom making, soap making, quilling, blacksmithing, woodworking, and whittling are among the activities you might see. Live bluegrass music, draft-horse and donkey pulls, horse-drawn wagon rides, barn tours, colonial games, an antique car show, a craft show, and special activities for children are part of the fun. Food and refreshment vendors are abundant—or you can bring a picnic.

Inside the Staebner's authentic Amish-built barn is their amazing museum of artifacts that show the evolution of farming technology and reveal interesting facts about the lives and labors of three centuries of farm families. Years ago there were more farms in New London County alone than there are in all of Connecticut today, and the Staebners have collected 4,000 old-time tools, implements, and farm vehicles, kept inside and outside their 5,000-square-foot, two-story rustic museum building. Many objects are at least a century old, including woodworking tools, looms, spinning wheels, drills, wooden water pipes, butter churns, weapons, milk cans, rakes, axes, yokes, and toys. If you'd like to visit at other times of year, call ahead to make an arrangement for a guided tour of the fields and cow and goat barns or a wagon or sleigh ride over their picturesque cornfields.

Hopeville

One of the small village centers that compose the town of Griswold, Hopeville is just a bit more than a turn in the road. A rural and oddly reassuring enclave to those who live in hectic places, it was once the site of a number of mills producing grain, lumber, and woolens; now it's the home of one of northern New London County's most popular family parks.

Hopeville Pond State Park (all ages)

193 Roode Rd., Jewett City (Route 201); park office: (860) 376-2920; campground: (860) 376-0313. Sports field open year-round. Park open Apr 1 to Oct 31, sunrise to sunset; per-vehicle entrance fee ($$) on weekends and holidays. Campground open mid-Apr through Sept 30; campsites ($) must be reserved through Reserve America (877-668-2267). Alcohol-free park and campground; no pets allowed in campground.

Located just east of Hopeville, a tiny village in the northern township of Griswold, this park is noted for its glacial geology and its excellent trails and forest roads created by the Civilian Conservation Corps in the 1930s.

Freshwater fishing, swimming, and boating are possible uses of Hopeville Pond, an antique woolen millpond used in the early 19th century. The trails, of course, are perfect for hiking, and a sports field with a picnic pavilion encourages use by families who like nothing better than an old-fashioned reunion-cum-ballgame. No food concession operates here, so pack in your own grub. The state has provided picnic tables, drinking water, and restrooms with changing areas, and a boat-launch ramp is in the campground.

Hopeville Pond's campground has 81 wooded sites that are perfect for tenters and small RVs. Reserve early; this is a very popular site, especially on weekends.

Voluntown

As you know by now if you've read any parts of this book consecutively, Connecticut has a vast amount of acreage set aside as protected public land. A huge chunk of that land is Pachaug State Forest, spanning six towns in this region and accessible from Route 49 just a short distance north of its junction with Route 138/165 in Voluntown. Pachaug is an Indian word meaning "turn in the river," and it is the pretty Pachaug River and its tributary, Misery Brook, that meander through the forest. It is the largest protected site in the state and a great place for family camping and outdoor recreation.

Pachaug State Forest (all ages)

219 Ekonk Hill Rd. (off Route 49); park office: (860) 376-4075; DEP Eastern Division: (860) 295-9523. Open year-round. Regular campers and horseback campers don't need reservations, but they pay a nightly fee ($). Day use is free, except on weekends and holidays between Memorial Day weekend and Labor Day, when the per-vehicle charge is $$–$$$.

Entering the forest on Route 49, you will cross the Pachaug River and disappear for days into a veritable wilderness of greenery—24,000 acres' worth. Most folks stay just long enough to soak up some of the beauty here and take it home with them in their souls. In these green woods and its waterways, you can hike, bike, canoe, bird watch, swim, horseback ride, and picnic to your heart's content. You can also skate, snowmobile, snowshoe, or cross-country ski, weather permitting.

Two separate campgrounds at Green Falls and Mount Misery provide wooded sites for tenters who decide to soak up the green overnight. You can haul in the motor home, too, but no hookups or dumping stations are available. The park and forest service provides drinking water, toilets, a boat ramp, and a horse camp. Backpackers and youth groups can do back-country camping, too, but both kinds of adventurers must call for a permit. Be sure to roam these rocky hills on more than 30 miles of trails past interesting habitats. A particularly great trail is the Nehantic Trail to the top of Mount Misery. From the east side of the parking area, it can be reached by way of a loop that takes you through a rhododendron sanctuary (which blossoms abundantly in late spring, generally after the second week in June) and a southern white cedar swamp, and then meets the trail to the breezy, slightly balding top of the sorry-sounding mountain. If you don't feel like a moderate workout, you can also drive to within 200 yards of the summit. Most definitely, if you're looking for a little wilderness in this busy state, come to its largest forest. You'll be amazed at how loud the quiet is.

Preston City

If you take Route 165 south from Voluntown, you'll end up in Preston, another rural enclave sought only by those travelers who reject the I-395 highway, which passes only a handful of miles to the west. At the junction of Routes 165 and 164, you should do yourselves a favor and take a right and drive north on 164 a few miles. Designated a scenic road for very good reasons, it leads past centuries-old farms and homesteads and the pretty Preston City Congregational Church—you won't be sorry you took a little detour before returning to head west again on Route 165 to the city of Norwich.

Maple Lane Farms (all ages)

57 Northwest Corner Rd., off Route 164, south of Route 165 junction; (860) 889-3766; 24-hour pick-your-own information: (860) 887-8855; www.maplelane.com. Open daily in season, 8 a.m. to noon, plus Tues and Thurs 4 to 7 p.m. Call ahead for field conditions. They supply containers, saws, baling, and other necessary supplies. $–$$.

Once 140 acres of overgrown pasture around an abandoned dairy farm, Maple Lane is now a thriving family farm with a marvelous spirit of confidence, abundance, and generosity fueled by hard work and determination. Share the positive energy by coming here to pick your own fresh blueberries, raspberries, cut flowers, and pumpkins, plus cut-your-own Christmas trees. Show up to pick your own, or call ahead and place an order for what you want them to pick for you.

Plucking sun-ripened raspberries on a clear summer day may inspire young gardeners to set down a few plants of their own. Who knows? It may well be you yourself who's struck with farm fever in this stunning country setting that kinda makes you want to trade in the Volvo for a John Deere.

Scenic hayrides are given on Sat and Sun from mid-September through Oct, from 9 a.m. to 4 p.m. ($). At holiday time, 35 acres of trees are available for cutting from Thanksgiving weekend through Christmas Eve. Hot cocoa and cookies are provided on the weekends. Call ahead to be sure of the crops and activities offered each season.

Where to Eat

Buttonwood Farm Ice Cream. 471 Shetucket Turnpike (Route 165), Griswold; (860) 376-4081; www.buttonwoodfarmicecream .com. Open March 1 to October 31, this cheerful, crystal-clean roadside establishment offers more than 40 flavors of top-quality farm-fresh ice cream every day from 1 to 8 p.m. (and sometimes later). Try the Forbidden Silk Chocolate or the Purple Cow. From late September and most of October, take a tractor-drawn hayride ($) through their fields, 10 a.m. to dusk on weekends; 4 p.m. to dusk on weekdays. $

Village Pizza Family Restaurant. 353 Route 165 in Fleming shopping center; (860) 887-1930. Spotless and perfect for families, this place is not just for pizza. Come also for Italian specialties, fresh sauces, chicken, veal, and seafood specials, salads, and a double helping of friendly service. Open for lunch and dinner Tues through Sat 11 a.m. to 10 p.m. and Sun until 8 p.m. $–$$

Where to Stay

Roseledge Herb Farm B&B. 418 Route 164; (860) 892-4739 or (888) 996-7673; www.roseledge.com. Stop just for tea and fresh-baked goodies or stop for the night, the perfect endpoint of a country day. A 1720 farmhouse with fireplaces in every room, homemade soap in the baths, hearth-cooked foods (on occasional winter evenings), feather beds and trundle beds, goats and sheep, fresh-from-under-the-hen eggs, a charming tearoom for guests and visitors alike, and room galore for very welcome children. Join innkeepers Sandy and Gail Beecher for the morning chores—goats have to be fed, eggs have to be collected—or explore the herb gardens, the beehive, and the barn. Pull out an old sled if it's snowing, play in the sandbox if it's not. $$–$$$, ask about mid-week specials.

Norwich

A small city with the unfortunate distinction of being the birthplace of Benedict Arnold, Norwich has heretofore maintained a pretty low profile as far as tourism is concerned. But there's a new wind blowing on the Rose of New England these days. Pride in the city's active role in the Patriot cause, the production of woolens for Union uniforms in the Civil War, the importance of its shipping and manufacturing history, and its remarkable concentration of homes and public buildings of architectural importance have led to a deliberate attempt by city leaders to pull the city out of the doldrums.

Helped by a great number of forward-looking individuals plus a hefty bit of money garnered from the gaming done not far away on Indian lands, Norwich is making serious efforts to win the affection of travelers. The best attractions for families are listed below.

For further information on this colorful and interesting city, contact the Norwich Tourism Office at (860) 886-4683 or (888) 4-NORWICH, or check the calendar of events and other details about parks and attractions on the website www.norwichct.org. Ask for two brochures: the *Kid's Guide* and *Norwich A–Z*. The Norwich Arts Council is also a great resource for visitors; call them at (860) 887-2789.

Slater Memorial Museum (ages 6 and up)

108 Crescent St. (Route 2), on the campus of the Norwich Free Academy; (860) 887-2505; www.norwichfreeacademy.com/museum. Open year-round Tues through Fri from 9 a.m. to 4 p.m. and on Sat and Sun from 1 to 4 p.m. Closed Mon and holidays. $, children under 12 free.

Scheduled for gradual completion during 2011, a major and stunning reconstruction project here provides universal access to the galleries inside the Romanesque edifice that houses a remarkable collection. Founded in 1888, the Slater is *the* place to take the children if you think it may be a while before you can take them to the Louvre, the Vatican, or any other of the world's finest sculpture galleries.

Here you will find a notable and beautiful collection of 150 plaster cast statues of famed sculptures from around the world. Among these exact replicas of Greek, Roman, and Renaissance masterpieces are *Aphrodite* (the so-called Venus de Milo), Donatello's *David,* and Michelangelo's *Pieta.* Although the plaster casting doesn't exactly do justice to the luminous and satiny quality of the marble originals, I still can't overstate the beauty of these magnificent pieces; truly, if you are at all interested in having your children see the unbelievable genius of Michelangelo, Donatello, Verrocchio, Luca della Robbia, and others, save yourself the airfare and come here.

The museum also houses a wonderful collection of American art from the 17th to 20th centuries, plus American Indian artifacts and Oriental, African, and European art and textiles. The American Rooms are period rooms that trace American history from colonial to Victorian days. The redesign of the building has resulted in the reinstallation and restoration of some of its holdings and has also allowed the creation of a new visitor's center, gift shop, and, perhaps, by the time you arrive, a refreshment kiosk.

Mohegan Park (all ages)

On Mohegan Park Road, with access from four different points; best entrance may be at corner of Judd and Rockwell Streets near the rose garden; (860) 886-2381. Open year-round 9 a.m. to sunset. Free.

With walkways, trails, bicycle/stroller path, picnic areas with grills, pavilions, gazebos, statuary, and fountain, this 385-acre woodland park can be a nice family destination.

Near the park's fairly large pond is a good-size swimming area and a small beach perfect for young children. Popular with both families and area day camps, it can get crowded, but restrooms, a concession, and a play area with swings make it workable for

On the Waterfront

The waterfront district of Norwich lies at the head of the Thames River. On Hollyhock Island, off Route 82 (West Main Street), is the **Marina at American Wharf** (www.americanwharf.com; 860-886-6363), which features riverfront walkways, a gazebo, benches, picnic tables, and barbecue pits that are available to the public. Its seasonal **Surf 'n Turf Cafe** (860-887-8555) is typically open from late April through late October, for lunch and dinner daily, plus Sunday brunch, with seating inside and outside on the promenade; the marina pool, however, and other amenities are for members only. Off Chelsea Harbor Drive, across the waterway, **Howard T. Brown Memorial Park** also has a gazebo, picnic areas, fishing pier, and free concerts on selected Friday evenings in summer. Special events in this historic area, including a Fourth of July celebration, a Taste of Italy Festival, and a Winter Festival Parade, have helped to encourage its revitalization.

Indian **Burial Grounds**

On Sachem Street off Route 32 is the tiny parcel of land that is the final resting place of Uncas, the Mohegan warrior and statesman who befriended the European settlers and gave to them the land that became the city of Norwich. It lies on the left side of the street, very close to the corner as you enter from Route 32.

families, and it is certainly a clean, safe place for an afternoon swim. It is open from June 1 to Labor Day and for skating, weather permitting, in winter.

The award-winning roses in the park's formal gardens, accessible from sunrise to sunset at no charge, at the corner of Rockwell Street and Judd Street are in bloom from late May through October, peaking in June and early July. You'll enjoy grassy paths among patterned beds and trellises showcasing more than 2,500 bushes in 120 varieties. The picnic shelter at the side of the 2-acre garden is a nice place to stop with a bag lunch.

Dodd Stadium (ages 4 and up)

14 Stott Ave. in Norwich Industrial Park; (860) 887-7962; www.cttigers.com. Apr through Sept. Weekday and Saturday games typically at 7:05 p.m.; Sunday games at 1:05 p.m. Check website for complete schedule and directions to stadium. $$.

If you like baseball, come here for a taste of the great American pastime. Near-sellout crowds are attracted to the games the Connecticut Tigers, the single A affiliate of the Detroit Tigers, play against other affiliates. The 6,000-seat stadium and lots of special events and promotional giveaways at nearly every game make this a fun, easy way to watch the sport.

Special packages offer snack-bar meal and ticket combos that make it easy to have a baseball birthday party—and you can arrange for a happy-birthday message to be announced or posted on the scoreboard.

Where to Eat

Illiano's Grill. 257 West Town St. in Yantic section; (860) 889-6163. Pizza Illiano-style is always a hit, as are all the other Italian favorites at this small Eastern Connecticut chain. $$–$$$

Where to Stay

Comfort Suites. 275 Otrobando Ave.; (860) 892-9292 or (800) 847-7848. 119 suites with fridge, microwave; indoor pool, fitness room; complimentary continental breakfast. $$$–$$$$

Courtyard by Marriott. 181 West Town St.; (860) 886-2600. 120 units with suites, restaurant, indoor pool, fitness room. $$$$

Holiday Inn Norwich. 10 Laura Blvd.; (860) 889-5201 or (800) 272-6232. 127 units, restaurant, indoor pool, fitness room. $$$

Montville/Uncasville

Just south of Norwich perched above the Thames River is the small town of Montville and its village of Uncasville, best known for their age-old connection to the Mohegan people. A visit here has a Native American focus.

Tantaquidgeon Indian Museum (ages 4 and up)

1819 Norwich–New London Turnpike (Route 32); (860) 848-0594. Open Apr to Oct, Wed through Fri, 10 a.m. to 4 p.m. and Sat 10 a.m. to 3 p.m. Closed from noon to 1 p.m. daily. Donation.

Filled with stone, bone, and wooden objects used or made mostly by the Mohegan Indians, this museum, now operated by the Mohegan Tribal Office, is located in the heart of Mohegan territory. It also includes baskets, ladles, and bowls made by skilled Mohegan woodworker and basketmaker John Tantaquidgeon, a direct descendant of Uncas, a 17th-century sachem of the Mohegans, and the father of famed Mohegan Medicine Woman, anthropologist, and ethnobotanist Gladys Tantaquidgeon. Although the emphasis here is on the Mohegans and other Eastern Woodland tribes, the collection also includes artifacts from Native American peoples of the Southwest, the Southeast, and the Northern Plains. Pottery, rugs, dolls, tools, beaded bags, shoes, a beautiful canoe suspended from the ceiling, and other objects are among the items in this unique collection. The culture and history of each group are explained throughout the exhibits.

Fort Shantok (all ages)

450 Massapeag Side Rd., off Route 32, Uncasville. Open 8 a.m. to sunset year-round. Check www.mohegan.nsn.us for more information.

The Montville area is rich in the history of the Mohegans. Drive north again from the Tantaquidgeon Museum on Route 32 to the area called Mohegan Hill (not actually clearly marked). In Fort Shantok (clearly marked), you will find the remains of the fortified village of the great Mohegan sachem, Uncas, and the 300-year-old sacred Mohegan burial ground. Here you can see the graves of the Tantaquidgeons and other descendants of Uncas. A stone monument marks the site of the 17th-century fort, and several small trails lead hikers along the banks of the Thames River, which flows past the edge of the park.

The park's large, open recreational areas are available to picnickers, anglers (there is a stocked pond here), and ballplayers, but the fort and burial ground area is a sacred site. Visitors are welcome to explore it respectfully. Please do not picnic in this shaded, peaceful area. Feel free to enjoy the riverside pathways as the Mohegans still do, as a place of quiet meditation. Annual events such as the Wigwam Powwow in the third or fourth week of August are also open to the public. The powwow features a Mohegan dance competitions, drumming, Native American cultural exhibits, native foods, crafts and craft demonstrations, and storytelling. Admission is **free.**

The Dinosaur Place (all ages)

1650 Hartford-New London Turnpike (Route 85); (860) 443-GEMS; www.thedinosaurplace .com. The outdoor areas are open daily, rain or shine, from 10 a.m. to 6 p.m. from mid-Apr through Oct; at 9 a.m. from Father's Day through Labor Day; and weekends only, 10 a.m. to 6 p.m., or dusk, in Nov, weather permitting. Last admission is one hour prior to closing. The Splashpad is open 10 a.m. to 5 p.m., weather permitting, daily from Father's Day through Labor Day. Outdoor admission is reduced after 4 p.m. Indoor activities are offered from 10 a.m. to 5 p.m. daily from Father's Day through Labor Day, and at the same hours on Sat and Sun only, year-round, as well as major Monday holidays and school vacation weeks. The gift shop is open from 10 a.m. to 6 p.m. daily, year-round, except when this whole operation is closed on Easter, Thanksgiving, December 25, and January 1. Admission fees are charged for visitors age 2 and older to the outdoor areas ($$ in the spring and fall seasons; $$$ in the summer season); separate fees are charged for each indoor activity area ($). No admission charge for the gift shop, the Fossil and Mineral Gallery, or the Fluorescent Room.

What started as a retail/commercial establishment designed as much to produce income as it was to be an activity center motivated to educate and entertain young minds, this pairing of related entities has grown to be a true attraction. Families come here in droves to explore natural history and the beauties of the Earth—in particular, the great big beauties we call dinosaurs. Outside are nature trails around a pond called Raptor Bay; 30 life-size dinosaur replicas inhabit this space called Dinosaur Crossing, and you pay admission ($$) to it near the complex's expanded snack bar and picnic area. Outside now too are an expansive playground and an amazing 10,000-square-foot water-play area called Monty's Splashpad, where 30 dinosaur-themed water features sprinkle and splash young visitors in the summer months. Changing rooms and restrooms complete the outdoor area. Inside, the Fossil and Mineral Gallery includes fossils, petrified wood, real dinosaur eggs, crystals and other minerals, and life-size dinosaur skeleton casts. The Fluorescent Room, the largest such gallery in the state, features fluorescent minerals. In the activity areas, each of which has a separate fee and a take-home souvenir, visitors can dig for gems in the Jackpot Mine, pan for "gold" in Thunder Creek, or unearth a dinosaur skeleton in the Bone Zone. Combination packages are available in these activity areas, and birthday parties are very popular. The rest of the enormous indoor space is devoted to an amazing array of scientific toys, games, craft kits, fossils, rocks, and minerals for sale. You can even eat lunch or dessert in the store's Cobalt Cafe.

Old Lyme

A curious mix of authors, painters, and mariners inhabits Old Lyme, a lovely village that revels in its artsy reputation as well as its nautical one. It's no surprise that Old Lyme can employ the phrase "colony" to describe itself—it has long attracted residents who fall neatly into one or more of these three categories.

One of the earliest and most permanent of these groups was the artists who gathered at the home of Florence Griswold from 1899 until decades past the turn of the 20th century. Known as the Lyme Art Colony, the folks who lived at Miss Florence's beautiful late-Georgian mansion played with light, color, and texture until they successfully settled upon characteristics later to become known as American Impressionism. J. Alden Weir, Childe Hassam, Henry Ward Ranger, William Chadwick, and many others perfected their brilliance here.

Florence Griswold Museum (ages 4 and up)

96 Lyme St.; (860) 434-5542; www.flogris.org. Open in Jan through Mar, Wed through Sun, 1 to 5 p.m., and Apr through Dec, Tues through Sat, 10 a.m. to 5 p.m. and Sun 1 to 5 p.m. Artist studio open Apr through Oct only. $–$$, children under 6 free.

Located on 11 acres next to the lovely Lieutenant River, this historic, soft-yellow mansion holds a magnificent collection of the works of the above-mentioned artists as well as related changing exhibitions throughout the year. You may wander the upper gallery rooms of the museum unescorted, but a guided tour of the downstairs period rooms, which are newly reinterpreted, is given first. If children are in the group, the gracious docents tell stories that capture young imaginations.

The museum also includes restored gardens, marvelous exhibition spaces and a wonderful museum shop in the Kreible Gallery at the riverside, and, in the mansion, several period rooms with Miss Griswold's furniture and personal effects. Especially wonderful are the original paintings on the panels in the dining room, the interpretation of an artist's bedroom at the height of the colony's popularity, and the restored studio of William Chadwick on the grounds. Visitors are encouraged to stroll and relax on the adjoining properties as the famed artists once did; you may even set up an easel and paint whichever of the lovely vistas catches your artist's eye.

The Hartman Education Center is the site of frequent programs for children as well as adults. On Sunday from 1 to 5 p.m., children can participate in hands-on Impromptu Encounters with Art, learning about some aspect of Impressionism or painting en plein air. A Midsummer Festival, which is a joyous and colorful collaboration of regional farmers and hand-crafters, includes varied activities and entertainments for children. Be sure to come for this very popular two-day festivity that includes activities and art shows at the Lyme Art Association gallery and the Lyme Academy of Fine Arts; it is typically the third Friday and Saturday in July.

Return in late November and December, when the mansion is decorated for Christmas. Story readings, special tours, art-making activities of interest to children, and holiday teas are offered throughout this low-key seasonal festivity.

McCulloch Farm (all ages)

100 Whippoorwill Rd.; (860) 434-7355; www.whippoorwillmorgans.com. Open daily from 10 a.m. to 4 p.m. but advance calls are appreciated. Annual all-day events in spring and very early fall. Call or check website for dates. Free.

One of Connecticut's hidden treasures is the oldest continually operating and largest Morgan horse breeding farm in the state. Visitors are more than welcome, but a call ahead ensures that someone here is able to give you a tour. Half a dozen or more foals are born here each spring, and you can see and pet them and their elegant parents nearly any day year-round. The farm itself is a Connecticut pearl—450 acres here are protected under a Nature Conservancy easement, and—lucky you—are yours to explore. Although it's not maintained as a tourist attraction, its recently restored carriage paths lead through quiet corners where you may see wild turkeys, guinea hens, and many birds and butterflies of the Eastern Woodlands. The owners kindly ask that you enjoy the property respectfully. They prefer no pets or picnicking, and there is no hand-feeding of their magnificent Whip-poorwill Morgans.

Come in May for Foals and Flowers, a three-day Open Barn event held every Memorial Day weekend, when visitors are welcomed into the barns for a close-up look at the new-born animals. Return in the fall for Foals and Foliage, also a three-day Open Barn event, held every Columbus Day weekend, when you can see the weanlings just before they are ready to be separated from their mothers. Both events are **free** to the public. No call ahead is required.

Sound View Beach (all ages)

Hartford Avenue off Shore Road (Route 156); Parks and Recreation, in summer only: (860) 434-2760. Open 8 a.m. to 9 p.m. Free street parking or parking fee ($–$$) at public and private off-street lots.

A wide, popular beach in the midst of a busy beach colony that looks like a throwback to earlier decades is great for playing or relaxing on a summer day or for strolling in autumn or winter. No coolers are allowed on the beach, there are no changing facilities or life-guards, and the only restrooms are portable toilets. Even so, tons of families come here, and on summer weekends the joint is hopping as the delightfully summery and slightly seedy arcades, amusements, snack bars, and restaurants along Hartford Avenue are crowded with visitors. The Carousel Shop sells sunscreen, sunglasses, ice cream, beach chairs, floats, and beach toys. They also operate the brightly painted (but small) 1925 car-ousel, which runs nightly from 7 to 9 all summer. One ride is $1, 12 rides are $10, and so on up to 100 rides for $65 for parties or fanatics.

For food, try the beachy fare at whatever seasonal restaurants and snack bars may be open on Hartford Avenue. Be sure to have an Italian ice from Vecchitto's.

Lyme **Art**

The **Lyme Academy of Fine Arts** (84 Lyme St.; 860-434-5232) and the **Lyme Art Association** (90 Lyme St.; 860-434-7802) have no articulated special focus for children and families, but both have ongoing exhibits in their galleries, plus classes, demonstrations, workshops, and lectures that may be of interest. Both are open year-round, but hours vary. Call for a schedule. Other shops and galleries on Lyme Street allow visitors the opportunity to see and pur-chase the work of local artists.

Ewe'll Love **This**

Sankow's Beaverbrook Farm in Lyme, at 139 Beaverbrook Rd. off Route 156 about 5.5 miles north of Route 1, opens to visitors seven days a week year-round so that families can enjoy their handmade woolens, farmstead sheep cheese, yogurt, and cottage cheese—and their 600 sheep and lambs. In spring, the 175-acre farm is fairly hopping with newborns; on the Saturday and Sunday after Thanksgiving, come for the annual Farm Day to see shearing demonstrations, take a horse-drawn hayride, buy freshly made gelato, browse their wool shop and buy country crafts from local artisans, and sample fresh meats and cheeses. Farm Day is held rain or shine. For more information, call (860) 434-2843 or (800) 501-WOOL, or check the website at www.beaver brookfarm.com.

Where to Eat

Boom. 90 Halls Rd. (Route 1), in the Old Lyme Shopping Center; (860) 434-0075. The third in the very lively and successful trio of coastal Connecticut's Boom restaurants, this one is as welcoming and delicious as the others in Westbrook and Stonington. Seafood is a standout here; Angus beef dishes are popular too, and the sweet-potato ravioli is a favorite. Children's menu. Lunch Mon through Sat from 11:30 a.m. to 2:30 p.m.; dinner, Mon through Sat from 5 p.m.; Sunday brunch only, 11 a.m. to 3 p.m. $$–$$$. Be sure to stop next door at the **Turning Page Bookstore** (860-434-0380).

HallMark Drive-in. Route 156; (860) 434-1998. An Old Lyme tradition, this classic shoreline shack specializes in fresh seafood, burgers, grinders, chicken, house-made ice cream and yogurt—even breakfast. Umbrella-shaded tables overlook the marsh so you can savor the salty air. Open Mar to Nov. $

Where to Stay

Old Lyme Inn. 85 Lyme St.; (860) 434-2600 or (800) 434-5352. This lovely country inn located in the historic village area welcomes children and pets to the no-smoking estab-lishment. Two of the 13 spacious rooms, all with private baths, have sofa beds, making them comfortable for families. Continental breakfast, inn restaurant and pub, entertain-ment, landscaped grounds. $$$$

East Lyme/Niantic

Though East Lyme actually extends northward several miles from I-95 (exit 72 northbound, exit 74 southbound), it is the activity in the southern part of town that attracts the most visitors. The village of Flanders centers on Route 1 where it bumps north of I-95, but it offers no attractions for tourists, unless you count the Flanders Fish Market (see Where to

Eat) or Pauline Lord's wonderful (and organic) **White Gate Farm** (83 Upper Pattagansett Rd.; 860-739-9585; www.whitegatefarm.net), both of which welcome visitors; call ahead for a guided farm tour at the latter.

Niantic, East Lyme's second village, south of both Route 1 and the interstate, is the center of most activity. Take Route 161 south and explore it and the east–west Route 156 to gain a perspective on this shoreline stretch of beaches, marinas and fishing piers, and small shops and restaurants. In downtown Niantic, a 1.1-mile-long waterfront walkway provides wide-open views of Niantic Bay and Long Island Sound. Enter the walkway at Cini Park under the Niantic River Bridge off Route 156 or from the Hole-in-the-Wall Beach at Baptist Lane. Interpretive signboards along the walkway educate visitors about local history and habitats, and benches provide plentiful places to rest during your stroll. Bring a picnic and a blanket if you'd like to linger awhile at the tiny Amtrak Beach and watch the trains go by.

Rocky Neck State Park (all ages)

244 West Main St. (Route 156) or exit 72 from I-95; (860) 739-5471. Open year-round 8 a.m. to 8:30 p.m. From Memorial Day to Labor Day, parking fee is $$–$$$. Off-season visitors pay a weekends-only fee or no fee at all. The campground is open from April through September 30 ($).

Few better places exist for beachcombing and shore camping than Rocky Neck State Park. Its full mile of beach frontage on Long Island Sound provides swimming, saltwater fishing, and scuba diving opportunities; its 160 campsites provide a home away from home for professional beach bums, amateur naturalists, and the children thereof.

Interpretive programs, junior naturalist activities, and a full summer calendar of nature walks and slide shows are offered for campers as well as day visitors. Hiking and picnicking are also common pleasures for both campers and day visitors. An interpretive trail points out examples of shore flora and fauna. The state provides picnic shelters, bathhouses, food concessions, lifeguards, first aid, and telephones. Campers have dumping station, hookups, drinking water, and bathrooms with showers and toilets.

Like other state parks, Rocky Neck is safe and clean, but its windswept bluffs and gorgeous views of the Sound and offshore islands clearly create a special attraction. The park is one of the prettiest of public shoreline areas managed by the state. Its beautiful stone pavilion, constructed in the 1930s, has pillars cut from Connecticut's other state parks and forests. From dawn to dusk in winter, the park's trails and open spaces can be used for cross-country skiing, and there is no better place to simply enjoy a fall afternoon.

Children's Museum of Southeastern Connecticut (ages 1 to 10)

409 Main St.; (860) 691-1111; www.childrensmuseumsect.org. Open Tues through Sun (plus Mon in the summer and on most holiday Mondays when school is closed). Tues through Thurs 9:30 a.m. to 4:30 p.m.; Fri 9:30 a.m. to 6 p.m.; Sat 9:30 a.m. to 5 p.m.; Sun noon to 5 p.m. Closed major holidays. $$; infants up to age 1 free.

Among the shops on Niantic's Main Street is a small museum for young children. Families from the far reaches of the state probably have a similar establishment closer to home, but if you happen to be in the area or you live nearby, come at once.

Niantic **Shoppers**

If your family is of a more strolling/browsing nature, cruise the shops and galleries of Niantic. Not to be missed just a ways along on Route 156, outside of the main village, is the **Book Barn** (41 West Main St.; 860-739-5715; www .bookbarnniantic.com), which has 75,000-plus used books (even more in their downtown satellite store at 269 Main St.). Both stores are open every day except Thanksgiving and December 25, from 9 a.m. to 9 p.m. Folks browse for so long here that the proprietors offer complimentary snacks, cocoa, and coffee.

This popular play and experience center provides an opportunity to develop young imaginations. See how creative your children can be in hands-on activity centers and exhibits that explore the senses, the arts, the sciences, and the coastal environment and culture. The slides and building toys in the Nursery Rhyme Land play area are perfect for toddlers. The Discovery Room includes a crawl-in planetarium and a marine life aquarium. A wonderful model train exhibit depicts the real sights of the Connecticut shoreline and countryside, and a new exhibit celebrates the Niantic River watershed. Outside are two play areas with opportunities for water, sand, and bubble play as well as climbing. Changing exhibitions keep folks coming to see what's new. This is a great rainy-day place if you are camping or vacationing in the area.

Black Hawk II (ages 6 and up)

East Main Street (exit 72, left at Route 156, about 7 miles, under the bridge, into parking lot), Niantic Beach Marina; (860) 448-3662 or (800) 382-2824. Mid-May through Oct, daily sails at 6 a.m. and 1 p.m. $$$$, children under 12 half-price. No reservations necessary.

Fishing trips out on the Sound are the specialty of this boat. Use parental discretion as to whether your child is old enough to handle the excitement (and the equipment) necessary to hook a striped bass or a nice big bluefish. *Black Hawk II*'s crew and captain handle the driving, supply bait and setup, rent rod and reel ($) if you don't bring your own gear, and turn burgers and dogs at the snack bar on board if you don't bring your own picnic. **Free** instruction is available for beginners. They stay out five to six hours in the sun, wind, and even in light rain, so bring sweatshirts, caps, and sunscreen. It's first-come, first-served and quite popular. Arrive 45 minutes before sail time on weekends and 35 minutes before on weekdays.

Where to Eat

Constantine's. 252 Main St.; (860) 739-2848. This clean, friendly, family-run establishment has great overstuffed sandwiches, house-made soups, salads, a children's menu, plus great seafood, chicken, veal, and steak dishes. Lunch and dinner, Tues through Sun from noon. $$–$$$

Flanders Fish Market and Restaurant. 22 Chesterfield Rd. (Route 161), Flanders; (860) 739-8866. Cheerful, busy, and very casual, this place serves the best fish in town, plus lots of typical American fare appealing to kids. Open daily from 8 a.m. $–$$

La Belle Aurore. 75 Pennsylvania Ave.; (860) 739-6767. This pretty little American bistro has seasonal, locally sourced fruits, veggies, meats, and seafood, presented artfully, to ensure your dining health and pleasure. Brunch on weekends 8 a.m. to 1 p.m.; dinner Mon and Wed through Sat from 5:30 p.m. $$$–$$$$

Where to Stay

Inn at Harbor Hill Marina. 60 Grand St.; (860) 739-0331. Nine very lovely and spotless rooms perched high above the Niantic River are a best bet for families. Fireplaces and balconies in some rooms; private baths in all. Complimentary buffet breakfasts, use of kayaks, and boat cruise (in summer season). Open year-round. $$$$

The Niantic Inn. 345 Main St.; (860) 739-5451; www.thenianticinn.com. One long block from the water, this small seacoast hotel has 24 roomy studios with dining and living area, in-room fridge and microwave, continental breakfast. $$$–$$$$

Sleep Inn & Suites. 5 King Arthur Dr.; (860) 739-1994. Part of the Quality Inn group, this one has an indoor pool, fitness room, complimentary continental breakfast; kids stay free. $$–$$$

Waterford

Judging by the sights along I-95, Waterford offers an abundance of shopping—and not much more. From its setting right on the Sound, however, Waterford offers a couple coastal attractions you might want to check out.

Sunbeam Express Cruises (ages 4 and up)

Captain John's Sport Fishing Center, 15 First St. (or 381 Rope Ferry Rd., by GPS); (860) 443-7259; www.sunbeamfleet.com. Lighthouse, fireworks, and harbor seal cruises, $$$$. Children 4 and under free. Groups of 10 or more get a discount. Eagle cruises and whale watches can also be arranged for large groups, by charter only. Reservations are required so the captain can call you if weather-related cancellations are necessary. The boats leave promptly; please check traffic conditions and plan to arrive 30 to 45 minutes before departure.

Down at the docks on the Niantic River at Captain John's Sport Fishing Center, in business for more than 60 years, you can take a public lighthouse or seal-watching cruise, or, if you collect a large enough group of friends and family, arrange another kind of nature cruise.

Approximately 3,000 harbor seals and harp seals live in the waters of Fishers Island Sound and other areas of eastern Long Island Sound, and Captain John's three-hour harbor seal cruises, narrated by a naturalist, leave from the First Street dock in late March and April; check the website for the schedule and to make reservations. Throughout the summer season, Sunbeam offers several four-and-a-half-hour lighthouse cruises. Crossing

Sand and **Song**

The **Waterford Town Beach** at 317 Great Neck Rd. offers six free concerts on Wednesday evenings at 6 from late June through early August. The concerts are held in the recreation field, adjacent to the main parking lot and pavilions at the beach, just about a mile down the road from Harkness State Park. If you come just for the evening (after 5 p.m.), there is no charge to park. If you arrive earlier in the day, nonresidents pay a parking fee ($$–$$$). For a schedule of concerts, call the Waterford Parks and Recreation Department at (860) 444-5881.

the Sound through Plum Gut and across the Race, the narrated cruise highlights 11 lighthouses on both the Connecticut and New York shores. Cruises to see fireworks from late June through mid-July are also popular; check the website for current information.

By private pre-arrangement, the boats can be hired in February through about mid-March for naturalist-guided bald eagle charters ($$$$) that depart from Old Saybrook and head up the Connecticut River to see the birds that come from Canada to feed on white perch in unfrozen sections of the river south of Haddam. If your group is smaller than the minimum required, the captain may agree to combine your family or scout group with another party to create a large enough group to start the engines on this 100-foot boat. Each cruise highlights any wildlife you might see, from ospreys, herons, and other waterfowl to wild turkeys, fox, and deer on the riverbanks.

The crew typically brings lunches, snacks, and soft drinks aboard for sale in the galley, or you can pack a lunch (no alcoholic beverages). Pack a Dramamine, a ginger capsule, or a wristband if you get seasick and dress appropriately for the weather. Bring a sweatshirt even in summer, and winter gear at other times. The heated cabin helps to keep you toasty, but despite the large windows the best viewing is still outside at the rail, so be prepared—and don't forget a camera and binoculars. Restrooms are on board.

Harkness Memorial State Park (all ages)

275 Great Neck Rd. (Route 213); (860) 443-5725. Open year-round 8 a.m. to sunset. Daily parking fee ($$) in summer. Free from Labor Day to Memorial Day. Free mansion tours on weekends and holidays only from Memorial Day weekend until Labor Day; first tour, 10 a.m.; last tour 2:15 p.m.

On the gorgeous seaside site of a former private estate, the park itself is a feast for the eyes. Pack a basket of goodies and spread a picnic on the lovely grounds surrounding Eolia, a restored 42-room mansion once owned by oil tycoon and philanthropist Edward S. Harkness and his wife, Mary. Bequeathed to the State of Connecticut, the house is now open to the public in season for free guided tours. A picnic area and fishing area are offered for day visitors, but no swimming is allowed, due to a strong undertow.

Where to Eat

Sunset Rib Company. 378 Rope Ferry Rd.; (860) 443-7427. Sunset views of the Sound and river complete with great ribs, chicken, pastas, salads, burgers, and more. Indoor and outdoor seating. Open daily for lunch and dinner from mid-March to mid-September. $$

Unk's on the Bay. 361 Rope Ferry Rd.; (860) 443-2717. Close to the water and slightly more upscale than other family places, Unk's offers good food at fair prices. Open year-round Wed through Mon for lunch and dinner. $–$$$

Where to Stay

Oakdell Motel. 983 Hartford Turnpike, which is Route 85; (860) 442-9446. Immaculate roadside motel. 22 efficiencies; each room has a fridge, microwave, and private bath, and either 1 or 2 double beds. Outdoor pool and grills. Complimentary continental breakfast. $$$

SpringHill Suites by Marriott. 401 North Frontage Rd.; (860) 439-0151. Two queen-size beds and a pull-out sofa in most rooms make this hotel great for families. In-room refrigerator, microwave, coffeemaker; continental breakfast, indoor pool, whirlpool, exercise room. $$$$

New London

Like its sister city, Groton, across the Thames River, New London has a long maritime history that has influenced its development into a center of commerce and industry. Settled in 1646 as Pequot Plantation by John Winthrop Jr., it was by 1846 the second-largest whaling port in the world. Long a manufacturing and shipbuilding city, it offers an eclectic assortment of attractions of value to families. This guide touches just the highlights of New London. Be sure to contact the New London Visitors Information Service (860-444-7264) or New London Main Street (860-444-CITY) for maps, brochures, and walking guides to all of this 6-square-mile city's museums, historic sites, shopping areas, restaurants, and lodging choices. A look at the city's website (www.ci.new-london.ct.us) may also be helpful.

U.S. Coast Guard Academy (ages 6 and up)

15 Mohegan Ave. off Route 31; Public Affairs Office: (860) 444-8270. Campus open year-round daily 9 a.m. to 5 p.m. A Visitors Pavilion is open May through Oct 10 a.m. to 4 p.m. The separate museum operates year-round 9 a.m. to 4:30 p.m. on weekdays only. The *Eagle,* when in port, is open for guided tours Fri through Sun 1 to 5 p.m. Free.

If you have someone in the family with an interest in the Coast Guard, you should know that New London is the home of its academy. The beautiful 100-acre campus overlooks the Thames River. The academy has a museum and a visitor center that features a multimedia show on cadet life. Tours of the bark USCG *Eagle* are offered whenever it is in port. Dress parades and concerts by the Coast Guard Band are held on a seasonal schedule, usually on Friday at 4 p.m. in the spring and fall.

New London's **Historic Center**

You may also be interested in these important points of interest near or within New London's Historic District:

- **Fort Trumbull State Park.** 90 Walbach St.; (860) 444-7591. Built on the site of Revolutionary War fortifications, this park has spectacular views of the river and sea. Guided tours, fishing pier, visitor center. Park open year-round daily, 8 a.m. to sunset; fort and visitor center open Memorial Day through Columbus Day, Wed through Sun, 9 a.m. to 4 p.m. Free to park and stroll; visitor center and fort tours, $.

- **Nathan Hale Schoolhouse.** Foot of State Street. One of the two Connecticut schools where Hale taught before losing his life in the American Revolution. Open May through Oct, Wed to Sun, 11 a.m. to 4 p.m. Free.

- **Custom House Maritime Museum.** 150 Bank St.; (860) 447-2501. Oldest customs house in the United States, now restored with museum on the customs service. Permanent exhibit on *Amistad* incident. Frequent changing exhibitions. Open Apr through Dec, Tues through Sun, 1 to 5 p.m. and by appointment. Free; donations welcome.

- **Whale Oil Row.** Huntington Street. Restored row of 1832 Greek revival houses owned by whaling tycoons.

- **Starr Street Restoration Area.** Another row of Greek revival homes laid out in 1835 on the site of a ropewalk.

- **Shaw Mansion.** 11 Blinman St.; (860) 443-1209. Built for wealthy Captain Nathaniel Shaw in 1756 and used as naval war office during Revolution, this museum has very nice exhibits and programs. Open year-round Wed through Fri, 1 to 4 p.m.; Sat from 10 a.m. to 4 p.m. $.

- **Monte Cristo Cottage.** 325 Pequot Ave.; (860) 443-0051. Boyhood home of Pulitzer and Nobel Prize–winning playwright Eugene O'Neill. Great tour, but stories are sad and somewhat adult. Look for O'Neill's statue, sweetly portraying his boyhood, on rock overlooking the harbor on Eugene O'Neill Drive. Open Memorial Day to Labor Day; call for days and hours. $; children under 5 free.

Lyman Allyn Art Museum (ages 4 and up)

625 Williams St.; (860) 443-2545; www.lymanallyn.org. Open year-round, except Monday and major holidays. Tues through Sat 10 a.m. to 5 p.m., Sun 1 to 5 p.m. $, children under 8 free. The admission fee allows entrance to the doll exhibit in the adjacent Deshon-Allyn Mansion as well.

Like the New Britain Museum of American Art, the Lyman Allyn owns one of Connecticut's little-known but exceptional small art collections. The fine and decorative arts from America, Europe, Asia, and the South Pacific make this a perfect introduction to art history for young children. Located in a pristine setting near Connecticut College and the Coast Guard Academy, this beautiful neoclassic museum contains 30,000 pieces; some holdings of special appeal to children are an Egyptian falcon mummy and Native American artifacts. The museum's American collection is excellent. Take the kids on an art history tour of American style from the late 1600s through the Impressionism of the 20th century.

The museum also owns a notable collection of 19th- and 20th-century dolls and dollhouses. A portion of that collection is exhibited in the 1827 Deshon-Allyn mansion adjacent to the main museum. If you would like to see those enchanting displays, just call ahead and ask for an appointment. A docent will be happy to take you to the Deshon-Allyn during your visit to the main museum. The museum arranges special changing exhibitions with children in mind at least twice yearly, usually in the summer and between Thanksgiving and New Year's Day, and arty birthday parties can be arranged here. Outside on the museum's front lawn is a sculpture garden designed to demonstrate the evolution of art. Children are welcome to climb on, play in, and ponder each object in the park.

Hempsted Houses (ages 5 and up)

11 Hempstead St.; (860) 443-7949; www.ctlandmarks.org. Open for tours Memorial Day weekend through Columbus Day weekend. In May, June, Sept, and Oct, they are offered on

New London **Waterfront Park**

A beautiful, wide, half-mile-long esplanade is the highlight of Waterfront Park, located along the Thames River in downtown New London (111 Union St.; 860-447-5201). See historic sites, enjoy the activities of the ferry terminals, or soak up the views of the river and waterfront. A good place to enter the area is behind the railroad station near the Fishers Island Ferry or at City Pier at the foot of State Street. Free live entertainment and special events are frequent on the stage at City Pier Plaza; the new Children's Discovery Pier has permanent displays about local marine wildlife; *Amistad* Pier offers fishing space; and the Custom House Pier hosts vessels of all sizes, including tall ships and luxury cruise liners.

What's the Story at **Connecticut College?**

The picturesque campus and liberal arts tradition at **Connecticut College** draw students from every corner of the nation. Families are also drawn here to the arboretum (www.arboretum.conncoll.edu), which is open daily year-round from dawn to dusk, and to the Connecticut Storytelling Festival, held annually in late April at the Connecticut Storytelling Center. For three days, professional and student storytellers gather for performances, workshops, and story swaps. Stories from traditions around the globe are told to audiences of adults and children. The opening story "concert" on Friday evening is often specially directed to families. Admission is charged. For information, call (860) 439-2764 or check the website at www.connstorycenter.org/festival .html. $$–$$$.

weekends only from 1 to 4 p.m. In July and Aug, they are offered Wed and Fri through Sun at the same hours. $.

This "compound" in the historic downtown area includes one of the oldest documented houses in America; both homes are among the few New London structures to have survived the burning of the city in 1781 by the British troops under the command of Benedict Arnold.

The Joshua Hempsted House was built by Joshua Hempsted the elder in 1678 and is one of the oldest frame buildings in New England. Joshua Hempsted the younger, who was born the year his father constructed the house, kept diaries for more than 40 of the years he lived in the house. A rope maker and father of nine children, Joshua kept his diaries from 1711 to 1758, and these writings have contributed greatly both to the excellent interpretation of the house itself and to our knowledge of 18th-century colonial American life. The newer, 1759 Nathaniel Hempsted House is one of the most unusual historic homes in New England—it has 2-foot-thick stone walls, a gambrel roof, and an exterior projecting beehive oven. Its mysterious French connections, the subject of recent research, are revealed in the intriguing one-hour tours.

Hands-on activities for children are offered on special weekends once each month. On Labor Day weekend a special focus is made on women's work of the 18th century. A Hempsted Thanksgiving is typically celebrated the Saturday after Thanksgiving. Costumed docents, open-hearth cooking, and food samples are part of the celebration.

Garde Arts Center (ages 4 and up)

325 State St. For a calendar of events or other information, call (860) 444-6766; www.garde arts.org. For tickets, call the box office (860) 444-7373 or (888) ON-GARDE. $$–$$$$.

If you have never taken the kids to a real movie palace, the kind with gilded architecture and acoustics to spare, plush seats, and a giant movie screen, go to the Garde, downtown in the historic district.

New London **Sets Sail**

A variety of boats leave from New London docks. Check among these for the trips that best fit your family's interests and budget:

- **Block Island Express.** (860) 444-4624; www.goblockisland.com. 2 Ferry St. High-speed passenger-only service (70 minutes) to Block Island from New London. Bicycles and surfboards welcome, but no motorized vehicles. Late May to Oct.

- **Cross Sound Ferry Services.** (860) 443-5281; www.longislandferry.com. 2 Ferry St. Seven vessels offer passenger and vehicle service (80 minutes) to Orient Point, Long Island. An eighth vessel, the high-speed *Sea Jet 1*, offers passenger-only service (40 minutes) to Orient Point.

- **Viking Fleet.** Cross Sound Ferry dock at 2 Ferry St.; (631) 668-5700; www.vikingfleet.com. New London to Montauk, Long Island, May to Sept. Links to Martha's Vineyard and Block Island.

In addition to its noteworthy new and classic film series, the 1,500-seat theater presents nationally and internationally known live performing artists throughout the year. Select from a Broadway series and a Family Theatre series, plus country music, dance, and comedy series. Tickets to single performances are available as well.

Look closely at the upcoming season's announcements. At far more affordable prices than Broadway, the family can enjoy wonderful theater, dance, and more. This 1926 theater, by the way, has enjoyed a $19 million restoration/expansion that has transformed this already grand lady into a state-of-the-art performing arts center. See the beautiful results in its marvelous grand entrance and circular marquee that usher audiences into three floors of new and restored Moroccan-style lobbies. It's a great place to see a holiday spectacular like *The Nutcracker,* or check out the Young and Fun series of dance, comedy, magic, and other youthfully exuberant productions.

Ocean Beach Park (all ages)

1225 Ocean Ave.; (860) 447-3031 or (800) 510-SAND; www.ocean-beach-park.com. Access to the beach and park **free** year-round, dawn to dusk. Entertainments and concessions open Memorial Day weekend through Labor Day weekend, 9 a.m. to 11 p.m. Admission collected through a parking fee ($$$). Use of water slide, pool, lockers, and mini-golf involves extra per-person or per-family charges. Lifeguards and first-aid station in season.

For the kind of family fun wherein everybody gets wet, come to a place that offers not one but three ways to get soaked. Owned and maintained by the City of New London, Ocean Beach Park is both old-fashioned public beach resort and newfangled party/conference/banquet facility. The half-mile-long, white-sand beach that is the focal point of the park may be its best asset. A wide wooden boardwalk down the length of the beach leads past a full-service restaurant, an unremarkable food court, a pinball and electronic game arcade, a kiddie playground, and an 18-hole miniature golf course ($) complete with life-size spouting sperm whale.

Also home to a handful of old-school-style carnival-sized kiddie rides ($ for a rides bracelet), the park also has an amusement park–style water slide. A triple-run tower of serpentine slides, this is a humdinger of a ride and, with the exception of the beach itself,

Mystic Whaler **Cruises**

If you have the time and the budget, these cruises just may be the cream of the crop of boat excursions along the entire Connecticut coastline. The schooner itself is an awe-inspiring 110-foot beauty carrying 3,000 square feet of sail, and, whether on a three-hour lobster cruise or a seven-day odyssey, the crew cheerfully invites both landlubbers and skilled show-offs to hoist the sails, plot the course, or take a turn at the wheel. If you can spring for an overnight sea trek, you can choose from five accommodations options, from the tiny Sloop to the Great Room, which gives you a taste of life belowdecks for the common sailor, to the Clipper cabins, which provide skylights, private head and shower en suite, a sink with hot and cold running water, and a double bed.

The lobster cruises include steamed lobster and fresh clam chowder served on-deck under sail. Six-hour day sails include a hearty barbecue fresh off the on-board grill served while cruising Fishers Island Sound; if the wind is right, it includes a swim in a sheltered cove before returning to Mystic. Overnight sails of one, two, three, five, and seven days include such ports of call as Block Island, Shelter Island, Sag Harbor, Newport, Cuttyhunk, and Martha's Vineyard. Full-moon cruises, pirate-treasure adventure cruises, lighthouse cruises, and art cruises that encourage you to bring along your art supplies and camera are among the maritime mini-vacations that Captain John Eginton plans to tempt you aboard. It might be worth it to skip the crowds at Disney World and have the adventure of a lifetime on your own private getaway windjammer.

The *Mystic Whaler* sails out of New London's Waterfront Park. Cruises range from $80 to $890 per person. Children 10 and older are welcome on overnight voyages at full fare. Children ages 5 to 10 are welcome on day sails and evening cruises at half-fare, with the understanding that parents are wholly responsible for the child throughout the cruise. To obtain rates and reservations, check the website at www.mysticwhaler.com, or call (860) 536-4218 or (800) 697-8420.

may be the most popular attraction here. A height requirement of 46 inches helps keep the ride safe for all visitors. The three flumes begin about 50 feet up at the top of a challenging set of stairs, so depending on your speed and stamina in climbing those stairs, you may get maybe 20 runs down the flume of your choice in the two-hour time slot your slide bracelet ($$) buys you. Younger kids may enjoy a sort of fun/sort of hum-drum splash pad/sprayground, and folks who don't like salt water swimming will like the immaculate Olympic-size swimming pool. A bathhouse with changing rooms, lockers, and showers are also available. All of these have individual fees ($).

If you like quieter and less expensive fun, come in the evening when the parking fee drops or goes away; bring a picnic, take the nature walk to Alewife Cove, and check out the birds from the observation deck.

Where to Eat

Fred's Shanty. 272 Pequot Ave.; (860) 447-1301. Overlooking Thamesport Marina, this quintessential seafood shack, immortalized in Mark Shasha's children's picture book *Night of the Moonjellies,* offers boats, gulls, "long dogs," fries, great seafood, and burgers. Outdoor seating only. Open mid-March through mid- October for lunch and dinner daily. $–$$

Mangetout. 140 State St.; (860) 444-2066. Fresh, seasonal, organic soups, sandwiches, wraps, frittatas, smoothies, salads, and baked goods, with vegetarian, vegan, and gluten-free choices. Awesome and inviting for families. Open daily until 4 p.m., opening Mon through Fri at 8 a.m., Sat at 10 a.m., and for Sunday brunch at 11 a.m. $

Recovery Room. 445 Ocean Ave.; (860) 443-2619. A cousin to the equally wonderful Pizzaworks in Mystic and Old Saybrook, this place has the perfect menu and ambiance for

children. Open for lunch on weekdays from 11:30 a.m., and daily for dinner from 4 p.m. $

Zavala. 2 State St.; (860) 437-1891. Authentic—and deliciously gourmet-quality—Mexican cuisine near Waterfront Park. Tex-Mex choices may please younger diners. Lunch on weekdays from 11:30 a.m.; dinner daily from 4 p.m. $$–$$$

Where to Stay

Holiday Inn New London/Mystic. 269 North Frontage Rd.; (860) 442-0631 or (800) HOLIDAY. 136 units including 24 efficiencies, restaurant, indoor pool, fitness room. $$$–$$$$

Radisson Hotel New London/Mystic. 35 Governor Winthrop Blvd.; (860) 443-7000. 120 units with 4 suites, pub and restaurant, indoor pool, fitness room. $$$–$$$$

Groton

Back on an even keel since the U.S. Naval Reserve Station decided to stay in town, Groton remains a busy center of naval and defense-related industry. Its long history as such defines its attractions as well. Surrounded on three sides by the waters of Long Island Sound, the Thames River, and the Mystic River, Groton has been a leading shipbuilding center since the 18th century. For much of the past century, it has been most famed as the home of the Electric Boat Division of General Dynamics, the leading designer and manufacturer of nuclear submarines.

Historic Ship *Nautilus* and Submarine Force Museum (ages 3 and up)

Naval Submarine Base, Crystal Lake Road; (800) 343-0079 or (860) 694-3174; www.ussnautilus .org. Open year-round from May 15 to late October, Wed through Mon 9 a.m. to 5 p.m., and from November 1 to May 14 (but closed the first full week of May) Wed through Mon from 9 a.m. to 4 p.m. Also closed the last full week of October, plus Thanksgiving, Christmas, and New Year's Day. Wheelchair access to the submarine is limited. Free.

A visit to Groton has to include a visit to the USS *Nautilus,* the world's first nuclear subma-rine. The USS *Nautilus* Memorial at the U.S. Naval Submarine Base on Route 12 includes tours of the *Nautilus* and an award-winning museum that explores the history and technol-ogy of submarines.

Excellently presented in a state-of-the-art facility, the museum exhibits celebrate the achievements of the human mind in devising this technology. Children can stand in the re-created sub attack center and hear the sounds of battle. They can operate three work-ing periscopes. They can watch films of submarine history, and they can explore mini-subs outside and models inside. Other outstanding exhibits explain the important uses of the submarine both in defense and underwater exploration.

Aboard the *Nautilus* you will explore the sonar and torpedo rooms and the navigation and control room. You will visit the crew's living quarters, the galley, and the captain's quarters. The impact of the ship's huge size is somewhat lost due to the way it is moored to give visitors access, but, once inside, visitors will easily imagine life and work aboard this amazing vessel that explored beneath Arctic ice and the 20,000 leagues of the deep ocean.

Project Oceanology (ages 6 and up)

1084 Shennecossett Rd., at foot of Benham Road, Avery Point Campus of UConn; (800) 364-8472 between 9 a.m. and 4 p.m.; www.oceanology.org. Public oceanography cruises from mid-June through Aug 31 at 10 a.m. and 1 p.m. Seal-watching cruises, Sat only in Feb; Sat and Sun in Mar. Lighthouse cruises, 4 p.m., June through Aug on Tues, Thurs, and Sat and in Sept on Sat only. $$$. Reservations strongly recommended; a Visa or Mastercard number is required to hold your reservation. Note: No children under age 6 are allowed onboard for safety reasons.

The lure of the sea may capture you once again in Groton. If so, head to the Institute of Marine Science at the Avery Point campus of the University of Connecticut, where you can board *Enviro-Lab II* or *III* for a two-and-a-half-hour cruise called Project Oceanology Study Cruises. These summer expeditions are among the best family activities offered in the state, especially for those families that have a child interested in marine biology.

Enviro-Lab's instructors are marine scientists who accompany each group of about 25 passengers for an afternoon or morning of study. Using the same methods the scientists use in their work, you will measure and record data about the geology and biology you observe. You will learn the uses of nautical charts and navigation instruments. You will collect and test water, mud, and sand samples. You will pull trawl nets and examine the plants and animals you catch. All the while the crew and captain provide a wonderfully interesting narration about the islands, lighthouses, and watercraft that surround your area of exploration.

Also available through Project Oceanology are cruises for observing gray and harbor seals in Fishers Island Sound. These weekends-only winter cruises are preceded by a 20-minute slide presentation. Inquire also about the lighthouse tour to New London Ledge; the fare is the same as for other cruises.

In summer, be sure to wear sunscreen, a hat, and sneakers. Bring a sweatshirt or a windbreaker. In winter, dress appropriately for cold weather, even though the boat has a heated cabin. Project Oceanology's headquarters are in a waterfront laboratory building near its boat docks. A seawater aquarium system, classrooms, a library, several labs, and a hostel are housed there; a cafeteria where visitors can purchase snacks and lunches is available to day-trippers. You can also picnic on the campus before or after a cruise.

Bluff Point Coastal Reserve (all ages)
Depot Road off Route 1 (go to the very end of Depot Road under the railroad overpass to reach the parking lot). Open year-round from 8 a.m. to sunset. For info, call the rangers at Fort Trumbull in New London. Free.

Those who prefer to explore the shore on foot may do so at this beautiful park and natural preserve of 800 acres. From the parking area on Depot Road, you may need up to a half hour to walk the 1.5-mile trail through the upland forest to the rocky bluff for which the park is named. Below the bluff lie the mile-long barrier beach and tidal salt marsh. Saltwater fishing, beachcombing, bird watching, horseback riding, and hiking are popular here, as is cross-country skiing in the wintertime.

You can also bring in a car-top boat to launch from the sand ramp right into the water, and you may go shellfishing, scuba diving, snorkeling, and swimming. No lifeguards are here. This wonderfully wild place—perhaps the finest wild place on the whole coastline—is a marvelous setting for any kind of outdoor family fun. Pack in everything you think you may need—and leave none of it behind.

Fort Griswold Battlefield State Park and the Ebenezer Avery House (all ages)
57 Fort St.; (860) 445-1729. Battlefield and fort ruins open daily year-round 8 a.m. to sunset. The museum (860-449-6877) and monument are open Memorial Day to Labor Day 10 a.m. to 5 p.m. and from the weekend after Labor Day until Columbus Day on weekends only at the same hours. The Avery House (860-446-9257) is open only on weekends, June to Labor Day, 1 to 5 p.m. Free. Free guided tours available.

Revolutionary War buffs might want to visit this site of the 1781 massacre of American defenders by British troops under the command of Benedict Arnold. The fort includes ramparts, battlements, and buildings dating from the Revolution, and the view of the river is wonderful. For a view to beat all, climb the 134-foot monument. When you descend, visit the museum, which tells the story of the battle and includes exhibits on other elements of southeastern Connecticut history from Native American times through colonial settlement, the Revolution, the Civil War, and whaling days. Ask for the dates of the Revolutionary War reenactment in early September. This Living History Weekend demonstrates camp lifeways and military drills.

Also on the park grounds is the 1750 Ebenezer Avery House, which, in its original site on Thames Street, was a repository for some of the wounded patriots. Moved to the park in 1971, the house features a kitchen and weaving room that are furnished as they might have been in the 18th century.

Noank Village (all ages)
From Route 1 heading east out of the city of Groton, take Route 215 (Groton Long Point Road) south to the village of Noank.

One of Connecticut's most picturesque shoreline enclaves, 300-year-old Noank has real beach-town flavor in its quiet, narrow streets, historic buildings, and shops and marinas. If your idea of fun is wandering and wading at some low-key shoreline spots, you could spend a day here, where there's nothing to do.

Esker Point Beach. Groton Long Point Road (Route 215) and Marsh Road; (860) 572-9702. One of the prettiest points on the Connecticut coast, with a perfect small beach for children. Linger through the afternoon to catch the sunset. Wednesday evening concerts in summer. Parking fee in summer only, $$ on weekdays, $$$ on weekends.

Noank Historical Society Museum. Sylvan Street; (860) 536-3021. Open July 4 through October 12 on Wed, Sat, and Sun from 2 to 5 p.m. $.

Spicer Park. Spicer Avenue, off Route 215, overlooking Beebe Cove. Grills, picnic area. Nice spot for bird watching. **Free.**

Where to Eat

Abbott's Lobster in the Rough. 117 Pearl St., Noank; (860) 536-7719. Fifty-plus years of strictly casual (not at all fancy) seaside ambience with views of bobbing boats and offshore islands. Eat out in the breeze and sun on picnic tables or under the striped tent. Lobsters, steamers, clams, oysters, shrimp, steamed corn, barbecued chicken, hot dogs, and strawberry shortcake—nothing fried. Open May through Labor Day, noon to 9 p.m. daily, then Fri to Sun through Columbus Day, noon to 7 p.m. $$$

The Fisherman. 937 Groton Long Point Rd., Noank; (860) 536-1717. Nice meals here on Palmer Cove, from shore classics to innovative American with locally sourced seafood and more. Outdoor patio. Lunch and dinner, daily. $$$

Paul's Pasta. 223 Thames St., Groton; (860) 445-5276. The best pasta place in the county. Lunch and dinner, 11 a.m. to 9 p.m. Tues through Sun. $–$$

Where to Stay

Best Western/Olympic Inn. 360 Route 12; (860) 445-8000 or (800) 622-7766. 140 rooms, restaurant, fitness room, sauna. $$$–$$$$

Mystic Marriott Hotel and Spa. 625 North Rd.; (860) 446-2600 or (866) 449-7390. Located on Route 117 close to the Noank area of Groton, this 4-diamond AAA-rated establishment has 285 rooms, including 6 suites perfect for families. Portable cribs available. Indoor pool, fitness room, day spa; coffee shop; lounge (serves lunch); Octagon restaurant for breakfast buffet daily and dinner Tues through Sat. $$$$

Mystic

If I were to name the 10 towns in Connecticut that most typify the essence of New England, I surely would mention Mystic. Rich in history that harks back to the earliest days of the Connecticut Colony, it is a town that has witnessed the first of the difficult compromises between settler and native, the glory days of whaling and shipbuilding, the rise of industrialization, and the decline of agriculture. Throughout this history Mystic has remained a vital community composed of diverse citizens engaged in the simple craft of building an American tradition.

For many years Mystic has been a tourist destination, most notably because of Mystic Seaport, among the nation's most outstanding maritime history museums. Now home to other notable attractions, Mystic attracts more visitors than ever before in its history. Even its downtown, long unnoticed by out-of-towners, is a thriving center enjoyed by tourists as well as townies. Not an official political entity itself, Mystic lies on the shoreline, half in the town of Groton and half in Stonington along both banks of the Mystic River.

Mystic Seaport, the Museum of America and the Sea (all ages)

75 Greenmanville Ave. (Route 27), off I-95 exit 90; (860) 572-5315; www.mysticseaport.org. The seaport is open year-round, daily, except Christmas Eve and Day. From Apr through Oct, the hours are 9 a.m. to 5 p.m.; from Nov through Mar, 10 a.m. to 4 p.m. $$–$$$; children 5 and younger free. Half-price admission after 4 p.m. Second consecutive day is free. Family memberships.

The first stop in Mystic for most visitors, the seaport's 17 acres of historic buildings and recreations represent a 19th-century New England whaling and shipbuilding village. An incredible array of educational and entertainment activities is offered here throughout the year. From rope-making to printing to oystering, from sailor to chandler to merchant, the arts, crafts, and occupations of an early American seaport are demonstrated for visitors of all ages.

Horse and buggy rides, planetarium shows, sea chantey sing-alongs, chowder festivals, lantern-light dramas at both Halloween and Christmas, tall-ship tours, fine arts exhibitions, hands-on activities, and outstanding special events are key to the seaport's success. Summer camps, living-history workshops, boat excursions, and concerts are among the opportunities for families.

If you haven't already visited here, plan to do so soon. You may find yourself riding an early-20th-century bicycle, stitching a sailor's log book, or sampling a hearty New England stew. After your adventures, shop in the seaport's outstanding art gallery and gift shop for a memento of your trip.

Sabino **Mystic River Cruises** (all ages)

From the Sabino Dock at Mystic Seaport; use south parking lot across from Seaport main entrance; (860) 572-5351. Check the website for rates; call for reservations after 10 a.m. on the day of the sail. Ninety-minute downriver cruises daily at 5:30 p.m., mid-May through Columbus Day. For these cruises, tickets are $$$; reservations are required, but no seaport admission is necessary. Daily half-hour cruises leave on the half hour, from 11:30 a.m. to 4:30 p.m. from mid-May to Columbus Day. Tickets are $, plus required seaport admission; children under 6 free.

The *Sabino* is the last coal-fired passenger steamboat in operation. Built in 1908 in East Boothbay, Maine, for passenger service on the Damariscotta River, it now carries passengers on its double decks for a cruise back in time. Watch the crew shovel the anthracite coal into the glowing maw of the boat's steam plant, then shift your gaze to the historic homes that grace the banks of the peaceful Mystic River. For the evening cruise, bring aboard a sweatshirt and a picnic dinner (or ask about their boxed dinner and beverage service) and settle in for the one-and-a-half-hour journey downriver and into Fishers Island Sound.

Mystic Aquarium and Institute for Exploration (all ages)

55 Coogan Blvd., off I-95 exit 90; (860) 572-5955; www.mysticaquarium.org. Open daily year-round (except Thanksgiving and Christmas); check the website for the changing seasonal hours. $$$; children 2 and under free. Validated tickets good for three consecutive days. Family memberships.

Continually refined and updated, the exhibit areas at Mystic Aquarium have been configured to represent the trio of "islands" of marine life found across the globe: the estuaries, the coral reefs, and the upwelling zones. From a New England tidal marsh to a coral reef re-creation to a penguin paradise, the aquarium's indoor and outdoor exhibits focus on 4,500 mammals, fish, and invertebrates of the sunlit seas. With its focus on the vital importance of the essential elements of a healthy ocean ecosystem, the aquarium also continues its primary mission of education, research, and conservation.

The magic starts at the main entrance, with a 750,000-gallon beluga whale pool that features both the deepwater areas and shallow cobble beaches of the beluga's

Animal **Encounters**

The Mystic Aquarium offers programs that allow the public to have contact with their whales and penguins. Adventurers 5 feet tall and over can make arrangements to spend time in the pool with the aquarium's beluga whales. An expensive adventure for most families, it may still be a once-in-a-lifetime experience worth the splurge to animal lovers. Call the aquarium or check the website for more details on this exciting program. A similar program allows contact with the aquarium's penguins. Children over age 6 may participate. Click on Penguin Contact Program on the website for more details.

south-central Alaskan habitat. Other indoor and outdoor exhibits include sharks, seals, sea lions, hundreds of species of fish, and invertebrates of every sort. The outdoor seal, sea lion, and penguin exhibits are re-creations of the animals' natural habitats in the North Pacific and Africa. The skylit marine theater allows staff marine biologists to demonstrate the dramatic talents and capabilities of California sea lions. The aquarium has an exciting relationship with underwater explorer Robert Ballard in the Institute for Exploration, which introduces visitors to undersea technology, oceanographic exploration, and marine archaeology. Simulated deep-sea dives aboard a manned submersible include the sights and sounds that one might experience during a 12,000-foot descent; another exhibit shows the robotic and other technology being used to explore famed shipwrecks.

The aquarium also has an excellent gift shop/bookstore, which shoppers may browse without an admission ticket. Workshops, classes, and special events are held at the aquarium throughout the year.

Olde Mistick Village (all ages)

At the junction of Route 27 and Coogan Boulevard, immediately adjacent to the aquarium; (860) 536-4941. Open year-round daily, from Mon through Sat from 10 a.m. to 6 p.m. and on Sun from noon to 5 p.m. Summer and holiday hours are often extended.

A shopping center built as a re-creation of a circa-1720 New England village, its pretty paths, reproduction freestanding shops, and ponds, fences, stone walls, and waterwheels make for a very pleasant experience, whether you are browsing or buying. Several restaurants, cafes, and candy stores are here, and the shops offer jewelry, clothing, toys, handcrafts, kitchen goods, and so on. Be sure to check the performances at the wonderful Cornerstone Playhouse (www.cornerstoneproductions.org; (888-838-2906), a 240-seat theater that produces a holiday show and other musical comedy productions suitable for the family.

Olde Mistick Village is especially pretty in summer, when its ponds are busy with waterfowl, its gazebo is the site of **free** concerts, and its flowers and trees are in bloom. During December the village and its white New England church replica are aglow with holiday light displays, and various festivities and promotions in individual shops lure shoppers along the luminaria-lined pathways.

Denison Pequotsepos Nature Center
and Peace Sanctuary (all ages)

109 Pequotsepos Rd.; (860) 536-1216; www.dpnc.org. Open year-round Mon through Sat 9 a.m. to 5 p.m. and Sun 10 a.m. to 4 p.m. $–$$, children 5 and under free. Trails are open dawn to dusk; leave a donation in the box. Leashed pets are welcome. Picnicking is allowed.

If you need a break from the busyness and the marine and historical themes, visit this 200-acre preserve with 7 miles of trails through woods and meadows and past ponds. Wildflower and fern gardens are among the areas created to encourage homeowners to create their own backyard habitats. If you are very lucky, you may see otter, mink, or other mammals native to these parts. Birds, of course, up to 150 species, are everywhere.

Other Mystical **Attractions**

- **Denison Homestead Museum.** Pequotsepos Road; (860) 536-9248. If the seaport fails to satisfy a history craving, this unusual 1717 house might do the trick. Its rooms represent periods from the 1720s to the 1940s. Open June through Oct, Fri through Mon from noon to 4 p.m.

- **Williams Beach Park** at Mystic Community Center off Mason's Island Road; (860) 536-3575. Saltwater beach, playground, picnic and snack pavilions, and grills. **Free.** No lifeguards. Open June to Labor Day.

The Pequotsepos natural history museum includes indoor native wildlife exhibits on woodland, wetland, and meadow habitats; a wonderful live native butterfly exhibit is enchanting. Frogs, fish, birds, and reptiles are among the other animals here, and an outdoor flight enclosure provides homes for non-releasable owls. Be sure to stop in the Night in the Meadow Theater to experience a simulation of the sounds and sights in a meadow on a summer evening. The Trading Post gift shop sells field guides, birding supplies, and natural science materials. A full schedule of guided walks, summer camps for children ages 3 to 16, and field trips are listed on the center's website.

The center's Peace Sanctuary on River Road is about a mile away on the western bank of the Mystic. Atop rocky ledges, this wooded, 30-acre preserve offers trails overlooking the river. Ask for directions when you visit the main center. Open at no charge from dawn to dusk, it is well named and especially lovely to explore during the early morning and close to dusk when the birds are most active. If you come in May, you may witness the charm of the 400 pink lady-slipper plants that blossom here.

Downtown Mystic (all ages)
West and East Main Street (Route 1); Water Street; Bank Street; Pearl Street; and other nearby streets.

A few years back only the locals knew the secrets of the "real" historic center of Mystic. Now the whole downtown area rocks and rolls with the tourist crowd that has discovered the no-longer-neglected inner core of the village. If your appetite for the sea has simply been whetted by the sights upriver, head downtown to Route 1 via Route 27 and the famed counterweighted bascule drawbridge that leads you to picturesque Mystic center. Linger awhile on the bridge itself (park the car somewhere else first) and watch the jellyfish and other flotsam. Stay to see the hourly raising of the bridge and the passage of the yachts and sailboats as they cruise up- or downriver. Then stroll the boutiques, galleries, bookstores, candy shops, and restaurants. Discover your own favorite places, but be sure to take your time at the Mystic Army-Navy Store, the Mystic Art Association Gallery, Mystical Toys, the Mystic River Park, the Mystic Drawbridge Ice Cream Company, and the incomparable Sea Swirl seafood shack. You'll easily find them all in the 1-mile historic district.

Into the **Mystic Cruises**

It seems there is no end to boating experiences out of Mystic, but the crowds are here to support them. In case the others have failed to intrigue you, here are a few more options out of the Mystic Seaport shipyard (860-572-5341):

- *Brilliant.* On this 61-foot schooner, weeklong summer sail training camps for teens; sailing voyages for adults by charter only ($$$$).
- *Resolute.* On this 26-foot launch, half-hour cruises for up to six passengers ($).
- *Breck Marshall.* On this 20-foot catboat, half-hour cruises for up to six passengers ($, plus museum admission).
- *Araminta.* This ketch, with a skipper, can be chartered for day sails in Fishers Island Sound with up to three agile crew members ($$$$).

Return in mid-August for the Outdoor Art Festival, a two-day juried show of 300-plus artists who bring their wares to the sidewalks, parks, and riverbanks of downtown Mystic. Local vendors keep browsers on their feet with plenty of food and drink, and entertainment for all ages abounds throughout the festival scene. Downtown Mystic is serviced by a fun transportation option from Memorial Day to Labor Day: From 11 a.m. to 6 p.m. daily, Mystic Seaport's *Liberty* water-taxi leaves every 30 minutes from a dock behind the S&P Oyster House for rides ($) to or from the seaport (or just take a round-trip whirl, if you like).

Voyager Cruises (all ages)

15 Holmes St.; (860) 536-0416; www.voyagermystic.com. Public sails daily from May 1 to late October at 10:20 a.m., 2:20 p.m., and 5:30 p.m. $$$$, children under 2 **free.** Reservations highly recommended. Charters also available on this vessel and on the tall ship *Mystic.*

The *Argia*, a replica 19th-century gaff-rigged schooner, takes passengers on two- to three-hour day sails in scenic Fishers Island Sound. This beautiful white bird glides gracefully across these sheltered waters, providing a gentle ride that cannot fail to relax and refresh a weary day-tripping family. Beverages and light snacks are sold on board. You may also bring along a picnic lunch or dinner. If the majestic *Mystic Whaler* would break your bank, this more affordable option may be just right for a family cruise.

Where to Eat

Azu. 32 West Main St.; (860) 536-6336. Hip, contemporary, and festive, this downtown restaurant offers a sophisticated fusion-style twist on favorites from omelets to quesadillas to pizza—and much more, for lunch and dinner daily from 11 a.m. and for breakfast on weekends only from 7 a.m. $$–$$$

Latitude 41. 105 Greenmanville Ave.; (860) 536-9649. At the north entrance to the Seaport, this totally refreshed restaurant is great for New England-y and classic coastal dishes in an airy main dining room, two tavern-like front rooms, and an outdoor patio in season. Open daily for lunch and dinner. $$$–$$$$

Lis Bake Shop. 15 Holmes St.; (860) 536-9090. Trust me—just go. No matter what ails you, this is the cure. Absolutely delish baked goods—cupcake fiends will be in heaven. If those don't beckon, try the muffins, cookies, lemon bars, quiches, or breakfast sandwiches. It's wee, it's sweet, it's fresh—don't miss it. Outside patio; indoor counter and stools. Open daily from 7 a.m. to 5 p.m., except 1 on Sun. $

Mystic Pizza. 56 West Main St.; (860) 536-6194. Who can resist? It's convenient, the menu has lots more than pizza, and it's famous, so be there, just for fun. Lunch and dinner, 10 a.m. to 11 p.m. daily. $

Mystic Soup Company. 32 Williams Ave., #1; (860) 245-0382. Behind the Sea Swirl, at the back of the tire store, this (little) hidden wonder makes two hot soups daily and 16 different hot-pressed panini sandwiches. Yummy. Eat in at a couple of bar tables with stools or out at two cafe tables. Mon through Sat, 11:30 a.m. to 3 p.m. $

Pizzetta. 7 Water St.; (860) 536-4443. This cheer-filled place with admirable eco-conscious philosophies and practices makes terrific Neapolitan-style thin-crust pies with fresh house-made sauce. You can top your pie just about any way you want and it with a locally grown salad as well. Even the cleaning products are green. Open daily for lunch and dinner from 11 a.m. $

Sea View Snack Bar. 145 Greenmanville Ave.; (860) 572-0096. Gulls circle the red-painted picnic tables, the sun glints on the river, and the seaside-shack cuisine, served outdoors from March to mid-November, means rings, wings, dogs, nuggets, fries, burgers, seafood, and homemade chowder. Daily lunch and dinner from 11 a.m. $

Where to Stay

Howard Johnson Inn. 253 Greenmanville Ave.; (860) 536-2654. 77 units, including mini-suites, all with fridges and microwaves. Indoor pool. Seaport packages. $$–$$$$

Mystic Ramada Hotel. 9 Whitehall Ave.; (860) 536-4281 or (800) 272-6232. 150 units, 4 suites, restaurant, sauna, fitness room, playground, indoor pool. $$–$$$

Whaler's Inn. 20 East Main St.; (860) 536-1506 or (800) 243-2588; www.whalersinnmystic.com. 49 lovely rooms in the heart of downtown Mystic by the bridge. Homey ambience; children stay **free.** Complimentary continental breakfast. Three-diamond AAA rating. Four-star restaurant called Bravo Bravo. $$$–$$$$

Mashantucket/Ledyard

I'm not sure whether to call this Connecticut's oldest town or its newest, but it certainly is one that gets an awful lot of attention. Inhabited by Europeans since early in the 17th century and for centuries before that by Native American people such as the Pequots, the Mohegans, and the Narragansetts, the mostly rural town of Ledyard contains a village called Mashantucket. A federal reservation of the sacred tribal land of the Mashantucket

Pequot Tribal Nation, it is the center of activity in this otherwise quiet, forested landscape.

Visitors arrive by the busload to Mashantucket's most famous attraction: the Foxwoods Resort Casino. I don't recommend this complex as a family attraction, but many folks might disagree. Billed as the largest gaming (read "gambling") facility in the world, Foxwoods rises upward from Route 2 as if it were Oz itself. Besides the other ways you can part with your shirt here, there are two four-diamond high-rise hotels with spectacular pools, spas, and gourmet-quality luxury dining; nearly three dozen more affordable national-brand restaurants; a retail concourse of specialty shops; theaters featuring movies as well as live entertainment; and a video game arcade. This guide recommends a closer look at the simpler side of life in the Eastern Woodlands.

Mashantucket Pequot Museum and Research Center (all ages)

111 Pequot Trail, off Route 2; (860) 396-6800; www.mashantucket.com. Open Wed through Sat 10 a.m. to 4 p.m. (last admission 3 p.m.). Closed Thanksgiving, Christmas, and New Year's Day and the eves of each of those days. $$–$$$, children under 6 free.

Established with the goal of preserving Pequot history and culture, the Mashantucket Pequot Museum and Research Center is a must-see experience for all travelers to

Ledyard's **Ups and Downs**

Northeastern Connecticut was famed in the 19th century for the number of water-powered mills that sprang up along the banks of the Quinebaug and Shetucket Rivers and even along lower tidal rivers such as the Yantic and Thames. As a result, abandoned mill sites are not at all uncommon in these parts. Fully operational, restored sites are a rarity, however, and Ledyard has one to show off for you. Located near Lee's Brook in Sawmill Park on Iron Street, which is Route 214, the unusual **Ledyard Water-Powered Up-Down Sawmill** has been restored to the way it might have been when it was built by Israel Brown in 1869. Water levels on the mill's pond site are highest in spring and fall, so operation is seasonal, even though the park is open daily year-round and the public is welcome to enjoy its picnic tables and grills. If you visit during the operational seasons, you can see the vertical waterwheel that turns the gears that move the up-down saw. This mill is still used to cut large logs into lumber. Demonstrations are given on Saturday from 1 to 4 p.m. during April and May and from mid-October through November. Also on this site are an operating shingle mill, an unrestored gristmill, and a blacksmith's forge. Admission is free. For further information on this National Historic Site or for information on the 1793 Nathan Lester House and Ledyard's Historic Districts, call (860) 464-2575.

Connecticut. Nearly $150 million went into the research, planning, and construction of this amazing complex.

From its lobby of warm woods and polished granite floors imbedded with seashells to its wooded outdoor trails (which lead toward the casino), you will be totally absorbed in a glorious yet graceful celebration of the Mashantucket Pequot tribal history and the natural history of their beloved land. Steps from the entrance lobby is an enormous glass and steel Gathering Space, open to the woodlands and the sky and home to beautiful, life-size dioramas representing the native people who have inhabited that exterior landscape for more than 10,000 years. Above your heads on the second level of the Gathering Space is a full-service restaurant offering Native American and traditional American cuisine, and not far away is a 185-foot stone and glass tower that provides sweeping views of the Mashantucket Pequot reservation.

Depending on the ages and interests of your group, you may need five or six hours to thoroughly explore the remarkable exhibits here. Your tour begins with an escalator ride through a simulated glacial crevasse complete with chilly temperatures and the sounds of howling winds. Traveling back to the Ice Age, learn how the movement of the glaciers shaped the land and how life began on the barren areas exposed when the ice caps melted. Time-traveling forward, see a life-size re-creation of an 11,000-year-old caribou kill; learn how the native people adjusted to the warming climate 8,000 to 3,000 years ago. Discover the ways the people adapted woodland resources for food and shelter. Traveling ever closer to our present time, walk through a 22,000-square-foot re-creation of a 16th-century coastal Pequot village, featuring dozens of realistic, life-size figures engaging in everyday activities that demonstrate the lifeways and beliefs of the Pequot civilization. Immersed in the light, sounds, and even the aromas of this village culture, you will be transported to a nearly lost but not forgotten time.

From there, explore the re-creation of a 17th-century Pequot fort discovered in 1992 just yards from the present-day museum. Stroll through an indoor and outdoor 18th-century Pequot farmstead, re-created on an acre of land right outside the museum walls. Step through the cabin door to an orchard and herb garden and learn about farming techniques and tools. Throughout the museum, watch films exploring such topics as food, wigwams, wampum, canoes, and Pequot history. (Note to parents: The excellent short film *The Witness*, recounting the story of the Pequot massacre at Mystic, is unflinching in its graphic portrayal of this brutal event. You may flinch more than a few times, and youngsters under age 10 may be disturbed by the violent nature of the film.)

You may be emotionally drained when you exit the theater if you have chosen to see the heartbreakingly honest *Witness*, but there is still much more to see. You can immerse yourself in exhibits describing the Reservation Period and the 18th-, 19th-, and 20th-century struggles and lifestyles of the Mashantucket Pequots. The changing exhibition gallery usually features contemporary Native arts or traveling exhibitions from other collections and native cultures. Two excellent research libraries include an outstanding collection for children; a 400-seat auditorium offers live performances, films, and lectures. A regular calendar of activities and demonstrations for children is planned throughout the year.

Where to Eat

The Mashantucket Pequot Museum has both a full-service restaurant and a snack bar. The casino itself has 30 restaurants, mostly national chains. Along Route 2 between Stonington and Ledyard are a small variety of eateries. Here's one local favorite.

Valentino's Italian Restaurant and Pizzeria. 725 Colonel Ledyard Hwy.; (860) 464-8584. With an emphasis on take-out New York–style pizza, this small restaurant also serves calzones, pasta dishes, salads, appetizers, and seafood, veal, and chicken dishes for lunch and dinner daily from 10:30 a.m. $$–$$$

Where to Stay

Abbey's Lantern Hill Inn. 214 Lantern Hill Rd.; (860) 572-0483; www.abbeys lanternhill.com. 7 rooms and a cottage in a contemporary country-style bed-and-breakfast in the countryside. Private baths (some with Jacuzzis); private decks or patios; complimentary full breakfasts on weekends; continental-style fixin's on weekdays. Children are warmly welcomed, and well-behaved pets are welcome in the cottage. No smoking indoors. $$$–$$$$

Mystic KOA. Route 49, North Stonington; (860) 599-5101 or (800) 624-0829; www .mystickoacampground.com. RV sites a few tenter sites, and affordable rental cabins, with multiple sorts of hookups, make this a good bet for camping families. Very close to I-95, if you are a light sleeper. Pools, playground, recreation hall, mini-golf, shuffleboard, and more. Daily, weekly, and seasonal rates. $

Two Trees Inn. 240 Lantern Hill Rd.; (860) 312-3000 or (800) FOXWOODS. This lodge-style alternative to the glitzy hotels of the Foxwoods complex is also owned and operated by the Mashantucket Pequots. Standard rooms and two-room suites. Indoor pool, fitness room, restaurant. Complimentary continental breakfast. $$$–$$$$

Stonington/Stonington Borough

Nestled between the coves near the easternmost boundary of the state, just about 5 miles east of downtown Mystic by way of Route 1, Stonington Borough is very quaint, very New England, very evocative of the days of sea captains and West Indies trading ships. Close your eyes and see the little girls playing hoops and graces, the little boys in knee pants shinnying their way up the flagpoles. Hear the clip-clopping of the horses, the whoosh of the gas lamps, the clanging of the bell buoys. It's easy to imagine in the Borough.

Once you have crossed the bridge to the borough, park anywhere and just stroll—it's a great walking town. At the Velvet Mill on Meadow Street, stop to see the mind-boggling artistry being done at the amazing glassblowing studio of Jeffrey P'an (860-535-0307), then wander through the shops and galleries on Water Street. Let the salty air lead you down

The Blessing **of the Fleet**

Perhaps the quaintest and most touching annual event in Connecticut is the blessing ceremony that offers spiritual protection to the fishermen who still ply these waters for the seaborne bounty that provides to them a living and to us a feast. Held on the last Sunday in July, the event begins with the Fisherman's Mass offered at 10 a.m. at St. Mary's Roman Catholic Church on Broad Street in the village. Then a brief dockside ceremony precedes the bishop's boarding of the decorated fleet's lead vessel, which moves into the harbor for the bishop to bless each of the remaining boats as they pass by on their way out beyond the breakwater. Out in the Sound, the families of deceased fishermen toss into the sea floral tributes formed like broken anchors. Visitors of all faiths are welcome to join the celebration; see www .stoningtonblessing.com for details of this year's event, which sometimes includes a street parade and dock festival.

to DuBois Beach right on the Point, and let the kiss of the sea breeze tease any stubborn knots from your work-worn shoulders. Refuel your engines at one of the cafes or restaurants offering great coastal sustenance, then choose from the attractions best suited for families.

North and west of the Borough, in Stonington proper, you will also find plenty to fill a weekend. In spring, see the watery environment come alive at Barn Island. In fall, check out the cider mill. And at any time at all, plant your feet on Terra Firma, a one-of-a- kind place for family fun.

Old Lighthouse Museum (ages 4 and up)
7 Water St.; (860) 535-1440; www.stoningtonhistory.org. Open daily May through Oct from 10 a.m. to 5 p.m. Open by appointment Nov through Apr. $, children under 6 free. Includes admission to the Palmer House.

Inside the 1832 stone lighthouse at the foot of the village, you can learn about the history of Stonington and its role in the War of 1812. You can see treasures brought back to Stonington by the captains of the China trade route. You can learn about the railroad that once transferred passengers from sailing ships to river steamboats. You can even climb the tower of the lighthouse itself for a marvelous view of the harbor and the fishing fleet that still works in these waters.

Captain Nathaniel B. Palmer House (ages 6 and up)
North Water and Palmer Streets; (860) 535-8445; www.stoningtonhistory.org. May through Oct, Tues through Sun 10 a.m. to 4 p.m. (last tour at 3 p.m.) and by appointment. $, children under 6 free. Includes admission to the Lighthouse Museum.

B. F. Clyde's Cider Mill

On a crisp day in early fall when the apples are at their peak and the cider is at its sweetest, head to **B. F. Clyde's** (860-536-3354) at 129 North Stonington Rd. in Old Mystic and watch this huge, steam-powered mill (the only such machine in the United States) press the amber juices from the apples that fill barrel after barrel to the brim. The whole place, in operation since 1881, is a National Historic Landmark. Sweet cider, hard cider, and the apples themselves are for sale, and on weekends especially there's always a crowd that adds to the aura of festivity here. Jams, jellies, honey, maple syrup, fudge, pies, breads, cornmeal, and local produce attract shoppers from near and far. Open daily 9 a.m. to 6 p.m. from Sept 1 through Oct 31 and then closing at 5 p.m. until December 31. Pressings are typically scheduled, on an as-needed basis, at 11 a.m. and 1 and 3 p.m. on weekends and at 1 and 3 p.m. on weekdays from mid-Sept through Nov, weather permitting.

Home of the discoverer of Antarctica, this 19th-century mansion at the far north of the village has 16 rooms filled with many examples of the clever architectural design work of the crafty captain himself. Better known for his success in the China trade and his discovery of the southernmost continent in 1820 in the relatively small sloop *Hero* while on a sealing expedition, the captain filled his elegant home with a variety of innovations and contraptions that intrigue young and old visitors. Lively one-hour tours relate the many adventures of Nat Palmer and his also-daring brother Alexander. Be sure to climb to the top of the cupola to have a look at the glorious view.

Barn Island State Wildlife Management Area (all ages)
Palmer Neck Road; (860) 445-1729 for area supervisor John Lincoln. Free.

The easternmost village in the lower part of the county just before you cross the Rhode Island border on I-95, Pawcatuck is just a speck of a place officially in the town of Stonington. For centuries an agricultural enclave with fields lapped by the sea, it has within its boundaries the state's largest coastal property managed for conservation and wildlife purposes. Situated on Little Narragansett Bay between Wequetecock Cove and the Pawcatuck River, this pretty 1,000-acre refuge has 4 miles of trails and unpaved roads across the tidal marshes and upland oak forest. Because of the unusual population of native and migratory birds here, the area is popular for bird watching. Saltwater canoeing and kayaking are especially pleasant in the quiet inlets here, and you can also fish, usually without too many other anglers to disturb your serenity. Hunting is allowed in the fall and spring, so in those seasons, wear brightly colored clothing. In any season, socks and shoes are the best footgear.

To reach the refuge, take Green Haven Road south from the traffic light on Route 1 where the sign says Barn Island State-owned Boat Launching Area. A nearly immediate left on Palmer Neck Road takes you past Wequetecock Cove and down to the shore. Be sure to tread lightly in this haven. Don't feed the wildlife or disturb their peace, and please pack out all your trash. This refuge is one of the state's best-kept treasures.

Terra Firma Farm (all ages)

330 Al Harvey Rd.; (860) 535-8171; www.terrafirmafarm.org. **Open year-round to the public, Mon through Sat, for visits and self-guided tours, from 9 a.m. to 5 p.m. Closed Sun. Saturday programs ($$$$ per child; registration required) from May through Dec; 10 a.m. to 2 p.m. Two-hour parent-planned-and-chaperoned birthday parties available daily from 10 a.m. to 6 p.m. ($$$$); weekly day camps throughout summer for ages 3 and up ($$$$); after-school programs throughout academic year for grades K-8 ($$$$); private full-day kindergarten program for locally based residents. For the safety of the farm animals, do not bring pets, alcohol, drinking straws, or balloons; smoking is prohibited.**

Run, don't walk to this amazing nonprofit facility established in 2003 as a community farm and educational academy on 22 acres of rural farmland owned by Connecticut Landmarks. Lessees Brianne Casadei and Ethan Grimes created Terra Firma Farm to inspire young people to be agents of change in society, but they themselves are models of agency, and visitors to their very special corner of the world are likely to be changed forever by their life-affirming, world-respecting attitudes. Just get thee hither as soon as you can. You won't regret a minute spent here, at least not as long as you follow the simple rules of respect and safety spelled out courteously (check their website) for all visitors.

Not only is the farm beautiful to behold, but so are its animals—cows, sheep, rabbits, goats, pigs, turkeys, guinea hens, hens, roosters, and donkeys—and its produce—flowers, herbs, vegetables of every sort, meats, poultry, and eggs, all farmed organically under the standards of the CT NOFA's Farmer's pledge. You can buy a sponsorship of an animal, which helps support the farm, and you can also buy a seasonal share in the farm's CSA (community-supported agriculture) program, which allows you to pick up a box of farm-fresh produce for 18 weeks from June through September.

Mostly, though, a visit here will bring your children up-close-and-personal with all the creatures and features of a working farm. Explore the fields and pastures, help with chores, watch the animals, harvest foods fresh from the soil, take produce home to your table, and develop a working knowledge of the ways that foods are grown. Themed Saturday programs include seasonal activities such as animal chores, planting, harvesting, baking, canning, ice cream- and candle-making, and much more. Learn how important the work of the farmer is, and see how the health of the land is vitally linked to animal health and human well-being. This is an all-good place to be on a summer afternoon—or any day at all.

Where to Eat

Dog Watch Café. 194 Water St.; (860) 415-4510. In Dodson Boatyard, this bright and casual pace is fun for all ages, inside and out, with great views of boats, rigging, sea, sky. Classic shore menu for lunch and dinner daily from 11:30 a.m. $$–$$$

Noah's. 113 Water St.; (860) 535-3925. Three solid meals a day at this warm and casual place in the borough. Good cookin' with a down-home flair, served with a smile. The scrod melts in your mouth. Closed Mon. $–$$

Prime Time Cafe. 1 West Broad St.; (860) 599-3840. On the bridge overlooking the Pawcatuck River in downtown Pawcatuck, this brightly painted bistro-style restaurant serves breakfast from 7 a.m., lunch, and dinner from 5 p.m. daily. American cuisine, house-made and cooked to order. $–$$

The Yellow House. 149 Water St.; (860) 535-4986. Wonderful coffees and biscotti in a sunny space splashed with cheerful colors. Tasty sandwiches, tacos, quesadillas, soups, and other easy fare for children. Open daily from 6:30 a.m.; closes at 2:30 p.m. Mon through Fri, 3 p.m. Sat, and noon Sun. $

Where to Stay

Cove Ledge Inn and Marina. On Route 1 at Whewell Circle; (860) 599-4130; www .coveledgeinn.com. Right near the hub of a marina on the Pawcatuck side of Stonington, this 5-acre waterfront complex is picturesque and convenient. 4 efficiency apartments, 2 guest houses, 2 suites in restored vintage main house, plus 16 motel rooms. Outdoor pool; playground; continental breakfast; kayak rentals. $$–$$$$

Inn at Stonington. 60 Water St.; (860) 535-2000. If your children are 14 years old or older, this elegant 12-room inn in Stonington

Borough can offer luxurious comforts. Fitness room, fireplaces, kayaks, and bicycles. Complimentary continental breakfast. $$$$

General Information

Eastern Regional Tourism District/ Mystic Country. 27 Coogan Blvd., Building 3A, New London 06355; (860) 536-8822 or (800) TO-ENJOY; www.mystic.org.

Mystic and Shoreline Visitor Information Center. Building 1D in Olde Mistick Village; Coogan Boulevard off Route 27, Mystic 06355; (860) 536-1641. Open daily; Memorial Day through Columbus Day 9 a.m. to 6 p.m.; and during the rest of the year 10 a.m. to 5 p.m. Mon through Sat and until 4 p.m. on Sunday. Accommodations assistance.

CT State Visitor Information Center. I-95 southbound, between Exits 92 and 91; (860) 599-2056. Open from 8 a.m. daily year-round; restrooms (open 24 hours daily); staff in summer. Maps, state tourism guides, brochures.

Norwich Tourism and Main Street Office. 77 Main St., Norwich 06360; (860) 886-4683 or (888) 4-NORWICH; http://norwich ct.org.

Visit **Mystic website:** www.visitconnecticut .com/mystic_eastern.html.

New London Visitor Center, at the Trolley Waiting Center. Eugene O'Neill Drive, New London; (860) 444-7264.

Index

A

Abbey of Regina Laudis, The, 94
Abbey's Lantern Hill Inn, 288
Abbott's Lobster in the Rough, 279
Abigail's Grille and Wine Bar, 115
A. C. Petersen Farms Restaurant, 131
Action Wildlife Foundation, 82
Agave Grill, 129
Air Line Trail, 198
Alcove Motel, 87
Aldrich Contemporary Art Museum, The, 50
Alforno Brick Oven Pizzeria and Ristorante, 210
All Aboard Pizzeria, 93
Allegra Farm, 192
Allen Hill Farm, 243
Allis-Bushnell House, 169
Altnaveigh Inn, 226
American Clock & Watch Museum, 104
American Legion State Forest, 84
American Pie Company, The, 57
Amistad Memorial and the Freedom Schooner *Amistad*, 153
Angelico's Lake House Restaurant, 200
Angellino's Restaurant, 226
Anne Conover Nature Trail, 167
Anthony Jack's Wood-Fired Grill, 102
Antique Machinery Association's Fall Festival, 68

Appalachian Trail, 64, 76
Apple Harvest Festival, 103
Aqua Restaurant, 210
Araminta cruises, 284
Arch Street Dock, 7
Arena at Harbor Yard, 32
ArtFarm, 202
Aspen Garden, 89
Aspetuck Valley Apple Barn, 49
Audubon Center of Greenwich, 6
Aunt Chilada's Mexican Eatery, 173
Avon, 109
Avon Cider Mill, 110
Avon Old Farms Hotel, 112
Avon Old Farms Inn, 111
Azu, 284

B

Bagel Deli, The, 109
Bagelicious Bagels, 175
Baird's General Store, 72
Bakers Dozen Bagel Company, 112
Ballard Institute and Museum of Puppetry, 225
Ballard Park, 50
Bangkok, 53
Bank Street Book Nook, 93
Bank Street Theater, 93
Bantam Bread Company, 89
Bantam Lake and Sandy Beach, 88
Barker Character, Comic, and Cartoon Museum, 174
Barn Island State Wildlife Management Area, 290
Barnum Festival, 35
Barnum Museum, 34
Bartlett Arboretum and Gardens, 13

Bart's Deli and Restaurant, 117
Beardsley's Cider Mill and Orchard, 42
Beardsley Zoological Gardens, The, 34
Bear Mountain, 76
Beaver Pond B&B, 236
Beckley Iron Furnace, 65
Beech Tree Cottages, 171
Belgique Patisserie, 67
Bellamy-Ferriday House and Garden, 94
Bella's Cafe, 158
Below Deck, 28
Best Western Black Rock Inn, 31
Best Western Camelot, 141
Best Western/Olympic Inn, 279
Best Western/Regent Inn, 227
Best Western Stony Hill Inn, 50
Bethel, 45
Bethlehem, 94
Bethlehem Fair, 94
Bethlehem Post Office, 94
B. F. Clyde's Cider Mill, 290
Bidwell Tavern, 218
Bill's Seafood Restaurant, 210
Birdcraft Museum and Sanctuary, 29
Bishop Farm, 174
Bishopsgate Inn, The, 195
Blackberry River Inn, 81
Black-Eyed Sally's, 129
Black Hawk II, 267
Blackie's, 176
Black Rock Fort, 156
Blessing of the Fleet, 289
Block Island Express, 274
Bloodroot, 38
Bluefish baseball team, 32

Blue Jay Orchards, 48

Blue Oar River Bank Grille, The, 194

Blue Slope Farm & Country Museum, 254

Bluff Point Coastal Reserve, 278

Boathouse at Lakeville, The, 77

Bolton, 218

Bolton Pizza and Family Restaurant, 220

Bon Appetit Café, 23

Bonterra, 102

Book Barn, 267

Boom, 265

Boothe Memorial Park and Museum, 40

Branford, 159

Brasitas, 14

Brass City Ballet, The, 178

Brayton Grist Mill and the Marcy Blacksmith Shop Museum, 238

Breadloaf Mountain Lodge and Cottages, 71

Breck Marshall cruises, 284

Brick School House, 218

Bridgeport, 31

Bridgeport Bluefish, 32

Bridgeport Holiday Inn, 38

Bridgeport Sound Tigers hockey, 32

Bridgewater, 90

Bridgewater Village Store, 97

Brilliant cruises, 284

Bristol, 103

Bristol Center for Arts and Culture, 104

Brookfield, 54

Brooklyn, 242

Brooklyn Historical Society, 242

Brooksvale Park, 173

Brownstone Exploration and Discovery Park, 196

Bruce Memorial Park and Playground, The, 5

Bruce Museum of Arts and Science, 5

Bull's Bridge, 63

Bush-Holley House Museum, 8

Bushnell Memorial Hall, 126

Bushnell Park and Carousel, 124

Butler-McCook House and Garden and Main Street History Center, 126

Buttolph-Williams House, 140

Buttonwood Farm Ice Cream, 257

C

Cafe Atlantique, 146

Canaan, 77

Candlewood Lake, 54, 55

Candlewood Lake Authority, 55

Canfield-Meadow Woods Nature Preserve, 188

Canterbury, 244

Canton, 107

Canton Historical Museum, 108

Captain John's Sport Fishing Center, 268

Captain Nathaniel B. Palmer House, 289

Captain's Cove Seaport, 33

Carbone's, 129

Carmen Anthony Fishhouse, 62

Carmine's Italian Grill, 106

Catnip Mouse Tearoom, The, 84

Cedar Island Marina, 208

Centennial Inn Hotel and Apartments, 134

Centro Ristorante, 30

Chaffee House, 116

Challenger Learning Center, 32

Chapin Park Bed & Breakfast, 87

Charlie Brown Campground, 241

Charter Oak Landing, 126

Chatfield Hollow State Park, 206

Chatterly's, 87

Cheshire, 174

Chester, 187

Chester–Hadlyme ferry, 194

Chester Museum at the Mill, 188

Chief, 33

Children's Garbage Museum, 40

Children's Museum of Southeastern Connecticut, 266

Children's Museum, The, West Hartford, 130

Chocopologie, 21

Chuck's Steak House, 53

City Limits Diner, 14

Claire's Corner Copia Cafe, 158

Clam Castle, The, 171

Clarion Hotel, 107

Clarion Hotel & Suites, 174

Clarion Inn & Suites, 120

Clarke Outdoors, 74

Clinton, 206

Clinton Town Beach, 208

Clinton Town Marina and Cedar Island Marina, 208

Cloud Nine Deli Cafe, 210

CoCo Key Water Resort, 177

Colchester, 252

Collinsville, 107

Collinsville Canoe and Kayak, 108

Colony Grill, 30

Comfort Inn, 168, 211

Comfort Inn and Suites, 232

Comfort Suites, 260

Company of Military Historians Museum, 209

Comstock Covered Bridge, 197

Connecticut Antique Machinery Association Museum, 64

Connecticut Antique Machinery Association's Fall Festival, 68

Connecticut Archaeology Center, 225

Connecticut Art Trail, 8

Connecticut Audubon Center at Fairfield, 29

Connecticut Audubon Center at Pomfret, 239
Connecticut Audubon Coastal Center, 145
Connecticut Audubon Society Center at Glastonbury, 138
Connecticut Children's Museum, 149
Connecticut Coastal Access Guide, 25
Connecticut College, 273
Connecticut Eastern Railroad Museum, 248
Connecticut Fire Museum, 120
Connecticut Forest and Park Association, 199
Connecticut Herb Association's HerbFest, 217
Connecticut Historical Society, 126
Connecticut River Artisan's Cooperative, 187
Connecticut River Museum, 184
Connecticut River Valley Inn, 139
Connecticut's Agricultural Fairs, 75
Connecticut Science Center, 122
Connecticut Tigers baseball, 260
Connecticut Trolley Museum, 119
Consiglio's, 158
Constantine's, 267
Cooking Company Killingworth, 206
Cooking Company, The, 194
Cooper Creek Bed and Breakfast, 67
Copernican Space Science Observatory and Planetarium, 136
Cornwall, 72
Cornwall Bridge, 70
Cornwall Bridge Pottery, 70

Cornwall Bridge Pottery Store, 73
Cornwall Inn, 72
Cornwall Inn Restaurant & Tavern, 72
Corttis Inn, 234
Cottage House, 234
Courtyard by Marriott, 44, 179, 260
Courtyard by Marriott at Yale, 158
Courtyard by Marriott-Norwalk, 21
Courtyard by Marriott Stamford Downtown, 14
Courtyard Marriott Manchester, 122
Cove Island Park, 12
Cove Ledge Inn and Marina, 292
Coventry, 214
Coventry Country Store, 214
Coventry Regional Farmers' Market, 216
Coventry Visitor Center, 214
Creamery Brook Bison, 242
Cross Sound Ferry Services, 274
Crowne Plaza Hartford–Downtown, 129
Crown & Hammer Restaurant and Pub, 109
Crow's Nest Gourmet Deli, 186
Cruise to Nowhere, 7
Crystal Lake, 221
Curtain Call Theater at the Sterling Farms Theatre Complex, 11
Curtis House, 62
Custom House Maritime Museum, 271

D
Danbury, 52
Danbury Museum and Historical Society Authority, 52
Danbury Railway Museum, 52
Danielson Adventure Sports, 231

Darbar India, 162
Darien Windsurfing, 28
Day-Lewis Museum, 133
Day Pond State Park, 252
Days Inn, 51, 174, 211
Dayville, 230
Deacon John Grave House, 170
Dean Ravine Falls, 78
Deborah Ann's, 51
Deep River, 187
Deep River Muster of Ancient Fife and Drum Corps, 188
Delamar Greenwich, 10
Denison Homestead Museum, 283
Denison Pequotsepos Nature Center and Peace Sanctuary, 282
Dennis Hill State Park, 80
Derby, 180
DeRosa's, 26
Devil's Den Nature Preserve, 47
Devil's Hopyard State Park, 191
Dinosaur Place, The, 262
Dinosaur State Park, 138
Diorio Restaurant, 179
Discovery Museum and Planetarium, 32
Dock & Dine Restaurant, 207
Doc's Trattoria, 67
Dodd Stadium, 260
Dog Watch Café, 291
Dogwood Festival, 30
Domenic's and Vinnie's Apizza, 179
Dom's Broad Street Eatery, 117
Dottie's Diner, 62
Doubletree Hotel, 119
Down the Hatch, 57
Downtown Cabaret Theater, 36
Downtown Mystic, 283
Dr. Mike's Ice Cream, 48
Dudley Farm, 166
Dundon House, 33
Durham, 204
Durham Fair, 205

E

Early Bird Cafe, 51
Earthplace: The Nature
    Discovery Center, 24
Eastford, 240
East Granby, 114
East Haddam, 189
East Hampton, 195
East Haven, 159
East Lyme, 265
Easton, 45
East Rock Park, 148
East Windsor, 119
Ebenezer Avery House, 278
Econolodge Inn & Suites, 211
Edd's Place, 210
Edgerton Park, 157
Edgewood Park, 157
Edmondson's Farm, 217
85 Main, 239
80 Licks Ice Cream
    Factory, 205
Ekonk Hill Turkey Farm, 247
Elbow Room, The, 131
Eleanor Buck Wolf Nature
    Center, 140
Elements Bistro, 131
Elephant's Trunk Flea
    Market, 93
Eli Whitney Museum, 172
Elizabeth Park and Rose
    Gardens, 127
Ellsworth Hill Orchard and
    Berry Farm, 68
Elm Street Books, 15
Enviro-Lab/Project
    Oceanology, 277
Esker Point Beach, 279
Essex, 184
Essex Steam Train and
    Riverboat Ride, 185
Ethan Allen Hotel, 53

F

Fairchild Connecticut
    Wildflower Garden, 7
Fairfield, 27
Fairfield Inn, 31
Fairfield Inn by Marriott,
    119, 147

Fairfield Museum and History
    Center, 28
Falls Village, 77
Falls Village Station Nature
    Trail, 78
Farmington, 131
Farmington Canal Linear
    Park, 173, 175
Farmington Inn, The, 134
Farmington River Tubing, 85
Farmington Valley Arts
    Center, 111
Fat Cat Pie Co., 21
Fatherland, 136
Feather Hill Bed and
    Breakfast, 239
Feng, 109
Fife 'n Drum Inn, 68
Fife 'n Drum Restaurant and
    Inn, 67
Firebox Restaurant, 129
Firehouse Deli, 31
Fire Museum, The, 121
Fisherman, The, 279
Fish Family Farm Creamery
    and Dairy, 220
Flamig Farm, 115
Flanders Fish Market and
    Restaurant, 268
Flanders Nature Center, 62
Florence Griswold
    Museum, 263
Foreign Cargo, 63
Fort Griswold Battlefield State
    Park, 278
Fort Hill Farms and
    Gardens, 232
Fort Nathan Hale and Black
    Rock Fort, 156
Fort Shantok, 261
Fort Trumbull State Park, 271
Four Points Hotel by
    Sheraton, 24
Franklin, 254
Frank Pepe Pizzeria
    Napoletana, 31
Fred's Shanty, 276
Freedom Schooner
    Amistad, 153
Freund's Farm Market, 78
Friends and Company, 170

G

Garde Arts Center, 273
Garden Education Center of
    Greenwich, 9
Garelick and Herbs, 16
Gates, 16
Gay City State Park, 219
Gelston House, 194
Georgetown Saloon, 48
Georgina's, 220
Gertrude Chandler Warner
    Boxcar Museum, 239
Gillette Castle State Park, 189
Glastonbury, 137
Glebe House Museum and
    Gertrude Jekyll Garden,
    The, 61
Goodspeed Opera
    House, 191
Goshen, 81
Great Captain's Island, 7
Great Falls of the
    Housatonic, 78
Great Hill Overlook, 199
Greenwich, 4
Greenwich Historical
    Society, 8
Greenwich Point Beach, 6
Griswold Inn, 186, 187
Groton, 276
Guilford, 162
Guilford Art Center, 163
Guilford Craft Expo, 163
Gulf Beach, 146
Gunn Historical Museum and
    Library, 93
Gurleyville Grist Mill, 222
Gustave Whitehead
    hangar, 33
G.W. Tavern, 97

H

Haddam, 189
Haddam Meadows State
    Park, 192
Hadlyme Country Store, 194
HallMark Drive-in, 265
Hamden, 171
Hammonasset State Park
    and Meigs Point Nature
    Center, 168

Hampton Inn-Milford, 147
Hampton Inn & Suites
    Manchester, 122
Hank's Restaurant, 243
Happiest Paddler, 197
Harbor House Inn, 10
Harbor Yard stadium, 32
Harkness Memorial State
    Park, 269
Harkness Tower Carillon
    Concerts, 151
Harriet Beecher Stowe
    Center, 128
Harris Hill Farm, 93
Harry's Place, 254
Hartford, 122
Hartford Marriott Hotel–
    Farmington, 134
Hartford Marriott Rocky
    Hill, 139
Hebron, 218
Hebron Maple Festival, 219
Hempsted Houses, 272
Henry B. DuPont III
    Planetarium, 32
Henry Whitfield State
    Museum, 164
Heritage Inn, The, 98
Heron American Craft
    Gallery, 63
Hillside Motel, 109
Hill-Stead Museum, 131
Hilton Garden Inn Norwalk, 22
Hilton Garden Inn Shelton, 44
Hilton Hartford Hotel, 129
Historic Ship Nautilus
    and Submarine Force
    Museum, 277
Historic Wharf Lane
    Complex, 145
Holbrook Farm, 49
Holiday Inn, 53
Holiday Inn Express, 44,
    103, 162
Holiday Inn Express–Bradley
    Airport, 120
Holiday Inn New London/
    Mystic, 276
Holiday Inn Norwich, 260
Holiday Inn Stamford
    Downtown, 14

Holiday Inn Waterbury, 179
Hopeville, 255
Hopeville Pond State
    Park, 255
Horse-Drawn Carriage and
    Sleigh Museum of New
    England, 192
Housatonic Meadows Fly
    Shop and Tightline
    Adventures Guide
    Service, 71
Housatonic Meadows State
    Park, 70
Housatonic River Outfitters
    Inc., 70
Howard Johnson Hotel, 147
Howard Johnson Inn, 285
Howard T. Brown Memorial
    Park, 259
Huck Finn Adventures, 107
Hunt Hill Farm Land Trust and
    Silo Cooking School, 93
Hurd State Park, 198
Hyatt Regency Greenwich, 10
Hyland House, 164

I
Illiano's Grill, 260
Imagine Nation Museum, 105
Indian Burial Grounds, 260
Indian Chair, 237
Indian Well State Park, 43
Infinity Bistro, 81
Infinity Music Hall, 79
Inn at Fairfield Beach, The, 31
Inn at Harbor Hill Marina, 268
Inn at Iron Masters, 77
Inn at Longshore, The, 26
Inn at Middletown, The, 203
Inn at Stonington, 292
Inn at White Hollow Farm, 79
Inn at Woodstock Hill,
    The, 236
Institute for American Indian
    Studies, 96
Interlaken Inn, Resort, and
    Conference Center, 77
International Festival of Arts
    and Ideas, 155
International Skating Center
    of Connecticut, 113

Isabelle et Vincent, 31
Island Beach, 7
Israel Putnam Statue, 46
It's Only Natural, 203
It's So Rich, 167
Ives Concert Park, 53
Ivoryton, 185
Ivoryton Playhouse, 185

J
Jacobs Beach, 165
Java Jive, 236
Javapalooza, 203
Jennings Beach, 27
Joey Garlic's, 134
Jones Family Farms, 42
Joseph's Steakhouse, 38

K
Karabin Farms, 103
Kayak Adventure, LLC., 28
Keeler Tavern Museum, 51
Kellogg Environmental
    Center, 181
Kensington, 134
Kent, 63
Kent Falls State Park, 66
Kent Iron Furnace, 64
Kent Village Center, 63
Kidcity Children's
    Museum, 201
Killingly, 230
Killingworth, 206
Kitchen Zinc, 158
Klein Memorial
    Auditorium, 36
Knapp's Landing, 41
Kudeta, 158

L
La Belle Aurore, 268
La Cuisine Market and
    Cafe, 162
Lake Compounce Theme
    Park and Entertainment
    Complex, 106
Lake Quonnipaug, 166
Lake View Restaurant, 218
Lakeville, 74
Lake Waramaug State
    Park, 91

La Quinta Inn and Suites, 136
La Quinta Inn & Suites,
    14, 158
La Salle Market and Deli, 109
Latitude 41, 285
La Vita Gustosa, 195
L. B.'s Family Restaurant, 234
Lebanon Historical Society
    Museum and Visitor
    Center, 252
Ledyard, 285
Ledyard Water-Powered
    Up-Down Sawmill, 286
Lee's Academy, 170
Lee's Riding Stable, 88
Lenny and Joe's Fish Tale, 170
Lenny's Indian Head Inn, 162
Levitt Pavilion for the
    Performing Arts, 26
Libby's Italian Pastry
    Shop, 158
Lighthouse Point Park and
    Carousel, 154
Lime, 21
Lime Rock tower, 65
Lis Bake Shop, 285
Litchfield, 87
Litchfield History Museum, 89
Litchfield Inn, The, 90
Little Captain's Island, 7
Little Stone House Cafe, 167
Local Farm Old-Style Life Skills
    Workshops, 73
Lock 12 Historical Park, 173
Lockwood-Mathews Mansion
    Museum, 19
Locust Tree B&B, 79
Lone Oak Campsites, 79
Long Beach, 39
Long Beach Skateland, 39
Longshore Sailing School, 28
Long Wharf Pier, 153
Long Wharf Theatre, 154
Longwood Country Inn, 62
Loon Meadow Farm, 80
Lord Thompson Manor, 234
Louis' Lunch, 158
Luddy/Taylor Connecticut
    Valley Tobacco
    Museum, 117
Lushe's SoNo Diner, 21

Lutz Children's Museum, 121
Lyman Allyn Art Museum, 272
Lyman Orchards, 204
Lyme Academy of Fine
    Arts, 264
Lyme Art Association, 264

M

Macedonia State Park, 67
Madison, 168
Madison Beach Hotel,
    The, 171
Maine Fish and Seafood
    Restaurant, 120
Main Stream Canoes &
    Kayaks, 86
Main Street Sweet
    Shoppe, 188
Manchester, 121
Mangetout, 276
Mansfield, 222
Mansfield Drive-In Theatre
    and Marketplace, 223
Mansfield General Store, 226
Mansfield Hollow Dam and
    State Park, 222
Mansfield Marketplace, 223
Mansion at Bald Hill, The, 236
Maple Lane Farms, 257
Maple Row Tree Farm, 49
Maple Tree Cafe, 115
Marcy Blacksmith Shop
    Museum, 238
Marina at American
    Wharf, 259
Maritime Aquarium at
    Norwalk, The, 17
Markham Meadows
    Campground, 200
Mark Twain House and
    Museum Center, 128
Mark Twain Library, 45
Marnick's Restaurant, 41
Mary Stuart House B&B, 82
Mashamoquet Brook State
    Park, 237
Mashantucket, 285
Mashantucket Pequot
    Museum and Research
    Center, 286
Mattatuck Museum, 176

Max a Mia Ristorante and
    Cantinetta, 112
Max Amore, 138
Mayflower Inn & Spa, 91
Me and McGee, 195
Meigs Point Nature
    Center, 168
Meli-Melo, 9
Merritt Parkway Motor
    Inn, 31
Merritt Parkway Museum, 39
Microtel Inn & Suites, 50
Middlebank II, 33
Middlebury, 179
Middlefield, 204
Middletown, 200
Midway Restaurant &
    Pizza, 242
Milford, 144
Milford Oyster Festival, 145
Min Ghung Asian Bistro, 139
MizzaPizza, 81
Mohawk Mountain Ski
    Area, 72
Mohawk Mountain State
    Forest, 72
Mohegan Park, 259
Monte Cristo Cottage, 271
Maple Lane Farms, 257
Montville, 261
Mother Earth Gallery and
    Mining Company, 54
Mount Riga Furnace, 65
Mount Riga State Park, 75
Mount Southington Ski
    Area, 102
Mount Tom State Park, 89
Mozzarella's Italian Grill, 232
Mrs. Bridge's Pantry, 236
Museum of Connecticut
    History, 127
Museum of Fife and
    Drum, 185
Museum of Fire History, 104
Museum of Greek
    Culture, 104
Music Mountain, 78
Music on the Green, 155
Mystic, 280
Mystic Aquarium
    and Institute for
    Exploration, 281

Mystic Cruises, 284
Mystic KOA, 288
Mystic Marriott Hotel and
    Spa, 279
Mystic Pizza, 285
Mystic Ramada Hotel, 285
Mystic Seaport, the Museum
    of America and the
    Sea, 280
Mystic Soup Company, 285
Mystic Whaler cruises, 275

N
Natchaug State Forest, 240
Nathan Hale Homestead, 214
Nathan Hale Inn, 227
Nathan Hale Schoolhouse,
    190, 271
National Audubon
    Society, 167
National Helicopter
    Museum, 41
Nature Conservancy's Devil's
    Den Nature Preserve,
    The, 47
New Britain, 134
New Britain Museum of
    American Art, 135
New Britain Youth
    Museum, 134
Newbury Inn, 57
New Canaan, 15
New Canaan Historical
    Society, 16
New Canaan Nature
    Center, 15
New England Air
    Museum, 118
New England Carousel
    Museum, The, 104
New Fairfield, 54
New Hartford, 85
New Haven, 147
New Haven Folk, 155
New Haven Museum,
    The, 152
New Haven Premiere Hotel &
    Suites, 158
New Haven's Little Italy–
    Wooster Street, 158

New Haven Symphony
    Orchestra, 154
New London, 270
New Milford, 90, 92
New Morning, 62
New Pond Farm, 47
New Preston, 90
Niantic, 265
Niantic Inn, The, 268
Noah's, 291
Noah Webster House/
    Museum of West Hartford
    History, 130
Noank Historical Society
    Museum, 279
Noank Village, 279
Norfolk, 79
Norfolk Chamber Music
    Festival, The, 80
Norma Terris Theater, 187
North American Canoe Tours
    Inc., 85
Northwest Park and Nature
    Center, 117
Norwalk, 17
Norwalk Inn & Conference
    Center, 22
Norwalk Museum, The, 20
Norwalk Oyster Festival, 21
Norwalk Sailing School, 28
Norwich, 258

O
Oakdell Motel, 270
Ocean Beach Park, 274
Oceanic, 18
Oddfellows Playhouse Youth
    Theater, 201
O'Hara's Landing at Twin
    Lakes, 75
Old Bethlehem Historical
    Society Museum, 94
Olde Bluebird Inn
    Restaurant, 49
Olde Mistick Village, 282
Old Lighthouse Museum, 289
Old Lyme, 262
Old Lyme Inn, 265
Old New-Gate Prison and
    Copper Mine, 114
Old Riverton Inn, 84, 85

Old Saybrook, 206
Old State House, 123
Old Store Museum, The, 56
Oliver Ellsworth
    Homestead, 116
Oliver's Tavern, 186
Olive Tree, The, 146
Om-FLY, 193
Oneco, 245
189 Sports Cafe, 57
On the River B&B, 85
Osbornedale State Park/
    Kellogg Environmental
    Center/Osborne
    Homestead Museum, 181
Osborne Homestead
    Museum, 181
Oscar's Delicatessen, 26
Outdoor Sports Center, 28
Ovens of Woodbury, 62

P
Pachaug State Forest, 256
Palace Theater, The, 178
Paley's Farm Market, 68
Pantry, The, 97
Paperback Cafe, 210
Passiflora Tea Room, 87
Pasta Vera, 10
Patriot's Park, 217
Paul's Pasta, 279
Penang Grill, 10
Penfield Beach, 27
People's State Forest, 83
Pepe's Pizzeria
    Napoletana, 158
Peppermill Steak and Fish
    House, The, 41
Peppertree Camping, 241
Perk on Main, 205
Phelps Tavern Museum,
    The, 112
Pickin' Patch, 110
Pink Sleigh, The, 210
Pizza Factory, 10
Place, The, 167
Plain Jane's, 49
Play, 93
Playhouse on the Green, 36
Pleasant Valley, 82
Pleasure Beach carousel, 34

Plow to Plate Farmers
    Market, 93
Pomfret, 237
Pomfret Center, 237
Port Jefferson, 37
Port Jefferson–Bridgeport
    Ferry, 37
Portland, 195
Portland Restaurant, 200
Portobello's Ristorante and
    Pizzeria, 87
Pratt Nature Center, 93
Preston City, 257
Prime Time Cafe, 292
Project Oceanology, 277
Prudence Crandall
    Museum, 245
Putnam, 237
Putnam Cottage, 9
Putnam Memorial State
    Park, 46
Putnam Wolf Den Trail, 237

Q
Quaddick State Park, 233
Quality Inn and Suites, 53
Quassy Amusement
    Park, 179
Quinebaug and Shetucket
    Rivers Valley National
    Heritage Corridor, 230

R
Radisson Hotel New London/
    Mystic, 276
Railroad Museum of New
    England/Naugatuck
    Railroad Scenic
    Excursion, 98
Ramada Inn at Bradley, 119
Recovery Room, 276
Red Carpet Inn & Suites, 176
Redding, 45
Redding Roadhouse, 49
Red Tomato Pizzeria, 171
Reid's Country Kitchen, 16
Residence Inn by Marriott,
    103, 118
Residence Inn by Marriott
    Hartford Downtown, 129
Resolute cruises, 284

Rickyl's Brookfield
    Luncheonette, 57
Ridgefield, 50
Ridgefield Playhouse, 50
River Bend Campground and
    Mining Company, 245
Riverdale Motel, 200
RiverQuest Expeditions, 193
Riverton, 82
Riverton Fishing Derby, 83
Riverton General Store, 84
Roaring Brook Nature
    Center, 108
Rocky Hill, 137
Rocky Hill–Glastonbury
    Ferry, 137
Rocky Neck State Park, 266
Rodeway Inn, 41
Roger Sherman Inn, The, 17
Roger's Orchards, 103
Romano's Macaroni Grill, 122
Roseland Cottage, 235
Roseledge Herb Farm
    B&B, 258
Rose's Berry Farm, 139
Rosie, 15, 16
Rossini's Italian
    Restaurant, 200
Roy and Margot Larsen
    Wildlife Sanctuary, 29

S
Sabino Mystic River
    Cruises, 281
Sakimura, 115
Salisbury, 74
Sally's Pizzeria, 158
Salsa, 92
Saltwater Grille, 89
Sandy Beach, 88
Sankow's Beaverbrook
    Farm, 265
San Marino Ristorante, 179
Sassafras Restaurant & Ice
    Cream Parlor, 44
Satan's Kingdom State
    Recreation Area, 85
Saybrook Monument
    Park, 207
Saybrook Point Mini-Golf
    Course, 207

Saybrook Point Park, 207
Schoolhouse at Cannondale,
    The, 23
Schooner Sound Learning
    Cruises, 157
Schooner SoundWaters, 11
Scranton Seahorse Inn, 171
Sea Mist II cruises, 161
Sears Park, 198
Seaside Center, 5, 6
Seaside Park, 37
Sea View Snack Bar, 285
Selden Neck State Park, 198
Seven Angels Theatre,
    The, 178
Shallowbrook Equestrian
    Center, 221
Sharon, 68
Sharon Audubon Center, 69
Sharon Farm Market, 69
Shaw Mansion, 271
Sheffield Island Cruise and
    Lighthouse Tour, 18
Shelton, 41
Shelton History Center, 42
Shepaug Bald Eagle
    Observation Area, 97
Sherman, 54
Sherman Historical
    Society, 56
Sherman Playhouse, 57
Sherwood Island State
    Park, 25
Shoreline Greenway Trail, 160
Shore Line Trolley
    Museum, 159
Short Beach Park, 39
Shubert Performing Arts
    Center, 154
Sikorsky Bridge, 39
Silo Restaurant, The, 134
Silverman's Farm, 49
Silver Sands State Park, 146
Simon's Marketplace, 189
Simsbury, 112
Simsbury Inn, The, 115
Ski Mount Southington, 102
Ski Sundown, 86
Skyline Restaurant, 119
Slater Memorial
    Museum, 258

Sleeping Giant State Park, 172
Sleep Inn & Suites, 268
Sloane-Stanley Museum, 63
Small Boat Shop, 28
Soapstone Mountain, 221
Somers, 220
Som Siam, 167
SoNo Arts Celebration, 19
SoNo Historic District, 19
SoNo Switch Tower Museum, 19
Sound Sailing Center, 28
Sound View Beach, 264
SoundWaters Coastal Education Center, 11
Soup Alley, 23
Southington, 102
Southport Beach, 27
Southwest Cafe, 51
Special Joys Bed and Breakfast, 218
Spic and Span Market, 27
Spicer Park, 279
Splash! Festival, 19
SportsCenter of Connecticut, 43
SpringHill Suites by Marriott, 270
SpringHill Suites Milford, 147
Squantz Pond State Park, 56
Stamford, 10
Stamford Center for the Arts, 11
Stamford Marriott Hotel & Spa, 15
Stamford Museum and Nature Center, 12
Stanley-Whitman House, 132
Stanton House Inn, 10
Stanziato's Wood-Fired Pizza, 53
Starr Street Restoration Area, 271
State Capitol Building, 125
Steep Rock Reservation, 96
Stepping Stones Museum for Children, 20
Sterling, 245
Sterling Bluegrass Festival, 247

Sterling Farms Theatre Complex, 11
Sterling Park Campground, 246
Stewart B. McKinney National Wildlife Refuge, 18
Still River Cafe, 242
Stoggy Hollow General Store and Restaurant, 236
Stone Museum, 83
Stonington, 288
Stonington Borough, 288
Stony Creek, 159
Stony Creek Market, 162
Stony Creek Village, 161
Storrs, 224
Strada 18, 21
Stratford, 38
Stratford Ramada, 41
Strong House, 116
Strong-Porter House, 218
STV *Unicorn*, 33
Sugar Hoot Bake Shop, 93
Sunbeam Express Cruises, 268
Sunrise Resort, 195
Sunset Rib Company, 270
Super Natural Market and Deli, 107
Sweet Evalina's, 236
Sweet Harmony Café & Bakery, 203
Sweet Pea's, 85
Sweet Spot, The, 93

T

Table Rock, 237
Taco Loco, 38
Take Time Cafe, 38
Talcott Mountain State Park, 113
Tantaquidgeon Indian Museum, 261
Tapping Reeve House and Law School, 89
Taste of Asia, 16
Taste! Organic Connecticut, 217
Tat's on Summer, 14
Terra Firma Farm, 291
Thankful Arnold House, 191

TheaterWorks New Milford, 93
Theatre Three, 37
Thimble Islands cruises, 159
Thomas Griswold House, 165
Thomaston, 98
Thomaston Opera House, 99
Thompson, 232
Timexpo: The Timex Museum, 177
Topmost Herb Farm, 216
Town Grove, 76
Town Line Sugarhouse, 241
Toymaker's Cafe, 79
Toys Galore and More, 63
Trattoria Roma, 44
Travelers Tower, 126
Trees in the Rigging, 186
TriArts Sharon Playhouse, 69
Trumbull Marriott, 38
Turning Page Bookstore, 265
Tuscany Grill, 203
Tutti's Ristorante, 26
Twin Oaks Café, 69
Two Trees Inn, 288
Typhoon, 203

U

UConn Dairy Bar, 227
Udderly Woolly Acres B&B, 139
UI Fantasy of Lights, 156
Uncasville, 261
Unk's on the Bay, 270
Upper Housatonic Valley National Heritage Area, 65
U.S. Coast Guard Academy, 270

V

Valentino's Italian Restaurant and Pizzeria, 288
Valley View Riding Stables, 231
Vanilla Bean Cafe, 239
Vazzy's, 38
Vecchittos, 203
Vespucci's, 176
Viking Fleet, 274
Village Pizza Family Restaurant, 257

Vinnie's Pizza, 180
Vito's, 141
Volsunga IV, 161
Voluntown, 256
Voyager Cruises, 284

W

Wadsworth Atheneum, 124
Wadsworth Falls State
    Park, 204
Walnut Beach, 146
Walnut Hill Park, 135
Wandering Moose Cafe,
    The, 74
Warrup's Farm, 48
Washington, 90
Washington Depot, 90
Waterbury, 176
Waterbury Symphony
    Orchestra, The, 178
Waterford, 268
Waterford Town Beach, 269
Water's Edge Inn and
    Resort, 211
Webb-Deane-Stevens
    Museum, 140
Weir Farm National Historic
    Site, 22
Wentworth Old-Fashioned Ice
    Cream, 173
Wesleyan Potters, The, 202
West Beach, 208
Westbrook, 206
Westbrook Inn B&B, 211
West Cornwall, 73
West Cornwall Bridge, 73
West Hartford, 130
West Hartford Inn, 131
West Lane Inn, 51

Weston, 45
Westport, 24
Westport Arts Center, 24
Westport Country
    Playhouse, 25
Westport Historical
    Society, 24
Westport Inn, The, 27
West Rock Nature
    Center, 148
West Rock Ridge State
    Park, 147
Wethersfield, 139
Wethersfield Historical
    Society, The, 139
Whale Oil Row, 271
Whaler's Inn, 285
Wheatmarket, The, 189
When Pigs Fly, 69
Whistle Stop Cafe, The, 189
White Gate Farm, 266
White Hart Inn, The, 77
White Memorial Foundation
    and Conservation Center
    Museum, 87
Wickham Park, 121
William Benton Museum of
    Art, 225
Williams Beach Park, 283
Willimantic, 247
Willimantic Brewery and Main
    Street Cafe, 249
Willimantic Food Co-Op, 249
Wilton, 22
Wilton Historical Society's
    Heritage Museum, 22
Windham, 247
Windham Textile and History
    Museum, 248

Winding Trails Recreation
    Association, 133
Windsor, 116
Windsor Historical
    Society, 116
Windsor Locks, 118
Winvian, 91
Wolf's Den Family
    Campground, 195
Woodbury, 60
Woodbury Ski and Racquet
    Area, 61
Woodcock Nature Center, 23
Woodland, The, 77
Woodstock, 234
Woodstock Fair, 235
Wooster Square Green, 157

Y

Yale Center for British
    Art, 150
Yale Collection of Musical
    Instruments, The, 151
Yale Guild of
    Carillonneurs, 151
Yale Peabody Museum of
    Natural History, 151
Yale University Art
    Gallery, 150
Yale University Visitor
    Information and Walking
    Tours, 149
Yellow House, The, 292

Z

Zavala, 276
Zhang's, 171
Zip's Diner, 232